# A Very Private Woman

# A Very Private Woman

*The Life and Unsolved Murder of Presidential Mistress Mary Meyer*

Nina Burleigh

Bantam Books
*New York · Toronto · London
Sydney · Auckland*

A VERY PRIVATE WOMAN
A Bantam Book / October 1998



Jacket photograph credits:

Top photo by Toni Frissell courtesy of *Vogue*. Copyright © *Vogue* 1935 (renewed 1963, 1991) by the Condé Nast Publications, Inc.

Bottom left photo by Cecil Stoughton, U.S. Army Signal Corps photographer on active duty assigned to the Office of the Military Aide to the President.

Bottom right photo copyright © *Washington Post* by permission of the D.C. Public Library.

*Book design by Laurie Jewell*



Library of Congress Cataloging-in-Publication Data
Burleigh, Nina.
A very private woman : the life and unsolved murder of presidential mistress Mary Meyer / Nina Burleigh.
p. cm.
Includes bibliographical references and index.
ISBN 0-553-10629-5
1. Meyer, Mary, 1920–1964—Death and burial. 2. Mistresses—United States—Biography. 3. Kennedy, John F. (John Fitzgerald), 1917–1963—Relations with women. 4. Presidents—United States—Mistresses. 5. Murder—Investigation—Washington (D.C.)—Case studies. I. Title.
E842.1.B85 1998 98-6731
973.922–dc21 CIP

*Published simultaneously in the United States and Canada*

---

Bantam Books are published by Bantam Books, a division of Bantam Doubleday Dell Publishing Group, Inc. Its trademark, consisting of the words "Bantam Books" and the portrayal of a rooster, is Registered in U.S. Patent and Trademark Office and in other countries. Marca Registrada. Bantam Books, 1540 Broadway, New York, New York 10036.

---

PRINTED IN THE UNITED STATES OF AMERICA

BVG 10 9 8 7 6 5 4 3 2 1

# Acknowledgments

There are three women without whom this book would not exist. Mary Stapp's research provided historical depth, and her insights are to be found throughout these pages. Deborah Clarke Grosvenor, my agent and friend, gave me her sharp editing eye, as well as her shoulder at crucial times. My editor, Beverly Lewis, worked tirelessly on the book and gave it the benefit of her calm intelligence, and I thank her for that and for her initial belief in the project.

I appreciate every one of Mary Meyer's friends and peers who talked to me, but especially Myer Feldman, Kary Fischer, David Middleton, Kenneth Noland, Eleanor McPeck, Peter Janney and Marie Ridder, who gave so generously of their time and memories.

Kevin Walsh kept me out of blind alleys, both literal and figurative.

I would also like to acknowledge Mark Allen; Christine Brooks; James Giglio; Dan Goodgame and my former colleagues at the Washington bureau of *Time* magazine (especially Chris Ogden and Doug Waller for early authorial advice); Dovey Roundtree; Tony Summers; David Wise; Michaele Weissman for slogging through a first draft; librarians at the Washingtoniana Room of the Martin Luther King Jr. Library; Ronald E. Whealan at the John Fitzgerald Kennedy Library; the staffs at the Library of Congress Manuscript Reading Room, the Columbia Historical Society, the National Security Archives, Daniel Brandt and Public Information Research, Inc., and the New York history room at the New York Public Library.

Journalists Philip Nobile and Ron Rosenbaum did initial spadework and interviews that paved the way.

# Contents

# A Very Private Woman

# Introduction

Anyone wanting to write about a member of the silent generation of women that mothered the baby boom and married the cold warriors confronts a peculiar obstacle: Many of these women believe their lives were utterly unremarkable. The cold war wives review years spent raising children and keeping house, arranging dinner parties for dignitaries, making art, or getting jobs. They find their personal histories bland compared to their husbands', men with war wounds on their bodies and secrets of state in their brains, men whose turf ranged from Havana to Moscow and Paris to Bucharest, and whose work altered world history.

When the woman in question had an affair with a married president of the United States and then died violently, the obstacle of humility is compounded by embarrassment and sorrow. Mary Pinchot Meyer's sister and closest friend say they burned her diary, and a CIA official destroyed her other papers, obliterating her voice from history. Her closest surviving friends made an informal pact not to discuss her. Many people who will talk are persuaded—for reasons that have more to do with Mary's access to powerful men and with the tenor of the times than with available facts about the woman herself—that Mary Meyer "knew things" she wasn't supposed to know, and that her death is somehow related to that knowledge. Still others are quite happy to talk, but thirty years and advancing age have dimmed their memories. The protectiveness of her friends, the shame and sorrow of her family, and the political intrigue during her years in Washington have combined to make her life and death mythic, a part of the Kennedy assassination conspiracy legend.

Most of Mary Meyer's female peers outlived their husbands, men who drank hard and were often addicted to nicotine. These women devoted their later years to creative endeavor. In their seventies, avian and fine as porcelain, they take themselves and their work very seriously. They lived the earlier part of their lives unnoticed in a half-lit world of great refinement and delicate sensibility, eclipsed by the cold warriors and their nihilistic contest of rocket fuel and warheads and plutonium. These women painted or sculpted or wrote poetry or studied and suffered the husbands who strayed or ignored them or drank too much, or whose secret deeds were only revealed by congressional inquiries years later. Their children rebelled and got lost in drugs and the turmoil of the 1960s before coming home. They survived much.

Mary Meyer's death was a tragedy for her two surviving sons and for her sister and close friends. It was a tragedy from which the affected have tried to recover in different ways. One of those ways has been a protective silence. Like high priestesses guarding the Eleusinian mysteries, those ancient Greek fertility rites of blood and sex, her friends have protected the mystery of their lost friend's life, and with it the secret history of their group, once so important and now fading into old age, death, and history. They want Mary's story and the reasons behind a mad scramble for her diary after her death interred with her. In so doing, they protect the living as much as the dead. The image of their once-powerful set shall not be damaged while they live. Their very silence has perpetuated the mystery of their late friend more effectively than anything they might have said. Mary Meyer became a silhouette in her own story.

As the years passed and the secrets of the CIA dribbled out, Americans came to believe the cold warriors were capable of supreme acts of oversight and evil. To some minds the intelligence agency assumed the role of the invisible hand and became a controlling entity behind ever more complicated, interconnected webs of events inside America. This impression was amplified by the excessive secrecy of those times and by the official and unofficial guarding of those secrets over the years. Mary Meyer's name appears in classified documents that are still being released. Among documents relating to Mary Meyer that have been released by the CIA is a completely redacted ten-page document on CIA stationery, probably related to her husband's job. Another is not dated and is titled merely "Background Information." It is "a review of the appropriate Office of Security files" and contains her vital statistics and an explanation of the circumstances of her death. There may be other material on her at the CIA. A Freedom of Information Act request made to the CIA by the author could elicit more results in coming years.

But among the great secrets of the cold war in Washington—and there were many, not the least being the CIA's "family jewels" of assassinations and coups—there was another buried secret: sex. As hard as it might be to imagine it today, Washington was a sexier town in the years of the cold war. Flirtation was an art. Marriage was respected and divorce rates were still low, but the late 1950s and the early 1960s were the dawn of a new era in male-female relations, and traditional relationships were being tested. Experiments were undertaken, hearts were broken. The women of Mary Meyer's generation and class always operated with propriety, though. If their husbands and friends and even they were conducting themselves like characters from a John Updike novel, that was certainly nothing for the historians to note.

Sex is one reason why they feared Mary Meyer's diary. But Mary Meyer's whole life was no more about sex than anyone else's.

In my research and writing, I have tried to give Mary Meyer's life as much respect and dignity as historians automatically grant to important men. The life stories of women throughout recorded history are often the domestic histories of men, and this is no less true of the women of Mary's generation and class. Women figure in the private lives of famous men, in their beds and in the raising of those men's children and the keeping of their homes. More rarely they are compatriots or collaborators in the public sphere. Historians are interested in mistresses for what they reveal about the lives of the important men with whom they consorted. I have attempted to describe a woman, her men, and her times—and the effect of those times and men *on her.*

Mary Meyer's style was questing. She was an experimental, doubting woman, a woman with a will of her own, and those qualities made her unusual, especially in the convention-worshiping 1950s and especially among her female peers in Washington. Although she was not ordinary in terms of looks and means, her story is one that ordinary women will be able to recognize. It is an arc that many women in her generation experienced: A confident, athletic girl grew up to marry and bear children, became dissatisfied with her life, and embarked on a path toward the beginnings of personal authority and independence. It is an arc that Kate Chopin named in the title of her book *The Awakening*, and this name is entirely applicable to Mary Meyer's life. But Mary Meyer's own awakening was cut short by murder.

This book is roughly divided into four sections that examine Mary Meyer's life and world through the men with whom she was associated: her father, her husband, her lovers, and finally, the man acquitted of her murder. I did not plan this approach when I envisioned the book. But because her papers were destroyed, parts of her life story must be deduced from clues in the more public lives of the men in her life.

Researching this book, I had some breakthroughs in interviews and other primary research that cut through the fog of mystery and allowed me to glimpse the real woman. Whenever someone remembered a particularly telling anecdote, whenever I spotted a piece of her handwriting, whenever I saw a new photograph of her or one of her paintings, I felt like an archaeologist brushing away at a lump of sand and suddenly finding just a single marble finger or a nose, from which I could try to imagine the rest of the sculpture. These scraps became pieces of a three-dimensional woman that I was constructing in my mind.

Some Georgetown women who knew Mary well did agree to interviews but insisted on being identified as confidential sources. The honesty and memories of several former Kennedy aides were helpful and contained a few surprises. Family letters and papers at the Library of Congress, as well as the Secret Service gate and phone logs at the John Fitzgerald Kennedy Library, provided other vital clues. It was especially exciting to find various letters in the Pinchot family and Cord Meyer collections at the Library of Congress with a sentence or even a note written in Mary's rounded, back-leaning hand. These little missives were vital. They turned out to be the only primary relics of Mary's own thinking that would be available to me.

I was also shown a small group of Mary's paintings by an individual who preferred to remain anonymous. These canvases showed Mary at different stages in her art, first struggling amateurishly and then painting with more assurance. It was clear that by the end of her life she was just beginning to develop her own style.

Small new details increased my understanding. Mary Meyer's experiment in Reichian therapy, for example, and her fascination with art and styles that were new and even bizarre were keys to how she thought and was perceived. She was not satisfied within the limits of propriety set by her class and she became less so as she matured. Although Mary went to the Reichian therapist for only a few months, the fact that she was willing to try something so controversial and so sex-drenched began to explain what it was about her and her times that her friends were so reticent about. Although the intervening decades saw the proliferation of many nontraditional therapies and a sexual liberation undreamed of in 1959, to Mary's contemporaries this was dangerous stuff.

Early on, trying to discern Mary Meyer's real personality behind the fog of words such as *charming* and *lovely*, I grasped at any straw. At one point I fed all my information on Mary—from her handwriting to her childhood illnesses, from her father's personality to her own attitude toward nudity—to John Gittinger, a CIA psychologist now retired and living in Oklahoma, who had for many years assessed the personalities of Soviet agents with just such random bits of information. Gittinger kindly ran the facts through his formula and came up with a personality theory, as he had when the CIA sought to uncover the weaknesses of enemy spies and leaders of nations.

In 1950s CIA acronym-speak, Gittinger said that Mary Meyer was an "IFU" type, meaning she exhibited the personality traits of an "Internalizer, Flexible and Uniform." Decoded, that meant in very broad terms that Mary Meyer was self-oriented and kept her own counsel, was open to experiences but tended to be unfocused, and had difficulty detaching herself from the familiar as a girl, thus needing to develop a close, nurturing relationship early in adulthood. Gittinger also deduced that she may have had some guilt feelings about being an unhappy mother, that she might have had an overdeveloped sense of responsibility, and that she would have at some point in her life rejected the mores she had been brought up with. As it turned out, I was able to confirm some of this assessment.

Of course, the real reason for the embarrassment about Mary, the real trepidation her friends feel when asked to talk about her, stems not from her own personality quirks but from her relationship with President Kennedy. They fear their intelligent, well-bred friend will be tarred with the bimbo brush for history. I sympathize with their fear. Women who have affairs with important men are often relegated to a certain lower status, while the men retain respect, if they do not acquire more veneration than before. It is important to say at the outset that Mary Meyer's relationship with the president was first and foremost a real friendship.

Researching Mary Meyer plunged me into a world new to me, that of the Kennedy myth and its legion of admirers, detractors, and scholars. Before I started this project, I had a very simple and clear idea about President John F. Kennedy. I was three years old when he was shot and I remember that day because it was the first time I ever saw my mother cry. As a child and an adult, respect and sorrow were the main feelings I associated with President Kennedy.

It soon became necessary to wade into the billions of words that have been written about every aspect of President Kennedy, from the magazine glamour to the sober academic histories to the tabloid sleaze and conspiracy theories. I was daunted by the sheer volume of information and surprised by some of the implications about the hidden side of a man and an administration that in my mind had been an idealized legend of decency and hope shattered by hate. I sought out scholars and writers and researchers to help me separate fact from gossip, unfounded conspiracy theorists from the serious questioners. I am satisfied that I found such people.

I decided early on that Kennedy warranted only a single chapter in Mary's life, because it seemed to me that in a full life of forty-four years, there was more to the woman than a relationship with one man, even if he was the president. The more I learned about Mary, the more I realized that was the appropriate weight to give her relationship with Kennedy. Novelists may write volumes describing the events of a few days, weeks, or months, but restricted as I was to the available facts, I feel a chapter is sufficient.

Nonetheless, those who are looking to understand more about Kennedy will find Mary Meyer of interest. In Mary Meyer's attitudes and lifestyle, in her freedom and simplicity and experimentation, we see the seeds of attitudes that came to represent the decade of the 1960s. We may speculate that the president who so enjoyed her company shared some of those attitudes.

Finally, I did not set out here to solve the crime of Mary Meyer's murder, and I have not done so. The acquitted defendant is still alive in 1998, but he says he doesn't remember anything about his arrest near the murder scene. The Washington, D.C., police decided the case was solved and did not save the evidence, so it is impossible to apply new technology to the old bloodstains. The closest there was to an eyewitness is dead. I was able, through police and court records and interviews, to piece together the life story of the acquitted defendant in the case. I found his record interesting, and I believe that his life story, because it intersects so fundamentally with Mary Meyer's, is an important part of this book.

# 1

# Murder in Georgetown

*Who wants to read about a bunch of unhappy women?*

A PROMINENT WASHINGTON ATTORNEY

October 12, 1964. The sky over Washington was crisp as a blue flag snapping in the breeze. Viewed from above, the city was verdant. Great swaths of parkland, tended gardens, and traffic circles gave the urban landscape an elegant southern flavor. After the steaming summer, the foliage had been slow to turn. The tall, imposing dome of the Capitol faced the Washington Monument across the Mall, two white chess pieces on a green board.

At 1600 Pennsylvania Avenue, the president's house was still a symbol of the tragedy of John F. Kennedy's assassination less than a year before. From the turrets and widow's walks of embassies, from the Truman Balcony of the White House, from the Capitol and the top of the Washington Monument, the city below was all trees and marble. "The City of Magnificent Distances" was what someone had called Washington in the nineteenth century. But this postcard view did not reveal everything. Obscured by the spreading treetops, dwarfed by the monuments and federal architecture, down on ground level Washington was a poor city. Whole sections of it were crumbling under decades of poverty. Many black people who were part of the city's majority lived in slum houses erected almost a hundred years earlier by black refugees from the Civil War. This Washington was one tourists rarely saw. Some black families remained without plumbing or electricity. Few had telephones. Crime, rats, and tuberculosis infested the hidden city.

Two bridges at Q and P Streets linked old colonial Georgetown with the federal city of Washington. The spans, resting on concrete arches that soared hundreds of feet above Rock Creek, were reminiscent of ancient Rome in their scale and whiteness. On the narrow streets of Georgetown, civility ruled. Important men slept here and worked by day across the bridges. The old cobblestones and red brick sidewalks were quiet and vacant but for a maid or a woman visiting friends. Along the walls of the townhouses and mansions, light quivered against leaded glass panes and disappeared in pools of shadow behind draperies shielding Russian icons, African wood carvings, Persian carpets, and Chinese prints the occupants had collected on their global forays. Late roses bloomed; vines of ivy and bamboo stalks shared space against the old stone walls.

It was an ideal day for walking. In a converted garage studio behind the red brick house owned by journalist Ben Bradlee, a woman was painting. She had short blond hair, full lips, and blue eyes quick to see humor. She was two days short of her forty-fourth birthday, but she usually passed for at least a decade younger. Her two teenage sons had recently moved back to their boarding schools in New Hampshire and Connecticut. Divorced and with children away at school, she was alone again in her house. Free to choose her companions, she sought out artistic, vivid people. The night before, she had entertained British theater director Peter Brook, who was in Washington to direct the hit play *Marat/Sade*[1]. But inside her studio was where she felt most alive. The shelves were lined with paint and tools, her collection of music boxes and other small objects, stones and leaves and sometimes a flower from her garden. She could run her hands along the rough edges of her work table and down to the silky head of Mommacat, an alley cat who gave birth every six months. Her latest kittens mewled from a box in the corner. It was time to tack up another Free Kittens sign on the door. Looking out the window, she registered the blue of the sky and filed the color in her mind. This morning she had poured pale blues and grays onto an unsized canvas on the floor in a style that other painters were making so famous it eventually got a name: the Washington Color School.

Around noon she propped up the painting before a fan to let it dry. She put on a gray mink-and-lambswool sweater, then a light blue angora sweater over it, donned her Ray-Bans, pulled on a pair of kid leather gloves, and in her paint-specked canvas sneakers and pedal-pusher slacks set off for her daily walk on the Chesapeake and Ohio Canal towpath. She left the little studio in the alley off N Street and strolled down the cobblestoned hill toward the Potomac River, passing rows of trim townhouses with their red and gray doors and brass knockers.

As she crossed M Street a long black car with official plates slowed and the rear window rolled down. One of the capital's most prominent women, Polly Wisner, wife of Frank Wisner, head of the CIA's worldwide covert operations for many years, waved and called out a greeting in the refined accent of a 1930s movie star, all broad *a*'s and dropped *r*'s—"Good-bye, Maahry." The car passed on. Polly was on her way to London, where her husband would be stationed for a few more years with the agency. She would be the last friend to see the artist alive.[2]

Soon the woman was on the canal towpath. She passed below the old brownstone trolley car garage that the CIA had turned into a site for training third-world police forces.[3] She passed a white male jogger who worked at the Pentagon. She continued walking farther away from Georgetown and civilization until she encountered someone near a small cottonwood tree. Two mechanics working on a disabled vehicle on the street high above the path heard her screams and her last words: "Someone help me."[4] Before they could look over the stone ledge and down into the woods, two shots rang out. The first bullet to her head would eventually have killed her but didn't immediately; bleeding from the wound, she clung to the small tree and tried to fend off her attacker with her free hand. As she lost consciousness she probably saw white. There are so many shades of white—cloud white, shell white, sail white, sand white—but this was like no white she had ever known, more painful than the blinding white of sunlight. She fell. The gun was applied once more to her shoulder blade and the bullet tore into her aorta, shutting off the blood to her heart, turning everything black in one breath, shutting out color, ending her life, and leaving her dead body to police and to the speculation of the ages.

The National Cathedral is built of gray stone at the highest point of Wisconsin Avenue, overlooking Georgetown. Light streaks its echoing nave, pouring in through stained-glass windows that depict the history of America from the Indians to the astronauts. The construction of the cathedral took a century, and parts of it were still unfinished in 1964, when two hundred mourners gathered inside the cathedral's Bethlehem Chapel to pay their last respects to Mary Eno Pinchot Meyer on what would have been her birthday, October 14, 1964. It fell to her brother-in-law to do much of the funeral planning. Ben Bradlee hired the undertakers and arranged for the organ music at the service. The altar was framed by white lilies and chrysanthemums, and their heavy scent filled the air in the crowded chapel. The coffin was draped with a flag. Some of the deceased artist's friends felt the journalist had overdone it a bit, given Mary's taste for simplicity. But the setting was appropriate to the mourners, many of whom were accustomed to official pomp.

Most of the men and women at the service that day were members of Washington's upper echelon, consummate insiders and veterans of the social scene swirling around the Kennedy administration. The mourners were as accustomed to wending their way across third-world tarmacs to waiting planes as they were to undergoing psychoanalysis, attending private clubs, receiving White House invitations, and dressing for dinner. They placed monogrammed matchbooks in the crystal ashtrays at their homes. The women were witty and conversant in the latest political gossip, and they wielded power decisively with the guest lists for their dinner parties. Their men were some of the nation's most influential fixers, lawyers, diplomats, politicians, spies, and journalists. Family money made their government salaries superfluous. Many of them lived in Georgetown.

The Potomac River, not politics and statecraft, initially gave colonists a reason to settle at what became Georgetown. Slaves, ice, and coal were all shipped and unloaded at the waterfront in the early years, but tobacco was the port's mainstay. In the eighteenth century tobacco was shipped up the river from southern plantations and stored in Georgetown warehouses on its way to England. The tobacco trade conferred prosperity on many a local merchant. The "George" of Georgetown was England's King George II, but the name might as well have referred to Scottish merchant George Gordon, owner of the port's largest wharf warehouse.

In 1871 Congress annexed Georgetown to the newer federal capital city of Washington. A few decades later its separate name was officially erased. But Georgetown retained its identity long after it became part of Washington. Residents always listed addresses in "Georgetown" without mentioning the District of Columbia. For years Georgetown was considered a slum, but by the 1960s the area was beginning to have a certain status. It was on its way to being Washington's Beacon Hill. A restoration effort begun in the 1930s had transformed the neighborhood into a white upper-class enclave within a city. The change was rapid and sweeping. Blacks made up twenty-two percent of the neighborhood in 1940, but by 1960 they were less than three percent. They were replaced by white men returning from World War II and their families. With the advent of the cold war, a generation of elite young men who might previously have gone back to the family business or to Wall Street were attracted to Washington. The old townhouses in Georgetown were conveniently located, charming, and cheap. Real estate agents bought whole blocks and sold them to the new white arrivals. Soon the only vestiges of the black community in Georgetown were a few churches, to which parishioners traveled every Sunday from their new homes across town.

Georgetown in 1964 was a cozy place where people left their doors unlocked. But the community was home to too many important people to be truly quaint, and too full of classified information to be called friendly. Dean Acheson, Allen Dulles, Robert McNamara, and Frank Wisner were among the powerful men with addresses in the little colonial village. A new being, the national media celebrity, was also an inhabitant: Joseph Alsop, Ben Bradlee, Walter Lippmann, Rowland Evans, and Art Buchwald were among them. The professional intimacy among the spies, policy makers, and journalists reflected a social continuity. They dined at each other's homes, wrote letters of introduction for each other's children and wives traveling abroad, and recommended each other's sons to Harvard, Yale, or St. Paul's School.

By October each year, Washingtonians who summered in the country—Maine, Maryland, and Virginia were favorite retreats—had returned. Georgetown women and children traditionally left the city during the summers, which were so uncomfortably humid before the age of air-conditioning that diplomats received hardship pay if they were posted to the American capital. The men stayed in the sweltering city to attend to affairs of state or to run national magazines and newspapers. Summers in midcentury Washington were such a men's club that one of the Georgetown women who stayed behind was designated head of "The Wives' Protective Association" by the other wives.[5] They were half serious. The capital's moral tone was set by Congress, where in the secretly swinging 1950s and early 1960s senators and representatives were accustomed to the occasional assignation with a willing woman from the typing pool or reception desk. Private morality rarely matched public appearance.

Mary Meyer's murder stunned the little community. While she was not one of the city's premier hostesses, Mary was a well-liked member of a social group that had formed around the cold warriors and the Kennedy administration. She was from a prominent family and related by marriage to one of the city's highest-profile journalists. Her ex-husband was one of the top officers at the CIA. She had been a fixture at the Kennedy White House and—a fact known to a few—one of the late president's lovers.

After the mourners filed in and took their seats, after the whispering and sniffling sounds of grief had died down, another Yale graduate, dressed in the white and red vestments of a suffragan bishop in the Episcopal Church, walked to the altar. Bishop Paul Moore was a family friend who had known Ben Bradlee, Mary Meyer, and her ex-husband, Cord Meyer, since the 1930s. He spoke of Mary's "honesty, her friendship, her rare sensitivity, that beauty which walked with her and which flowed from her into each of our lives." He then called for forgiveness in a six-minute oration. "We cannot know why such a terrible, ugly irrational thing should have happened. We can only sense that it was in some way bound up with sin and sickness of the entire world . . . somewhere perhaps in a pattern invisible to anybody else except God Himself," he said. Then Moore asked for prayers for "that demented soul" who caused the "senseless tragedy."[6] But many were not prepared to forgive the murderer, and the less liberal members of the crowd were incensed at the minister for bringing politics into the chapel by trying to portray the alleged killer as a victim and the killing as an act perpetrated by poverty and injustice.

There was much quiet murmuring in the cathedral that afternoon about the accused. Some people did believe the police theory—that Mary was the unlucky victim of an assault randomly committed by a twenty-five-year-old day laborer named Ray Crump Jr., who was arrested not far from the murder scene. Others were uncertain. Mary had been a sometimes reckless woman with access to the highest levels of the American government. There were so many spies at her funeral. It was less than a year since the assassination of President Kennedy. The Warren Commission's report concluding that Lee Harvey Oswald had acted alone in shooting the president in Dallas had been released just two weeks before Mary's murder. Most people didn't question its conclusion, at least not yet. But this murder, coming so soon after the assassination, was disquieting. "It was strange, especially the way the police and newspapers rushed to judgment about who did it. It felt wrong," said one of Mary's friends.[7]

One man sobbed unconsolably throughout the ceremony. Cord Meyer was a wounded World War II hero now overseeing a network of CIA front groups, and until that day many in Georgetown had not realized how much he still loved the woman who had divorced him seven years before. Meyer was a tall man whose boyish handsomeness had hardened into a gray statue of itself. The glass eye that replaced the one destroyed by shrapnel from a Japanese grenade stared always straight ahead. He was a man who had started life with a map, and only in middle age had he begun to realize that the map didn't fit the terrain. Instead of the life of public service and acclaim he had envisioned for himself, he was buried deep in the secret bureaucracy of the CIA, his service to his country forever classified. Throughout the early 1960s, including in newspaper articles about his ex-wife's murder, when Cord Meyer was mentioned he was always referred to simply as a "government employee." Within a month of her death he left on a trip abroad, identifying himself on his passport application as a "writer" on a "pleasure" trip. There was some truth to the cover. Cord Meyer considered himself a writer whose novels were forever delayed by the demands of his government job. The passport application had also required him to answer the question "Are you now or have you ever been a member of the Communist Party?" He typed "No."[8] Well-bred and intelligent, Cord was known around town as a confrontational man whose worldview was growing more hawkish by the day and who sometimes drank too much and disrupted dinner parties with his arguments. His passionate need to win every disagreement was legendary. He was also a collector of modern art who could recite the poetry of Stephen Spender.

Cord Meyer was comforted at the funeral by two men from the top of the CIA. Richard Helms, a thin, impeccably mannered man who would eventually head the CIA, had taken the day off to attend the service. He and Cord Meyer were colleagues but also warm personal friends. Cord Meyer had sponsored Helms and his wife for membership in the Waltz Group, which hosted dinner-dances for the Washington elite several times a year. The two went back more than a decade in the CIA and had weathered many crises together.

The fact that Mary's death concerned the CIA bigwigs is noted in a declassified, heavily redacted FBI memo regarding the rescheduling of a meeting between CIA director John McCone and Helms and FBI officials. The reason for the meeting is not stated in the memo, which was written by an FBI agent named William C. Sullivan, J. Edgar Hoover's number-two man. "On 10/14/64, Helms advised the Liaison Agent that it will be impossible for CIA officials to meet with me and Supervisor [name redacted] on 10/14/64, and suggested that the meeting be held at 10:00 a.m. 10/15/64. Helms explained that both he and Angleton have been very much involved with matters pertaining to the death and funeral of Mrs. Mary Pinchot Meyer. She is the woman who was murdered on the canal towpath near Georgetown on 10/12/64. She was the former wife of Cord Meyer, a CIA official."[9] In an interview, Helms could not recall exactly what personal involvement the memo noted beyond his attendance at the funeral.

The "Angleton" referred to in the memo was Cord Meyer's closest friend and fellow Yale graduate, James Jesus Angleton, second only to J. Edgar Hoover as the nation's greatest collector of personal secrets. Angleton had been personally close to Mary as well. He occupied the post of CIA counterintelligence chief, charged with deciding which of America's spies might be traitors. Half Mexican, half Anglo-Saxon, Angleton was stooped and cadaverous, with fingers stained yellow from years of heavy smoking. Angleton's passions included Italy and anything English, dry-fly fishing, and raising orchids. He had a reputation for paranoia. He never opened the blinds in his office and kept the drapes pulled on top of them. He was rarely seen. CIA official David Atlee Phillips said Angleton was so reclusive, Phillips mistook another man for Angleton for fifteen years. His pronouncements were taken seriously. Some called him "the CIA's answer to the Delphic Oracle."[10]

Among his many responsibilities in the fight against global Communism, Angleton made it his business to stay on top of the private affairs of the denizens of Georgetown, men and women with complicated lives so intimately connected to the heart of the national government that they seemed obvious targets for any enterprising Communist looking to do blackmail or, worse, recruit a traitor. On the day of Mary's funeral Angleton already had in his possession the diary and letters that told the story of Mary Meyer's personal life. They had been handed to him by journalist Ben Bradlee in an act motivated equally by family embarrassment and patriotic duty. Later Angleton would boast that he had also bugged Mary Meyer's telephone and bedroom.[11]

Angleton served as an usher at Mary's funeral, leading the mourners to their seats in the chapel, but he felt Bradlee had devised the funeral more to impress social Washington than to honor the dead woman. He smiled when he saw one of Mary's close friends, Otakar "Kary" Fischer, a Czech immigrant who edited a scholarly journal of Soviet studies called *Problems of Communism*. As he walked Fischer to his seat, Angleton surveyed the gathered members of Georgetown society and whispered in disdain, "We were her true friends, you know."[12]

Cord Meyer oversaw a large staff at the CIA, which accounts for the presence of so many spies at the funeral. In the two decades after World War II, the CIA had grown far beyond its initial executive charter, and nearly beyond the will of the men who created it. The agency operated from a new building in Langley, Virginia, and its huge budget and vast projects were unknown to the American people. The responsibilities of the labyrinth they had constructed were already starting to drive some of the men mad, many to drink, and more to cut moral corners.

In ten years many of the men involved in the CIA's early years would become sinister figures in the public mind as revelations about secret plots tainted their images. But as the pews filled for Mary Meyer's funeral, these figures from the agency were still in the fullness of their power and were aware of many things the American public would learn only years later. They knew of the CIA's attempts to assassinate Castro and other foreign leaders. One of these leaders, Rafael Trujillo of the Dominican Republic, had already been killed with American-supplied weapons. They were aware of the CIA's drug experimentation on unwitting civilians, carried out in the mistaken assumption that the Communists had already developed "mind-control" drugs of their own. They were secretly influencing the politics of countries across the planet, from Iran to Italy and much of Latin America. Cord Meyer had most recently been organizing phony labor strikes and student protests in Brazil and the Dominican Republic to thwart Communists. Angleton knew that the CIA was illegally opening the mail of American citizens corresponding with people in Communist-controlled countries. In fact, as he would defiantly tell congressional investigators a decade later, he was overseeing the operation.

Journalists also filled the pews at Mary Meyer's funeral. Many had been personally close to John F. Kennedy, and they would soon become household names thanks to television or best-selling books. They would flourish for decades. These newsmen often knew more than they could print. Chief among them was Mary's brother-in-law, Ben Bradlee, the son of a Boston banking family and a rising star in national journalism. He was Harvard-educated and spoke French fluently but camouflaged his pedigree behind a streetwise front. With his macho manner, savvy, and profanity, he epitomized the finger-snapping cool of the Hollywood Rat Pack, a style much favored by the late president. On first meeting Bradlee, one male acquaintance thought that *Newsweek*'s Washington bureau chief was a bookie.[13]

Mary's younger sister, Tony, was Bradlee's second wife, and he was her second husband. Together they were raising six children in a big red brick house on N Street. As a golden couple during the Kennedy years, they had frequently dined alone with the president and his wife, Jackie, in the White House. Tony was an ethereal blonde like her sister, but she was taller, more angular, and more reserved than Mary. A careful and sometimes even spectacular dresser, she was more restrained and formal than her older sister. She had been particularly close to Jackie Kennedy, as both women had so often been together in the background while one of their men made history and the other recorded it. At the funeral Tony sat next to her mother, Ruth Pickering Pinchot, a New Yorker and former journalist herself, whose reclusiveness would increase after the tragedy of her older daughter's death.

*Washington Post* publisher Katharine Graham, recently widowed and still new in her powerful role, came to pay last respects. Rowland Evans, the newspaper columnist, and his wife, Kay, a close chum of Mary Meyer's, were in the chapel. Like Mary, Kay Evans had been a favorite guest at White House parties, and the two women had, on at least one occasion, shared a table with the president. Columnist Joseph Alsop Jr., an influential figure, attended the funeral with his wife, Susan Mary. His letters of foreign policy advice to Kennedy were taken as seriously by the White House as Alsop himself took his wines and eighteenth-century French furniture. White House correspondent Charles Bartlett, who worked for the *Chattanooga Times*, was extremely well connected in Washington and also came to the funeral. He and his wife, Martha, had introduced John F. Kennedy to Jacqueline Bouvier. Kennedy aides Arthur Schlesinger and McGeorge Bundy were also in the pews.

Many of the mourners were artists who knew Mary from gallery openings and cultural events. One of Mary's former lovers, abstract painter Kenneth Noland, had traveled down from New York, where his career was, as he would say later, "in ascendancy," and where he was being introduced to fame by the formalist art critic Clement Greenberg. Noland's affair with Mary had coincided with one of his most productive periods. The funeral was the first and last time Noland met Cord Meyer, whom the artist later recalled as "very spooky."

The Assistant Director of the Washington Gallery of Modern Art, Alice Denney, who had exhibited Mary's work several years before, was in the chapel, along with her assistant Eleanor McPeck. The two women were horrified by the murder, but the presence of all the intelligence agents at the funeral intensified the sinister undertone for them. They had never seen this side of Mary's world. "It seemed terribly inappropriate," said Eleanor McPeck. "It was unlike Mary. I never would have thought of her in a cathedral, much less going to church."

Poet Reed Whittemore, a college friend of James Angleton's at Yale and now poetry consultant to the librarian of Congress, was there with his wife. Mary had been expected to attend a Whittemore reading on the night of her murder. William Walton, a former war correspondent and artist who had been a close friend of Ernest Hemingway's in Europe, was in the pews. He had been rewarded for running Kennedy's New York campaign with entree to the White House, where he advised Jackie about the mansion's decor. He had served as Mary Meyer's "walker," in the parlance of the times, the man who escorted her to intimate evenings in the White House on the pretext that she was his date. Artists who were wives of famous Washington men also attended the funeral. Arthur Schlesinger's wife, Marian Cannon Schlesinger, was a portrait painter who had played tennis with Mary at the White House. She came, as did V. V. Rankine, who was married to a British diplomat and writer stationed in Washington and had shared a studio with Mary.

A tight-knit group of women in the chapel were Vassar graduates who had spent their college years in the early forties with Mary beneath the old oaks and maples on the campus in Poughkeepsie, New York. They were a refined, elegant lot with the confidence conferred by old money. Most of them were wives of World War II veterans, and mothers, and Mary's independence, divorce, and slightly Bohemian lifestyle had been a source of light, vitality, and amusement to them. Clustering at the funeral, they still could not believe their vibrant friend was dead. The group of Vassar women "sat together in a daze," recalled Mary Skidmore Truesdale.[14]

The Vassar women kept apart from the other Georgetown wives, the ones to whom the label "socialite" might be applied without giving offense. In high school and college the Vassar women had enjoyed that lifestyle, but afterward they had eschewed it as shallow. Many had been debutantes, but they were loath to mention those days to each other, even though they all knew when to wear white gloves and when to take them off. One of them was surprised to learn years later that Mary had been a debutante. "We really didn't care about that stuff," she said.[15] They felt themselves to be educated, which they were, and engaged in dynamic, interesting lives. A few were working in professions. One of them, Katharine Graham, had just become publisher of the *Washington Post*.

Anne Chamberlin was one of Mary's closest friends, a gamine journalist who worked for *Time* magazine. Chamberlin had covered Jacqueline Kennedy while Mrs. Kennedy waited, pregnant, in Hyannisport for her husband to win the Democratic nomination in 1960. Chamberlin, born Anne Nevin, was divorced and adventurous, much like Mary. She had spent part of her Vassar years driving across the Andes in Peru and living in Paris.

Mary Draper Janney, a dark-eyed historian who taught at a private suburban Washington day school, had roomed with Mary at Vassar. She retained her 1940s style into the 1960s, even though she was married and the mother of three children, and her students thought of her as a capital-city version of Lauren Bacall, with her rumpled, mannish suits, whiskey voice, and habit of lighting up cigarettes in class. She was married to CIA man Wistar Janney. Mary Janney sat in a pew near another Vassar classmate, the bouncy blond Scottie Fitzgerald Lanahan—F. Scott Fitzgerald's daughter—and her husband, Washington attorney Jack Lanahan. Also representing the Vassar contingent was Cicely d'Autremont Angleton, an heiress with high cheekbones, raised in Arizona, who had graduated two years behind Mary. A suburban mother of three herself, Cicely sat between her husband, Jim, and Cord Meyer.

At the funeral in spirit but not in person were James and Anne Truitt, two of Mary's closest friends. James Truitt had recently moved to Tokyo as the Japan bureau chief for *Newsweek*. His wife, Anne, was, like Mary, an artist and a mother. Anne's meticulous self-consciousness was the polar opposite of her late friend's buoyancy. Mary trusted the Truitts so much she had confided in them about her relationship with President Kennedy. Crew-cut James Truitt came from a prominent Maryland family and was known equally for his intelligence, eccentricity, and social grace. He was a heavy drinker and personally close to both Angleton and Cord Meyer. Anne Truitt had been raised on Maryland's Eastern Shore in a genteel southern family and graduated from Bryn Mawr. As her husband's erratic behavior increased, Anne Truitt channeled more of her emotional struggle into art.

The night after Mary Meyer was murdered, a single telephone call from Japan to Washington had sparked a chain of events that would shroud Mary's life and death in mystery for decades. As they sat at home in stunned silence, Ben and Tony Bradlee had received a phone call from Anne Truitt in Japan. It was a matter of some urgency, she told Tony Bradlee, that they find Mary's diary before the police got to it and her private life became a matter of public record. Anne Truitt repeated the warning to counterintelligence chief James Angleton. Although the Angletons and the Bradlees did not have all the details about Mary's relationship with the late president, they knew enough about her lifestyle to agree with Anne Truitt. The papers of the dead woman must not wind up in the wrong hands. No one knew what Mary, in her wild late years, had written down, what letters she had kept, or whose private thoughts and actions she had committed to paper. A frantic search began.

Mary Meyer's murder in the heart of Georgetown and the national security community took on the aura of the unknowable that pervaded her life as the wife of Cord Meyer. When she died, the CIA was locked in a covert intelligence war conducted as intensely inside Washington as in the alleys of Saigon. Paranoia and a thrilling sense of global power surged through the nation's capital, especially among her male peers. "There was an enormous issue about secrecy then," recalled Myer Feldman, who served as deputy special counsel to the president in the Kennedy administration, and who attended Mary's funeral. "There were spies everywhere in the town, spies for Israel, spies for France, spies for the Russians."[16] Many of these men thoroughly enjoyed themselves, often conducting business in Washington over three-martini lunches in plain view of anyone who cared to watch the cat-and-mouse game. Women who dined at Jackie Kennedy's favorite restaurant, La Salle du Bois on M Street, might, if they paid attention to their fellow lunchers, watch the occasional envelope passed under the table between an Iron Curtain diplomat and an American intelligence agent or State Department official. Under one of those tables, CIA official Robert Amory Jr. had received the text of Khrushchev's speech to the Warsaw Pact nations in which Khrushchev criticized Stalin.[17] The FBI had planted microphones under the restaurant's tables to try to catch traitors and foreign spies. Some of the waiters were federal agents. In cold war Washington, real life was stranger than fiction.

All that intrigue was very sexy. Sexual adventurousness was part of the Georgetown style. Its denizens viewed themselves as morally sophisticated and European, in contrast to the Eisenhower Republicans. "These people felt they were just a couple years away from Hemingway," said C. Wyatt Dickerson, the husband of socially prominent television broadcaster Nancy Dickerson. "A lot of them had experience with Paris in the 1950s. They came back to Washington and thought that wife swapping separated them from the country folks."[18]

Washington has always attracted ambitious men absorbed in competition with each other. The cold warriors, possessed of atomic-era "ballsiness" and wearing their machismo like World War II officers' epaulets, were consumed with power. They styled themselves after James Bond or the Rat Pack, men adorned with numbers of women. If their women did not find this attractive, they were very unhappy women. "The husbands just overshadowed us completely," said June Dutton, long divorced from Kennedy administration official Fred Dutton. "Most of the men felt too important to involve their wives in what they were doing. There was no room for partners in it. We were just decorations and isolated. The men all gathered and talked, and women were left to talk about children and schools. The wives were just wives."[19]

Mary Meyer was an enigmatic woman in life, and in death her real personality lurks just out of view. Her life was domestic and private, as were the lives of her female friends. As independent as she seemed to her female friends, it is unlikely any of the men in Mary's life ever thought of her as an equal. She and her friends were surely affected by the condescension of their men, an attitude that has survived the decades since her death. "Who wants to read about a bunch of unhappy women?" one of their ex-husbands, a prominent Washington attorney, said when told that any book about Mary Pinchot Meyer would also involve the lives of her friends.[20]

During the Kennedy years, women remained in the background. The prevailing notion was that they were "tomatoes," "the females," present for male amusement. Women in Mary's group accepted the way things were. They were refined women, willing mothers of the baby boom (Mary's sister, Tony, had six children). Although they lived in Washington and were often well educated, they never asked to share power with their husbands in any public way. Asked whether her opinions mattered to their dinner guests, one leader of the Georgetown social scene, Susan Mary Alsop, took a puff from an ever-present Merit cigarette, laughed dryly, and without hesitation replied: "Not in the least. I was modest in nature, and I thought I was with people who knew a lot more than I did."[21] After her dinners, in a time-honored tradition, Mrs. Alsop always retreated with the women into a room separate from the men.

In their female-centered world, the women had their own code of behavior. They were skillful flirts, practitioners of a lost art. They had to be. Men were the only route to economic and social power. Without a powerful man, a woman would almost certainly fall out of the circle. Certain women became leaders, and their whims and behavior were copied the way girls do in a high-school clique. Journalist Barbara Howar has described this scene as it revolved around the perpetually pregnant Ethel Kennedy, wife of the attorney general. Ethel attracted a coterie of female friends, wives of other powerful Washington men, who wanted nothing more than to be just like Ethel. "They emulated each gesture and expression, dressed alike, thought alike, accepted or rejected each new face or fashion in the manner of their idol, and as if by some secret signal from above, would gobble you up or ignore you, fold you to their bosoms or cut you dead."[22]

Here and there a nonconforming individual appeared. One of them was Mary Pinchot Meyer. She was born in 1920, the year women got the right to vote. She wore manners and charm like a second skin, but there was a reserve to her as well. Few people got beyond her outer self to see the inner Mary. She was complicated. She wanted freedom and personal authority, but she lived in a time when society distrusted those qualities in women. Men gave her entree to smoke-filled parties where conversation was vivid and the presence of power quickened her blood. Often these men were incapable of emotional openness, and this gave her an aura of loneliness. Like many of the men and women in her group, she might have been depressed at a time when that illness was not much discussed or diagnosed. She fought against melancholy with psychoanalysis and sheer will. She was attracted to glamour and the dramatic, yet she herself radiated simplicity and warmth. She had a special effect on men. One man once said she reminded him of a cat walking on a rooftop in moonlight.[23] She was cool and poised, and she paid attention to men and made them feel interesting. She flirted *and* "went all the way," in the parlance of the times. And she became a White House insider at a time when belonging to the Kennedy clique was the apex of a Washington woman's social achievement.

Her death was all the more tragic because of its timing. Born into luxury, attractive and well educated, she appeared on the surface to have led a charmed life. But she had endured a family suicide, marriage to a difficult wounded World War II veteran, unforgettable personal losses, and then a divorce. Through it all she had retained the vitality and energy her friends loved and admired. And in her last years she had begun to carve out a niche for herself as an independent woman, an unusual creature for her time. She was killed in the prime of her life.

It was not her personality but her access to Kennedy and to other prominent men that ultimately made her a figure of mystery and power after her death. A journalist suggested years after her murder that Mary Meyer had been "the secret Lady Ottoline of Camelot," referring to the British pacifist. Mary might actually have been a force for peace during some of the most frightening years of the cold war, but only in death did Mary Meyer really leave the confines of the private world she shared with her female friends and become part of a legend.

# 2

# Grey Towers

*Keep an anchor to windward in case of revolution.*

AMOS PINCHOT, 1933

Floating candles in the shape of white lilies sent small ripples of reflected fire around the surface of the Finger Bowl. Crickets chirped accompaniment to the soft conversation of the Pinchot brothers and their families and guests, seated around the water table in the arched brick pavilion that served as a summer dining room at Grey Towers in the 1920s and 1930s. The water table was three feet deep and the pool within was framed by an oval stone wall with a wide shelf where the plates, cutlery, linen, and glasses were arranged on woven mats. A large piece of coral on the bottom of the pool recalled a sailing trip to the South Seas. Uniformed servants delivered the food on balsa wood rafts decorated with gold and indigo peacock plumes, and the dishes floated from diner to diner with a gentle push. Often the Sunday night fare was baby peacock, raised in cages on the grounds of the northeastern Pennsylvania estate so that the birds never walked and thus did not become tough. Cornelia

Bryce Pinchot, the wife of Pennsylvania governor Gifford Pinchot, liked to tell her guests that a platter of peacock tongues, as served to kings in classical literature, really did make a fine dish. More plebeian fare was also served, fresh from the garden—tomatoes, potatoes, lima beans, asparagus, peas and carrots.[1]

The children at this table could never resist the urge to play with the rafts of food. The Pinchot brothers, Amos and Gifford, and their wives chided Mary and Tony and their first cousin Gifford for pushing the floating platters too hard in the water, making waves and marring the serene effect. As the dinner dragged on, the children grew restless. They heard their ponies whinnying in the meadow near the tennis courts and the dogs barking at some wild creature near the edge of the pine forest filled with deer and black bear, bald eagles, osprey, and bobcat. The little girls could hear the waterfall and think about swimming lessons with their elder half-sister, Rosamund.[2] At Grey Towers the women were practicing nudists, and they often wandered the grounds near the pool and waterfall naked, to the great delight of the servants.[3] When Mary was a girl, Rosamund sometimes rode horseback in the buff as well, a sylph galloping about in moonlight. In years to come, men and women who visited the estate with Mary were always slightly shocked or charmed, depending upon their degree of conventionality, when she casually stripped and dove into the pool above the waterfall.

As they sat around the Finger Bowl in the gathering dark, the little girls could also imagine the rattlesnakes they'd been warned of and the boots they must wear and the snakebite kits they had to strap on if they went into the woods, though they had yet to encounter a snake. And they thought of the tennis games their father was so keen on playing with them. The way to the grass tennis courts was through the long walled garden, where tart raspberries and rhubarb grew. The fruit trees there had been first cultivated by their grandfather, and the little girls loved to reach up to pluck Seckel pears and eat them as the juice ran through their fingers. They were sometimes put to work, too, plucking the Queen Anne's lace from the meadow behind the garden so the horses would not eat it and become sick.

Finally dessert was served, and the Pinchot girls tried to stifle their giggles and avoid their father's eye, for he might be laughing too. Their aunt Cornelia had ordered the servants yet again to create a baked Alaska, a piece of sheet cake piled with ice cream molded around a bottle, coated with meringue, and baked. Just before the dessert was sent floating out on its balsa raft, the butler dropped a little water and dry ice into the bottle, so the confection smoked like a tiny volcano as it circled the pool.[4]

Around the Finger Bowl the Pinchot family tried to entertain in style and served guests a glass or two of luxurious—since illegal—liquor or wine. The governor and his wife were, of necessity, politically "dry" during Prohibition, but they didn't let the amendment stop them and their guests from enjoying a nip here and there. The adults engaged in an ongoing and sometimes tense discussion about the storage of bottles of gin, whiskey, and wine in Amos's little house on the estate grounds, in order that the Gifford Pinchots' residence not be tainted. Acquiring, storing, and sharing liquor were Pinchot family obsessions during Prohibition. "If it's not too much trouble can you keep my whiskey and dole it out when my guests are thirsty?" Cornelia wrote Amos in 1921. A year later Cornelia formally apologized for giving some of the Pinchot whiskey to her friends instead of back to him. Amos often worried that the gardener would find the stock and report it back to the townfolk.[5]

As night fell around the Finger Bowl, the terra-cotta urns in the pavilion with their showers of flowers and ferns disappeared into the gloom. Purple wisteria dripped petals onto the Finger Bowl. In the gardens around the estate, where white lilies and blue delphinium and various roses bloomed in tended profusion, and grapevines flourished in the "graperie," an occasional bird rustled in the towering butternut and white pine trees. When the guests retired, they would notice that the flame shapes of the stone finials on the low walls around the gardens and pool and tennis court were repeated indoors, carved on the dark maple newel posts on the wide stairway.

Mary was a healthy, athletic, and outgoing child who learned horseback riding and was spoken to in French almost as soon as she could walk and speak; her mother was "Maman," and her nanny was "Mademoiselle."[6] When she was a toddler, her short curly hair was white-blond, and wherever she went a uniformed nurse trailed her with her baby sister, Tony, in a carriage. The two sisters' special pet was a scruffy fox terrier named Benjy.[7] At Grey Towers, Mary had a personal garden within the larger garden, and she started a butterfly collection. She and her father put out sugar water to trap butterflies, then killed them with ether and pinned them to a board. By the time she was twelve years old she had dozens of beautiful insects on display.

Mary was the first daughter in Amos Pinchot's second family, and if she grew up to become a strong-willed woman, some of her fire certainly came from her father. Amos Pinchot was a major figure in the history of progressive politics in the twentieth century. A wealthy gadfly with great passion and idealism, he burned with the spirit of free inquiry and the rights of the individual. A New York lawyer who rarely practiced law, Amos was known as a champion of the underdog, a man who preferred lost causes to compromised ideals. His motto was a comment made by one of his friends, the Progressive senator Robert La Follette, who said of his own reforming efforts, "Defeat was a matter of no consequence."[8] Like Mary's future husband, Cord, Amos could be described, with either admiration or disgust depending on one's political views, as dogmatic. The youngest of three Pinchot children, educated at Yale in the family tradition, in his youthful days Amos Pinchot had been considered a New York society swell, a man who "always did love elegance and the formalities of social life."[9] With his pince-nez, tailored suits, and mustache twirled slightly at the ends, he cut a stylish figure throughout his life.

He belonged to a variety of social clubs, from Yale's Skull and Bones to Teddy Roosevelt's New York hunt club, the Boone and Crockett. He was a talented tennis player and remained aggressive on the court even after a hip injury incurred during the Spanish-American War, when his horse fell off a cliff in Puerto Rico. He had signed up for service as a private because he believed Spain was exploiting Cuba.[10]

He had his political awakening when he supported his older brother Gifford, who in 1910 was chief of the U.S. Forest Service and opposed the granting of Alaskan coal reserves to a wealthy member of the Taft cabinet. Amos saw the contest in epic terms, not as one between men but between the forces of private power and the public interest. Thus began his lifelong crusade against "the privileged," a group of which he himself, living on inherited wealth, was a member in good standing.

Amos Pinchot lived his life tilting at windmills, or as his friend Max Eastman once put it, trying to stem Niagara with placards.[11] He took on the nation's big-money powers, supporting the notion of public utilities and the breakup of large segments of land. He believed private monopolies ought to be abolished by law, not merely regulated. But there his idea of the role of government ended.

Amos Pinchot was an individualist, never a socialist. He wrote that government ought to be limited to "the furthering of the interests of the individual." He was known as a publicist, not of the fluffier sort, but a serious man who wrote about serious ideas for educated people. In the *New York Times* his confrontational style provoked readers to write letters accusing him of everything from lunacy to anarchism. Pinchot delighted in provocation, but he always rejected the revolutionary label. He considered himself firmly in the liberal reformer camp.[12]

Around the Finger Bowl at Grey Towers during the Depression, the national economic crisis was present in minds but not circumstances. Sunday evenings at Grey Towers, however, were very unlike the hardscrabble Sunday night suppers in most of 1930s America, where average people were having trouble maintaining the necessities of life. The leafy grounds, just an hour and a half by train from the Amos Pinchot family's Park Avenue apartment and the breadlines of

New York, were an enclave of gracious living. Located on the Delaware River, the estate offered grass tennis courts, a swimming pool, fishing, horses, and music lessons on 3,600 acres that included a privately owned waterfall, Pinchot Falls, trickling over dark rocks for a third of a mile through an old forest of pines and black cherry trees. Black locust trees lined the mile-long drive up to the house from the edge of the town of Milford.

Devoted as they were to public ownership of land and utilities, the Pinchots could guard their own property rights fiercely. The family controlled the fishing rights in the Sawkill, which they stocked with trout, and the use of the waterfall. The Milford locals were allowed to swim at the falls, which was where Tony and Mary met "different people," as Tony put it.[13] But the locals had to follow strict rules. They could not use live bait or bring guests up from the village. At one point in the 1930s, the family considered leasing the brook so they wouldn't have to keep paying a night watchman, without whom "you know what will happen," Gifford wrote to Amos, but that idea was never carried through.[14]

The Pinchot family had done well financially in America without doing much harm to people or the environment and without drawing great attention to its wealth, remarkable achievements in the era of the industrial robber barons and conspicuous consumption. Growing up at Grey Towers, Mary Pinchot was exposed to upper-class manners and mores as well as radical American politics. The silver spoon always contained a dose of skepticism. While the family paid respect to social conventions, it was never slavishly social. From these vaguely Bohemian beginnings, on an idyllic estate frequented by some of the country's most important men, Mary's place in society was so secure that decades later she became a member of the Kennedy in crowd without the straining that marked most Washington climbers.

The family roots were three generations deep by the time Mary was born. The Pinchots were descended from a French immigrant,

Cyrille Désiré Constantin Pinchot, born into the middle class of France in 1797. As a nineteen-year-old captain in the French army, the Pinchot family patriarch was involved in a plot to spring Napoleon from St. Helena. When that attempt failed, he escaped on a fishing boat to England, then moved to America. He bought four hundred acres in Milford, which already had a significant French population, and became the tax collector.[15]

Cyrille's son James Pinchot increased the family fortune with a wallpaper business and by marrying well. James wed the former Mary Jane Eno of Simsbury, Connecticut. Her father, Amos Eno, owned large tracts of New York City real estate and built the first Fifth Avenue Hotel, nicknamed at the time "Eno's Folly." Mary Jane Eno's brother Richard wrote the first traffic laws, preparing the city of New York and by extension the entire country for the automobile age. Richard Eno had inherited a million dollars from his father and traveled widely in Europe, noting the traffic situation in London, where common courtesy seemed to govern the public thoroughfares, unlike New York City. In 1903 he published "Rules for Driving," the first comprehensive traffic regulation system in the world. New York City adopted it.

After making millions in the wallpaper business, James Pinchot retired at age forty-four and turned to philanthropy, travel, and conservation. He and Mary Jane had three children: Gifford, Antoinette, and finally Amos, born in Paris in 1873. In New York they lived in Gramercy Park, where their wealthy neighbors included the Hewitts, Coopers, and Minturns. Theirs was the New York of Edith Wharton: squalid, run by corrupt political bosses, pestilent along the waterfront, and yet at the upper reaches a very formal society of afternoon visits in carriages with footmen in red-topped boots and side-whiskers.

In summers the family left the heat and smell of New York and went to Milford, where James Pinchot had built Grey Towers, a French château-style, L-shaped castle with three towers and a servants' wing. The house, with nineteen bedrooms and twenty-three fireplaces, was built in 1885 of local fieldstone for $40,000 by the American architect Richard Morris Hunt. It became the aristocratic manor above the peasant town of Milford. The Pinchots' various acquaintances in American art, literature, and politics often visited the country mansion. A horse was kept in the stables for their close friend General William Tecumseh Sherman.

James Pinchot was generous to Milford. He endowed a building in the center of town on the site of his old dry goods store and dedicated it to the Yale School of Forestry. Eventually he established a field study area and a forestry camp on the grounds of the Grey Towers estate.

Of the two sons, Amos and Gifford, Gifford took the more political course in life. He inherited his father's interest in forestry, took botany courses at Yale, and studied forestry at France's national forestry school in Nancy. Back home, he designed the forest at Biltmore, George Vanderbilt's North Carolina estate. He spent years traveling around the United States studying forests and publishing books: *The White Pine*, *Adirondack Spruce*, and *Timber Trees and Forests of North Carolina.*

The tall, intense Gifford became a close friend and advisor to Teddy Roosevelt, who appointed him the first chief of the U.S. Forest Service. The issues he faced there involved larger political debates about the role of government and private versus public control of natural resources. During his service the number of national forests in the United States increased six times, to 193 million acres in 1910. While he helped acquire land for the federal government, Gifford Pinchot did not always side with the conservationists; he angered pioneering naturalist John Muir by supporting San Francisco's efforts to acquire a piece of Yosemite National Park as a reservoir.

Gifford's career with the federal government ended in 1910 when he accused one of President Taft's political appointees, Interior Secretary Richard Ballinger, of involvement in fraudulent claims to Alaskan coal reserves. Taft sided with his cabinet member and fired Pinchot. A few years later, Gifford and Amos led the fight to unseat

Taft. When the Republicans renominated Taft, the Pinchot brothers helped form the "Bull Moose" or Progressive Party, which nominated Roosevelt for the presidency in 1912.

Gifford eventually ran for governor of Pennsylvania and won on the Republican ticket in 1922. During his first term he established himself as an ardent supporter of Prohibition and a foe of the big-utility interests. He was reelected governor in 1930, and his road-building program eased the state's Depression-period unemployment by giving jobs to thousands. His motto became "Get the farmer out of the mud." He harbored presidential ambitions for several decades but never achieved national office.

Amos Pinchot, named after his mother's father, was not as politic as his older brother and also more intrinsically progressive. He twice backed the presidential candidacy of Wisconsin populist Robert La Follette. La Follette's ticket called for establishing government ownership of railroads and allowing Congress to override the Supreme Court. Journalist Walter Lippmann would brand La Follette's platform "violently nationalistic and centralizing."[16] In Amos's adult years, there was a great deal of political ferment even within the Progressive Party about the rights and limitations of large corporate entities, partly due to a lack of clarity in the 1890 Sherman Act. Amos was aligned with a radical group within the party that wanted monopolies abolished outright and supported public ownership of forests, water-generated power, utilities, and railroads. But the party refused to attach those trust reforms to its platform, as some influential members believed monopolies were inevitable and ought to be permitted but regulated.

In 1912 Amos ran for Congress himself in the Eighteenth District of New York, fully aware that his chances were close to nil in the overwhelmingly Democratic area. He used the opportunity to proselytize for the Progressive cause, pulling out a chair on a sidewalk and talking to crowds about the evils of big business. Of his foray into campaign politics, he later wrote that he was surprised at how many people wanted to listen to him. But he was a notoriously poor public speaker who swallowed his words and got bogged down by the reams of statistics he always carried up to the podium.[17]

Eventually, in 1914, Amos's fight with the protrust forces within his party burst into the open. Amos himself publicized the rift, believing that true Progressives would follow his lead and force the money interests out of the party. Instead the reverse occurred, and no one followed his lead. Teddy Roosevelt publicly repudiated him. Progressive Party officials asked him to resign.

Amos went on to fight American involvement in the First World War. His view was that the war (and later the Second World War as well) was being waged at the behest of the big-money powers and had no higher purpose than serving the economic interests of the privileged at the expense of the common man. In 1916 he became chairman of the Committee on Real Preparedness and served on the executive committee of the American Union Against Militarism in 1917. He also became treasurer of the defense committee for the magazine *Masses*, which had been banned from the mails for its antiwar positions. Through his involvement with *Masses* he became outraged at the attacks on the civil liberties of war protesters. That outrage led him in 1917 to help found the National Civil Liberties Bureau, which eventually became the American Civil Liberties Union.

*Masses* was a literary and artistic magazine founded by the writer and critic Max Eastman. Nicely designed, it was devoted to the premise that social revolution could be joined with artistic endeavor. Eastman and three staff members, including the journalist John Reed, were tried twice for sedition in connection with the magazine, but both trials ended in hung juries. Amos called the magazine one afternoon as it teetered on the edge of financial ruin and supposedly told Eastman he put out "a swell magazine." Eastman and Reed immediately went to Amos's law offices, where he gave them several thousand dollars to stay afloat. He later paid to spring Eastman from jail, where he was being held on libel charges.

Through his association with Eastman and *Masses*, Amos the Park

Avenue lawyer entered a new world—a young, downtown New York community of writers and artists that included Sinclair Lewis, Edna St. Vincent Millay, and many, many lesser lights. "*Masses* reflected . . . the gay and innocent flavor of pre-war cultural radicalism: bearded Wobblies attending tango teas in Greenwich Village. Anybody who was anybody wrote for *Masses*," according to *The New Republic*. Many of Eastman's writers and associates were openly Communist. "The Russian revolution then seemed to them the fulfillment of their humanitarian dreams. Their world had a gaiety and a speciousness about it. Its inhabitants were a cohesive group—Bohemian, enchanted by art, tireless in talk, intoxicated by everything," wrote David Boroff in the *National Observer*.

Eastman was later a fixture in Mary Pinchot's life, providing an example of left-wing activism throughout. He eventually visited Soviet Russia and became disillusioned with the Communist system as he witnessed Stalin's brutal rise. He remained close to Leon Trotsky and even served as Trotsky's literary agent in New York until Trotsky was assassinated in Mexico. As a literary critic, Eastman disparaged T. S. Eliot, James Joyce, and Gertrude Stein for what he termed their excessive obscurity. His influence as a critic waned after he published his attack on the moderns in an article in *Harper's* in 1929 called "The Cult of Unintelligibility."

Among Eastman's Bohemian crowd, Amos met his future wife. In 1919 Amos divorced his first wife of nineteen years, Gertrude Minturn, a daughter of a prominent New York family with whom he had had two children, Rosamund and Gifford, to marry Ruth Pickering, thirteen years his junior. Ruth was a Greenwich Village writer and the daughter of a middle-class businessman. Their first daughter was born a little more than a year later, in New York City on October 14, 1920, and was named Mary Eno Pinchot after her paternal grandmother.

Divorce at the time was still taboo, and Amos, prickly and sensitive to public opinion, was subject to social reproach for the rest of his life. Even years later, Amos's divorce was a source of amusement for the New York tabloids, apparently eager to humiliate a man of his wealth and stature. In 1927, when his oldest daughter, Rosamund, returned from a European trip, the celebrity press arrived to photograph her coming down the gangplank. Both Amos and his ex-wife showed up at the dock to greet their daughter. A photographer for the *New York Daily News* snapped a picture of the awkward threesome, and the paper ran the picture with a snide story about the embarrassing surprise meeting of Rosamund Pinchot's divorced parents. Amos fired off a letter to the paper's owner, Joseph Medill Patterson, noting that he had known Patterson's mother but that the family blood had obviously begun to run thin, as clearly her son had "no respect for the decencies and dignities of life."[18]

Descriptions of young Ruth were similar to those that would be applied by another generation of men to her daughter Mary. When Amos met Mary's mother, Ruth Pickering was still the "lithe, strong, beautifully proportioned, ash blonde with a petulant mouth, [and] most lovingly tender and far-seeing blue eyes" who had captivated Max Eastman as a young man.[19] She was also "a poet—a girl who concealed under a great deal of silence a rare and individual gift of speech," wrote Eastman, who never acted on his feelings toward her.

Ruth had grown up near Eastman in Elmira, New York, in a Quaker home with her parents, two sisters, and two grandmothers. Her father had inherited his father-in-law's paint business as it stood on the verge of bankruptcy, and throughout Ruth's childhood the Pickering family was economically straitened trying to pay off old debts. Her mother worked as the company bookkeeper. In an article titled "A Deflated Rebel" for *The Nation*'s 1926 series called "These Modern Women," Ruth described her childhood self as a "continually rebellious" tomboy who grew up to become more a pragmatist than a feminist. As a girl she befriended her poor and uneducated neighbors against the advice of her powerful Grandma Haynes, whose approval was doled out stintingly. Ruth rebelled against the matriarch in spirit and letter. "I sought out the toughest companions of the neighborhood. I played with boys summer and winter, whose bravado, being normal, seemed of a far less glorious nature than my own."[20]

After studying at Vassar and Columbia University, Ruth Pickering worked at a variety of jobs, including brief stints in secretarial and factory work, always in it for "the experience," as she put it, more than the work itself. She eventually discovered she liked writing and editing. She was an editor and staff writer for *The Nation* when she met Amos Pinchot. Thirty-three years old, she had remained single and lived the life of a modern career woman. Just before her marriage and move to Park Avenue she lived in a room in a rented red brick Greenwich Village townhouse with Max Eastman, his sister Crystal Eastman and her husband, and Eugen Boissevain, the future husband of Edna St. Vincent Millay.

With two strong individualists for parents, Mary was destined to respect people with strongly held views who marched to the sound of their own private drummers. Ruth Pickering's preoccupation with individualism eventually led her to renounce even the group cause of women's rights. After marriage she decided that her youthful feminism had been merely an extension of her own ego, with no higher purpose. "In the early days of my marriage the formulas of feminism pestered me because I allowed my husband to support me," she wrote in *The Nation* in 1926. Ruth justified herself by concluding that exchanging rebellion for financial security had matured her by allowing her the leisure to write what she wanted to write. "I have traded my sense of exhilarating defiance (shall we call it feminism?) for an assurance of free and unimpeded self-expression (or shall we call that feminism?). In other words I have grown up."[21]

Although she wrote about the labor movement before her marriage, after her marriage and Mary's birth Ruth turned to more traditionally feminine topics and became a dance and art critic. Her articles convey a serious appreciation of modern dance and art and a wry sense of humor. In a tongue-in-cheek 1921 *New Republic* article headlined "The Economic Interpretation of Jazz," she wrote about the effect of high rents in New York on modern dancing and music. "Music and dance have become more restricted, the intensity increasing in direct ratio to the rise in rents. . . . And men and women are obliged to cling closely together in order to move at all. . . . And what then is to be done with the allotted space for one pair already congested? Nothing save to lay her cheek against his cheek for further crowding. And so it goes on—the heat engendered in these overpacked rooms with no air leading inevitably again to the lower-necked gown. One moral question after the other becomes a question merely of rents."[22]

In the Roaring Twenties, modern dance represented a symbolic physical escape from the Victorian corset of the previous generation. Reviewing two books about Isadora Duncan in the February 1929 issue of *The Nation*, after the dancer's death, Ruth, by then raising her own two daughters, praised Duncan for her freedom of expression and her goal of teaching children to, in Duncan's words, "through dance, music, poetry and song express the feelings of the people with grace and beauty." Ruth was especially impressed by the dancer's devotion to individuality. Wrote Ruth: "She was teaching her children to be free and to be fine and to be natural. . . . Freedom was her religion and most specifically freedom for the unique woman that was Isadora."[23]

Amos and Ruth's devotion to individualism and personal freedom became a distinguishing characteristic of their oldest daughter. Mary Pinchot was born into a world of modern adults who were leaving Queen Victoria behind and entering the age of Freud. Ruth and Amos tried to encourage formality, manifested in good manners, along with freedom and creativity in children. Ruth was a gentle but distant mother who concentrated on her own work with a self-absorption that did not involve her children. From her, Mary learned first about women's independence.

But Ruth also deferred to her husband, Amos, who was older and the source of her economic freedom. Throughout Mary's childhood, men of great worldly power organized her life and the lives of all the women around her. Although politically progressive, Amos could never abandon the social conventions of the age in which he was educated. The two poles represented by her parents pulled Mary in two directions all her life. Little Mary adored her powerful father and would spend the rest of her life trying to replace him with other powerful men. When she grew up, she was always attracted to men who wanted to direct her or dismissed her relevance altogether. As with many women of her generation, any authority or artistic aesthetic she developed would come only later in life, if at all. This did not mean, however, that she lacked self-confidence or her mother's desire for independence. The example of her parents' strong beliefs and the cushion of Pinchot family money, especially in her early years, conferred on her a fearlessness and assurance that she retained throughout her life.

Pieces of Mary Pinchot's childhood history during the 1920s and 1930s are recorded in the letters of Amos and Ruth and the Gifford Pinchot family. The letters chronicle the daily life of a well-to-do family. Like other wealthy Americans, the Pinchots traveled frequently and had several different places of residence; they communicated with each other almost daily via engraved stationery about many matters: family illnesses, the repair or replacement of household items, the baby's latest word. Ruth wrote frequent letters to Amos during the early part of their marriage, when she was at one family dwelling and he at another, keeping him up to date on their baby girl's progress. From the Hamptons, the summer Mary was two, Ruth wrote: "Mary is the baby wonder of the beach. She has been on the beach morning and afternoon each day. She sits on the floor putting pebbles into a pail and yelling furiously 'I like Daddy.' She is so pretty with her curly hair and fresh red cheeks."[24] The next summer, writing from a vacation at the Eastmans' in upstate New York, she wrote, "Mary is a perfect little bully. She knows she can make Elizabeth cry easily and she teases her all the time. She's the aggressor and a devil."[25]

Ruth moved comfortably into the upper-class Pinchot world. The family money relieved her for the first time in her life of the necessity of work, and the effect was liberating. "Since I no longer have to work, I am no longer lazy," she wrote in an essay published in *The Nation*.[26] But she never grew entirely at ease with servants and the messy details of their hiring and firing. Coming from a family where every penny earned was counted, Mary's Quaker mother could be irritated by the lavishness at Grey Towers.

At Milford, the château was occupied by Gifford and his family. It had a dozen workers. The little house on the grounds occupied by Amos and his family had a cook, a cleaner, and a nurse. Both brothers had butlers. The little Pinchot girls grew up accustomed to the presence of servants. Tony never learned to cook and years later, when she and her second husband, Ben Bradlee, had President Kennedy over, she begged her aunt Cornelia, who was living in Washington then, to lend her a cook. But Mary grew up to learn and enjoy cooking.

There was apparently some tension between Ruth and her more aristocratic sister-in-law. Writing from the Hamptons while Amos was in Milford arranging for the little house to be electrified, Ruth talked about obtaining some furniture from the château for the little house at Grey Towers (designed at the turn of the century by Mead, McKim & White, designers of New York's original Penn Station), which was occupied by Amos's family: "Leila might be able to sacrifice a couple of lamps when she's got a governor for a husband don't you think?"[27] Ruth was also aware of rivalry between the two brothers. The younger brother was keenly interested in politics but lacked the politician's personality. Of his brother Gifford, Ruth assured her husband: "Everyone who knows you both is quick to see the superiority of your intellect."[28]

In 1924 Ruth gave birth to her second daughter, Antoinette, called Tony. From childhood, little Tony was the more reserved and shy of the two sisters. She had more childhood illnesses, and many of Ruth and Amos's worries in the 1920s concerned Tony's latest bout with mumps, scarlet fever, and even appendicitis. One summer the family trooped to Fire Island, because Tony was underweight and peaky and seemed to need the sea air.[29] Physically, Mary had the strong chin and bone structure of the Pinchot family, and Tony, with her heart-shaped face, took after her mother.

Ruth loved her children but relished her solitude and her writing time, and so Amos was more of a presence in their lives than their mother. Amos's attitude toward his daughters was attentive and loving, but also austere and strict. He often planned their days for them. The girls regarded their mother as gentle and their father as the disciplinarian. Neither parent was particularly warm. Amos left the hands-on details of their upbringing to a succession of nannies when he could. When Mary was seven, Amos wrote happily that "the new governess, very calm but firm, impresses the children with the advisability of doing necessary things like eating and going to bed."[30]

Throughout Mary's childhood Amos continued to donate his legal services to various cases involving civil liberties, and he threw his political support behind one cause or another. His last third-party attempt, the Committee of 48, collapsed in 1920, but he never tired of organizing for the causes he believed in, no matter how unpopular. He was involved in the defense of the Italian anarchists Nicola Sacco and Bartolomeo Vanzetti, two Italian immigrants arrested while distributing anarchist literature and charged with robbery and murdering a shoe factory payroll clerk in Braintree, Massachusetts, in 1920. The men, a shoe factory worker and a fish peddler who could barely speak English, went to the electric chair in August 1927, but not until after their case had polarized right and left. Their trial before the Massachusetts Superior Court had been conducted in an atmosphere of Red-scare hysteria. The judge had vowed to "get those anarchist bastards" and the jury convicted them of murder. They had lingered in prison for years while supporters tried to free them. In 1925 a man under sentence for murder confessed that he had participated in the crime as part of a gang, and academics and lawyers from across the country became involved in appealing for a retrial. Jurist Felix Frankfurter, in a magazine article that inflamed conservatives, charged that the case had been based on circumstantial evidence. Sacco and Vanzetti became martyrs for the left, and before they were executed, mass demonstrations were held and bombs exploded in New York and Philadelphia. The executions became an international issue and led many on the left to lose faith in the American system of justice. After the men were put to death Amos wrote editorials attacking politicians and journalists who had condoned the executions, including Walter Lippmann.

Amos also spent the better part of Mary's childhood years working on a two-part book about his anticorporate philosophy. The first part, which he planned to title *Big Business in America*, was to be filled with his own personal accounts of sinister experiences with the money bosses. He worked on it throughout the latter half of the 1920s and into the thirties. The result was a jumble of outlines, notes, anecdotes, and quotations that were never gathered into a cohesive text. In 1933 he started in on a companion work, which he called *The History of the Progressive Party, 1912–1916*. The notes and text for that work were eventually compiled and edited by a family friend, Helene Maxwell Hooker, and published after his death.

Mary was closer to her father than Tony was. Amos wanted his daughters athletic, and of the two younger ones, Mary was more inclined toward sports. Amos taught her to play an aggressive game. Decades later, her tennis-playing friends in Washington were amazed when the soft-spoken, gentle woman suddenly turned ferocious on the tennis courts, wielding a vicious serve and mean backhand. Amos's war injury prevented him from moving very fast on the courts, but he would hit the ball back to his daughter with great force and speed. He was such a tennis fan that he often took the girls and their friends to watch championship tennis at Forest Hills. His hip injury prevented driving as well, so the family had a chauffeur until gas rationing during World War II made the cost of a car prohibitive.

Another woman at Grey Towers who taught Mary by example about female power in a world of men was her aunt. Cornelia Elizabeth Bryce Pinchot, known in the family as Leila, was a thirty-three-year-old American aristocrat when she married Gifford. Her father, Lloyd Bryce, was a congressman, a writer, and Teddy Roosevelt's ambassador to the Netherlands. Her mother was the granddaughter of iron magnate Peter Cooper, who founded the Cooper Institute (now Cooper Union). Cornelia was raised in Newport society but grew up to spurn the traditional role of well-bred wife. She marched in suffrage parades and helped her husband get elected in 1922 by getting women voters in Pennsylvania organized for the first time since they had won the right to vote. In 1928 she ran for Congress herself on a platform similar to her husband's: support for Prohibition and opposition to utility monopolies. She was defeated but went on to work in support of women and organized labor, and in the 1940s she became the United States representative to the International Women's Conference. She spent her last years active in Washington, D.C., social life, and chaired the Washington chapter of Americans United for World Organization, a group that called for atomic disarmament.

Cornelia was a 1920s superwoman, a supremely self-confident feminist who seemed able to do and have it all. She gloried in the kind of adventure available to rich young women. In her twenties she left Newport society and traveled with a friend across the continent, visiting American cities and towns and collecting, as she put it, "big-game hunters, reactionary Senators, Socialists, stodgy captains of industries, single taxers, a whole-hog Tolstoian, college professors and editors galore." In an essay for *The Nation*, she described her exuberant form of feminism: "My feminism tells me that woman can bear children, charm her lovers, boss a business, swim the Channel, stand at Armageddon and battle for the Lord—all in a day's work!"[31]

Cornelia was responsible for the Italianate and baroque touches added to Grey Towers in the 1920s. She saw a painting of a water table in Italy and decided to copy one, hence dinners around the Finger Bowl. She imprinted her own style on the château, adding trompe l'oeil decoration, paintings, and theme rooms. Her visiting room on the first floor was done in blue paint and wallpaper with a nautical theme. At The Hague she purchased a sixteen-by-ten-foot painting of ships at sea, a depiction of a Dutch naval battle, and had the canvas embedded into wet plaster in the wall of the room. Near the ceiling she hung some of the mounted game fish caught by the governor and his family and friends in the Florida Keys. A tiled path out the door picked up the oceanic theme and led from the visiting room through bowers of wisteria to the outdoor dining area and the

Finger Bowl. She put in a moat around the house, stocked with goldfish the family fed with bread.

Life at Grey Towers was both leisurely and formal. A silent campaign film called *Governor Pinchot and Family Enjoy Their Daily Exercise* shows, in grainy, speeded-up film time, what the estate was like in the 1920s. The camera scans the swimming pool, where Ruth and Rosamund, Amos's eldest daughter, in white bathing costumes and caps, teach two little girls, Tony and Mary, how to swim. Then they all climb out of the pool and pose, tableau-style, the women lounging with their legs stretched toward each other and the men standing on each side like pillars in their summer whites and straw boaters. The nannies and cooks wear crisp white uniforms.

With her deep-set blue eyes and strong chin, Amos's adored Rosamund, a curvaceous five-foot-nine blonde, had the Pinchot features Mary also inherited. Rosamund was a teenager when Mary was a child, and throughout Mary's childhood her half-sister provided a model of sophistication and glamour. Rosamund taught Mary how to ride at Milford. Her long, muscular legs and full figure were in contrast to prepubescent Mary's childish body. School chums of Mary's recall that she was in awe of her adventurous and beautiful half-sister and somewhat overshadowed by her.

At seventeen, Rosamund was "discovered" by Viennese producer Max Reinhardt, who spotted her on the deck of a luxury transatlantic ocean liner, the *Aquitania*, as he was heading to the United States to stage a New York production of *The Miracle*. Rosamund was returning home from a trip to Europe. Reinhardt chose her to play the part of the nun, and she was an overnight sensation, the socialite-turned-actress. Her photograph appeared frequently in stylish magazines, and for a few years she was a budding starlet.

Gifford and Cornelia Pinchot's only son, Giff (brothers Amos and Gifford both named their sons Gifford, so at times there were three Giffords on the estate), was a few years older than his youngest girl cousins. He and his friends rode horses, and he had his own forge where he practiced the blacksmithing he had learned from one of the village hands. Mary and Tony were strictly admonished to stay away from his playhouse, the Bait Box, where Gifford was conducting a long experiment examining the tiny pond and moat creatures with his microscope. Young Gifford grew up to become a doctor, left Pennsylvania, and eventually donated the large house and some of the grounds to the U.S. Forest Service.

Bookshelves in the Pinchot homes were lined with classic and modern prose and poetry, including all of Henry James's novels, ancient and modern history, studies in anthropology, works about mystical and conventional religion, psychology tomes, and dramatic works from Sophocles to Shakespeare to Ibsen and O'Neill. The books of A. A. Milne sat next to the complete poetical works of John Milton. Some of the volumes had notes in the margins written by either Ruth or Amos. Amos was especially fond of Shakespeare's sonnets and the works of the Greek tragedian Euripides, and he reread them throughout his life.

Writers, artists, and men of law and politics often visited the family at Milford and in New York. The Pinchot girls grew up around family friends who included Max and Crystal Eastman; Louis Brandeis; Roosevelt's secretary of the interior, Harold Ickes; and the flamboyant heiress Mabel Dodge. Mary's domestic world was cozy but vicariously cosmopolitan. She got letters and presents from her aunt Antoinette, married to a British nobleman and always on the move between London and some exotic destination. Her uncle Gifford took a South Seas sailing trip in 1929 on the family yacht and brought back all manner of treasure, including a sea turtle and the balsa wood rafts and coral for the Finger Bowl. Amos took frequent trips to the Florida Keys to fish, and sometimes the girls went along. Her half-sister, Rosamund, was always steaming off to Europe or California.

In New York during the winters of her childhood, Mary Pinchot lived on Park Avenue. Park Avenue became fashionable after World War I, when the trend toward apartment living among society people began. Most of the buildings were quite new. They were all stolid and square, a dozen or more floors rising into the sky. Park Avenue itself was divided by medians of fenced, well-tended grass, flowerbeds, and shrubbery. Only noncommercial traffic was allowed, no buses or trucks. The *WPA Guide to New York City*, written by Depression-era writers, claimed city planners described Park Avenue as "a superslum" because of the unappealing sameness of the design going into the new buildings. "Its architecture is noteworthy for its lack of imagination, one building resembling another like peas in a pod. Although the apartments have all the modern conveniences, adequate provision for light and air and view was generally neglected," the WPA guide said. Still, it was all rather swish. "Uniformed doormen tend top-hatted men and begowned women in their journey from foyer to car, car to foyer," the WPA writers wrote disdainfully.[32]

In October 1929 Amos Pinchot moved his family from a large apartment at 1125 Park Avenue, which occupied half of an entire floor, to a slightly smaller one at 1165 Park Avenue that occupied one fourth of a floor. The difference between the buildings was insignificant but the amount of space was somewhat less, and in the unforgiving eyes of New York society, the move meant the Amos Pinchot family had dropped a rung or two on the ladder. Amos put the best spin on things, however. In a letter to his sister Nettie he described the new apartment as "all freshness, lightness," with east and south light in all bedrooms, "and the Provencal furniture we bought at Cannes makes it livable."[33] Frayed rugs and patched draperies were the only visible signs of the family's financial straits. They were also a symbol of old money.

For the Amos Pinchot family, the 1930s were relatively hard times. The Pinchot family in general was not entirely unaffected by the economic disaster. Some renters of their New York real estate holdings, short of cash, had stopped paying rent, and the family had been forced to take second mortgages on some of the buildings. Amos was responsible for the family trust. He had taken on the role of family trustee when he realized that he liked to practice law only in connection with causes in which he believed. Amos began the decade with a protracted battle over the proceeds from the Eno family trust. Later, when that was settled—and not to his satisfaction—the income from family holdings in New York real estate began to shrink.

Amos suffered the darkness of the 1930s in his own way. He fretted and began to drink more—a habit that eventually got out of hand. He took out his anger in fits of temper at his daughters. The tradition of public service in his family and his own progressive politics probably compounded the guilt and helplessness he felt walking the streets of New York, passing once-employed people selling apples for five cents apiece. Experiencing financial setbacks himself, he knew other Americans were undergoing much worse. He tried to think about how to improve their lot. In 1931, in the darkest pre–New Deal days, he wrote to his brother Gifford urging him to go forward with a proposal to provide work on road camps for the unemployed in Pennsylvania. "You could be the first American leader to lay down and act on the proposition that the government has an obligation to supply people with work, when they want it and can't get it elsewhere. This is going to be a milestone in American history."[34]

Until Franklin Delano Roosevelt's New Deal, America suffered and waited for the Depression to end. A great sense of betrayal and resentment filled the land. The 1920s had seen the idolization of the dollar. When the gay party crashed to a halt and millions were thrown out of work, there was an outpouring of hatred toward the upper classes, toward the bosses and bankers and the system that had let so many down. Many American intellectuals regarded the Depression as an opportunity for a rethinking of the entire American economic system.

Amos, with his characteristic extremism, expected and predicted the worst. In one 1933 letter to his brother he advised him to "keep an anchor to windward in case of revolution."[35] He was not alone in that view. "The Depression led many intellectuals to believe some sort of social and ideological apocalypse was at hand," wrote Robert McElvaine, a chronicler of the Depression years. In 1932 fifty-two prominent writers, critics, and professors signed an open letter calling for a Communist president. Among the signers were Sherwood Anderson, Theodore Dreiser, Malcolm Cowley, John Dos Passos, Langston Hughes, Edmund Wilson, and Lincoln Steffens.[36]

Between 1929 and 1933, unemployment rose until more than a quarter of the American workforce was out of a job. Hoover and the Republicans had followed a plan of inaction. The idea was to let the

Depression take its course, that it was healthy for the market to drop and that it would improve by and by. One of Hoover's solutions was to launch an ad campaign to cheer up the unemployed and buy some time until the whole problem corrected itself. An ad that appeared in major periodicals displayed an unemployed worker with the following copy underneath: "We're not scared, either. If you think the good old U.S.A. is in a bad way more than temporarily, just try to figure out some place you'd rather be. . . . I'll see it through—if you will!"[37]

Amos Pinchot was not among the boosters, and his growing pessimism and anger were a nasty cloud over the houses where Mary lived as a girl. He never retreated in his attack on the monopolies. But in the mid-1930s he started to display a passion for positions that were on the fringes of populism, that resentful no-man's-land where the left met the right. He advocated a social-credit system of banking, in which the monetary and credit power would go into the hands of a nonpartisan authority. He carried on a correspondence with Ezra Pound, who was already flirting with fascism in Europe, about the evils of the monetary system. Pound's letters to him are a collage of insult, flattery, opinion, and economics. In one letter Pound wrote, "Yes I am with you, power to coin money is and of a right should be vested in Congress." In 1936 Pound wrote: "I suspect the WHOLE of yr/generation in the U.S.A. was fed on second rate English slop. . . . You are an old man but you have not been a coward. On at least a number of occasions you have showed courage."[38]

By the time Mary was fifteen, her father was listening to and admiring Father Charles Coughlin, the right-wing Catholic priest and radio broadcaster whose vitriolic populism was a hit with disaffected, xenophobic Americans before World War II. The "Radio Priest," as he became known, signed a contract with CBS in 1930 and at his most popular, in the mid-1930s, estimates gave him almost forty million listeners. He started out attacking Communists; then he turned his attention to the bankers. Eventually he linked the two and railed against both capitalism and Marxism, claiming that he supported a Christian democracy. He was behind FDR and the New Deal at first, but by 1936 he claimed the whole administration was "a government of the bankers, by the bankers and for the bankers." By the late 1930s he was openly supporting fascists and calling for a corporate state based on the model Benito Mussolini had installed in Italy. When he began praising Adolf Hitler in 1940, he was already losing his followers.

In letters to his uncle William Eno—who was showing signs of anti-Semitism—Amos in 1938 indicated some admiration for Coughlin. "I suppose you heard Coughlin yesterday. His delivery has greatly improved but he is getting himself into a death struggle with some very powerful foes." Elsewhere in the same letter, Amos wrote about the anti-Semitism sweeping the country. "The American Jews would be wise if they made themselves as inconspicuous as possible for the next few years. There is no doubt about the anti-Jewish wave of sentiment. It's a pity but a fact which must be reckoned with."[39]

William Eno, the father of traffic regulation, was not so circumspect. In a letter to Amos in 1938 he complained that most of Roosevelt's advisors were Jews and wrote that the Jews were taking over most of the business and media organizations in New York. "Think this over and you will see why we may wake up someday and follow Hitler," Eno wrote.[40]

Initially Amos supported FDR and the New Deal, but he soon decided the new administration was usurping too many powers for the executive branch and heading toward dictatorship. He objected in radio speeches and in pamphlets to FDR's labor policies, his court-packing bill, and his reelection to a third term. He particularly feared the consequences of wage, price, and farm-production controls. In an April 1937 open letter to FDR published in the *New York Times*, Amos laid out his objections to both the judiciary bill, which he called "sinister," and the National Recovery Act, which, he wrote, would lead to a managed economy under "a personal government which places the fate of labor, industry and agriculture in a bureaucracy controlled by one man. . . . I am forced to conclude that . . . you desire the power of a dictator without the liability of the name."[41]

Amos felt some personal responsibility for the direction the country was taking, because he had so forcefully advocated public ownership of some monopolies. But the massive expansion of the federal bureaucracy under Roosevelt offended his fundamental belief that government should limit itself to furthering the interests of the individual. He did not believe the New Deal was helping the unemployed. He was convinced FDR was leading the country into a war, and, just as he had been two decades earlier, he was ardent in his opposition to getting involved in Europe's problems. He was one of the founders of the America First Committee, which was devoted to keeping the United States out of World War II. (It disbanded immediately after Pearl Harbor was attacked.)

As late as 1941 Amos still held out hope that America could stay uninvolved. In a letter to William Eno that year he wrote: "I believe we will stay out of the war in spite of the desperate efforts of the administration and the Jewish leaders. . . . It would be monstrous folly . . . to exhaust the country's resources and manpower in fighting and reforming half the civilized and part of the uncivilized world."[42]

Mary and Tony were growing up to be beautiful young women among the lilies and orchards of Milford, and they were aware of their father's worries only as an ominous but distant storm. There came a night at Grey Towers in the late 1930s when the adults gathered around the radio. The girls were old enough to understand the import of what was happening, although the impact it would have on their generation and their own lives was beyond their imagination. It was September 1, 1939, and Mary was almost nineteen. Hitler had just invaded Poland. France and Britain were declaring war on Germany. Fascism was rampant in Europe. Spain was in the last throes of a civil war General Franco would win. It looked as if a contest between good and evil was under way. "There was news that boded no good," recalled family friend David Middleton, who was with Mary that evening. "It was a continent away and we were still just kids. But there was this sense of history and doom. It was a hot, late summer night. I remember it vividly. The moon was coming up and you could hear the crickets and the radio was crackling and we looked to the east and there was this light in the sky."[43]

# 3

# "Pinchot"

*She wants something new. You know the type. Bored with life, looking for excitement at any price—as though life weren't complicated enough as it is.*

MARY PINCHOT

When she was twelve Mary Pinchot was enrolled at the Brearley School, a private girls' preparatory school on the Upper East Side of New York, a few blocks from her family's Park Avenue apartment. Founded in 1883 by Harvard educator Samuel A. Brearley, the Brearley School was known for academic rigor as well as exclusivity. Over the years it educated the daughters or granddaughters of Henri Matisse, Franklin D. Roosevelt, Katharine Graham, Eugene O'Neill, Margaret Mead, and President John F. Kennedy. During Mary's years, Brearley girls came from New York's WASP elite and the community of German Jewish immigrants whose daughters were not welcome at other private schools. It occupied all ten floors of a red brick elevator building built in 1929. During the thirties and forties the Quaker headmistress, Millicent Carey McIntosh, abandoned the practice of dropping girls not up to the academic work and instituted a program whereby those having difficulties received special help. Under her leadership, the school historians claimed in a centennial report, the admission system "became as truly competitive as it was humanly possible to make it." There is no evidence the school excluded girls not of the upper classes, but few of Mary's classmates were from families of lesser means than hers.

Tuition was eight hundred dollars a year. Girls wore a uniform of white blouse and dark skirt and took the basics—English, math, geography, history, science—and languages, both classical (Greek or Latin) and modern (German or French). The school also offered music, drama, and art. The school medic was Dr. Benjamin Spock, who became the preeminent advisor to mothers in Mary's generation. The parents' board of trustees included Mrs. Stephen Vincent Benét, wife of the poet. The faculty were mainly graduates of the Seven Sisters schools, Columbia, or Oberlin.

The *New York Times* devoted a full page to Brearley's fiftieth anniversary in November 1934, when Mary was a fourteen-year-old in ninth grade. The headline read "New Emphasis on Self-Reliance for Girls at Brearley" and quoted Millicent Carey McIntosh as saying the school was trying to prepare women for professions because "women no longer wish to depend on male relatives." That was still a rather novel notion and the newspaper couldn't help but snicker a little. The *Times* reported: "To educate girls to be fit companions for educated husbands is still part of the school's goals but if a male visitor is so thoughtless as to indicate approval he is quickly reminded that point of view is archaic. The goal now is much more comprehensive; it is the fullest development of the girl herself—chiefly for her own sake although it is assumed her husband will benefit also. . . . The description of Brearley girls that most readily catches the visitor's ear is 'amusing.' " Headmistress McIntosh defined the word as "avoidance of over-intensity." To that end, the school offered dancing classes with Arthur Murray in the tenth-floor gym.[1]

Millicent Carey McIntosh and the other Brearley faculty were slightly out of step with the times in their emphasis on self-reliance in girls. On the same day it covered Brearley's fiftieth anniversary, the *Times* ran an article on the recommendations of the New Jersey supervisor of schools, who criticized the practice of awarding girls letters for sports because it made them too competitive. Such awards were bad for girls, he said, because they "make them self-centered and upset them. Girls should have as their prime object the development of sportsmanship and character rather than competition and reward."

Such worries did not trouble the girls or the faculty at the Brearley School. The centerpiece of the school's social life was the basketball team, and Mary, whose classmates called her "Pinchot," played an aggressive game as a forward. She was also on the tennis team, and several years in a row she brought a championship trophy to the school. She had an athlete's body, "a good body for movement," a Brearley chum, Frances Kilpatrick Field, recalled, and her athleticism made her popular because the Brearley girls were devoted to their teams.[2]

Brearley also tried to give its well-heeled girls a taste of life below their station. Students were dispatched on field trips to the Lenox Hill Neighborhood House, a settlement house for Russian, Italian, and Irish immigrants. Millicent Carey McIntosh was naturally careful to tell the *New York Times*, "This is in no sense social work." Rather, the visits to Lenox Hill were proper social calls. "Our girls enjoy the activities of the house. It gives excellent Italian operas for example," the headmistress told the newspaper. "We invite groups to visit us here. They come with their children and all of us enjoy ourselves thoroughly."

At Brearley, Mary and her friends whiled away lunch hours learning to smoke cigarettes at a local sandwich and soda shop. Smoking was so pervasive that Brearley provided the seniors with their own smoking room, a sunny space on the seventh floor overlooking the East River. Although she never became a chain-smoker, Mary smoked socially throughout her life. The girls decorated the room with a framed photograph of Fred Astaire in a top hat and an old radio-Victrola on which they played, over and over again, "Loch Lomond."

They listened to Yankees games and the Yankees-Giants World Series on the radio in the fall of 1937, and lounged on the sun-faded couches, smoking and singing along to the radio. There were some constraints on their carefree existence. The Depression was on, and even Park Avenue girls were told to be aware of the value of a dollar. "We thought of college—earning a living was part of the picture," the class of 1938 wrote in its senior yearbook. "We took summer jobs and we budgeted our personal living expenses."[3]

Mary Pinchot shone at Brearley. She was smart, fit, amusing, not too intense; in other words, the model Brearley girl. Her classmates selected her as "Miss Brearley" in 1938, the girl closest to the school's ideal. "Pinchot, looking cute at any time," was how her fellow students described her in the 1938 yearbook. "She had lots of beaus," recalled Frances Field, who walked to school with Mary from their Park Avenue apartments. She was invited to weekend dances at the boys' schools, Groton, Choate, and St. Paul's, more often than her friends. On those weekends, the girls traveled to the New England campuses and boys vacated their dorm rooms and slept in the gym, leaving little notes behind on pillows for their dates. On one such weekend, Mary was William Attwood's date to a dance held at Choate. Attwood grew up to become President Kennedy's U.N. ambassador and later publisher of New York *Newsday*. On that snowy night Mary Pinchot first met a skinny, funny boy named John F. Kennedy, a few years her senior.[4]

The Brearley class of 1938 thought they were sophisticated when it came to the facts of life. "We learned about married life through an epidemic of pregnancies among our teachers," Mary's class wrote in its "farewell message." By the time they were fourteen, chaperones and nannies were not trailing them around all the time, and Mary and her Brearley friends explored New York on their own. Mary's neighborhood was still an uncongested, friendly place to its residents. New York itself was a playground, an extension of their elite world on Park Avenue. Their favorite store was Saks Fifth Avenue. They toured the museums and the parks. There was still little crime. And there were so many boys. "Our landscape was already so dotted with men that coming out had little glamour," the Brearley girls wrote in the 1938 yearbook.

By her midteens Mary Pinchot was finding society more interesting than butterfly collecting at Grey Towers. She spent less and less time with her family in Milford and more time with friends in the Hamptons, closer to New York. In these years, the distance between Mary and Tony grew. Tony would eventually attend Brearley also, but four years behind her older sister.

The teenage Mary was much in demand as a houseguest.[5] The four social "seasons" were still the rule in society, and Mary Pinchot followed her friends through the rituals, even as they made fun of them. Spring, or the *"petit saison,"* was for horse racing, summer for the Hamptons or other cooler country climes, fall for riding to hounds, winter for the debutante balls, and deep winter for Palm Beach or sport fishing in the Keys.

Her teenage years were a whirl of debutante balls at the Waldorf-Astoria and the Ritz-Carlton followed by dates at clubs where young people drank and danced to swing orchestras and rhumba bands. Cab Calloway entertained at the Cotton Club. The girls and their escorts drank and danced at the Waldorf's Sert Room or the Stork Club or trooped over to the Rainbow Room to see silly tricks performed by "King the Wonder Dog."[6] Mary was irresistibly attracted to the party life. "She was invited to everything, she was so popular," recalled Frances Field. Life revolved around lipstick and ball gowns and silk stockings. Mary Pinchot first met her future husband at one of the many debutante balls during those years.

The pace of prewar socializing in New York increased as war loomed. Barbara Blagden Sisson, one of Mary's Brearley chums, recalled: "We lived at a terrible rate prewar. We didn't know if we would be alive."[7] Mary's coming-out year, 1938, was arguably the year the New York debutante scene seemed most glamorous to the rest of America. Two days after Christmas, New York society gathered in the main ballroom suite of the Ritz-Carlton for the biggest debutante ball of the season. Mary Pinchot, recently turned eighteen, was among the four hundred guests. The room was decorated in gold and white, the color of snow and candles. The college boys who served as escorts wore tails and white ties. The debutante, Brenda Duff Frazier, and her mother received guests in front of a dark red floral arrangement and cornucopias draped with California lichen and erupting with lilies. The debutante herself wore a dress of heavy white duchesse satin with a hoop skirt. She was festooned with ostrich plumes.

During the cotillion, Mary and the other debutantes performed various dances they had been practicing at dancing school for months. For the coaching quadrille, Brenda Frazier, who was personally worth eight million dollars, held white ribbon "reins" attached to the necks of four men who led her around the ballroom floor. She was so nervous she dropped them. Flashbulbs flickered every few minutes as cameras recorded the event for newspapers and national magazines, the organs that had transformed the post-Depression New York society girl into a fairy-tale princess.

Brenda Frazier's debut was not the first ball of the 1938 season, but it was the largest and the most publicized. Brenda, dark eyes demurely downcast beneath penciled brows and with deeply rouged lips, had been on the cover of *Life* magazine the month before, accompanied by a large fawning photo spread on the New York debutante season. That winter, four hundred debutantes were introduced to New York society at teas, balls, and dinners. The national press lapped up the glamour and fed it back to a public weary of grim times and receptive to fantasy.[8]

Many of Mary's friends made their debuts on a grand scale, but she did not; Amos refused to pay for a huge coming-out ball. But he didn't dispense with the custom entirely. Mary was presented at home at a small afternoon tea. She was not unaware of the inanity of the endless round of parties. One frequent escort, David Middleton, recalled her very much wanting to be seen at the places of the moment but never being fully satisfied. "Her attitude was, 'I've been to the debutante parties and I've had enough of that.' She was in that sense inquiring, exploring. There was also a little of 'What to do?' Ultimately she was trying to find out 'What do *I* do?' because she wasn't a person who would be content to be peripheral. You had this kind of a paradox between 'socialite' and what she wanted to be."[9]

The 1930s were a decade that saw the rise of movie-star celebrity. Grimy Depression America craved stardust and found as much of it in the society scene as it did in Hollywood. Mary was thrilled by the attention. Once David Middleton escorted her to "21" and gossip columnist Walter Winchell mentioned sighting the lovely debutante's appearance in a booth. Mary was beside herself at the item in the next morning's paper. "Rosamund, I think, was her role model," said Middleton. Mary was forever in awe of her half-sister's celebrity. Rosamund was always turning up in movie magazines and in 1934 had signed a six-month contract with Metro-Goldwyn-Mayer and moved to Hollywood. Mary enjoyed photographic attention as well. While a teenager, she modeled clothes and hairstyles for *Vogue*. Frances Field remembered that Mary got a little extra money for clothes from the sessions. One *Vogue* shot by fashion photographer Horst shows Mary in her late teens in glamorous profile with upswept hair and diamond earrings, an ice princess with full lips and a distant gaze.

By the 1930s modern celebrity culture and mass media had altered the function and style of the debutante balls. Old New York society surrendered to commercial reality, and nearly every ball had a publicist to shepherd photographers toward the prettiest or richest girl. The press agent for one of the balls was actually retained by three industries: velvet merchants, jewelers, and orchid growers.[10] The debutante scene could be crass and cruel. The *Park Avenue Social Review* of November 1938 offered a running commentary on the brutal social game. "No matter which way we turn these days the spotlight remains focused on the debutante of '38–'39. From now until the beginning of the *petit saison* every function is arranged primarily for her benefit. This is her year to 'shine' if 'shine' she ever will, a year of constant vying, of petty jealousies. It is entirely up to her whether she becomes one of the 'glamour' girls of the season or one of the 'duds.' "[11]

The glitter and glamour of the balls masked some unpleasant truths about high society. Brenda Frazier, the dark-haired *Life* cover deb of 1938, tried to commit suicide with sleeping pills in 1961. She later wrote an article for the magazine headlined "My Debut—A Horror." She wrote that after years of psychoanalysis, when she looked at photographs of her coming-out party she saw "the mockery of the fixed smiles . . . and how many people there are in the world who were doomed like me by unfortunate childhoods to adult lives plagued by fears and inner emptiness."[12]

Those very fears plagued Amos Pinchot when he watched his daughter on her gay rounds. The deprivations of the Depression had barely affected his daughter's lifestyle. New York was grim with rumors of war and his daughter was frolicking from weekend to weekend, her mind only on the next dance or dinner date.

At home Amos sometimes took out his bleak mood on his daughters. One night in the late 1930s the Pinchot apartment on Park Avenue echoed with shouts when Amos criticized Mary about her social life. Mary held her own and argued back until her father slapped her in the face in front of her mortified date.[13] Amos's violent act could have been the result of heavy drinking, which he indulged in more and more as he grew older. He also felt legitimate worry for his family's financial future. The family fortune had been diminished, and Amos believed he might not be able to afford college for his daughters. He also feared the country was going to war. But it was the loss of his daughter Rosamund from which he would never recover.

Rosamund landed only one small role in one Hollywood film, though she did appear eventually in some French films. But she was tall and voluptuous when the style for American female stars was still the thin-lipped wraith. She was also not much of an actress. On her return to New York she announced she was retiring from acting, a development the New York newspapers covered with much interest. She and Amos bought some New York real estate together, including an old theater (possibly with the idea of giving her a venue). In 1935 and 1936 she returned to acting and performed in summer stock in New York and Massachusetts. She married a gadabout wealthy lawyer named William Gaston whose family owned textile mills in Gastonia, North Carolina. She had two children with him, but she soon fell in love with the Broadway producer Jed Harris, also a major Hollywood figure, whose bisexuality doomed their affair. Despondent over her failed movie career and romance, in the spring of 1938 Rosamund rented a house on Long Island alone and killed herself inside a running car in a closed garage. She left two sons under the age of ten.

Rosamund took her own life during Mary's senior year at Brearley. Mary was whirling through the schedule of debutante parties and the suicide was not mentioned among friends, much less in the press. The *New York Times* in those years did not publish the obituaries of suicides, so the death passed without publicity. But it would have deep and lasting effects on Mary, whose world until then had been unblemished by any sort of pain or tragedy.

Rosamund's suicide broke Amos. She had been his favorite child, and after her death Amos drank more and fell victim to a series of ailments that hospitalized him. Mary, who had been spending much time away from Milford, became a more frequent companion to him at Grey Towers. She loved her father and now was able to prove her worth to him. As Amos descended into a clinical depression Mary tried to cheer him up, though she continued to make the rounds of parties and none of her friends knew about the private pain in her family. In letters Amos wrote during those years, he mentioned Mary more often than Ruth or Tony.

In the fall of 1938 Mary followed her mother to Vassar. The campus in Poughkeepsie, with its ancient trees between two lakes, crisp country walks, streets of antique shops, dress stores, and inns, and its long tradition of women's education, was intimidating at first. Mary wrote home that she didn't much like it. But by her second semester she was used to the rhythm of women's college life. Weekdays were for classes such as "The Meaning of Morals, Beauty, Truth, God—open to freshmen by special permission," Gary Cooper movies, and studying. Weekends were for New Haven or Princeton and football or basketball game dates. It was all familiar ground, New York society transplanted to upstate New York and Connecticut. Half the girls at Brearley went on to Vassar, so Mary was still among childhood friends. And the young men they visited on weekends were often the same boys who had been their escorts at the cotillions.

The writer Mary McCarthy graduated from Vassar several years before Mary Pinchot arrived. She described the freshman girl's sense of awe at first passing through Taylor Gate, where Yale men in roadsters were parked waiting for the upper-class women in their pale sweaters and pearls, "tall, dazzling . . . impeccable, with stately walks like goddesses." Entering Vassar was like entering "a Forest of Arden and a Fifth Avenue department store combined." The college was founded in 1861 by a self-made and self-educated Poughkeepsie brewer named Matthew Vassar, and by the 1930s the school had a reputation as the archetypal American women's college, "less intellectual than Radcliffe or Bryn Mawr, less social and weekendish than Smith, less athletic than Wellesley, less Bohemian than Bennington," McCarthy wrote. The very name of the college signified "a whiff of luxury and the ineffable, plain thinking and high living."[14]

At Vassar, Mary met women who became her lifelong friends. She lived in the dorm known as the North Tower, considered the most glamorous campus residence. During the week, the women all wore bobby socks and saddle shoes, but for dates they daubed on Chanel No. Five, powdered their noses with Elizabeth Arden, and imitated Margaret Sullavan. Their favorite swing band was Tommy Dorsey, and they were deeply disappointed when he couldn't play for their junior prom and they had to settle for a band leader named Glenn Miller, though they were pleasantly surprised at the outcome. Sophisticated girls, they voraciously read *The New Yorker* and the *New*

*York Times*. Most of all, they were devoted to Yale. They hung the Yale motto, "For God and country and Yale," around the Vassar campus.

"Doesn't it feel refreshingly feminine to wear stockings and a dress and to be on our way to purely unintellectual doings?" asked the 1942 *Vassarian* editors above a photograph of a train packed with fur-clad young ladies headed to Princeton and New Haven. "We may have a test lurking somewhere in the near future, and come Sunday night and the 7:40 we will feel like Death, but what else do we look forward to with such anticipation and what else is there to recall with equal glee?" In the 1941 yearbook, the same notion had been expressed: "We are forced to conclude that Yale and Princeton have more appeal for Vassar than Vassar does for itself." The sense that men's endeavors were more appealing than women's would be reflected in the way Mary and her contemporaries lived in the decades to come.

Many Vassar girls arranged their schedules so that they had no classes on Friday, the better to catch an early train to New Haven. They went on any pretext—a blind date was enough. Once they arrived they expected to be taken care of. Sometimes the men put them up at hotels, and certainly they would pay for their dinners. "Going Dutch" was not done. In return the girls were good company, but nothing more was expected. There was a great deal of drinking and dancing to swing bands and much heavy kissing, but also an innocence among the Vassar girls. "We were all virgins, as I recall," said Mary Truesdale, who often took the train to New Haven with Mary. "Everybody was a virgin. I remember sitting in Main Hall waiting for somebody to come back who was going to go the whole way so I could see what it was like."[15]

In those years, finding a suitable husband was still a significant and quietly approved part of a Vassar girl's education. But there was a distinction at Vassar between the women who were seriously considering professions and those headed for early marriage and no work. Mary fell into the latter category. She was such a beauty that her classmates elected her to the Vassar Daisy Chain, an honor that consisted of donning a white dress and parading around campus on Commencement Day with similarly clad nymphs linked by a chain of daisies. "She was someone you liked to have around to look at," said classmate Frances Prindle Taft.[16] On the other hand, some of her collegiate sisters, women who would go on to have professional lives, found her rather vapid. "She was not the type who entered into college or class activities. She wasn't active but she wasn't snooty either. She was decorative as far as we were concerned," said one Vassar 1942 graduate.[17]

It is possible that the family tragedies of Rosamund's suicide and Amos's depression and alcohol abuse caused Mary to withdraw somewhat from college activities and shed the lively, highly involved personality she had projected at Brearley. Because the girls in her social class did not discuss private family matters such as suicide and alcoholism, it is impossible to know whether those were the reasons Mary Pinchot was not, at Vassar, the widely admired and popular girl she had been at Brearley. But Vassar itself encouraged and rewarded a different kind of girl than the breezy prep school athlete.

Vassar inspired in its girls a reverence for, if not always the eventual practice of, a kind of independence of thought and spirit. The faculty was dominated by unmarried women, and students were expected to have ideas and express them with confidence. The young women were by and large the daughters of the upper and upper-middle classes who would soon marry Republican lawyers like their fathers, but the school urged its students to "do" something with their lives. It produced, Mary McCarthy wrote, women who were simultaneously two persons—"the housewife or matron and the yearner or regretter." The Vassar girl would feel "she has let the college down by not becoming famous or 'interesting,' " McCarthy wrote. The most revered Vassar graduates were not the humdrum professionals, women who had become doctors or teachers, but those who had distinguished themselves in more dramatic ways, such as the poet Edna St. Vincent Millay (Vassar 1917) or the first woman to enlist in the marines, Major Julia Hamblet (Vassar 1937). Vassar girls in Mary Pinchot's generation learned to admire daring. "An *arresting performance* in politics, fashion, or art is often taken by the Vassar mind to be synonymous with true accomplishment," McCarthy noted.[18]

Mary embarked on the study of plant pathology with the vague plan, inspired by the teachers at Brearley and encouraged by the spinster professors at Vassar, to go into medicine and become a doctor. But she had a creative side, one more in keeping with the secret hope of Vassar girls of the time, to distinguish herself as different from other women, and a strong will quietly hidden under good manners and a pretty face. "She really did whatever she wanted to do," recalled Mary Truesdale. "She took any classes she liked. She was there when she felt like it. She always walked with authority and held her head high. She looked like she knew where she was going and what she wanted to do. She was full of ideas and had her own way of looking at things."[19]

Her college friends saw a good-natured girl who kept to herself and was slightly offbeat. She didn't like to be onstage, but she enjoyed painting and in prep school had already won a few awards for her artistic ability. She had a silly sense of humor. Frances Field, her Brearley classmate, also attended Vassar. She remembers an incident during their senior year when three girls and Mary were all studying for finals together in the same room. The tension was palpable and the room quiet as a vault. Suddenly Mary stood up to go to the bathroom. As she was walking out the door she leaned over and took a bite of some tulips in a vase by the door, calmly chewing them as she walked away. "She was very serene," Field recalled. "Never loud."[20]

In a short story called "Futility," which she wrote when she was twenty-one and published in the *Vassar Review and Little Magazine*, Mary described the boredom of party life and imagined a strange solution to it. In the story, a young woman named Ruth Selwyn sips a martini at a party in an apartment with a chartreuse couch, a white fur rug, an aquarium inset above the mantelpiece, and "chicly cadaverous" guests who are "being too killing about Noel Coward's love life." Utterly bored, she fantasizes about an imminent operation that will make every sensation "new and exciting and different and interesting." On her way home, she passes a florist shop where orchids are displayed in the window. "They look as though they had been grown in damp underground caves by demons. They're evil sickly flowers with no life of their own, living on borrowed strength."

The next day Ruth Selwyn visits a Dr. Morrison, who performs an operation on her that connects her optic nerves to the auditory receptors and vice versa. In the voice of Dr. Morrison, Mary Pinchot mocks her own boredom. Explaining the operation to his nurse, the doctor says, "I wouldn't be trying it either, except that, well, she's been coaxing and phoning and trying to persuade me every day now for the last three weeks. She wants something new. You know the type. Bored with life, looking for excitement at any price—as though life weren't complicated enough as it is."

After the operation Ruth walks outside and hears the clicking of her own heels on the pavement, which appear in the form of a troop of soldiers in plumed helmets marching alongside her. A green crossing light sounds like a bugle call. When she looks at a print of van Gogh's sunflowers she hears Stravinsky's "Sacre du Printemps," and when she looks at peonies she hears the "purr of a dove." A church bell tolling sets off a series of colorful images, "with each ring a spectrum, starting with deep royal blue and ending with pale, pale blue." But soon the colors get jumbled up with the marching soldiers and some pigs who joined her after she hummed "The Three Little Pigs."

The little story ends badly for Ruth Selwyn. Exhausted by the clamor assailing her crossed senses, she returns to the apartment with the chartreuse couch and lies down upon it. As another evening of drinks and empty chatter begins, she closes her eyes. Like Sleeping Beauty, she goes into a permanent sleep, except there is no prince on the horizon. The last line is: "And because her eyes were closed, she heard nothing to disturb her, and slept forever on the chartreuse couch."[21]

The story essentially describes a condition known as synesthesia, a crossing of sensory experiences that poets have mined for metaphors for decades and that drug users discovered to be one physical aspect of an LSD experience. It is unlikely that Mary Pinchot was one of the estimated one in a hundred thousand people who experiences synesthesia naturally. Richard E. Cytowic, a psychoneurologist, has studied them and found that as a group, they are able to function normally. According to his studies, such people are often unusually artistic and drawn to creative fields. It is more probable that the idea of synesthesia was introduced to Mary in discussions on art or literature at Vassar. In fact, another later Vassar graduate, young Jacqueline Bouvier, indicated her own familiarity with the theory in a prize-winning essay for *Vogue* in which she analyzed how the French poet Baudelaire developed "the theory of synesthesia" in some of his works.[22]

Mary was very briefly involved with college politics in her junior year when she joined a club called the Polit Board, Vassar's major political entity. The group invited speakers to campus and brought together left and right for heated discussions. Her interest was no doubt encouraged by Amos, by this time seething at FDR. Mary was trying to be somebody, and that somebody was her father. But her interest in politics was tepid at best. In a *Vassarian* photograph of the club, she looks small and distinctly out of place, a dainty blond child-woman gazing dreamily from the side of a heavy wood table among a group of fiercely earnest girls in saddle shoes staring into the camera. Amos had by then decided the president was being advised by "Marxian intellectuals, the most pestiferous and useless class that ever cumbered this sad world."[23] In November 1939 he wrote a letter to his brother Gifford that mentions Mary's political world. "Vassar seems to be very much interested in communism. And a great deal of warm debating is going on among the students of Mary's class, which I think is an excellent thing. People of that age ought to be radical anyhow."[24] A few years previously the same issue had come to the attention of another Vassar parent, Agnes Meyer, mother of the future publisher of the *Washington Post*. Writing to her daughter Katharine in 1935, Agnes suggested Katharine organize some of the Vassar girls and create a campus club to battle "the emotional trend toward communism amongst the girls."[25]

With Mary off at college, Amos began to suffer from a variety of ailments and grow increasingly depressed. In 1940 he wrote to his only son, Mary's half-brother, Gifford, "These are emergency times. Real estate is going to thunder. I have felt very downcast about the condition of my finances, which are exceedingly bad." He speculated that it might be impossible for Mary to finish at Vassar and for Tony to go at all.[26] Mary stayed around him during the summer of 1940 and tried to cheer him up. They fished for trout in the Sawkill at Grey Towers. In June Mary and Amos flew together to California after Amos attended the Republican convention in Philadelphia, which nominated Wendell Willkie. In July she took singing lessons and performed in a small concert at Milford. She practiced at home and Amos watched over her progress. "Her teacher seems rather pleased with her voice. In any event the training will improve her speaking voice and also her health. The exercises, breathing and others, are quite strenuous."[27]

In the fall of 1940 FDR was elected to a third term, beating Amos's candidate, Wendell Willkie. The world was at war and America was sidling toward conflict, with Amos Pinchot firmly opposed. Hitler's machine was rolling across Europe, capturing more and more territory and beginning the reign of terror against Jews and dissidents. In September 1940, Germany, Italy, and Japan signed their tripartite agreement. Still Amos held to the notion that America could stay out of the fray.

In September 1941 Amos wrote a long letter about Mary to his son, Gifford. He lamented her failure to keep in shape for tennis but approved her plan to study medicine. "A long hard row to hoe, but she really wants to do it. Good women doctors are rare and generally quite successful. My friends assure me there is a fine opportunity for women doctors in this city." Mary was then just a few weeks short of her twenty-first birthday, when her trust fund—worth about $65,000 in stocks and bonds by 1964—would come under her control. Amos wrote that she planned to keep it in trust, all but five hundred dollars for clothes and other expenses.[28]

That winter the war debate abruptly ended and Amos's protestations looked both wrong and unpatriotic. On December 7, 1941, the Japanese bombed U.S. naval and air bases at Pearl Harbor, Hawaii. Simultaneously the Japanese attacked U.S. bases in Guam, the Philippines, and Wake Island. Only after the attack did the Japanese formally declare war. The next day the United States declared war on Japan. Two days later Germany and Italy declared war on the United States. Just before Christmas, Winston Churchill conferred with Americans in Washington about a joint British-American military command. By year's end, America was officially at war. The nation was about to come face-to-face with what columnist Walter Lippmann called "ice cold evil."

For Mary Pinchot and her generation, Pearl Harbor meant the dance was over. Yale men went off to basic training. Many Vassar women from the class of 1942 joined the war effort themselves: The WAVES were created in 1942, and women also helped train troops in communications, joined the Red Cross, and worked at the many stateside factories that were shorthanded with the men gone. The era of Rosie the Riveter, of the spunky 1940s woman in a kerchief and coveralls or a cinch-waisted business suit with big shoulders, commenced.

The war had a profound effect on Mary's social world. The national emergency dictated that there would be no Vassar prom to celebrate the spring of 1942. Even the lights on Times Square were dimmed so as not to light the harbor for German U-boats. Mary also had more personal worries during her last year at Vassar. Her father was physically ill and unraveling mentally. The onset of war had compounded his medical and psychological problems. As an America Firster, he was badly proven wrong by the attack on Pearl Harbor. He began spending more time in seclusion at the Connecticut estate of his uncle William Eno.

At the Connecticut house on a hot summer afternoon in 1942, a few months after Mary's graduation from Vassar, Amos locked himself into a second-floor bathroom, climbed into the bathtub, and slit his wrists. The suicide attempt failed. Amos was found by his uncle and taken to a hospital in time to be revived with five blood transfusions. But news of the attempt made the *New York Times*, and his mental instability was now public knowledge.[29] His cherished dignity destroyed, he never recovered his physical or mental health and spent the rest of his life in hospitals.

Her father's suicide attempt and deterioration transformed Mary's young life. Two of the most important people in her world—her father and her older half-sister—had decided that life was not worth the trouble. The Pinchot family's tragedies remained deep but private wounds. Mary probably survived the anguish by separating herself from other people's unhappiness, an ability that would become pronounced in later years. Only those close to her ever detected the darkness underlying the light and easy facade; years later, after Mary's own tragedies had come to pass, James Angleton compared the Pinchot family to the ill-fated House of Atreus in *The Iliad*. Mary contained her feelings in the habit of her social class, which held it improper to grieve too long, especially over an event as socially reprehensible as a suicide attempt.

After college, Mary's life was dominated by women. The streets of New York bristled with men in uniform waiting to be shipped out. Inside the offices, women in suits took jobs vacated by the soldiers. The Pinchot women went to work. The family fortune was on the wane, and although they had trusts, Mary and Tony and Ruth had to find ways to make ends meet. To make extra money, Ruth took in boarders at the Park Avenue apartment. Most of them were Mary's Vassar classmates looking to settle in New York, who paid a small monthly sum to sleep in one of the extra bedrooms. Ruth took a job as director of publicity at the YWCA. Tony, who would start at Vassar in the fall of 1942, worked at a women's magazine in the summer. Mary, her plans to go on to medical school dashed by the combination of war and the family disaster, went to work as a journalist.

One of the women who boarded at the Pinchots' apartment was

Mary Brier Goodhue, a Vassar graduate then working at one of the New York law firms, who went on to become a state senator in New York. Another boarder was Mary's college friend Anne Chamberlin. Goodhue remembers the apartment was spacious, plain, and comfortable, "not much art, not a museum," with three or four bedrooms and a maid's room—occupied by a boarder, not a servant—off the kitchen. The women did their own cooking. Ruth Pinchot was a gentle, attractive woman who had, Goodhue said, "many admirers" among the younger generation. Outside, the war was ever-present. Goodhue recalled that "You never saw a man in ordinary clothes." But the war improved women's chances of getting jobs and starting professional careers. Goodhue, who had a law degree from the University of Michigan, would not have landed her job with a prestigious New York firm if not for the war. "If the men had been home, they would have never hired any women," she said.[30]

Mary took a job at United Press and became a feature writer. She was immediately designated as a success and assigned to go out and interview people when most women and men her age were consigned to the desk. She had her own column. "She was very confident and independent," said Vassar classmate Barbara Gair Scheiber, who also worked at United Press. "There was something very singular about her. Now I know she couldn't have been as confident as she seemed, but I felt then that whatever Mary wanted to do she would do." At the office, Mary inspired envy. She flitted in and out of the office in stylish clothes and executed her columns with a self-taught peck on the keys; no one at Brearley or Vassar took typing. "There was an element of defiant fearlessness to her," Scheiber said. "She had this very throaty big laugh and a smile. There was this enjoyment, a twinkle and a laugh, but also a sort of coolness. There was some removal, like someone living in her own tower."[31]

In New York during the war years Mary was a young woman who came into her own, briefly. An experimental side emerged in her personality, poking out its head and looking around. There were suddenly no powerful men in her life to direct her. She was free to explore the world on her own. Socially, she tried to distinguish herself from the other college girls by associating with people from the movies, people her sister Rosamund would have found interesting. She befriended Polish documentary filmmaker Henwar Rodakiewicz. And she was seen around New York on the arm of actor Walter Pidgeon, who was old enough to be her father. That got the attention of the gossip columnists. She flirted with politics as a social experiment, trying to expand her group of friends and probably meet men. One man who worked for the Congress of Industrial Organizations in those years invited Mary to a large party thrown by the labor unions. He remembered her as a merry date with little interest in or knowledge of the intricacies of labor politics.[32] Her presence at this event may have led to her briefly joining the American Labor Party. Her association with labor supporters generally, and probably her father's leftist history as well, would later bring her name under suspicion during the McCarthy-era witch-hunts that ensnared her future husband. Although those who knew her then scoff at the notion that she might have been a political rebel, the FBI and its informers took her seriously enough.

Barbara Gair Scheiber had more reason than others to feel jealous of Mary Pinchot. During the war years there was a shortage of young men in New York, and Mary turned the heads of those that remained. The men and women who worked at United Press frequented a legendary Irish pub, Tim Costello's on Forty-third Street and Third Avenue, around the corner from their office. Until the war, Costello's had been a dark and smoky newsman's haunt that rarely saw female patrons, much less Vassar girls. Now that women were taking some of the vacant newspapering jobs, they too bellied up to the bar. Tim Costello was very protective of the women and especially of the fine-boned girl who so incongruously graced the bar with a Lucky Strike in one hand and a drink in the other. Most of the men who frequented the pub were too old to enlist and therefore uninteresting to the young women, but there were a few younger swains. One of them, Bob Schwartz, wore a Navy uniform but was stationed stateside to work for the military newspaper *Yank*. He was a tall, dark, and sexy intellectual, and some of the girls from the United Press office soon fell for him. Barbara Gair Scheiber was a little disappointed when Mary won him.

Schwartz had just arrived in New York from Salem, Ohio, when he began to see Mary Pinchot at the bar alone, with the hulking Irish proprietor hovering protectively. She was coolly perfect from afar but witty and self-assured up close, and if a man got close enough, he saw a twinkle of mischief in her eyes. "Everybody wanted to pick her up, but she was a little forbidding," Schwartz remembered. "She was wildly beautiful in the Grace Kelly sense." Finally Schwartz got an introduction to the mystery woman from a mutual friend who was "awed" by her. Schwartz, with the benefit of five decades of hindsight, recalls that he himself was not awed, although he found her "fascinating." Schwartz says that when he first approached Mary, "Tim Costello was standing by but he knew me and he knew what I was about, so it was okay."[33]

Mary and Bob Schwartz fell in love, and Schwartz became her first long-term lover. They stayed together for three years and for much of that time they lived together in Schwartz's room at the Shelton Hotel, on Forty-ninth Street and Lexington Avenue, where all the young men who worked for *Yank* were housed on one floor and paid twenty-five dollars a month for their rooms. "It was a wonderful room, perfect for two," Schwartz recalled. It was also a scandalous situation for a young woman of Mary's generation and one that would have been entirely shocking had there not been a war on. But Mary did not care. She probably took great delight in blithely stepping out of a hotel room every morning into a hallway filled with admiring young men. With her father ill and oblivious, she was suddenly and for the first time in her life acting entirely under her own authority.

A middle-class Jewish midwesterner, Bob Schwartz could not have been more different from Mary's father or the boys with whom she had danced away her college years. Ruth Pinchot "had a little problem with my Jewishness," Schwartz recalled, but she was always cordial and didn't make any attempt to discourage Mary. The relationship between mother and daughter at this point was "respectful,"

Schwartz thought, and even deep, but hardly warm and not a "patty-cake" kind of relationship. "Ruth was the kind of woman who commanded respect. Mary was very proud of the fact that her mother had been one of the first suffragists," Schwartz remembered.

Mary introduced Schwartz to her world. The couple sailed around Long Island in her cousin Gifford's yacht, or spent whole weeks together on sailboats chartered by Schwartz and Henwar Rodakiewicz, who was dating one of Mary's former roommates (and Ruth's boarders) at the time. The couple went to Milford every weekend. To Schwartz, Grey Towers was a dreamy, idyllic place where his girlfriend swam nude and they could slide down a waterfall with three levels of cold bubbling pools beneath the whispering pines. She told him stories of a dead but glamorous older sister who had acted in French films and ridden horses at full gallop around the grounds at midnight so her little sister could hear the pounding of hooves from her bed. He was captivated.

Schwartz saw his girlfriend as "militantly wholesome, not wild" like the half-sister she had so admired. She had a seriousness and a questing nature. To Schwartz she was "profound," a young woman who was thinking about higher questions, the meaning of love, life, war, and death. "There was no crap to her," he recalled. "She was not light."

In thinking about the higher questions, in 1943 she was not alone. Two world wars in four decades had scratched hope and scrambled belief. Young men were dying. The world was a dreary place. Questions about meaning were becoming popular. In 1942 Albert Camus published *The Stranger*, and a year later Jean-Paul Sartre published *Being and Nothingness*, introducing nonacademic readers to the notion of existentialism. In the visual arts, there was a great energy emanating from the Museum of Modern Art and a group of New York artists developing the abstract style. Dutch artist Piet Mondrian had emigrated from Holland in 1942, followed by other European émigrés, including Josef Albers, Hans Hofmann, and László Moholy-Nagy, who revitalized the abstract style. The world war was much on their minds, and to express the underside of human existence, these artists turned to Jung and his theories of archetypes and dreams. The first abstract paintings had relied on enigmatic images from mythology and dream states. By the late 1940s and early 1950s the forms gave way to the splashes and splatters and lines for which abstract expressionism is known.

Mary was always more interested in relationships and the ethics of human behavior than in politics. Schwartz thought her interest in art was part of an aesthetic continuum that started with her interest in relationships and psychology. Schwartz recalled that Mary's mother, Ruth, was deeply involved in politics, but that Mary was less so. "Politically she was beyond leftist," Schwartz said of Mary. "She was concerned with the ethics and aesthetics of life. She was concerned about what was proper not in the sense of manners but in the larger sense of what it meant to be a human being." Mary was so serious about these questions that Schwartz could not joke with her about them for fear of arousing her anger. "She would say, 'Why are we really here?' And I'd say, 'I don't know, I'm from Ohio.' And she would not have any of that. She required that we be serious about being serious."

Mary was a devoted pacifist. She made Schwartz read a book about a World War I soldier sent to Verdun knowing that every one of the forebears in his aristocratic British family had been slain in battle. "She got into all that: 'Isn't this stupid? What are we all doing killing each other?' To say she was antiwar is to really not understand her. She was essentially aesthetic."

Meanwhile, Mary's father was deteriorating. His lucidity gone after the suicide attempt and his physical strength depleted, Amos lingered in hospitals in a state of poor mental and physical health. Mary spoke of him rarely, but with affection and sadness, Schwartz said. Since Schwartz was adamantly anti-Hitler and saw nothing defensible in Amos's America First position, he and Mary hardly discussed her father. Schwartz felt that Mary disagreed with her father's politics but respected his passion and dedication.

In early 1944 Amos had so declined that his immediate family—Ruth, Mary, Tony, and Amos's son from his first marriage, Gifford—had to decide whether to act on a doctor's recommendation that

Amos undergo a lobotomy. They decided against it.[34] Amos died of pneumonia in February 1944 and was buried in Milford. "Amos is buried on a high hill under the trees and stars," Ruth wrote.[35] His friends sent sympathy letters to Ruth suggesting that death was a kind of release: "Poor old Amos!" wrote Newton Stokes. "His life was a strange mixture of happiness and unhappiness—with the emphasis in the late years at least on the latter."[36] The effect of her father's death on Mary is not recorded, but it was probably a relief for her as well as the rest of the family, since Amos had been essentially gone from them already for two years. In one of Ruth's letters she notes that Mary was able to get back to Milford in time for the funeral, but it is unclear from where. Schwartz does not recall the death.

As journalists, Mary and Schwartz traveled together. One of the longest trips they took was in 1944, a transcontinental train ride from New York to San Diego, where they stayed for several weeks. Schwartz had an assignment to interview the survivors of a ship that had been destroyed. All but seven of a thousand men had perished. While Schwartz interviewed his survivors, Mary carried out her assignment from *Mademoiselle* and interviewed Paul Popenoe, one of the founders of the new family education movement on college campuses designed to teach proper marital and family relationships. Courses in marriage were becoming popular in the early 1940s. The classes advised young women that the psychologically healthy role of a woman was to be lover, mother, cook, cleaner, and nurturer. They taught American college girls how to "play the role" of women as if it were a new science.

Women of Mary's generation, traumatized by the war and unable to see beyond the end of the disaster, eagerly sought advice for a "modern marriage." Although they had been educated and were theoretically prepared for fuller lives than that of homemaker and wife, the social scientists advised that that was unhealthy and against what was scientifically proven to be "natural." And science, in those modern years, was believed to be as powerful as God, if not to have replaced the deity altogether.[37]

Mary was intrigued by the new "science" of love and marriage and was excited about interviewing Popenoe, then teaching at Occidental College in southern California. "He was a step ahead of most people, and that would be Mary," Schwartz said. "She had found somebody who had a singular insight which he'd built into a philosophy—and she wanted to know more about him. She wouldn't just do a Sunday feature piece on marriage, she would go deeper."

The ensuing article, headlined "Credits for Love," appeared in *Mademoiselle*'s August 1944 issue. Mary's take on the new classes was noncritical, even approving. "Young women and men too have decided there's a lot to be learned from textbooks about a subject traditionally reserved for lyrical poems," she wrote. The marriage course at Occidental, she reported, held first place in popularity among students. "That old argument about marriage vs. a career, incidentally, has petered out to almost nothing since the war," she reported. "Girls seem to have decided, now that it's almost impossible to keep a husband on this side of the ocean, that a husband and children are enough for any woman. 'Career girls are always a vocal minority,' said one of the teachers, a Mrs. Freeman. 'This year we have none at all.' " Popenoe told Mary one of the main reasons marriage courses hadn't spread even faster across college campuses was that " 'it is so hard to find proper teachers. . . . There are so many old maids on most faculties. It's hard for them to root for home and family.' "[38]

Mary's other articles were typical of the fare in print for women then as well as now, with practical sexual knowledge a constant subtext. Her debut article, on venereal disease, had been published in the March 1944 issue of *Mademoiselle*. Later that year she wrote about recent studies that claimed the state of the weather at conception was an accurate predictor of health or intelligence in babies.

As the young women back home read *Mademoiselle* and thought about marriage, sex, and children, war raged all over the world, inspiring scientific advances that were altering the culture, morality, and environment of the nation and the world. Mary Pinchot came of age during a period of rapid scientific development provoked by the need for more war supplies and better weapons. In 1942 Enrico Fermi accomplished the first self-sustaining nuclear fission chain reaction and in a coded message informed FDR, "The Italian navigator has entered the new world." The atom bomb was just around the corner. Napalm, a jellylike mixture of palm oil and gasoline that stuck to its target until it burned out, was invented at Harvard in 1942. New anesthesias were developed that could not only ease the pain of a wounded soldier but also make childbirth relatively painless. The pesticide DDT was invented and sent immediately to the military to reduce the numbers of insects spreading malaria and typhus in tropical outposts, though the environmental effects of this and some other developments were not noticed for decades. On other levels, deprivation and rationing produced new ideas. With meat scarce, the casserole became a popular dish. A billion pounds of plastic were produced in 1941, replacing metal in every possible way. Shortages changed styles: Hems went up, and the nylon stocking was invented to replace silk. More women also began wearing slacks in public.

Even as science advanced on a material level, the psychic effects of war were not even named. Men came home from Europe and the Pacific emotionally traumatized. A *Good Housekeeping* article in 1945 advised women about what to do, and in it the writer expressed all that America felt about manhood, and all that would be repressed in the decade to come. Headlined "What You Can Do About the Returning Vet: Will He Be Changed?" the article advised: "After two or three weeks he should be finished with talking and with oppressive remembering. If he still goes over the same stories, reveals the same emotions, you had best consult a psychiatrist. This condition is neurotic."[39]

The women of Mary's generation wanted scientific know-how to heal their men's nightmares of war. But there was no easy cure for the torment beneath the veterans' stoic faces. It was up to the women to soothe away the bad memories and lead men back into lives that had a semblance of peace and security. "We had a lot of war," said one of Mary's Vassar and Brearley classmates, Barbara Sisson. "Our parents were in World War I and our husbands went to World War II.

Our sons faced Vietnam." In 1937, when they were seventeen, Sisson and Mary and some other Brearley girls had put on a production of *The Trojan Women.* They spent their lifetimes experiencing the play's truth. "How little we knew when we acted in that play what we would be facing ourselves," Sisson reflected.[40]

As the men returned, the working women were sent home. It happened in factories and newspapers with equal dispatch. In 1945 female auto workers in Detroit who were laid off to give jobs back to returning veterans held a protest march demanding the end to discrimination based on sex. In Washington, journalist Marie Ridder threw her typewriter at a young man named Phillip Geyelin in the Capitol Hill offices of the *Philadelphia Evening Bulletin* when she realized he had come to take her job.[41] (Geyelin later became editorial page editor of the *Washington Post.*) But for most women, the return of the men to their rightful place was a relief. Now they could resume their real business as wives, mothers, and nurturers. Even Vassar graduates believed in that happy ending. "I'd say the majority of us thought that's exactly what we would do," said Barbara Gair Scheiber. "Of course, some of us felt we really wanted to have interesting careers, but at the same time we would be failures if we didn't get married by age twenty-five."[42]

No woman was immune to that belief, and no woman could resist the attraction of a uniformed, battle-hardened young man who had fought the good war. As the war ground on, Mary and Bob Schwartz began to drift apart. He was heartbroken. "Our relationship was one of those phases in life, but I think we were meant to go a bit longer," he said decades later. Schwartz blamed himself. But in fact Mary was already on to someone else, a genuine movie-size war hero.

# 4
# THE IDEALISTS

*Our real choice is not whether we are going to get world government; we are going to get it in a very few years. It is fundamentally the question of world government by conquest and empire or world government by voluntary and rational consent.*

CORD MEYER

The bride wore a white-and-green printed crepe afternoon dress and carried a bouquet of white daisies and freesia. Her blond hair hung in a wave to her shoulders, pinned back at the temples. For jewelry she wore a single strand of pearls and her glasses hung on a cord around her neck, ready in case she needed to read anything. The groom wore his marine lieutenant's dress uniform and a wide, goofy smile on his wounded face. The small gathering of family members assembled at Ruth Pinchot's Park Avenue apartment in the early afternoon of April 19, 1945, was all informality and brightness. Outside spring was beginning. Pale green tipped the tree limbs in the Park Avenue meridian. Across the ocean, the war had turned for the Allies and in less than two weeks Hitler would commit suicide in his bunker. That spring heralded a brief season between the death of Hitler and the dropping of the atom bomb when people let themselves believe in the possibility that there might be no more war. Protestant theologian and writer Reinhold Niebuhr, a friend of Ruth's, was acquainted with the groom and thought him a promising young man, as did everyone else in the room. Niebuhr had a few years before published *The Nature and Destiny of Man*, in which he tried to explain the Christian and Western concepts of individuality and history. His theories defined Communism and fanaticism as the two great evils to arise from the Western way of looking at history. Communism, he had written, was a secularized version of messianism, "the hope for a heaven on earth."

The wedding ceremony commenced. Niebuhr, an intellectual, not a minister, stumbled a few times as he read the restrained Anglican lines from the Book of Common Prayer: "The union of husband and wife in heart, body and mind is intended by God for their mutual joy; for the help and comfort given one another in adversity; and, when it is God's will, for the procreation of children and their nurture in the knowledge and love of the Lord. Therefore marriage is not to be entered into unadvisedly or lightly, but reverently, deliberately." At the appropriate times, the bride and groom responded in even and deliberate voices.

They were a happy but not a giddy couple, two people possessed of conviction about the rightness of what they were doing. The assembled shared that feeling. "Amos would have felt that Cord was right for Mary and she for him, I know," Ruth Pinchot wrote to Cornelia a few weeks later.[1] The rings were exchanged and then the vows were sealed with a kiss, for which Mary Eno Pinchot Meyer rose way up on her toes and Cord Meyer bent down. His lean, uniformed arms reached around her waist. Mary had her own handsome hero, a man of passion and experience and ideas who was obviously going to succeed. His wound only made him all the more beguiling. He had come through a night of death and he believed in a higher calling. Behind the boyish grin and the impeccable manners was a ferocious intensity. On that happy day she could not suspect that he would eventually repudiate his young dreams. And she could also not imagine that the implacable will she so respected would strain their marriage.

After the ceremony the small wedding party strolled a few blocks up Park Avenue to a family friend's larger apartment for an afternoon reception, where a wedding cake and champagne were waiting. On the street, New York's press photographers were already waiting, having heard of the rush-rush wedding of debutante Mary Eno Pinchot to Cord Meyer, son of a wealthy New York family and a decorated war hero. The popping flashbulbs caught the young couple, all broad grins and laughter, on the sidewalk. Her gloved hand never for a moment unlatched itself from the starched crook of her new husband's sleeve.

All of New York's newspapers mentioned the wedding of the two socially prominent twenty-four-year-olds. The *New York Times* called Mary "Writer, a Member of Noted Family" in its headline. Society columnist Cholly Knickerbocker banged out a column about the lovely Mary Eno Pinchot's nuptials that slyly insinuated this was an awfully sudden marriage. In fact, the couple had been dating for months. Cord had proposed to Mary by telephone from Washington, where he was interviewing for a job as assistant to U.S. delegate Harold Stassen at the upcoming United Nations convention in San Francisco. He didn't want to take his first job without knowing whether the girl he loved was going to marry him. The ambitious groom-to-be remained in Washington until a few hours before his wedding to secure his job as Stassen's assistant. The quick ceremony was arranged to fit Cord's schedule. The couple sped off to Washington that night and spent one more together in the capital before Cord headed to San Francisco on a train with the rest of the U.N. delegates. Mary followed him a few days later by plane, carrying her own press credentials for the event. The gossip columnists gilded the romance—the dashing war hero heading off on a mission to solve world problems, scooping up a lovely princess on his way. The *Daily News* cast the wedding as a martial event ordered by a young officer.

"In Washington, D.C. for conferences with Commander Stassen, he long-distanced his proposal Wednesday night, got a yes and then demanded immediate action."[2]

The tabloid's military-style description of the surprise wedding was apt if not entirely accurate. Cord Meyer was a decorated marine lieutenant who later in life became known for his confrontational style. Mary dated him throughout the winter of 1944–45, after he emerged from a veterans' hospital where he was being treated for shrapnel injuries and fitted with a glass eye. As part of his recuperation he had been resting in New York, playing squash to become accustomed to his partial blindness, and dancing and drinking to recover his spirits. He and Mary and any friends who were not away on wartime duties prowled the New York clubs. They were trying to recapture the tempo of the prewar years, but much had changed.

During those long nights the young couple talked for hours. They discussed the catastrophe of war, the meaning of death, and the human capacity for peace. Cord had an intensity that intrigued Mary and the deep seriousness she thought she wanted in a man. He was a literary talent whose writing was already being published in national magazines. He was also a man of action who had emerged from war deeply committed to peace. The psychic energy from his wounding was still pulsing in him and he was casting around for a way to act on his resolve. As Mary watched his face and listened to him talk with an almost religious zeal about the wrongness of war, there was no doubt in her mind that here was a man who had the courage to put his ideals—so similar to her own—into action. A month apart in age and both attractive, literary, and to the manner born, they seemed like soul mates. And there was something more: In many ways—but especially in his devotion to an impossible ideal—Cord was a lot like Amos.

The Pinchot family had its suicides, and the Meyer family had its own skeletons. Cord's great-uncle Harry Thaw was famous for murdering architect Stanford White (whose firm had designed Amos Pinchot's little Milford house) in 1906 over a beauty named Evelyn Nesbit. When Cord was nine, his father had a breakdown and was briefly institutionalized.[3] Even when Cord was an adult, his father's mental troubles were evident in the anguished dreaming shouts that echoed through the New Hampshire summer home on nights when Cord was home. But in the morning no one mentioned them.[4]

The Meyers were wealthy and socially connected, and like the Pinchots, they had spent the Depression years in relative ease. Like Mary, Cord was a fourth-generation American descended from a successful European immigrant. His great-grandfather Cord Meyer emigrated from Germany in 1845 and began working as a grocer in Brooklyn. He soon owned a wholesale grocery business and a sugar refinery. Cord's father was a foreign-service officer in Washington when his first set of twin boys was born. Cord's mother, Katharine Thaw, belonged to the Pennsylvania Thaw family, which possessed a major coal fortune. Cord and his twin, Quentin, and their parents lived in diplomatic residences in Havana and Stockholm until their mother had a second set of twins and the family returned to America. Cord senior rejoined the family real estate business. The Cord Meyer Company was one of the preeminent landholders in New York, responsible for developments on Long Island and Forest Hills. The Meyer real estate holdings had increased a fortune made in sugar refining by a company called Meyer and Dick that had operated in Cuba during the previous century.

Cord and Quentin (named for his father's friend Quentin Roosevelt) attended private school in Switzerland and then St. Paul's School. St. Paul's was considered one of the two or three most desirable private preparatory schools in the country. Located in the snowy New England town of Concord, New Hampshire, the school was academically rigorous and socially almost monastic. Boys were required to go to chapel three times a day and were imbued with high Episcopalian formality. Both boys played hockey, but Cord was less athletic than his twin and he took the goalie position only after long study of the game by reading.

Cord Meyer as a boy was an artist. Headmaster Gerald Chittenden noticed the boy's sensitivity and lyrical talents and concluded that "Cord is fundamentally a poet."[5] He edited the St. Paul's School newspaper, *Horae Scholastica,* and wrote poetry and articles for it.

After graduating second in his class, he went on to Yale, where he continued writing poetry and edited the *Yale Literary Magazine*. His intellectual reputation grew. He won the Alpheus Snow Award, given to a student deemed to have contributed the most intellectually to Yale, and graduated summa cum laude.

There were signs in the child of the argumentative man Cord would become. The St. Paul's headmaster never forgot young Cord's tempestuousness. "As a boy he had a fixed habit of going off the deep end; he blew like a half gale," said Gerald Chittenden in an interview in the 1940s. "He may sometimes have been a little absurd in those days but when he cooled down, as he sometimes did, he amused himself as much as he did the rest of us." The headmaster went on to describe a boy who was driven to fury by cynicism and who on questions of morals and morale "was always right." The boy exercised his will as a dormitory supervisor.[6]

On the Yale campus during Cord's years there, discussion about the war in Europe raged and men bitterly argued questions of isolationism and pacifism. Cord considered for a time becoming a conscientious objector should the United States enter the war. After Pearl Harbor was bombed, the question of objecting to the war suddenly became obsolete. He enlisted in the marines in the fall of 1942.

Cord's father had been an army airman in World War I, and military service was assumed of the four Meyer sons. Meyer's father told interviewers later that of the boys, he felt Cord would be the least able to take the stress of war. "If any of them crack up under it, it will be Cord," his father thought as the four sons enlisted. His mother believed he would be killed, since he was the most sensitive of the boys.[7] But he signed up anyway, being a young man of conviction, to fight in a war that to many looked like a battle between good and evil.

David Challinor, Cord's roommate at St. Paul's, credited the preparatory school itself for promoting a desire for public service in its pupils. "I think boarding school instilled an idealized obligation into this extraordinarily privileged, elite group of young men. It was less so for women, whose only option was to get married. For the men there was a very subtle obligation. You owed something back for this unbelievably privileged life you led."[8] While many of these men would patriotically give their lives or limbs in World War II, the rigid code had its dark side. Cord and his social peers had endured few deprivations in their young lives and they could easily be accused of being soft. Aware of that possibility, schools such as St. Paul's, with their iron rules of honor, ethics, and manhood, drilled everything soft out of their pupils. Some historians have blamed upper-class machismo for a variety of military disasters engineered by men of Cord's generation, from the Bay of Pigs to the Vietnam War.

In March 1943 Cord left Quantico at the age of twenty-two with a second lieutenant's rank and became a machine gun platoon leader. He was sent to the South Pacific. The Pacific islands were crucial because they ensured the flow of oil from the Dutch East Indies to Japan and also served as a line of defense against attack on Japan itself. Capture of these islands was part of General Douglas MacArthur's Pacific strategy to bring Tokyo within range of American bombers. The action was extremely dangerous, as the Japanese fought desperately and refused to surrender even when their ranks were thinned and there was no hope left. To the horror of Americans invading the islands, Japanese soldiers scrambled with suicidal fervor into the line of machine gun fire, wielding sticks or rocks if they had lost their weapons, until they were all mowed down. Even wounded men on crutches joined the surges. One American veteran described the scene on Saipan as similar to a movie cattle stampede. Bulldozers had to be brought ashore to bury the thousands of Japanese corpses.[9]

In a letter to his parents published in the *Atlantic Monthly*, Cord described the banzai charges on American troops on Eniwetok Island, where he was in the first wave of the American assault. The once-sensitive boy was in awe at the brutality and his participation in it. "Finally we killed them all. They never surrender. I have no regrets over killing them. They are or seem inhuman. We kill them with as little feeling one way or another as one might kill mad dogs." As an officer, Cord watched his own troops die as well. "As we buried our dead I swore to myself that if it was within my power I should see to it that these deaths would not be forgotten or valued lightly," he wrote. "No matter how small a contribution I should happen to make it would be in the right direction."[10]

In July 1944, on the beach at Guam, Cord would make an awful contribution. The Guam shore was not broad enough for a massive frontal attack, so the Americans were sent onto the island in smaller groups. The attack on Guam lasted two weeks—the longest battle in the Pacific theater—and the American leaders recognized they would lose many men. "My aim is to get the troops ashore standing up," Vice Admiral Thomas F. Connolly had promised.[11] Beyond that it was up to their luck and their God. Cord went ashore with the first wave on the night of July 21. He and the men in his platoon waded ashore in the dark and, their boots soggy with water and under the crushing weight of their rucksacks, dug into the sand to wait for the Japanese attack they were sure was going to come. In his foxhole, Cord listened to the breeze in the palm trees and felt with a certainty in his gut that he was going to die. In a short story he wrote about the experience, he recalled that in the middle of this fear he felt an urge to stand up in the sand and announce to the enemy that they were all just men and that war was absurd. He did not stand up, but sometime during the night, a Japanese grenade rolled into his hole. It blew up in his face as he tried to fling it away from him, killing his partner and severely wounding him.

Lying in the sand immobilized, his head bloodied and fragments of teeth washing out of his mouth, Cord first thought he had lost the sight in both eyes forever. He felt in the dark for his weapon to put himself out of his misery but decided against using it. In a short story that eventually won the O. Henry Award, he described his thoughts. "He saw war clearly as the finished product of universal ignorance, avarice and brutality. A little out of adolescent vanity, but more because he had failed to become a conscientious objector, as he ought to have done, he chose to accept the consequences in an effort to redeem by personal valor a lost consistency of purpose."[12]

When the sun rose over Guam in the morning Cord was still conscious but unable to move or speak. Marines surveying the damage discovered he was still alive only when someone took his pulse. A doctor on the beach pronounced that he had about twenty minutes to live, and the marines sent an official telegram to his parents announcing he had died; a later telegram eventually corrected the first. He was taken to a rescue station on a nearby coral reef and revived with blood plasma. After time in a hospital near Pearl Harbor, he was transferred to a naval hospital in New York. For his injuries he received the Purple Heart and Bronze Star.

By the fall of 1944 he was home and resuming his acquaintance with Mary Pinchot. Mary spent most of that fall and winter with Cord; the boarders at her mother's apartment rarely saw her. Mary Goodhue was working at a law firm and occasionally discussed the law with Cord, who was taking law classes at Yale. He had quickly decided he didn't like the law, mainly because he had such a hard time reading with one eye. "I thought Mary and Cord were a good pair, a sort of natural pair," Goodhue recalled. "They had broad interests, worldwide. They weren't small, picayune people."[13] Paul Moore, a St. Paul's and Yale chum of Cord's, was also wounded in the Pacific and back in New York recuperating in the fall of 1944. He and Cord played squash together and socialized, two veterans-about-town with their dates. "We were happy to be back and we were doing a lot of drinking," Moore said. Mary "danced exquisitely" and was the kind of young woman who attracted attention when she walked into a club. "She was an extremely bright and responsive conversationalist, up on current events. And Cord was bright and amusing."[14]

Cord's abilities as a writer had already been discovered by the editor of the *Atlantic Monthly*, Edward Weeks, who was introduced to Cord Meyer Sr. by New York State Parks Commissioner Robert Moses. Weeks read Cord's war letters home, was struck by the vividness of his language, and decided to publish them while Cord was still overseas. But the writing life alone did not satisfy the wounded man. He needed a platform and a point of authority from which to write. Reinhold Niebuhr, who taught at Union Theological Seminary, tried to interest Cord in the seminary, but Cord was not interested in religion, either. There were no answers for him in the Bible, even if he did have the moral certitude of a preacher. The newly returned Cord Meyer was serious about one thing, world peace, and he threw himself wholeheartedly into any efforts he believed could ultimately ensure it. In 1945, the new United Nations looked to him like the place to start.

The day Cord and Mary got married, Cord was appointed as one of two wounded veterans to accompany the U.S. delegate to San Francisco for the U.N.'s formative convention. There were high hopes for the gathering. Idealistic men such as Cord saw it as a blank slate upon which to write a grand scheme for a permanently peaceful planet. World federalists, of which Cord would soon become one, believed the new organization could be a supranational authority with power to settle regional conflicts before they became world wars. This hope-filled event constituted Cord and Mary Meyer's honeymoon.

The scene in San Francisco was more international than anything provincial 1940s America had ever seen. It was a glorious, eclectic gathering of men and women of all skin colors and styles of dress, from turbans to saris and kimonos to dashikis, who had crossed the world to come to America, the great liberator of the earth. The Allied diplomats had been raised to celebrity status, and people stood in line for hours to catch glimpses of Russia's Molotov or England's Eden. The attention they got was the subject of much journalistic mirth. "Women sigh for a look at Anthony Eden," wrote one columnist.[15]

People also lined up on the street outside the window of the I. Magnin department store, where movie actor Charles Boyer was broadcasting live on the radio, and screamed to get the autographs of such Hollywood attendees as Orson Welles and Gracie Allen. Besides delegates and their staffs and wives, the event had attracted every sort of person from the serious to the crazy. Foreign-policy students and American Indians in tribal dress rubbed shoulders on the sidelines with religious fanatics and poets, and all of them looked for someone to lend an ear. The helpful associations of middle America, the Kiwanians and the Rotarians, turned out to offer their advice, joined by the League of Women Voters, the American Bar Association, and any other national organization with the means to attend.

Mary attended as a journalist with press credentials from the North American Newspaper Alliance. The convention, held at the opulent San Francisco Opera House and the more boxlike Veterans Center, was a press extravaganza. There were twelve hundred accredited journalists, or six for every delegate. Press credentials were prized possessions, and Mary was probably fizzing with the thrill of being an esteemed observer at a historic event with the leisure to soak up the sideshow. The press was treated with at least as much deference as the delegates. *New Yorker* writer E. B. White became a friend of both Cord and Mary at the conference. He described the scene for journalists as one as full of fantasy as the city air was full of fog. "If you hold a press card in San Francisco, you can go far," he wrote. "Far" included free food, free police-escorted shuttle service around the city, and entree to any of the big meetings. "You find yourself falling into the vicious habit of attending meetings merely to establish your right to be there," White said.[16]

Behind the official scenes there was much gaiety, and the journalists took full advantage of it. "Statecraft Was Well-Lubricated" read one headline below a cartoon of a throng of multinational diplomats holding cocktail glasses.[17] White observed six cases of Seagram's tagged for one delegation. The Russians brought their own massive quantities of caviar and vodka. One journalist joked that most of the delegates and diplomats were "looking for peace at the bottom of a glass." Yet there was an awesome "sense of destiny and obligation" about the conference, White wrote. "The accusing eye of millions of homesick young soldiers, the hungry gaze of millions of famished children, are trained on this hill tonight. Theirs is a fixed stare, which no one can evade."[18]

Cord took little pleasure in the lighter side of the convention. The memory of dead comrades and his own trauma was still fresh. He was also growing pessimistic. The convention was rife with politicking and double-crossing. Raw power was wielded by the Big

Three—the United States, Russia, and England—leaving small countries voiceless and licking their wounds. Cord, as Stassen's assistant, was immersed in the sometimes tragic details. He had to listen to the pleas of those with noble but lost causes, such as Polish anti-Communists and supporters of Ukrainian independence who were going to be defeated by the Soviet Union's delegation. Worse, he quickly lost faith in the whole enterprise when he realized the Big Three, with France and China, were going to carry through on a plan to retain veto power over the world body. Cord believed that only if national sovereignties submitted to a higher authority could another war be averted. The formation of the United Nations Security Council spelled the end of his hopes for the utility of the United Nations in carrying out his chief objective, ending war. He told reporters for the *New York Times* that the convention was merely a step in the right direction, and concluded that the veto power was just another alliance of the great powers and one that would surely lead to another war.

Among the press representatives was a young man Mary remembered from a prep-school dance and Vassar weekend dates—John F. Kennedy. He was attending on Hearst newspaper credentials, and he and Mary got reacquainted as young peers among the hordes of older journalists and pundits. Kennedy's relationship with Cord was not as warm. Cord talked to the *New York Times*, but he turned down a request for an interview from Kennedy. Kennedy wrote his skeptical reaction to Cord's ideas into a notebook: "Admittedly world organization with common obedience to law would be the solution. Not that easy. If there is not the feeling that war is the ultimate evil, a feeling strong enough to drive them together, then you can't work out this international plan. Mustn't expect too much . . . There is no cure-all."[19]

John Kennedy and Cord Meyer got off on the wrong foot at the United Nations convention, and Kennedy never got over his dislike for Cord.[20] The bad blood between the two men might have come from Cord's arrogant personality, Kennedy's friendship with Cord's new wife—a woman whose questioning style of thinking and upper-class poise matched his own—or simply rivalry between two equals. The two men actually had much in common. They were from moneyed East Coast families, were well educated, and had war wounds and medals for heroism. And both already seemed headed for national prominence.

Just before the convention ended in May, Cord Meyer received word that his twin brother had been killed in the American assault on Okinawa, in one of the final battles of the war. Cord initially held the unlikely hope that his brother was the subject of a false report, as he himself had been, but Quentin's death was soon confirmed. Cord's brother had been hit by a Japanese grenade while trying to retrieve a wounded soldier from the line of fire. After Cord heard the news, a passage from an e.e. cummings poem, "Buffalo Bill's," kept running through his mind: "and what i want to know is / how do you like your blueeyed boy / Mister Death." For days he was despondent, unable to express himself even to Mary. He wrote later, "My wife tried to comfort me. I could do nothing for a time but sit in my hotel room."[21]

Stassen quickly let his assistant leave the convention to mourn. Cord and Mary boarded a train in San Francisco and took it through the Sierras to a ranch in Montana owned by the Meyer family. There the couple spent a month sunbathing, fishing, and having the vacation honeymoon they had missed in San Francisco. Mary was already pregnant. Their first child, whom they would name Quentin, would be born in January, just a few days shy of nine months after their wedding date. At the ranch, Cord began writing an article for the *Atlantic Monthly* in which he argued that the United Nations delegates had not accomplished as much as was being claimed, and that only by giving the U.N. power over nations would it ever work. But the force of his article was about to be lost in an event of historic significance. While the young couple relaxed on the ranch in mid-July, the United States secretly detonated the first atomic bomb at Alamogordo Air Force Base in the red desert of New Mexico.

In August Mary and Cord boarded a train for the journey back east. En route Cord continued to work on his article and Mary edited it. The piece was twice as long as it was supposed to be. Mary took out paragraphs and Cord promptly replaced them. They argued on intellectual ground, turf on which Cord could never give an inch. Cord responded to her criticism of his work with derision. The man who had shared his ideals with her and listened to her with what she thought was understanding and respect just months ago had vanished. He was so vehement and cutting that at one point during the editing process she burst into tears and ran to the ladies' room.[22] Sobbing, she fought down waves of early-pregnancy nausea. The American plains, yellow and dusty under the late summer sun, rushed by outside the train, just as they had on another transcontinental train trip with Bob Schwartz a few years before. Back in the sleeping compartment, if she put her head on the pillow facing the window, the fields and tiny towns blurred into long stripes of color.

Reaching Chicago in the late afternoon, they changed trains. In the shadowy bustle of Union Station, the young couple stood on steady ground for the first time in a day and a night and there heard a newsboy shrilly hawking an extra edition. Men and women had stopped what they were doing to read the news over each other's shoulders. A single atom bomb had demolished the entire Japanese city of Hiroshima, killing tens of thousands in a ball of flame and wounding many more. The war was almost over. The newlyweds' argument on the train suddenly seemed petty as the implications of the new weapon hit them. Back aboard and on their way to New York, the screech of wheels on track mimicked screams. Cord told Mary then that he had heard of work on the atom bomb during his half term at Yale Law School the previous fall. The use of the new weapon confirmed his belief in the need for a federated world. The improbability of that after the squabbling and power plays he had just seen in San Francisco merely depressed him, but he didn't tell that to his young wife until his depression had grown much darker.

After the news of Hiroshima settled in, followed quickly by the superfluous horror of Nagasaki, Cord decided the U.N. convention was already obsolete, since the gathering had occurred without the delegates' knowledge of the new weapon of mass destruction. In an essay published in the *New York Times* in September, Cord described the bomb's belittling effect on veterans such as himself. "The pillar of smoke over Japan on August 8 spelled in large letters for all who dared to read, not only the end of that war, but the end of our own security, no matter what our military strength." Referring to his own wound, he continued, "I feel now as if I had been hit by David's slingshot in an archaic battle in a long-vanished past."[23]

In the fall of 1945 Cord and Mary, now six months pregnant, moved to Cambridge. There Mary took a job as an editor for the *Atlantic Monthly*, and at the suggestion of *Atlantic* editor Ed Weeks, Cord began writing a book about the effect of the atom bomb on world affairs, to be called *Peace or Anarchy*. His short story about the night of his wounding, "Waves of Darkness," was accepted by the *Atlantic*. He continued to read and write poetry, study Shakespeare, and jot down ideas for novels, plays, and short stories. The Harvard Society of Fellows awarded him a three-year grant to write. Through the fellowship, he was invited to dine weekly with prominent intellectuals and men of letters who came to the university, among them Alfred North Whitehead, Vladimir Nabokov, and T. S. Eliot.

That November, just after his twenty-fifth birthday, Cord was gripped by a black depression, the first of many episodes. He and Mary spent the Thanksgiving holiday together with his parents; it was the first Meyer family holiday without Quentin, and death was never far from Cord's thoughts, whether his brother's, his own close escape, or the deaths of millions threatened by the new weapons. The fact that Mary was about to bear their first child was not an occasion for joy at that moment. In his journal he wrote, "Talked with Mary of how steadily depressing is our full realization of how little hope there is of avoiding the approaching catastrophe of atomic warfare. . . . [T]he little child that is soon to be born shall live to see only sorrow and trouble."[24] Mary saw Cord's darkness and tried to cheer him up. It was a task she was familiar with, having served her father in the same capacity a few years before. And endless propaganda had prepared her for the duty of providing comfort to a returning veteran.

Although there is no written record of Mary's feelings during this period, the fact that she was pregnant probably increased her own sense of concern about nuclear weapons and the fate of the world. As a committed pacifist who thought all wars were indefensible, Mary must have shared Cord's fears about the possibility of mass destruction.

Even so, his bleakness must sometimes have been oppressive. After all, together they were bringing a child into the world. It was already becoming her job to attend to practicalities and live in the present, because she had married a man who would not or could not do that.

The atom bomb, while it had ended the war, inspired what Norman Cousins, editor of the *Saturday Review*, called "a primitive fear." In an ominous 1945 editorial headlined "Modern Man Is Obsolete," Cousins expressed the notion that science had exceeded mankind's ethical capacity. "Modern man has exalted change in everything but himself," Cousins wrote.[25] Like Cord, he saw the answer to that dilemma in world government with a radical plan for world peace.

At the dawn of the cold war, young Cord Meyer was regarded by some as an internationalist visionary. In his book *Peace or Anarchy* and in excerpts published in the *Atlantic*, Cord proposed that the United Nations be granted authority to oversee nuclear power installations inside member countries. The U.N. also needed to be given the authority to prevent war "and the armed power to back it up." He proposed that the U.N. Security Council be transformed into a cabinet without veto power and that the body create a world court before which individuals could get fair and legal trials.

Just after moving to Cambridge in the fall of 1945, Cord was invited to a conference in New Hampshire, organized by Supreme Court justice Owen J. Roberts and Wall Street lawyer Grenville Clark, on the effects of the atom bomb and the possibility of world government. Clark became the elder statesman in the world government movement and continued promoting it into the 1960s, long after Cord had moved on to less idealistic pursuits. The group drafted a letter, published in the *New York Times*, that urged supranational authority for the U.N. That involvement soon led to Cord's being invited to speak around the country on world federalism, and he became the young spokesman for the growing movement.

Mary and Cord settled into a pattern of married life typical of postwar couples their age: They followed his career, and Mary committed herself to his dream and bore their children. In 1946 the birth rate rose twenty percent over the previous year. Mary, determined not to be as distant as her own mother had been, did not turn her babies over to a nanny. She became an efficient, practical mother. In the fall of 1947 Mary gave birth to a second child, Michael. Mary bore the brunt of the child care during these early years, because Cord was often traveling. When Cord was around, Mary put him to work and they split the nightly feedings, alternating nights. Cord later joked that the feedings seemed like a waste of time: You got out of bed to feed the baby, it all came up, and then you started over again.[26]

In New York and in Cambridge, Mary had the occasional companionship of old friends from Vassar who were also married and mothering babies. The women would meet at playgrounds with their toddlers and trade anecdotes of family life. There was little time or inclination for talk of higher questions or of art. Still, Mary managed to keep her hand in some creative pursuits. She took morning classes at the Art Students League in midtown New York for one month each in 1948 and 1949, and there she came into contact with the abstract expressionists working in New York. One of her life drawing classes was taught by a Russian émigré named Nahum Tschacbasov, who encouraged his students to invent freely and examine underlying organic structure, focusing on "pure color, space and volume," as he put it in a League catalogue.

In May 1947, Cord, not yet twenty-seven, was elected president of the world federalist movement. The five American world federalist organizations had coalesced into one, United World Federalists. Cord and Mary moved to New York so he could take charge. Within a year, under his leadership and determination, the number of world federalists doubled to more than thirty thousand people in nearly six hundred chapters around the country. The group attracted a number of prominent citizens. Among the members and sympathizers were Harper and Row publisher Cass Canfield, Norman Cousins, Justice William O. Douglas, Harris Wofford, who would one day be associate director of the Peace Corps, and future California senator Alan Cranston. Albert Einstein allowed his name to be used on the organization's letterhead and personally solicited funds for the association.

With their combined trusts and probably occasional money from Mary's mother, Ruth, the couple could afford to do without much of a salary, although they did not live lavishly. In New York, they lived in Ruth's Park Avenue apartment, where they had a housekeeper, but they did not go in for the amount of household help both of them had known as children. Mary continued to cook and raised her children mostly by herself. She was sanguine about Cord's frequent trips. He was engaged in a crusade and she was enthusiastically supportive. His absence was the price they paid for a goal greater than her own needs and desires. His involvement in world affairs was a ticket to a broader world for her, too. When she could, Mary went down to his offices and volunteered. As Cord's fame grew, Mary seemed satisfied to travel in his wake and accept his reflected glory. Her picture appeared next to him in the September 1948 *Mademoiselle*, the couple posed on a staircase, leaning on an ornate wooden banister and looking down at the camera, above the headline "Steps to Peace." "Mary and Cord Meyer work together for the gravest need of our time—freedom from war and the threat of war," the caption read. "Mary, a Vassar graduate, was assistant fiction editor of the *Atlantic Monthly*. Now she writes for UWF (United World Federalists) and directs volunteer workers, having put aside, for the moment, her free-lance writing."[27]

Cord's radical pacifism was born of his war experience. He knew world federalism was a shout into the wind, but the memory of his wounding and dead comrades compelled him to carry on. No one besides Mary saw Cord's despair. Among colleagues, he developed a reputation for being tireless and not terribly attentive to other people. He smoked a full pack of cigarettes before ten A.M. He was so concentrated when writing that he habitually left briefcases and clothes in airports and hotels. He could work for hours in a straight-back chair in the middle of a train station. He was on the road more often than he was home. A friend of Cord's from those years told a reporter for *World Government News* that Cord was an extremely distant husband and father—which was, to the friend, all to the good: "A large share of his efficiency comes from his gay attractive wife's sympathy with his work. No matter how heavy his schedule, Mary Pinchot Meyer has never intervened. Instead she has spent months in volunteer work at the office. 'It's a lucky thing that Cord has the wife he has,' says one of his friends. 'She understands exactly what he's trying to do, and she is just as good with people as he is with ideas.' " The unnamed friend went on to note that Cord didn't pay much attention to the small details of family life, but that it was for the greater good. " 'It's far more important, of course, to think through every aspect of world affairs than it is to remember how old your children are—not very many wives would realize this. By the way, ask him exactly how old Quentin and Michael are now—he can outline his plans for Luxembourg brilliantly, but I don't think he can tell you that.' " The question was put to Cord, and indeed, he could not answer.[28]

As the movement grew, so did Cord's stature and the demand for his appearances. Soon he was making four speeches a week, an elegantly suited but casual young man on the podium who always spoke with a cigarette burning between his fingers. Cord Meyer was a natural public speaker who never used notes. He spoke in long sentences with no temporizing phrases or generalizations. His war wound increased the moral authority that had been his since childhood, and his idealistic righteousness was especially persuasive with college students and with women. He became something of a sex symbol for world peace. One college woman who joined the federalist movement recalls having a poster of him in black leather jacket and eyepatch on her dormitory wall.[29] In a 1947 *Glamour* article, photographs of twenty-seven-year-old Cord Meyer and twenty-nine-year-old JFK were placed side by side for a feature story called "Ten Men Who Care."[30]

In 1946, just a month after Winston Churchill made his famous "Iron Curtain" speech delineating the coming cold war, Cord Meyer addressed a convention of world federalists from the Seven Sisters colleges, sponsored by *Mademoiselle*. For Cord, the atom bomb, not fascism, was the new common enemy. "The initiative lies squarely with the United States," he told the adulatory young women. "We discovered the weapons, we used them and it is now our move. So long as we continue with these weapons we can expect only a deterioration of relations among the countries of the world. Our real choice is not whether we are going to get world government; we are going to get it in a very few years. It is fundamentally the question of world government by conquest and empire or world government by rational and voluntary consent." He also told them civil wars had been made obsolete in the atomic age. "The old right that people had to resort to revolution against their tyrants is virtually lost with the nature of modern weapons and the fact that you need such tremendous industries to make them; you can't revolt at the barricades with an old rifle."[31]

That summer the United States conducted aboveground atom bomb tests on Bikini Atoll. Cord Meyer seemed to his audiences to be a ray of sanity in a dangerous, doomed world. They left his lectures thinking it was possible that if everyone pulled together and tried to get along, the madness might not lead to the inevitable holocaust. Yet even as he became a symbol of hope, Cord was tormented. At the height of his popularity he wrote in his journal: "Between the shelled beaches and the Armageddon of atomic war I live out my useless days in horror."[32]

As his stature increased, Cord Meyer the idealist was beginning to crumble. A few years earlier he had expressed himself on the war vividly and with great emotion. Now, in his writing on world federalism and the atomic bomb, he became pedantic. Cord had gone straight into the public fray with a message he was unsure of himself. The young man felt weary and was torn by doubts about whether world federalism could ever work. Aloft on planes carrying him away from his wife and children to yet another speech, he engaged in an interior dialogue about whether his life's true path lay in public service or in private, scholarly contemplation, yet observed that "my peculiar temptation is not money but notoriety and fame. This must be put aside. It corrupts and takes the mind from the object."[33] Even as he wrote this, his picture was appearing in newspapers in Hartford. He argued with himself but seemed incapable of acting. "I fear that the capacity to react to art or poetry is one that we lose through disuse," he wrote.[34] Later he wrote: "That story or play about a young man trying to decide what to do with his life definitely should be written. Use Eliot's Dry Salvages as a starting point."[35]

He wrote notes for essays that condemned both war and the American system, which he saw could be corrupt and shallow. He later considered a piece on the reasons for low morale of soldiers. "The answer lies in the complete degeneracy and rottenness of our way of life. Profits, material comfort never were a cause worth dying for and never will be and they knew it. . . . The troops have been lied to for too long."[36]

He never did publish anything of the sort. Those were the last written outbursts of the hopeful angry man who had won Mary Meyer's heart. He knew himself to be susceptible to the seductive claims made by Communists about the capitalist system. He felt the emotional force of their argument. A classless society probably appealed to his strong sense of morality. But Cord was a privileged beneficiary of the capitalist system and he could never oppose it. Such a route would never lead to the public acclaim he secretly craved. In the years to come, like a man protesting too much, he devoted his considerable energies to defending a system whose rotten aspects he recognized against the cunning tactics of the Communists.

Cord first came to know those tactics as a member of a young veterans' group. At the U.N. convention he had met another young wounded veteran named Charles Bolte, who had lost a leg in Europe.

Bolte was dedicated to achieving a postwar role for America that would justify the sacrifice of men in his generation. Bolte set about organizing veterans and created the American Veterans Committee (AVC), which supported a continuing international role for the United States.

In the spring of 1946 Cord learned that the Communist Party was attempting to take over the AVC by running its members for leadership posts. The first political battle against what Cord described as "hard-core party members" took place in the unlikely venue of Des Moines. Rather than let gullible American veterans, who might mistake the Communists for ordinary liberals, simply vote them up or down, Cord set out to defeat them with every weapon he had, including surveillance and political tricks. He and his allies "maintained a twenty-four-hour watch" on the hotel room of their Communist opponents' leader "in order to identify as many as possible of the individual communist leaders," he later wrote.[37] Cord and Bolte offered a slate of candidates for the AVC leadership committee, and they "attempted to avoid dissipating our voting strength by ensuring that all those who agreed with us voted for the entire slate and did not exercise independence of judgment."[38] Cord realized his tactic was undemocratic. "In some ways our strategy was a departure from the democratic ideal of free and open debate. But it was forced upon us by the disciplined political machine the Communists employed."[39]

Led by Cord, the non-Communists triumphed in Des Moines. A second skirmish occurred a year later in Milwaukee, when a young veteran and psychology student named Timothy Leary sat in the audience and became disgusted by the Red scare infecting the ranks. Cord rolled over the Communists there again. The final battle was fought in Cleveland in 1948. By then tension between the East and West blocs over the Marshall Plan, the Soviet coup in Czechoslovakia, and the Soviet blockade of Berlin had defined for even the most politically oblivious veteran the difference between the United States and Communist Russia. Any Communists still lurking in the AVC were quickly exposed by their stands on those big issues. At the end of the day in Cleveland, the AVC amended its bylaws to deny membership to members of the Communist Party.

Cord later said he learned about the dangers of "utopian" Communist thinking at the AVC. "The communist is perhaps the most unrealistically Utopian of all reformers in his conviction that ownership of the means of production by the workers will in itself bring about a new era of harmony among men. It is this fanatical conviction that leads him into the most dangerous of all illusions—the belief that he is justified in using any means to achieve his end."[40] Cord too understood the thrall of utopian ideas. His world government would have been one.

The world federalist movement reached its apex in 1948, with an international convention in Luxembourg. Mary flew there with Cord, leaving her two sons in the care of a nanny. She made the rounds of the meetings emanating money and glamour. Her expensive clothes and gracious manners were unusual among the earnest band of hopeful one-worlders.[41]

By the end of the 1940s, Cord was disillusioned with the world government movement. The postwar world was not going to be united but was already disintegrating into two blocs, East and West, Communist and capitalist. In January 1949 the Soviet Union and its East European allies established a Council for Mutual Economic Assistance, and shortly after that NATO was formed. That same year China became a Communist republic. The battle lines were drawn. The nation's brightest men were gravitating toward Washington and a chance to prove their mettle in this new undeclared war. Comparing himself to them, Cord felt left behind. Theoretically world government would work, he felt, but only if the government was run on Western, market-oriented, democratic principles with the rule of law in force. In the bifurcated new world, with totalitarian Communism on the other side, international federalism looked like appeasement.

In the fall of 1949 Cord and Mary moved back to Cambridge, where he picked up his Harvard fellowship again. During his years on the road as a celebrity, his relationship with his wife and family had suffered. Now Mary was eight months pregnant with their third son and he barely knew the first two children. She wanted him to share the child-rearing burden. He had begun to feel uncomfortable playing the crusader. In a journal entry at the start of 1950 he wrote, "It is a mistake to become totally engrossed in this matter to the exclusion of everything else. And that is what I have done, forgetting that love between individuals, that small acts of kindness and respect, that the pleasures of artistic enjoyment and creation, that all these things and more are an essential part of one's life to be omitted only at the cost of that feeling of barren sterility I feel now."[42] One of Cord's friends would say years later, "Early fame ruined him."[43]

Back in Cambridge, Mary began taking art classes at the Cambridge School of Design and found she liked it and had a certain ability. American art was coming into its own at this time. In New York, Jackson Pollock was starting to drip and throw paint onto canvas. But in Cambridge, Mary was changing diapers and minding two—soon to be three—young children. She gave birth to her third and last son, Mark, in early 1950. The time she could spare for painting was always contingent upon the children's needs; guilt was a monster at the door of any mother following a muse into solitary work at the beginning of the baby boom. Mary also had at hand the memory of her mother, remote, writing at a desk behind a closed door during Mary's own childhood.

Cord made a last-ditch effort to get out of the public eye and find some "quiet work" in academia. But he also contacted friends in government and the field of foreign relations. A job with the State Department or White House would put him where the action was and still allow him to continue to write and think. He corresponded with Averell Harriman at the White House and Secretary of State Dean Acheson, but his affiliation with the world federalists made him too controversial for the State Department. In March 1951 he turned down an opportunity for academic work, a teaching fellowship to study the broad topic of the future of humanity, offered by the University of Chicago. Cord was no longer interested. He was already on to a more exciting job in Washington.[44]

In the 1940s and 1950s the American intelligence service was almost a graduate extension of the Yale secret societies. Its officers were socially as well as professionally connected to one another. Forty-two members of Cord's class of 1943 went into the Office of Strategic Services—the World War II organization that preceded the CIA. Nine went on to the CIA.[45] Several Yale graduates, with alumni Tracy Barnes and Richard Bissell at the helm, eventually masterminded the CIA's Bay of Pigs disaster. By the 1960s the relationship between Yale and the CIA (and between the CIA and many other universities) had begun to decline. Cord Meyer would personally go to great lengths in the 1970s to try to stop the publication by Harper and Row of a book by a younger Yale alumnus, Alfred McCoy, on the connections between the CIA and the heroin trade.[46]

In 1951, thanks to a meeting between his father and CIA director Allen Dulles on the Hamptons summer social circuit, Cord interviewed for a CIA position. Using his American Veterans Committee victory as proof of his commitment to fighting Communism, he won over the CIA director, who offered him a job so classified Dulles couldn't discuss it with him in any detail until he was hired. Cord thought it over and decided to take it. In his memoir he cites as the deciding factor Allen Dulles's "cosmopolitan, sophisticated" manner, a social resonance that came from the fact that Dulles belonged to all the private clubs Cord Meyer's family also called their own.[47]

It is unclear what Mary thought of the CIA at this point in her life, but since it was being organized by a group of like-minded liberals, she was probably as supportive of the agency's goals as Cord was. And she was all for the move to Washington. Her sister, Tony, and many of her Vassar chums were already in Washington, most with their husbands in the government.

The philosophical underpinnings that accompanied Cord Meyer from world federalism into the CIA did not require any great alteration. The core belief of world federalists—that a higher and more rational authority should resolve the conflicts of individual nations—was not antithetical to the core belief of most cold warriors at the CIA. The cold warriors believed *themselves* to represent the more rational, higher authority to whom small sovereign countries in danger of falling to Communism would want to submit for their own good. And Cord's politics were never really revolutionary. He had chafed in the role of outside agitator. He believed, as he had told the college girls in 1947, that civil rebellions against tyranny had been made obsolete by the atomic bomb. The era of armed revolt, of the triumph of weaker groups with strong ideas over military might, was over for him.

Cold war policy architect George Kennan called the atom bomb the most serious danger in the history of mankind and the most serious insult to God.[48] As the United States and Russia began to face off over the corpse of Germany, their differing visions of postwar Europe dressed the stage for the coming decades of brinkmanship. Nuclear tension set in almost before the ink was dry on agreements ending World War II. Just two months after Hiroshima, in October 1945, the American Joint Chiefs of Staff had drawn up a secret plan that outlined the destruction of twenty of the largest Soviet cities with atomic bombs. The mixed industrial targets, including Moscow, "would exploit the maximum capacities of the weapon, produce the quickest, most direct and certain effects on Russia's immediate offensive capabilities," the paper stated.[49] In 1951 President Truman for the first time authorized the Defense Department to take control over the nuclear and nonnuclear components of nine "Fat Man" bombs.[50] The cold war had commenced.

Americans wanted men in charge who inspired confidence. The men who stepped forward, such as Cord Meyer, had their authority conferred by Yale, the work ethic, and the stiff upper lip. They were straight arrows in an era when deviance of any sort was regarded nervously. President Eisenhower accurately defined the national mood when he said upon his election in 1952, "The great problem of America today is to take that straight road down the middle."[51]

A war-tired people wanted normalcy, but an ominous array of

weapons of mass destruction, nuclear, biological, and chemical, were being planned, built, and tested around the world. Sightings of unidentified flying objects increased dramatically as the air forces of both the United States and Russia raced to design the best, fastest, and most invisible vehicles for their bombs. Audiences flocked to see B movies in which mad nuclear scientists accidentally set off radiation leaks leading to mutations that created killer slime, giant insects, or an incredible shrinking man.

It was the era of propaganda and mind control, of *The Manchurian Candidate* and *The Invasion of the Body Snatchers*. The notion of brainwashing seized the national imagination. The competing ideologies, capitalism and Communism, depended on the belief systems of individuals. If those beliefs could be altered, then there would be no need to use the new doomsday technologies.

At the start of the new decade, both Mary and Cord were thirty. They had been married five years. Mary continued to be her husband's occasional editor while he criticized her attempts to write fiction. They began a dangerous little psychological game straight out of *Who's Afraid of Virginia Woolf?* She would read his private journal and write her comments on his thoughts in the margins. These little marginal notes reflect her sense of humor and her impatience with her husband's ponderous pessimism. In March 1950 Cord wrote, "There is a special pleasure in the objectivity that one wins by the imaginative creation of other characters to face the dilemma that one is tired of wrestling with in terms of personal decision and action." In the margin, in red ink in her left-leaning, rounded script, Mary Meyer underlined the words "tired of wrestling" and wrote, "You are a romantic! We're all in the same bed honey—Pooped!" Left with the raising of three boys under the age of five while Cord was off all day with his books, she knew the literal meaning of "tired of wrestling."[52]

In Cambridge, Mary and Cord had settled into a pattern of behavior that increased her domestic responsibilities even further. Cord played the absentminded professor, hapless and melancholy, and Mary became, by choice or default, the practical, efficient mother.

When they moved into their rented house, the landlord asked Mary whether her husband intended to put up any paintings and would need to hammer nails into the walls. Mary laughed uproariously and replied that her husband did not know how to use a hammer and would not be putting up any paintings; if any art was going up on the walls, it would be her doing. On another occasion around the same time, the couple and their sons were driving somewhere in the Massachusetts countryside when they got a flat tire. As Cord told the story later, he got out of the car and wandered around a bit, wondering what to do. When he turned around, Mary was on the ground replacing the tire herself, to his masculine humiliation.[53]

As the pressure on her to be the practical one in the household grew, Cord's melancholy and self-absorption began to look self-pitying and ridiculous to her. At one point Cord wrote of the growing Korean conflict, "I am without hope. And yet I live from day to day as before." In the margin Mary wrote in a large, loopy script, "When you say you are without hope you imply that you thought humans were not what they are—humans."[54] In 1951, just before they moved to Washington, he tried his hand at writing a poem. He called it "Proper Tribute," a four-stanza paean to a beautiful woman who wears her beauty "carelessly like a bright dress / Lent for a night by some indulgent guest." The last lines were "What damage in poor hearts her passing wreaks / And how for her desire sleepless burns." In the margins Mary drew an arrow to the last line and observed: "She bites her fingernails, fails to shave under her arms, has no sense of humor and is a totally mundane soul—but silence fires the imagination of the spiritually timid."[55]

Domestic security was exalted on every level—nationally, in the suburban streets, and especially inside the home. Whatever marital dissatisfaction seethed between Mary and Cord, they had three children under the age of five and a life together. The postwar ethic was all about home and family. Beneath that placid surface, though, nuclear annihilation was a submerged threat. The Soviets tested their first atom bomb in 1949, and a year later the United States was raising the ante with the hydrogen bomb. Americans read a government pamphlet called "You Can Survive" about how to build a bomb shelter. They might have filed it next to copies of the best-selling *Your Dream Home*. Children practiced duck-and-cover exercises at school. Air raid sirens wailed in weekly tests across the land. Mary Pinchot Meyer and her husband, Cord, entered the new decade doing what those who could afford it did: They put the best possible face on it and moved to the suburbs. But McLean, Virginia, was not just any suburb. It was across the Potomac River from Washington, D.C., the strategic command center of the cold war.

# 5

# CIA Wife

*We CIA wives were all exhausted women, worn to the bone.*

— CICELY ANGLETON

On a summer afternoon in 1952, four American tourists were lost in a French postcard, with CIA official Cord Meyer behind the wheel. The countryside was all winding narrow roads traveled by farmers in horse-drawn carts and shaded by old trees. Cord took the curves at high speed to provoke the terrified laughter of the wives. A long lunch of more red wine than pâté and bread, and a possibly incorrect French road map, left them hilariously lost. "Where is Chartres?" they laughed inside the car. "*Où est Chartres?*" Their unpracticed tongues massacred the language of the European aristocracy. The men stopped and tried to ask directions in their American-accented French from farmers, innkeepers, and anybody else they could hail. But even when they made themselves understood, they could not comprehend the French response. They drove for hours, circling through the same picturesque hamlets, passing what seemed to be the same cows and the same haystacks. Mary and Cord and their companions, Tom and Joan

Braden, were just like the other American tourists stumbling around France that summer except that the husbands were officers in the United States intelligence service, in Europe on a mission. Braden, a tall, bony Iowan and World War II intelligence veteran, headed the International Organizations Division of the CIA, and Cord Meyer was his recently hired assistant. Braden was surprised to discover his sophisticated Ivy League–educated protégé didn't speak French any better than he did. They were in France meeting with leaders of trade and labor unions considered ripe for infiltration by the Communists. They offered American money and support to those who promised to repel the Communist influence within their ranks.

Their wives were oblivious to their business. They knew their husbands worked for the CIA. Each woman might be called a cleared wife—a woman the agency believed to be a safe repository for any secrets her husband might mutter in his sleep. The CIA denies it had a formal clearing process for wives, but some of the wives believed there were background checks performed on them.[1] Two CIA documents have been released mentioning Mary. One is a completely redacted paragraph with a single sentence at the end left visible that reads: "There is no indication that Mary P. Meyer was ever a member of this organization." The other is a one-paragraph "summary" of her life statistics, titled "A Review of the Appropriate Office of Security Files Relating to Mary Pinchot Meyer." The two documents seem acknowledgments that Mary Meyer had been investigated or "vetted" by the CIA to some degree.[2]

Cleared or not, the men in the early years of the CIA didn't confide in their wives much anyway, and the women didn't ask too many questions. In the summer of 1952 Mary Meyer and Joan Braden were just along for some shopping and sightseeing. They returned home without seeing the medieval monument. The great architectural feat known as the cathedral of Chartres had to wait for another day. More *vin rouge*![3]

Cord Meyer had signed up with the CIA to do psychological and intellectual battle with the Communists, a task for which he was uniquely qualified. The world federalist movement had given him access to the minds of one-world utopians, pacifists, and left-leaning intellectuals, the very men and women the CIA was most worried about. The International Organizations Division was dedicated to infiltrating academic, trade, and political associations across the globe before they were taken over by Communists. The goal was to control potential rebels, to co-opt the leadership, and to steer the left generally toward capitalist ideals, not Communist ones. To achieve this, the CIA hired informants, channeled money into the organizations, and eventually created its own front groups.

For Cord Meyer and his colleagues the early battles were in labor and political organizations in European countries, especially France and Italy, where Communists seemed to be gaining political power in the early 1950s. By the end of the decade, Cord was infiltrating groups ranging from those in South and Central America to organizations in Asia. Eventually the funding was directed toward American student and labor groups in the domestic battle against Communism.[4]

Cord had demonstrated at the American Veterans Committee his talent for working in secret to eliminate Communist influence in an autonomous organization. Questions about constitutional rights or democratic principles had not troubled him, since he believed, as did many cold warriors, that the Soviet Communists would take over whole European countries from within if they were not opposed by the CIA, also from within. Years later Cord wrote in his memoir, "The fact that our assistance had to be kept secret did not disturb me. . . . Discretion and secrecy were required if our assistance was not to be self-defeating."[5]

Within the CIA, Cord Meyer soon came to be regarded as creative and inspired, on a par with the top four or five crafters of CIA policy during the 1950s. CIA officer Dick Bissell called him "the creative genius behind covert operations."[6] He oversaw the secret funding of intellectual groups, most famously the National Student Association, but also the Congress for Cultural Freedom, which engaged some of the best minds in the Western world by providing forums for discussion throughout the 1950s and 1960s. The congress published a respected journal, *Encounter,* and involved such intellectuals as poet Stephen Spender and critic Frank Kermode, who for years were unaware of the source of their money.[7]

Cord's connections to liberal intellectuals served him well, and his operations involved some surprising names. He oversaw one operation in which a young Gloria Steinem received CIA funds to organize the American student presence at the Vienna Youth Festival, an event expected to be under Soviet influence. Steinem's contact with Cord was *Time* editor C. D. Jackson. Steinem later explained that in 1958 private funds were hard to find for attendance at a Communist youth festival, so she accepted money from the CIA via the National Student Association. Steinem's organization, the Independent Service for Information on the Vienna Youth Festival, eventually was paid $85,000 and continued to receive CIA support through 1962.[8]

Cord Meyer's infiltration of domestic groups was eventually exposed. In 1967 a student member of the National Student Association revealed in *Ramparts* that the association had been accepting money from the CIA for years. The news prompted larger American newspapers to investigate and expose a vast picture of the CIA front groups, including dummy foundations set up to channel millions of dollars in federal money.

Cord's efforts were often directed at the world labor movement, where Communist propaganda might fall on receptive ears. He maintained relationships with anti-Communist leaders of the American labor unions. Some of the most revered names in the American labor movement, among them George Meany of the AFL-CIO, were involved in Cord's network. Tom Braden gave fifty thousand dollars in fifty-dollar bills to Walter Reuther of the United Auto Workers so he could spend it on labor unions in Germany. According to Braden, such measures were necessary in the early 1950s because the Soviet Union operated seven "immensely powerful" front groups in Europe for students, women, labor, and journalists.[9] In Latin America, Cord created a CIA conduit to local affiliates of labor unions, and through them the CIA was able to keep tabs on potentially revolutionary movements in countries controlled by dictators favorable to the United States.

CIA money was also disseminated domestically to trade unions around the United States, including the Communications Workers of America, the American Newspaper Guild, and the National Education Association, which used it to fight Communism in their own ranks and abroad.[10]

In 1951 the CIA was still a clubby place with a relatively small budget. It was housed in temporary barracks along the Mall in downtown Washington, buildings left over from the war. The buildings were identified only by letters, "K Building" or "L Building," and were poorly ventilated. In winter they were chilly, and in the summer desk fans moved the sweltering air.[11] Despite the economical front, a series of presidential directives was exponentially increasing the agency's power in the early 1950s. Before the end of the decade, the agency moved to plush offices at Langley, won a large secret budget from Congress, and gained a clandestine foothold in back alleys from Saigon to Teheran. The men who ran it gained enormous power but never faced election politics or the restrictions of the constitutional process. At Langley, certain fundamentals were all that mattered. One was the possibility of nuclear war. The other was the assumption that the Communists were out to dominate the world and had to be stopped at any cost. Lore has it that the only piece of graffiti in the men's bathroom then was "$E=mc^2$."[12] The inscription on the lobby wall as one entered was biblical: "And ye shall know the truth and the truth shall make you free."

The secrecy of the CIA was justified in the early years because the cold warriors believed the KGB could infiltrate any organization, even the CIA itself. The unease was compounded by Senator Joseph McCarthy's televised hearings investigating allegations that there were Communists in high places. The International Organizations Division, where Cord Meyer worked, was regarded by some hawks as a nest of liberals who might be a little soft on the Reds. Tom Braden had ties to the progressive community, and Cord had been affiliated with the dovish world federalists and the intellectuals at Harvard. To manipulate the left required some affinity with it, but Cord was never as close to the left as he was accused of being in August 1953.

One afternoon in his second year with the agency, Cord was summoned to a meeting with Richard Helms, then covert operations chief Frank Wisner's deputy. Helms was a careful bureaucrat who rose to head the CIA during the pre-Watergate years. On that hot afternoon, Helms first offered his younger colleague a cigarette and then told Cord that he had "a rough one" to discuss with him. The FBI had been investigating Cord for several months and had come up with a list of charges that questioned his fitness for government service, based on his political associations. The charges were made by anonymous accusers, but Helms had to take them seriously; Eisenhower had decreed that it was up to the accused government employee to offer a defense against such charges. Kafka couldn't have set the scene better. Cord went white with rage. His enemies would forever remain invisible. He would have to resign until cleared.

The charges were a hash of his youthful associations and acquaintances. He was accused of consorting with one of his Harvard professors, a man who was in fact a leftist. His world federalist past and his AVC work were suspect, even though he had been fighting the Communists. His associations with the publisher Cass Canfield and the poet Richard Wilbur, both progressive but neither of whom was known to be a Communist, were part of the charges. And the charges claimed that his wife, Mary Pinchot Meyer, had once belonged to the American Labor Party—a relic from her wartime days as a New York journalist.[13]

Mary was unable to take the charges seriously. The notion that her buttoned-down, ambitious husband with his crafty antagonism toward the Reds was actually a leftist must have struck her as ludicrous. "My wife was inclined to treat the whole affair lightly and encouraged me to think that it must be the result of some misunderstanding or mistaken identity that could easily be explained," Cord recalled in his memoir. But the accusation seared him. A lawyer advised him to defend himself by writing an autobiography that explained his life history and his acquaintances. It took months to write and grew to the length of a short novel. He submitted it as his defense with the words, "Here's an elephant gun to shoot an ant." A secret court of CIA executives, including Dulles, convened to consider Cord's case. On Thanksgiving Day, three months after the ordeal began, it ended abruptly when Allen Dulles personally called Cord to tell him his employment had been found "clearly consistent with national security."[14]

For beating a suspicious-associations charge during the McCarthy era, Cord became legendary within the CIA. He had faced down an attack from the provincial, isolationist right and remained standing. The McCarthy attacks were as much against intellectuals and the East Coast elite as they were against Communists. Cord had made a perfect target. The fact that he had survived made him a hero not only of his generation but of his class.

But the ordeal was the final stroke in the demolition of the one-world idealist. Cord's patriotism would never again be questioned. His devotion to the American system and to the CIA eventually went beyond the pale. As the years passed, he grew more and more vociferously anti-Communist. At dinners and cocktail parties he buttonholed people who disagreed with him, jabbing a finger into their chests and arguing with a loudness and a ferocity that even his friends found rude.

When Mary and Cord moved to the Washington area, the city still had a distinctly small-town, southern flavor. The Virginia suburbs, where the Meyer family lived, were just being carved out of red farmland, and the locals still spoke in thick backcountry accents. The capital city itself was really two separate cities. Blacks were in the majority by the late 1950s, but the black and white communities were strictly segregated. The wide green divide of Rock Creek Park physically separated white Georgetown from the black quadrants, and the realtors' redlining and Jim Crow laws did the rest. Restaurants, theaters, and even recreational facilities were segregated. Until the 1960s open discrimination in the capital was a diplomatic embarrassment. In September 1950 Nigerian scholar Chike Obi, who possessed a Ph.D. in mathematics from Cambridge, was a guest at the White House. Two days after he arrived in Washington for his extended visit he abruptly left the United States, announcing that he hoped never to return. He and some other international students had been turned away from five restaurants because of his race before being allowed to sit down in a shabby café.[15]

As embarrassing as such incidents were, they never prompted action.[16] "D.C. Is Hardship Post for Negro Diplomats" was the headline in the *Washington Post* above a detailed story on the discrimination African embassy officials faced in the American capital during the 1950s. But race relations were a silent problem in Washington. Ignored by white Washington, street crime, juvenile delinquency, and housebreaking in the black neighborhoods increased annually as the number of unskilled black migrants to the capital kept rising. Housing was a problem. Urban renewal was destroying black ghettos, but real estate covenants kept out of better neighborhoods any blacks who could afford to buy there. Jobs were completely segregated. Even in the late fifties, not one Washington finance company or bank employed a black teller, clerk, or secretary except the black-owned Industrial Bank of Washington. Blacks were unofficially barred from holding jobs as ticket sellers in railroad stations, clerks in hotels, or laundry truck drivers. Most worked as janitors, elevator operators, servants, and laborers.[17]

The political and social center of white Washington was Georgetown and the internationalists who had moved there to wage the cold war. The Georgetowners could not have been less interested in the urban affairs of the capital city; their sights were set on China, Russia, and beyond. They were theoretically in favor of civil rights, but in practice the only contact they had with black people was with the domestics who traveled across town to work in their houses.

The friendships between Georgetown neighbors made for a

network between men who ran the State Department, the intelligence service, and the national media. In case anyone forgot how important they were, journalists reminded them periodically. Stewart Alsop, who lived in the heart of Georgetown himself, wrote a book in which he analyzed Washington power sets and divided people into groups, including "Bold Easterners" and "Prudent Professionals." The "Bold Easterners" were of course the group to which Mary and Cord and many of their friends belonged.[18] Alsop also penned an article in which he made the case that Washington and his friends and neighbors were at the very center of the world. In fact, the social connections with journalists were a crucial part of the CIA's propaganda machine. Chief among CIA friends were the Alsop brothers. Joseph Alsop wrote a column with his brother Stewart for the *New York Herald Tribune* and they occasionally penned articles at the suggestion of Frank Wisner, based upon classified information leaked to them.[19] In exchange, they provided CIA friends with observations gathered on trips abroad.[20] Such give-and-take was not unusual among the Georgetown set in the 1950s. The CIA also made friends with *Washington Post* publisher Phil Graham, *Post* managing editor Alfred Friendly, and *New York Times* Washington bureau chief James Reston, whose next-door neighbor was Frank Wisner.[21] Ben Bradlee, while working for the State Department as a press attaché in the American embassy in Paris, produced propaganda regarding the Rosenbergs' spying conviction and death sentence in cooperation with the CIA.[22]

Journalists were not penalized for crossing the line. On the contrary, those who betrayed the national-security establishment by divulging secrets were cut off both socially and from further information. Drew Pearson was dropped from the guest list of the Bankruptcy Ball, a Georgetown event attended by the foreign-policy set and many journalists, just for writing something unfavorable about Paul Nitze, a foreign-policy advisor to Truman and Kennedy.[23] Some newspaper executives—Arthur Hays Sulzberger, publisher of the *New York Times*, among them—actually signed secrecy agreements with the CIA. But such formal understandings were rare, and relationships between agency officials and media executives were usually social—"the P and Q Street axis in Georgetown," said one source. When Carl Bernstein reported that one CIA official had called Stewart Alsop a CIA agent, Joe Alsop defended his brother to Bernstein, saying: "I dare say he did perform some tasks—he just did the correct things as an American. . . . The Founding Fathers [of the CIA] were close personal friends of ours. . . . It was a social thing, my dear fellow."[24]

Cord Meyer developed and nurtured his own friendships among journalists. He seconded the nomination of *Washington Post* writer Walter Pincus for membership in the Waltz Group, a Washington social organization. Pincus went on to become the *Post*'s premier intelligence reporter. Cord also maintained friendly ties with William C. Baggs of the *Miami News* and foreign-affairs writer Herb Gold. Cord's ties to academia served him when he needed favors from publishers and journalists. In some accounts, he and *Time* writer C. D. Jackson together recruited Steinem. According to his journal, Cord dined at the Paris home of American novelist James Jones.[25] He was also close to *Chattanooga Times* writer Charles Bartlett throughout his life.

Cord and Mary lived across the Potomac from Georgetown in a comfortable, sprawling eighteenth-century white wood house locally known as Langley Commons, with a wraparound porch and an acre of sloping lawn only a few miles from the site of what was to be the CIA's new permanent headquarters at Langley. Langley Commons had served as an inn and post office and later as a makeshift hospital that housed wounded Civil War soldiers. Redecorating her house, Mary discovered some writing beneath wallpaper on one of the bedroom walls; it turned out that in several rooms wounded soldiers had scrawled their names and other graffiti with lead bullets. The house and lawn were shaded by a towering oak reputedly five hundred years old. White pines, lacy walnut trees, old hawthorns, and box elders also shaded the grounds. The terraced garden was old and filled with traditional perennials, and Mary tended what had been planted more than a hundred years before she arrived: crape myrtle, wisteria, single-bloom hollyhocks, bridal wreath, peonies, irises, and daffodils. The house, with its four bedrooms and two wings, had more than enough space for the family. It was never lavishly decorated or filled with knickknacks. It was a functional house, and Cord would sometimes joke about its simplicity. One friend of the family recalled that while the Meyers were interested in the arts, there was not much classical music played in the house. " 'Home on the Range'—Western music—was what they listened to."[26]

The Meyer family lived as did most other upper-middle-class families in Washington in those years. Cord's concerns were global and his responsibilities vast. Mary's life was by contrast limited and domestic. She became a devoted gardener. She took art classes and painted in the two-story shed she had turned into a studio on the grounds of the house. Cord lived in the world of James Bond and Hemingway. Mary admired the work of artist Helen Frankenthaler and had a casual artist's style in dress and manner. Women who knew Mary then recall that she "came alive" discussing art and literature. One of her favorite quotes was from the French writer Paul Claudel: "Order is the light of reason but disorder is the delight of reason."[27] Still, with small children to be watched, there was little time for philosophical discussions.

The young couple was politically progressive. Cord disliked religious institutions and none of their three sons was baptized, a fact that angered Cord's side of the family but wouldn't have bothered Ruth Pinchot. Being nonreligious was common among the young cold warriors in the Meyers' set, for whom secular humanism and Freud had replaced the creeds of their parents. Years later many of their children, including the Meyer sons, turned toward both institutional and nontraditional religions as a source of comfort and security.

Mary's own experimental side was by necessity submerged during these years, but she nurtured her art and Cord supported her. They had a black live-in maid who did housework and some cooking in order to give Mary the time to work on her art. Mary's painting was important to Cord, and he encouraged it. When the couple entertained, Mary usually cooked. Cord's innate argumentativeness was tempered by Mary's presence. "Cord always loved to start an argument after dinner," Marie Ridder recalled. "But she would always make a joke about it, and everyone would end up laughing. She lightened him." Ridder, a neighbor of the Meyer family in McLean, recalled that Mary had an agreeable effect on Cord, but sometimes even she could not divert him, and then she would be embarrassed by the scenes he created: "Cord could disrupt any dinner party."[28]

During the early 1950s in McLean, the couple appeared quite happy on the surface. Cord seemed genuinely interested in his wife, and she returned his affection. "One could see he loved her enormously," Ridder recalled. One family friend recalled meeting Cord and Mary together for an excursion to a photo exhibit at the National Gallery, followed by dinner at a Georgetown restaurant. "The photographs were very artistic," the friend recalled. "When we came out of the museum, Cord only cared about Mary's opinion. He kept asking her which one she liked best and why."[29]

But Mary's own creativity was tempered by the mundanities of carpools and visits to the dentist. The questing girl had been largely replaced by the capable wife, breezy, efficient, and in command. Like many other Vassar graduates from the class of 1942, she channeled her education and craving for drama into solid, family-oriented work and became a trustee at her sons' private day school. Along with the other mothers of children at Georgetown Day School, she ferried children to and from school and after-school recreation.

High casualness, a combination of tennis whites and set hair, was the prevailing style among the wives. The clothes mothers wore, even in their cars, "had to have structure, manners, backbone, character," journalist Connie Casey wrote in an article about her childhood years in Washington. "The Washington suit was often outlined at cuff or jacket bottom or skirt hem in a band of a different color, frequently black. These suits had well-defined boundaries, suggestive of treaties negotiated." For more formal affairs, women young and old struggled for "the balance between pretty and proper and ended up resembling the Mother of the Bride in Champagne beige or dusty rose."[30]

Mary was different. While everything in Washington pushed women away from the natural world, Mary did not get her hair set every week and she wore loose, comfortable clothes. Her short hair was always windblown, and she wore little makeup. "She always looked as though she had just come from a tennis game or a walk in the woods," said Eleanor McPeck. "She had the most extraordinarily vivid coloring—rosy cheeks and brilliant blue eyes," said Elizabeth Eisenstein. Other women hired gardeners and ordered up a hundred yellow daffodils when the mood was upon them. Mary loved gardening herself, working the earth with hands and spade. She carried the Pinchot women's Milford habit of nude sunbathing to McLean. She was comfortable with her body, even as she gained weight around her hips and middle that she was trying to lose. On summer afternoons she casually doffed her clothes and found a sunny spot on the lawn upon which to read. One Meyer son's young friend never forgot stumbling upon her in a moment that vastly expanded his nine-year-old understanding of the opposite sex. Her reaction to discovery by the gaping little boy was nonchalant. Peter Janney was permanently altered. "I saw her lying there on her stomach and she sort of turned and smiled and greeted me. She never said anything to me. She put me very at ease, but I was so embarrassed and awestruck. She was like the softest human creature I had ever experienced. She was just exquisitely soft."[31]

The most prominent Washington wives knew how to host dinner parties, their primary political function during the 1950s. At these dinners, the cold war was always a presence. "Everything goes on as usual except there's a great undercurrent of tension," one of the hostesses, Gwen Cafritz, told the *Washington Post* in 1959. "We're worried about the fate of Berlin."[32] Among the doyennes of Washington society were Joan Braden, wife of the CIA's Tom Braden, and Jean Friendly, married to *Washington Post* editor Alfred Friendly. The most powerful wife of them all in the 1950s was Polly (Mary) Wisner, the daughter of a moneyed Northeast family and wife of the

CIA's Frank Wisner. She married Frank before finishing college and became one of the foreign-policy set's most formidable hostesses. Throughout the 1950s, matters of state were discussed and decided in the dining room of her P Street house, a large brick townhouse built in 1830 and known as the Linthicum House. The world-scale decisions made at her dinners were sometimes leaked to journalists at the same time. Often after dinner on warm nights, the male guests—spooks, diplomats, and American and British statesmen—gathered in the colonial revival–style garden below the veranda and talked quietly of the cold war beneath the Venetian lanterns, lead cherubs, and boxwood. Polly deliberately stayed ignorant of the details. "I kept out of it. I was so afraid I would hear something or be told something that I would mention later, making a mistake," she said.[33] Her regular guests included George Kennan, top CIA officials Tracy Barnes and Richard Bissell, ambassador to Russia Chip Bohlen, and columnist Joseph Alsop.

Mary Meyer went to these parties when she had to. Although polite, she never became close to hostesses such as Polly Wisner. "I found her utterly charming. She was every single grace you'd hope your daughter to have," Polly said. "She was—a very old-fashioned expression—the epitome of a ladylike person. She had very good manners, a lovely voice, and great charm." Polly found Mary reserved and possessing "a great deal of dignity. She wasn't the type who would share her woes."[34]

Neither, of course, was Polly. Her husband, Frank Wisner, was manic-depressive in the years before psychiatrists had determined how to treat the disease. As the years passed, colleagues noticed his behavior becoming more and more bizarre. Wisner was overseeing a global propaganda and spy machine, what he called his "mighty Wurlitzer," and he respected the younger Cord Meyer for his subtle skill at the game. "He found Cord very smart, I think," Polly said. Her husband frequently invited Cord to drinks at their Georgetown house or to Galena, the family farm in nearby Maryland. But Cord was not empathetic. When Wisner was shakily recovering from a particularly deep depressive episode in 1958 that had required electric shock treatment and a six-month hospitalization, Cord approached him at a party and, poking his finger in Wisner's chest, excoriated his former boss, shouting furiously, "Look at you, you're a shell of the man you once were." The Wisners never saw him after that. Seven years later, Frank Wisner put a shotgun to his head one summer afternoon and pulled the trigger.

Mary and Cord were closer friends with some of the younger couples in Washington, including Mary's Vassar classmates and their husbands. The Vassar women felt a tiny disdain for the Washington hostesses, whose avocation seemed to them rather frivolous. Among the Vassar women was Mary's sister, Tony, then married to lawyer Steuart Pittman, who became assistant secretary of defense under Kennedy. Another college chum, Mary Draper, had married Wistar Janney, who worked at the CIA with Cord. Vassar girl Scottie Fitzgerald had married lawyer Jack Lanahan and lived in Georgetown. And Cicely d'Autremont had married James Angleton, chief of the mole-hunting office at the CIA and another of Cord's colleagues. Journalists such as James Truitt and his artist wife Anne and later Ben Bradlee were also part of the Meyers' circle. Through Truitt, they became friendly with *Washington Post* publisher Phil Graham.

Even among the cliquish Vassar women, Mary's social distance was unusual. She was simply not interested in the social whirl. Some of her old friends were put off by her Washington persona, so much more remote than theirs. "She was aloof and not as interested in keeping the friendships nurtured," Eleanor Lanahan, Scottie's daughter, said. "She made my mother feel a little bit too social. Unlike my mother who was very gregarious and more forthcoming, Mary had a grip on herself. She was poised."[35]

CIA wife Joan Bross recalled that Mary always recoiled at the prospect of making appearances at official dinner parties. "She always asked me how many people were going to be there," she said of her invitations to Mary. "She was thinking about serious things and hated small talk, I think. She was asking big questions such as, 'Why are we here?' "[36]

Mary did not really embrace the Washington social scene until she became a frequent guest at the Kennedy White House. Rather than make small talk with diplomats at Polly Wisner's, the younger families—the Meyers, Janneys, Truitts, Pittmans, Lanahans, and Angletons—spent a great deal of leisure time together. There were evening get-togethers, and sometimes the families took weekend camping trips to nearby beaches or mountains when the husbands could get away. They went to the Delaware shore and the Blue Ridge Mountains with their children. On Saturday mornings in the fall, the adults got together and played touch football in a park north of Georgetown while their children biked around the sidelines, then all retired to someone's house for lunch and drinks. Mary, still athletic, was always enthusiastically involved in these games. Jim Angleton and Cord and the boys fished together at Milford and in the Washington area. Cord went hunting for quail and pheasant with Wistar Janney. The Janneys had a pool, and on hot summer nights the parties were loud, drunken affairs, filled with laughter, dancing, and the sound of breaking glass and people being pushed into the pool. Mary loved to dance. Her favorite song became "Chantilly Lace," a snappy tune about a girl with "a pretty face, ponytail hanging down, a giggle in her talk and a wiggle in her walk." One admirer recalled that "the song suited her and she knew it." Angleton, for his part, loved dancing solo to Elvis Presley.

The boisterous partying of their parents left strong, sometimes bitter memories with the children. Describing the atmosphere of her parents' world in the mid-fifties, Eleanor Lanahan wrote, "From this point I feel I could give the correct flavor to the tale by suffusing these pages with a light mist of alcohol. Many a morning I wandered through the smoky twilight of the living room, like an archaeologist perusing hastily abandoned chambers. Clusters of stale drinks sat on the end tables. Ashtrays burgeoned with butts . . ."[37]

Peter Janney became an eclectic psychologist outside Boston, incorporating aspects of astrology, nutrition, and spirituality into his practice. His memories of youth in 1950s Georgetown remained infused with his childhood emotional reactions to the conflicting habits of heavy drinking and cool denial among the adults. "It was a circus," he recalled. "They used to drink so much." Janney blamed his father's premature death in the 1980s on his use of alcohol and nicotine.[38]

Heavy drinking was an occupational hazard for CIA men during the cold war. The capacity to hold one's liquor was deemed important because the Soviets were such notoriously big drinkers and American agents in direct contact with them were forced to try to keep up. The CIA even researched a whiskey placebo but gave up. "Everybody had a drinking problem," CIA psychologist John Gittinger said. "It wasn't regarded as a problem because most of them felt they could handle it. There was much more concern about tooth work or operations because they had the feeling that being under anesthetic would cause you to betray secrets."[39]

Jim Angleton was one of those heavy drinkers. He was also one of Cord's closest friends. Angleton's problems with alcohol and his penchant for imagining elaborate Communist plots were balanced by his charm as a friend, his familiarity with modern art, and his habit of quoting writers from Homer to Ezra Pound. His intellect and his interest in literature and art were matched in Cord. Cord often accompanied Angleton to his retreat in northern Wisconsin. Angleton made his own dry flies and raised trout fishing to a pursuit as complex as the hunt for Communists.

The revelation that his British friend Kim Philby actually worked for Moscow would propel Angleton in the sixties from garden-variety suspicion of the Soviets to a state that some in the CIA have compared to clinical paranoia. "That [defection] was a shattering experience to Angleton," Gittinger recalled. "From that period on he was the most suspicious man in the agency. My own feeling is the emotional wreckage of that close friendship made him mistrust everybody and colored his life from that point on."[40]

Angleton's "monster plot" theory held that the Russian intelligence service had already invaded every nook and cranny of the Western intelligence agencies with moles. His theories actually damaged the CIA by paralyzing its Russian section. Russian ex-spy Oleg Kalugin wrote a book about his thirty years in the KGB in which he said Angleton was considered by the KGB to be a sort of unintentional mole because his paranoia was having such a negative effect on the CIA. But Angleton was a favorite of CIA chief Allen Dulles, in part because of the gossip about Washington he was able to share. Angleton even bugged a dinner party given by a Treasury Department official's wife simply to amuse Dulles with the captured conversation.[41] "Dulles was sort of titillated by that stuff, and that's how Angleton won his confidence," journalist Victor Marchetti said. In years to come, Angleton would boast that he had placed wiretaps on Mary Meyer's phone and bugged her house, but it is unclear why he would have done it or whether he shared the information gleaned thereby with anyone at the CIA.

As chief of counterintelligence, Angleton was both "scholarly and cold-blooded." He authorized the writing of a handbook on interrogation that endorsed torture by various psychological and physical means, including chemical, electrical, and medical procedures. The CIA was fully aware that the detentions and methods were illegal, and the handbook instructed its users to notify "Headquarters" when it was being employed. The torture handbook remained in use until 1985.[42]

Cord and Angleton disagreed professionally. Cord never subscribed to Angleton's "monster plot" theory, and Angleton was leery of Cord's involvement with labor and student associations, fearing it would expose the CIA to infiltration.[43] But the two men remained very close personally. Each considered himself a humanist in a world of gray bureaucrats. Mary Meyer's friend Elizabeth Eisenstein thought Angleton had "a very fascinating, romantic, Bohemian side. Jim Angleton was the most romantic man I've ever known. His tastes ran to poetry and romance in general."[44] Eleanor Lanahan, whose father, Jack, hunted game birds with Cord in the Maryland and Virginia countryside, always regarded Cord as vaguely artistic. "He held up an egg one day and said, 'Isn't this an admirable shape?' I remember thinking that was so charming and out of the ordinary. He was also a great collector of modern painters." Eleanor Lanahan was impressed by the Barnett Newmans hanging in the Meyers' house. "That was very avant-garde for Washington."[45] Cord and Angleton were both close to poet Reed Whittemore, with whom Angleton had edited a poetry journal at Yale called *Furioso*. When Whittemore moved to Washington to become the poetry consultant to the librarian of Congress (now called the Poet Laureate), he joined the small group of CIA men and journalists who socialized with Angleton.

Mary's sons and nephews idolized Angleton. "He had more depth than any man I'd ever met," said one of Tony Bradlee's children. "He had extraordinary sensitivity and an interest in people." He was so nurturing of his friends that one of his nicknames was "Mother." Angleton was a hugely entertaining friend who saw life through the lens of classical literature. Mundane events—a family poker game or the way a dinner was cooked—often drew a cryptic scholarly allusion. Those who didn't know their Homer had to guess at his meaning. The spymaster played the piano at family gatherings at his suburban house and sometimes cooked barley stew with marrow bones for the Meyers.[46]

Angleton and his wife, Cicely, had two daughters and a son. As a couple, the Angletons were deeply attached, but the relationship was uneven and they separated several times. His own children were troubled by their father's remoteness. Cicely continued her education and after many years received a Ph.D. in medieval history. Kennedy White House social secretary Letitia Baldrige might well have been thinking of Cicely Angleton when she noted wryly that in the 1950s, "If you had a husband working for the CIA you learned to become a specialist in medieval art or gardening or something so you had your own life, because your husband would not talk to you."[47]

The Truitts were another socially prominent and artistically inclined Washington couple. Like Mary, Anne was a thoughtful, cultivated young mother and artist. She had been born into a Maryland family that lived on inherited wealth, and the family fortune had been devastated by the Depression. Also, like Mary's father, Anne's father had had problems with depression and alcohol. Anne's extremely refined sensibility eventually led her to art. Trained in psychology at Bryn Mawr, she painted and sculpted throughout the 1950s and showed her work in group exhibitions in Washington, but not until she was in her early forties did she suddenly arrive at the style of spare, painted wood sculpture for which she became known.

Anne's husband, James Truitt, was a journalist with *Newsweek* and later the *Washington Post*. He had a reputation as a serious intellectual and writer—and as a big drinker. People who knew him have differing recollections. "Truitt was incredibly smart, incredibly well read," David Middleton recalled.[48] Kary Fischer found him "porcine" and boorish. Serious Washington artists respected him, and he helped them with occasional published art criticism. Truitt had sophisticated and broad tastes in art. He collected Korean art and Japanese primitive art. He was eccentric and experimental. He kept an alligator in the bathtub of his Georgetown house for a time. Eventually he came to regard Mary Meyer as his spiritual sister, probably because her experimental nature was so like his own. Physically compact, he wore his sandy hair in an extremely short brush cut. Truitt often indulged his alcohol habit with his friend and colleague Phil Graham, the publisher of the *Washington Post*. Like Ben Bradlee, Truitt was a blue blood who also had the Rat Pack style down. Charming and genteel, cigarette always in hand, he still gave the impression of a man of street savviness and constant movement.

Anne was more severe in her presentation. She dressed in the style of Georgia O'Keeffe and favored southwestern attire, shawls, and large silver rings. Her relationship with Mary was complicated. She adored and admired her, but she was eventually hurt by her husband's attention to her friend. Anne became a mother relatively late in life, for those days. She was in her thirties when she and James Truitt had two daughters, Alexandra and Mary (named after Mary Meyer), and a son, Sam. Years later Anne wrote with revulsion of her role in the fifties-style marriage: "I had actually *eaten food earned by someone else*. I tasted something slimy and rotten in my mouth and felt a kind of servitude utterly familiar. With the force of a blow to my solar plexus, I felt clearly the position I had placed myself in: I had been beholden to James for the food in my mouth; I had been frightened that he would not put it there or in the mouths of the children; I had felt as if I owed him something because he kept me and the children—and that's the truth, I had owed him."[49]

The Angletons, Truitts, and Meyers grew very close, and they were especially bound together by their mutual interest in art and culture. They were deeply involved in Washington's relatively limited cultural life. One journalist who was assigned to cover the cultural scene in the late 1950s derisively called the whole city "a cultural backwater." But those who sought stimulation found it through the Institute for Contemporary Arts. The ICA was founded in 1946 by a poet, Robert Richman, with the intent of gathering writers, artists, and intellectuals from the United States and abroad and sending them on speaking engagements around the country, beginning in Washington. Headquartered at the Corcoran Gallery of Art, the ICA focused on cultural exchange. During the fifteen years it existed, many of the great figures of Western literature who came through Washington were hosted by the ICA, including Vladimir Nabokov, Stephen Spender, Octavio Paz, W. H. Auden, Christopher Isherwood, Richard Wilbur, Robert Frost, and Nadine Gordimer. The ICA also presented dramatic and dance performances and art exhibits. It sometimes brought together various cold war philosophers and atomic scientists to discuss the fate of the earth in the era of nuclear weapons. Mary Meyer and her friends were often in the audience.

A small group of Washington artists was working in the abstract expressionist style, and Mary met them through art classes at American University. The university's art gallery was one of the first in Washington to show the works of Jackson Pollock and other experimental New York artists. "Artists felt that they were on the brink of something new then and it was very exciting," recalled Ben Summerford, an instructor at American University who taught and befriended Mary.[50]

The art of the 1950s was a splash of individuality in a landscape of conformity and acquiescence to authority. American artists were confrontational, throwing their ideas in the faces of the gray suits. Artist Claes Oldenburg, one of the early creators of the "happenings" that would become more common as art events in the 1960s, opened a one-man show in 1959 by walking the streets of New York in an elephant mask, inviting public action and response. In literature the Beat poets were described in 1959 by *Life* magazine as "sick little bums" and "hostile little females." In music there was rock and roll, the dissonant bebop jazz of Thelonious Monk, Miles Davis, and John Coltrane, and the strange classical compositions of John Cage that relied on the random occurrence of sound and silence. In one Cage piece, twelve radios were tuned to different stations.

The New York artists working in the abstract style in the early part of the decade emphasized emotion in their action-packed canvases. As the decade wore on, their work became less and less referential and more incomprehensible to viewers. Art critics became prominent as interpreters and arbiters of taste. The preeminent art critic of the decade, the man to whom Mary's friends in the Washington art world looked for notice and approbation, was Clement Greenberg. The Washington artists Mary befriended in the early part of the decade would have paid dearly for Greenberg's attention. Before long, some of them did get it.

At home at Langley Commons, Mary worked on canvases in her studio shed, experimenting in the abstract style when she had time, but art came second to children. Like many mothers across America in that era, Mary felt that bearing and tending children was her most important job. And the women who produced the baby boom did not have children accidentally. They planned them, and spaced them close together so they could get on with their lives later. Although

Cord traveled and worked late hours, when the family was together they were "gregarious," recalled one relative. The Meyers spent a lot of time in Milford during the summers. Mary fished with the boys for trout in the stream at Grey Towers.

The three boys, all blond and blue-eyed, were growing up with distinctly different personalities. The eldest, Quentin, was smart, adventurous, and—more than the other boys—argumentative, like his father. Michael, the middle child, was not as intellectually quick as his two brothers, but he was an extremely popular boy, the kind of kid who drew other children to him. "Everybody wanted to be on Michael's team," recalled Peter Janney, who used to belong to what the kids called "the Mike Meyer gang." Physically and emotionally, Michael took after his mother more than his father. The baby, Mark, was shy, soft-spoken, and more lyrical and artistic than the other two. He was so shy when he was little that he often wouldn't speak for himself when in a group of people: he would whisper in Mary's ear and she would speak for him. "We called Mary 'Mark's spokesman,' " said one relative.

It was rare for Mary Meyer and the other CIA wives and their children to know exactly what their men were doing by day. A man who had just attended a meeting plotting the assassination of Castro or, in Cord Meyer's case, the staging of a phony labor demonstration in Guatemala came home at the end of the day, mixed a drink, ate dinner, and tried to interact with his family. But the men could never talk about how they had spent their time in the office. There was little give-and-take in those households. Husbands opened their souls to their martinis instead of to their wives.

The cold war years were trying times for CIA wives but also thrilling because of the women's proximity to power and international adventure. If the men couldn't talk to their wives, they did sometimes bring them along on trips abroad, and such travels set the women apart from the other housewives of the fifties. But the strains were enormous. Cicely Angleton, a white-haired poet now, will no longer discuss what she calls "those strange times." She has said her husband's job essentially destroyed their family life. Their son, her husband's namesake, still thought his father worked for the Post Office into his teens.[51] "I don't know how we lived through them," Cicely Angleton said of those years. She told her husband's biographer: "We were loyal women who got the short end of the stick. The husbands had careers, travel and outside interests, and we had none of that. The men were decent enough, but their nerves were shot. People's lives depended on them. It was so much more than a career."[52]

Jane Barnes, the daughter of CIA officer Tracy Barnes, a man who was deeply involved in the Bay of Pigs invasion and plots to assassinate Castro, believed that her mother was silenced by the sheer enormity of what was happening during the cold war. "Practically the hardest thing for my mother to do was hold a strong opinion. She knew there was this dire world horror going on, and it scared her."[53] Wives and children regarded the men as unassailable authorities. "We thought of Daddy as James Bond," Barnes said. Like many CIA men, Barnes loved the works of Ian Fleming and John le Carré. A neighbor once said to Barnes, "These books must be nonsense," and he replied, "On the contrary, they're understated."[54]

Mary did hold opinions and she was not afraid to express herself. Wives like Mary picked up tidbits here and there, through dinner conversation or listening to their husbands talk on the telephone. They were only half in the dark, whereas the rest of the country during the fifties was completely unaware of the agency and its work. Mary knew generally that her husband was fighting Communism within organizations such as the American Veterans Committee and labor unions. As the years passed she learned enough about the methods and aims of her husband and his colleagues to become openly critical of the CIA in a way that upset some of the other wives. Peter Janney recalled his mother becoming upset about Mary's anti-CIA remarks.[55] But she was never a politically strident woman and, like the other wives, probably never knew the full extent of the CIA's activities or the details of highly classified matters such as assassination plots and coups.

The CIA wives and children were in for a shock when Congress opened the Pandora's box of the CIA in the 1970s with a series of hearings into the agency's activities. A kind of retroactive paranoia afflicted them when a Senate committee exposed the "family jewels" of assassinations in 1976. Only then did the CIA wives and their children begin to understand, along with the rest of the country, what their husbands and fathers in the U.S. intelligence service had been up to. Jane Barnes recalls her mother's reaction. Tracy Barnes was already dead when the Church Committee released its finding that he had helped plot Castro's assassination. His wife was left with nothing but her memories for confirmation. "The guilt she felt," Jane Barnes said. "After the Church report she suddenly remembered how one night after they'd been out, he said, 'You know it would be so easy to shoot him from a crowd'—referring to Castro. It had alarmed her, but she only realized later it was something, it was *something*."[56] And once their husbands were exposed by the Church Committee, some of the women and children closest to the cold war action began to be able to believe anything at all about those years and their men. They imagined even more was possible than what had been uncovered by congressional inquiry.

Among Mary's friends, psychoanalysis became very popular. Women who couldn't fix their husbands worked on themselves. And bubbling beneath the very proper surface of their lives, beneath the engraved social invitations and art classes, there was always sex. Unmarried sex was still taboo, but progressive social science and popular psychology were telling Americans that sex was also the key to a healthy life. Kinsey's books on sexual behavior were best-sellers; his research stated that men were more sexually aggressive than women. The first issues of *Playboy* came out in the 1950s.

Among Washington men and women, flirtation was rampant. Sex was a diversion from the mundane chores of motherhood and the government bureaucracy. And it was the only real link between men and women in their bifurcated world. "A lot of people were dying to have sex with other people and they didn't do it," recalled Letitia Baldrige. "There was a whole lot of unmitigated lust, a lot of tension in the air that was not based on politics. It was based on whether people were attracted to each other or not. And they made no bones about it even though they weren't going to go out and have sex with each other." At dinner parties, there was a great deal of winking and whispering in ears. "One would say to another, 'You are really damned attractive,' and for the rest of those people's lives, they would run into each other and there would be a knowing twinkle," Baldrige said. "The having to behave made it all that much sexier."[57] But not everyone behaved all the time.

In Mary's set, extramarital affairs were under way in the 1950s. Her friend Anne Truitt was having an affair with an artist named Ken Noland, who was also married.[58] Even Cord would be accused of being "incurably promiscuous."[59] He was among those who earned a reputation as a married man on the make. Several women who first met Mary and Cord at their McLean house in the early 1950s fielded calls from Cord Meyer the very next day asking them for a date. One woman who became a close friend of Mary's never forgot her first impression of the couple. "When I first met Mary and Cord she was literally a golden girl. She had on these clothes that looked like wheat, and her hair was gold. Cord called me at my hotel the next day and asked to come and see me. I was shocked. She was so beautiful, and it was disgusting. He thought he was such an operator. I can't imagine she didn't care."[60] But if Mary was bothered, she didn't let it show. One family friend recalled Cord going on a mission to Germany one year. The friend wanted to give him the names of some female friends in Germany whom he might call, but first the friend asked Mary whether she felt comfortable about her husband's visiting with women on a trip abroad. Mary encouraged it. "She said she wanted him to have a good time," the friend recalled.[61] In any case, when Cord began attending CIA parties and Georgetown dinners without Mary, it quickly became clear to their friends that there were problems in the Meyer marriage.

After his triumph over the McCarthyites, Cord Meyer rose rapidly at the CIA. In 1954, when Tom Braden left the agency to become a newspaper publisher, Cord took his place as chief of the International Organizations Division. Within a few years he was overseeing a vast "black" budget of millions of dollars channeled through phony foundations to a global network of associations and labor groups that on their surface appeared to be progressive. Also as chief of the International Organizations Division, Cord was high enough in the CIA hierarchy to be privy to the top-level meetings about covert operations. He was in line to become deputy director of plans, the position that in James Bond movies is occupied by the spymaster "M."[62]

Cord was not immune to the pitfalls of his job. He drank a great deal (although not the three lunchtime martinis habitually enjoyed by his friend Jim Angleton). He also smoked constantly. His CIA colleagues nicknamed him "Cyclops" because of his war injury and watched, cringing, as smoke from the ever-present cigarette between his lips curled up into his unfeeling, unblinking glass eye. He drove a sports car and left many a hostess worried about how a man with one eye and so much alcohol coursing through his veins would fare on the road.

Cord continued to be pessimistic about the fate of the world and unsure whether government was the right place for his talents. He still fantasized about a happier life in "quiet work." In January 1954 he and Mary went to New York for several days, during which time he searched for a job in publishing. He got an offer from one of the big newsmagazines but none from the established book publishing firms he wanted to join. At that time he was committed to getting out of the CIA. "I intend to pursue the search and be out of the government by June," he wrote. "I've been buried long enough in the anonymity of the federal bureaucracy." He privately predicted "bad trouble soon" in Indochina but hoped to be away from the government before the need to get Congress to authorize troops.[63] But by November of 1954 he had done nothing about leaving. His resolve was weakened by his promotion to fill Braden's spot as chief of the International Organizations Division. The promotion flattered his desire for political recognition and he wrote in his journal that it kept him so busy he was barely able to stay awake at home at night. Still, he was unsatisfied. "Bam he lived as wow he died. It's no good really," he wrote to himself.[64]

During that busy summer of 1954 the Meyer family's golden retriever was hit by a car on the curve of highway in front of their house and killed. The dog's death worried Cord. He told colleagues at the CIA he was afraid the same thing might happen to one of his children, and he repeatedly warned the boys to stay off the road. He even considered moving the family, but the house was comfortable and it suited them.

In the summer of 1954 Mary and Tony, feeling left behind by their husbands and a little dissatisfied, set off on a European adventure. Their mother, still holding out for female individuality and independence in the midst of the baby boom, urged her daughters to cut loose. Ruth gave each of them a round-trip ticket on a ship to Europe and a thousand dollars in pocket money—a large vacation sum in 1954. "Ruth felt her daughters were being buried under their bourgeois marriages, and she wanted to give them a break," said one relative.[65]

The sisters went first to France, then traveled to Rome, where their light hair and American breeziness immediately attracted the attention of Italian men. Mary was delighted. Every sense was enlivened by the smells and sounds of Europe, the aroma of sweat and coffee and pipe tobacco and fish, the gurgling of fountains, the women in black with their rosaries and baskets, the food and wine. In Assisi, the sisters stayed in a hotel overlooking a convent. Mary was amused by her view of the street below, where on one side of a stone wall schoolgirls played, while on the other side men were brawling.[66] The sterility of McLean and Washington was obliterated by the riot of noise and color. The two sisters wrapped their hair in scarves, donned slacks, and drove to the Mediterranean. Children, husbands, pasts fell away in the breeze. They spent several weeks on the Mediterranean.

In Positano they came across an Italian gadabout who spent his summer days on a yacht with his dog, Mouglie, and had an affinity for young American college girls. If the girls were willing, he would bring them aboard and set sail for weeks at a time. He had a wealthy wife, a good Catholic who indulged her husband and stayed in Florence with his children. He also painted. Mary was enchanted. The record of the man's name has been lost, but various descriptions of who he was have survived. James Truitt told journalists he was an Italian count.

For the first time in ten years Mary was away from Cord and the children. Her half-sister, Rosamund, had committed suicide when she was the same age Mary was now, thirty-four. Perhaps it was this fact and the distance from her familiar life that revived the experimental person she had once been; perhaps it would have happened in Washington anyway. But she left Tony and joined the Italian on his yacht, where for several days they swam and sunbathed nude. The Italian was a carefree and uninhibited man whose gentleness differed greatly from the possessiveness and cold indifference of her husband. The Italian was soft, a little fat, and prematurely gray in his mid-thirties. There was certainly no serious talk of love or commitment. Much later she would tell Cord the brief affair that summer was "sexually satisfying" but nothing more.[67] Still, it was more than nothing. Mary might have been revisiting something the college girl on the chartreuse couch had known about the allure of sensory experience.

After Italy and a lusty *arrivederci* to the Italian, Mary moved on to Paris with Tony. There the sisters connected with the American expatriate crowd, a jolly group of journalists, diplomats, and spooks who loved nothing more than wicked women and long parties. "It was an unusual thing to have two respectable ladies from Washington roaming through Paris in an adventurous way, and they were roaming," recalled journalist Blair Clark, who met the sisters in Paris. Clark called their adventure "the husband-dumping trip." One journalist who encountered Mary during that month pronounced her "on the make." In Paris, Mary ran into an old Vassar chum, Anne Chamberlin, who was working for *Life* magazine. Tony fell head over heels in love with Ben Bradlee. He knew the sisters from Washington and invited them out one Saturday afternoon to a rented nineteenth-century estate, the Château Boissy St. Leger. The shabby and romantic château had sixty-seven bedrooms and a ballroom where Bradlee and the other Americans hosted three-day parties for British, French, and American friends. Mary and Tony spent an afternoon there, strolling the grounds behind a head-high stone wall. Blair Clark remembers that particular party as a "Fitzgerald-ish sort of affair" attended by Americans and Europeans with lots of leisure time on their hands. In the ballroom, a couple dozen people drank, jitterbugged, and danced the mambo—the latest American dance craze.

After the party, Mary went back to Paris and Tony spent the night talking to Ben Bradlee in a café. The next day Ben and Tony realized they were in love, but Tony wouldn't consummate the affair until after she had consulted her sister. That done, the couple spent the next day and night in a *bel endroit*, "exploring," as Ben Bradlee put it in his memoir, "hungers that weren't there just days ago and satisfying them with gentle passion, new to me."[68]

Blair Clark took Mary to a long, lazy lunch at Lucas Carton, a famous restaurant on Place de la Madeleine, on the day Tony and Ben were off together. Over sauces rich with butter and cream and a few bottles of good red wine, Mary whiled away the afternoon beguiling Clark with sexy stories. "I remember we talked about all sorts of things. I heard about their adventures in Italy. I remember telling her she reminded me of a Henry James character, an American adventuress abroad." Clark was impressed more by her free spirit than her looks. "She was handsome and attractive but she didn't strike me as a Powers model, as they used to say. She was a little flirtatious and I had the strong impression that she was in an adventurous mood romantically, though not necessarily toward me. There was very little talk about husband and family and children."[69]

Back in Washington, Tony's life changed almost immediately as she confessed to Steuart Pittman that she had fallen in love with another man. She moved into the basement of the massive house on Rhode Island Avenue owned by her aunt Cornelia Pinchot, now a widowed Washington hostess active in women's politics and atomic disarmament. Throughout the fifties her two nieces and their husbands had been frequent visitors to the grand brick mansion she had decorated in her trademark ornate style. In early 1955 one evening's entertainment included showing a home movie of the Pinchot family's South Seas sailing trip, and one of the invited guests was Katharine Graham. Mrs. Graham had asked to see the home movie, Cornelia wrote to her son Gifford, noting that Mrs. Graham was not entirely welcome: "She is obviously the Meyer Giff did not like."[70] The Pinchot sisters were always welcome at their aunt's house, though. The previous summer Cornelia had hosted a wedding party at the house and remarked in a letter to her son that Tony and Mary had come and that they and their spouses "are a great asset to any party." Mary "looked lovely in a very swank made-in-Rome dress," she reported.[71]

After the summer of 1954 Cord and Mary maintained their marriage on unstable ground. When Mary returned from Europe, Cord felt his wife was changed. Mary had probably recovered some of her old way of looking at life, and she was beginning to feel a sense of creative possibility. Her independent spirit was buttressed by her time away, and she delved more seriously into modern art.

In 1954 a group of new artists had begun to make their mark in New York. Jasper Johns painted *Flag*, a subversive depiction of the American banner. Mary traveled to New York to see the abstract paintings of Robert Motherwell and Robert Rauschenberg and others, and after her return from Europe she spent more weekends visiting galleries and museums in the city and staying at her mother's Park Avenue apartment. Mary's friends at American University frequently drove up to New York in caravans of station wagons and brought back some of the new paintings to exhibit at the university gallery.

As they had in their younger days, Cord and Mary continued to emotionally shadow-box in writing. Mary wrote a short story about a married woman rejuvenated after a brief love affair. Cord criticized it as "sophomoric in emotion and badly written," although he suspected it was autobiographical and so attacked it even more mercilessly.[72] Mary began her practice of confiding in her friends the Truitts. She told them about the affair with the Italian and thought her secret safe with them. In fact, James Truitt was keeping copious notes on Mary, a woman whom he found both desirable and fascinating.

In February of 1955 Cord traveled alone to Europe. In Lisbon he became filled with self-pity for the direction his life had taken and regret over his growing estrangement from his wife. "I'm changing not necessarily for the better," he wrote in his journal. ". . . I thought of how through rude indifference and selfish carelessness I had so alienated Mary and of how all my days would be as lonely and melancholy as this one if she left me."[73]

Later that year the Meyers got new next-door neighbors. The young senator from Massachusetts, John F. Kennedy, and his wife, Jackie, bought Hickory Hill, the estate several hundred yards down the road from Langley Commons. It was close enough that the family dogs wandered over and had to be returned. Soon Mary befriended the senator's dark-haired wife, ten years younger than she. One of the things the two women had in common was that Jackie Kennedy and her sister, Lee Radziwill, had also taken a parent-financed, sisters-only trip to Europe together, theirs in 1951, and written about it.[74] Jackie was often left alone. The senator was intensely ambitious and angling for a national nomination in 1956. He was also incorrigible in his skirt-chasing. He and a congressional pal had rented an apartment in downtown Washington, where they partied with groups of secretaries.[75] John Kennedy still had no use for Cord Meyer, and Cord would not support him politically even though both men were Democrats. But the men's wives shared an appreciation of the outdoors and occasionally went for walks together. Like Mary, Jackie had attended Vassar and had an interest in the arts.

The summer of 1955, Tony married Ben Bradlee in Paris. The Meyers attended the wedding, then traveled to Italy. In Positano the Italian was still anchored in the harbor, living on his yacht with an American college girl. Mary blithely introduced Cord to her Italian friend and then arranged for them all to move onto the boat and sail together to Capri and Naples. Cord, unaware of his wife's relationship with the man, agreed. Later, Cord remembered only that the man whom he called "the Italian" "painted casually and not very well," and had a dog who kept him company on the boat along with the "sequence of women he successively entertained."[76]

After Cord went home, Mary stayed in Italy on the pretext that she was going to remain with Tony in Paris. In fact, as Tony and Ben Bradlee both knew, Mary was actually staying in Italy to return to her Italian lover. She sailed with him alone for ten days, living as the recently departed American girl had, in a bikini on the azure water. The first summer with the Italian had been a mere sexual fling. This time was different. Mary was smitten with him and he with her.

As they floated together they spun out a dream future. The Italian had always wanted to live in the American West, in the land of the cowboys. Mary would help him emigrate to Canada, from where he could divorce his wife.[77] Then they would both fling away their pasts like gloves or champagne glasses, take her three children, and move to a farm in Idaho or Montana or Colorado or California, where they would paint together and experience the freedom of their fondest imaginings. Filled with the romance of these new possibilities and inspired by her younger sister's daring change in her life, Mary returned to McLean with her heart set on changing her own course.

A year passed, and Mary did nothing but plan and paint and quietly try to figure out the appropriate time and place to tell Cord of her secret desire. Her new neighbor at Hickory Hill made a bid for the vice presidential nomination at the 1956 convention. He failed, but many Democrats thought the handsome young senator was the real winner of the convention, not Adlai Stevenson. Back in McLean after the convention, Jackie gave birth by cesarean section to a stillborn child and was so ill a priest was called to give last rites. During the ordeal, Kennedy was away in France, recovering his confidence by sailing the Mediterranean with one of his congressional friends, Florida senator George Smathers, and a boatload of young female beauties. One of the blondes always referred to herself in the third person as "Pooh." Kennedy had to be persuaded to return to his wife three days after the stillbirth.[78]

In Washington the political balance was changing. In 1954 the Senate had voted to condemn Joseph McCarthy, and the nation's zeal for Communist-hunting was ebbing. The static tension of the cold war grated on people's nerves, and there was a yearning for new ideas. George Kennan, in an abrupt change of heart, in 1957 urged the United States and the Soviet Union to mutually withdraw from Europe, but the suggestion was ignored by the American government, and young politicians such as Senator Kennedy began to focus on ways to decisively beat the Russians in the cold war. Kennedy introduced into congressional debate in the late 1950s the concept of a coming "missile gap," justifying the building of an even greater stock of nuclear weapons. Through the early part of the decade, aboveground atom bomb testing had continued in the American West and in the Pacific. One American test on Bikini Atoll in 1954 went awry, injuring thirty-one Americans, several hundred natives, and some Japanese fishermen. A year later scientists proved that atomic fallout from that and other tests was hazardous to life in a seven-thousand-mile radius around the island.

The night of her thirty-sixth birthday, October 14, 1956, Mary and Cord went out to a cocktail party for drinks and then to dinner with their friends Anne and James Truitt. The Truitts were aware of Mary's plans with the Italian, and they had encouraged her to talk to Cord instead of merely treating him coolly and leaving him to wonder what was wrong. That night, after they returned home, she confronted him with the truth and laid out her plans to move to a western farm with the children and her lover. She loved the Italian and planned to make a life with him, she said.

Cord had suspected something was up. He was not about to accede to her wishes. The idea that an Italian gigolo would give his sons a good home on a western farm was preposterous. "My only hope is to allow time to dull her feelings and to permit reality to show through her presently intact illusion," he wrote in his journal, adding bitterly: "One cannot argue with someone who is in love with love."[79]

That fall Cord waited for her to get over the Italian and Mary waited for her husband to concede that their life together was finished. With the boys all in school, Mary painted at home as the garden slowly lost its color, the oak leaves turned yellow, and the walnuts in their green skins fell to earth. The first frost came. Cord and Mary kept up appearances for the boys. But Cord no longer went to art openings with Mary, and his CIA friends ceased inviting her to come to their parties and dinners for visiting dignitaries, since she was so clearly uninterested. Mary wrote long letters to the Italian and spent hours in her studio, mixing paint with daydreams and swathing it all on canvas. Her awakening was beginning.

Television had become a part of most American homes and was about to utterly change American politics. The signs were already there: In Toledo in 1954, the city water commission had investigated strange intervals of increased water usage and determined that they coincided with TV commercials, and that same year frozen TV dinners were introduced. In the fall of 1956 the young Senator Kennedy traveled to twenty-six states campaigning for the Stevenson ticket, all the while garnering adulation himself. At Ursuline College in Louisville, Kentucky, female students crowded Kennedy's car and screamed for him. "We love you on TV," they shouted. "You're better than Elvis Presley!"[80]

The era of television might have dawned in America, but the Cord Meyer family was not yet among the households with one of the new devices. The Meyer boys, like their peers, loved television, and when they were visiting friends they preferred sitting in front of the tube to playing outside. "They were starved for it," Peter Janney said. One incident in particular stood out. The two families were sitting in the Janneys' yard on a warm summer night when shy little Mark suddenly blurted out: "Goddamn, let's go in and watch TV!" The two families doubled over with laughter at the profane outburst from the normally silent child.[81]

Mary's two oldest boys, Quentin, now eleven, and Michael, nine, had got into the habit during that fall of 1956 of going to a neighbor's house after school to watch the westerns that were on TV in the afternoons. They were so captivated by the glowing box that they began coming home later and later each afternoon. Mary had recently laid down the law: If they didn't stop arriving home late for dinner every day, there would be no more television at the neighbors' for them.[82]

She might have been in her little shed painting on the late afternoon of December 18 when tragedy struck. Or she might have been putting dinner on the table, for she never left all the cooking and table setting to the maid, especially around this time of year. The holidays had arrived and the festive air had infected her boys with the usual excitement of Christmas. A decorated tree was up in the living room, and presents were hidden away in closets. The children were bursting with anticipation for the big day. The family always made much of Christmas, and Cord and Mary and the two grandmothers usually showered the three boys with a mountain of presents.

The light faded early that time of year. Across the curving road at the neighbors' house, Michael and Quentin reluctantly tore themselves away from the television at the last minute and ran for home, trying to make it back to the dinner table on time in compliance with their mother's recent order. The two boys crossed the road at a point on the asphalt curve near where the family golden retriever had been killed a few years before. The road was not lit and there was no shoulder. No driver could see the Meyer house, high on a hill behind trees, much less anticipate that a nine-year-old boy would suddenly run into the headlights' beam. The man who hit Michael stopped and began screaming helplessly, and this sound and Quentin's horrified cries called Mary to the roadside. She ran the twenty yards downhill to the road, and long before she arrived at Michael's side she could see her son, a crumpled heap on the side. When the ambulance came Michael was already dead and Mary, no doubt in shock herself, was consoling the hysterical man who had been driving.

No one can be sure what went through her mind in those minutes, but parents who have lost children say that the deep grief sets in only later, when the shock has worn off and the reality of a child's forever empty bed settles in. Waiting for the ambulance to come for her lifeless son, Mary might have retreated into the reflexes honed by her upbringing and the challenges she had faced in her life. She was there to be leaned on, even in her life's worst hour.

In the next few days, when family friends came to visit, she hugged their children to her, offered them comfort, and sent them up to her dead son's bedroom to select one of his toys to remember him by. She and Cord distributed Michael's Christmas toys to his friends in the Mike Meyer gang. Little Mark, only six and still deeply shy, did not fully understand what had happened to his older brother. People who visited Mary in those days saw a woman deep in grief, still trying to behave with her youngest boy as though the world were safe and his little life would continue undisturbed. In the years to come, Mary would grow ever closer to and more protective of Mark.

They buried Michael in Milford just before Christmas 1956, under the stars and trees near Amos, the grandfather he had never met. Cord traveled alone with the coffin on a train five hours from Washington to Milford. Mary traveled with Mark. Quentin, so like his father in intensity, could not attend.

A relic of Michael's short life remains on the shelves at Grey Towers in the form of a favorite book, *My Secret Garden*. Inside it he had written his name, Michael Pinchot Meyer, in a childish hand. Later, the surviving sons asked if they could divide up the rest of his toys.

It would take a few months for Cord to realize the boy's death was not going to bring his wife back to him. Mary, tumbling into a depression, might have found refuge in thinking about the Italian and their dream of a farm out west. But there was now a great weight pulling her away from all that folly, all that frolic.

# 6

# Experiments

*The first cause of the neurosis was the moral inhibition, its driving force the unsatisfied sexual energy.*

WILHELM REICH

*It took about a half hour to hit. And it came suddenly and irresistibly. Tumbling and spinning down soft fibrous avenues of light that were emitted from some central point. Merged with its pulsing ray I could look out and see the entire cosmic drama. Past and future. All forms, all structures, all organisms, all events were television productions pulsing out from the central eye.*

TIMOTHY LEARY,
DESCRIBING HIS FIRST LSD EXPERIENCE IN SPRING 1962

Alone in the gallery, Mary was surrounded by the art of friends and teachers. Stark black-and-white studies of light and form by art professor Ben Summerford suggested television images, dim memories, and dream states. Washington artist Kenneth Noland's large-scale *Candle* was luminous but did little to warm the room. There was something inviting about the painting called *Sea* by her friend and art professor Robert Gates; the large canvas of billowing blue forms seemed to shimmer as she turned her head. Mary Orwen, a friend, had contributed her abstract renderings of flowers and leaves. Lothar Brabansky, a German sculptor, was showing a bronze series on mothers and children.[1]

In October 1957 the artists whose work appeared in the new Jefferson Place Gallery represented "the most avant-garde group working in Washington today," wrote the *Washington Post* art critic who reviewed the gallery.[2] The gallery was the first commercial space in Washington devoted to abstract expressionist work by local artists. Gallery partners were students and professors at the art departments of Catholic University and American University.

For Mary, the little gallery served as both a sanctuary and a connection to other people while she weathered the worst of her grief. At the end of the 1950s depression was a plague in Mary's group. In the coming years three of her male friends would kill themselves the same way, with guns to the head. Others from her group, men and women, would be hospitalized for breakdowns. Alcohol and the stiff upper lip were the most common self-treatments. With her family history of emotional instability and the tragedies of her son's death and the disintegration of her marriage, Mary was not immune to despair and maybe even depression, which was still little discussed and rarely diagnosed. She had begun regular psychoanalysis with Washington's premier analyst, a man who was also seeing many other prominent Georgetowners.[3] In his office she went over her life piece by piece. But no amount of analysis could have erased the sense of powerlessness emanating from that one instant on the roadside in McLean, and nothing she did could have shut off for long the running cinema of her son's death. In her worst moments the preceding summers in Italy must have seemed brief flickers of light in a personal history of recurrent darkness: Cord's pessimism, her father's decision that death was preferable to life, Rosamund's suicide. "She was lost, and she needed something to be attached to and the gallery and art gave her that," said artist Kenneth Noland, who eventually became a lover.[4]

In the silence of the little gallery, Mary Meyer began her fight to gain and keep possession of herself. It was a struggle her close friends observed in her for the rest of her life. Art and eventually her own self-discipline became antidotes for despair. In those early years she sat near the gallery door on weekdays and waited for occasional visitors. She was "helping out," recalled gallery director Alice Denney.[5] When visitors came to the gallery they found a woman eager to assist in a quiet, well-mannered way, but with red-rimmed eyes and a fragility that made them cautious and tender around her. In the small town that was Washington, D.C., everyone knew what had happened and no one knew what to say. They all agreed it would take time. And perhaps no one ever got over the loss of a child, not really.

During the long hours when there were no visitors inside the gallery, Mary could simply absorb the silence. Surrounded by abstract art that made language irrelevant, she was in retreat. The past had snapped free like a cable in a high wind. Cord was gone, Michael was gone, the Italian was gone. She was cut loose and starting over.

The previous spring, with the forsythia blooming yellow around the giant old oak and bad memories in every room, Cord and Mary had put Langley Commons up for sale. In May 1957 they purchased together a townhouse on Thirty-fourth Street, in the heart of Georgetown. The little blue townhouse was actually a house, maisonette, and garage, all connected, with four bedrooms, one for each boy and Mary, plus a guest room. The garden in the back was long and shady but seemed to Mary to be filled with possibilities. The real estate records of the transaction listed Cord's occupation as "government clerk." It is unclear whether Cord intended to live there with Mary; he never did.

For a time after Michael's death Cord hoped his marriage might be renewed by the shared sorrow. But he soon realized Mary would never come around. His analysis of the problem was that his wife needed a weak and needy man to lean on her and he had become too strong. "This Italian, who has sworn to change his old ways and seek a new simplicity on the western farm, is a challenge to her protective instinct. She knows he needs her," he wrote.[6]

But that proved to be wrong. Late that summer the Italian broke it off, to Mary's great humiliation. By then the Meyer marriage was beyond repair. She had told all her friends of her plans with her lover, and reconciliation with Cord was impossible. That fall, less than a year after their son's death, Cord agreed to leave the family house and begin the separation required for a divorce. The night he left, he admitted to himself that his manipulative behavior might have been improper. "I was a jailer in an abstract cause and once the Italian had removed himself as he did two weeks ago, I had much less reason to persist. The worst thing was my own tendency to take a perverse pleasure in exercising my power over Mary and it's better for me and everybody around me to have done with that."[7] He moved into an apartment in Georgetown where, on his first night alone, he tried to believe his new solitude would resurrect his old writing talents.

The summer of 1958, Mary went to Nevada for a stay at Gus Bundy's divorce ranch. She filed for divorce in June in Washoe County, Nevada, and spent a few months in the Nevada desert waiting for it to be made official. The Truitts, on their way to Jim's posting to the San Francisco *Newsweek* bureau, stopped in Nevada and the three of them sunned together by the pool. Anne was already pregnant with her middle daughter, whom she would name after Mary. Mary later told Noland that while in Nevada she had a brief romance with a male opera singer who was also at the divorce ranch.[8]

In her divorce petition, her lawyers alleged "extreme cruelty, mental in nature, which seriously injured her health, destroyed her happiness, rendered further cohabitation unendurable and compelled the parties to separate."[9] Cord was furious at the legal description since he believed himself to be in the right and perhaps even the injured party. But he had agreed in principle to the divorce and someone had to be at fault in order for it to proceed. Cord borrowed his ex-brother-in-law Steuart Pittman's domestic separation agreement to design his own.[10] The men had an emotional bond; if they had just kept their wives home that summer of 1954, their families might still be intact.

Cord's Nevada attorneys accepted the decision of the divorce judge but specifically denied Cord was guilty of mental cruelty. At Mary's request, the divorce records were sealed.[11] Any evidence of the "perverse pleasure" Cord admitted he had taken in "exercising my power" over her would never be made public.

Mary's friends had always surmised that she had had a "terrible, rough" time with Cord.[12] The divorce was acrimonious and the children were used as weapons. "Cord was bitter. He acted like a seventeenth-century cuckold, said Mary was an unfit mother and compared her to the whore of Babylon," recalled one friend of both.[13] Mary would be able to survive financially on Pinchot money from her mother, but the children would tie her to Cord forever. Cord gave her physical custody of Quentin and Mark, now twelve and eight, but demanded and won the right to control their education. Mary never spoke ill of Cord, but there were acrimonious fights in private. One friend of the Meyer boys recalls witnessing a heated argument inside the living room of the Georgetown house, with Cord and Mary shouting at each other while the boys played in an adjoining room.[14]

Cord quickly took advantage of his control over the boys' schooling and moved them from Georgetown Day School, with its racial integration and relatively liberal principles, to the more staid and exclusive St. Albans School, an Episcopal institution more like Cord's own prep school. When the boys complained about the heavier homework load at St. Albans, Mary laughed breezily and cried, "Well, just don't do it!"[15] Eventually both boys were sent to boarding schools.

The couple's postdivorce relationships with other people were fodder for further battles between Cord and Mary. Mary still wrote cutting comments in the margins of Cord's journal when she got her hands on it. Next to his account of a 1958 trip through Madrid a few months after their divorce with someone identified only by her initials, Mary wrote the woman's name out in red ink that seemed almost to hiss.[16] In another, later note in which Cord mentioned the effect of new relationships on their sons, Mary wrote, "Jill Cowen, in his father's case," referring to Cord's ongoing relationship with a young aide in the Kennedy White House.[17]

It was while volunteering at the Jefferson Place Gallery that Mary embarked on a romance with Ken Noland. Noland was a boyish, sandy-haired southerner with a passion for abstract art, jazz, women, and baseball, not always in that order. Shortly after his eighteenth birthday he had enlisted in the Air Force and spent four years in the service. He trained as a glider pilot but never got close to combat. When he came home, with the help of the GI Bill he attended Black Mountain College, a tiny mecca for American artists in the middle of the North Carolina mountains. Many people in Noland's hometown of Asheville, just twenty miles from the college, thought of the school as a "behavioral sink of communism and free love."[18] The college never had more than ninety students and sometimes less than twelve, but it was extremely influential. A number of seminal American artists taught there, including musician John Cage, painters Willem de Kooning and Franz Kline, and dancer Merce Cunningham. Noland studied under European émigré Ilya Bolotowsky, an abstract artist.

With his southern accent and deliberately "hick" persona, Noland could not have been more different from Cord Meyer, at least on the surface. He did not fit naturally into Mary's more refined circle. That was part of his charm. Through her relationship with him, she learned a new style of abstract painting and observed his deeply serious attitude toward it. Noland practiced his art instead of castigating himself for wasting his talent, as Cord did. He had been in Reichian therapy and worked on his emotional life. He was financially insecure. When he started seeing Mary he was in the middle of a divorce involving three children, and drove a cab to supplement his income. Underneath the surface, Noland was another deeply ambitious man. He "carried the history of modern art around in his head," according to the abstract artist Robert Motherwell. He was working with single-minded determination to carve out his own style in the competitive art world.

Noland's entree into the New York art world was helped by the critic Clement Greenberg, whom he had met at Black Mountain College in 1950. Greenberg was an important influence on American artists in the 1950s. He explained modernism to a public desperate for interpretation of abstract art. A strong-willed and passionate man, he had a seductively simple way of looking at art; collectors and museums developed "an almost mystical faith in his judgment," and Greenberg understood how to use his power.[19] He became interested in Noland in the early 1950s and later became a patron saint to the Washington Color School artists.

Greenberg first took Noland and the older Washington artist Morris Louis to artist Helen Frankenthaler's New York studio in 1951. Though the two D.C. artists had been interested in the ideas and style of Jackson Pollock, they found their method in Frankenthaler, who, like Pollock, practiced direct physical contact with her canvases. Critic Barbara Rose wrote that Frankenthaler, while influenced by Jackson Pollock, preferred thinner paint. She began to work on the floor, rather than at an easel, because, she told Rose, "it became a physical necessity to get the pictures off the wall" and "you could work quickly without getting a drip."[20]

Noland was impressed by the method behind Frankenthaler's delicate pink and blue painting *Mountains and Sea*, a canvas drenched with oil paint thinned with turpentine so it looked dyed with color. Back in Washington, Noland and Louis set to work immediately. The two artists decided to try "jam" painting. For several weeks they worked together in a studio at the Center of the Arts, experimenting with the making of abstract paintings that didn't suggest anything else, pouring paint onto canvases laid on the floor or draped over objects, and improvising much as jazz musicians would in a jam session.

The road from Frankenthaler's studio to the famed circle paintings Noland created during his years with Mary Meyer was not direct, but Noland's work in the early 1950s began, along with Louis's work, to attract Greenberg's approval. Drenching canvas with thinned paint was what the critic would deem an "honest" use of materials and an ongoing development of painting that had begun with the impressionists. Greenberg supported American abstract art that did not refer to images outside of the work itself, and felt the focus of the viewer should be on the surface of the canvas and the quality of the paint. The flatness and coolness of the work thus created became known as the "color field" school of painting, and in the early 1960s, with Greenberg shepherding them toward it, collectors and museum curators began to buy and exhibit it.

The Jefferson Place Gallery, located so near the White House and Capitol Hill, had its share of patrons from the political world. Often the main ties between art and power were through the wives, many of whom either sat on gallery boards or were amateur artists themselves. For a time it seemed every other wife in Georgetown was either taking painting lessons or setting herself up in a studio, though most remained firmly in the dilettante class. Presidential candidate Adlai Stevenson was linked romantically with one of the Washington women who painted, Sarita Peet, who went on to marry artist Robert Gates, one of Mary's teachers at American University.[21] Undersecretary of State Dean Acheson's wife was a painter. Helen Stern, wife of lawyer Philip Stern and one of Mary's closest friends, painted. The wife of Estes Kefauver, Nancy Pigott Kefauver, was a painter. Tony Pinchot Bradlee, Ben's wife, eventually had her own show of sculptures. V. V. Rankine, the wife of a British speechwriter, shared studio space with Mary for a time. In a few years, Mary herself became one of the links between Washington artists and power politics.

Portraitist Marian Cannon Schlesinger, then married to Arthur Schlesinger, recalled that most Georgetowners were not all that interested in art but liked having artists in their midst to buttress their cultivated sensibility. "It was nice to think people were painting on the side," she said. "It was all a bit patronizing."[22] At the amateur level, there were often shows at Georgetown cafés and competitions with first-, second-, and third-prize ribbons for the winners.

Marital ties between politics and the arts brought support to real artists who were struggling without money or personal connections. Having a cabinet secretary as a guest on the opening night of one's show was all to the good. Better yet, the women's husbands often had the money to buy the work. "It was far simpler then," Ben Summerford said of Washington life. "There was not the sense of isolation between groups. When we opened the Jefferson Place, people in government were interested and bought paintings. We didn't even have to send out invitations."[23]

Among serious artists, the capital was ruefully regarded as a backwater. New York was where they'd rather be. Washington did not provide much of a market for modern art, recalled Alice Denney, who handled the work of many of the big New York abstract artists in Washington: "I couldn't sell a Jasper Johns then."[24] Mary Orwen, a founder of the Jefferson Place Gallery, recalled, "We used to always complain about it being so out in the country. We felt New York had everything. But when we started the Jefferson Place it got really exciting. We felt we were getting something started."[25] In their isolation from the mainstream of modern art, the Washington artists were able to carve out their own niche. Noland's geographical distance from New York, while a handicap in some ways, allowed him to make art separate from prevailing New York fashions, and therefore new.

Outside the Georgetown group of artistic wives and powerful husbands, the American government was hardly supportive of modern art, nor was the Washington community any more appreciative than the rest of America. The State Department in 1946 canceled a European exhibition of works by seventy-nine modern American artists after members of Congress complained that it was "Communistic." President Truman pronounced that "so-called modern art is merely the vaporings of half-baked, lazy people."[26] But by the late 1950s modern art was not regarded as subversive; rather, it was just silly, or at best baffling. In 1961 the Washington wives of a group of scientists and diplomats won fifteen minutes of fame when they decided to become abstract artists during their regular bridge games. Those who took breaks from the card tables went into the kitchen and splattered canvases with kitchen items—flour, syrup, ketchup, house paint, and anything else that would stick. After a few months they showed their "paintings" to their husbands, who found them amusing, and to a few Washington galleries, who showed interest and offered to buy them. Then they broke the story to the *Washington Evening Star*, which covered their stunt with tongue-in-cheek glee. "An Artistic Slam," said the headline. "Ten suburban bridge club women have pulled a fast one on modern art. . . . Among them they have 37 children."[27]

Living among the artistically uninitiated only drew the Washington abstract artists closer together. The art scene was so tight that at gallery openings "you'd know nine out of ten people at every one," said artist Ed Kelley, a former student of Noland's.[28] Artists congregated around two poles. At one pole was American University and Robert Gates, who taught both traditional and modern art. At the other was Catholic University, where Kenneth Noland taught. Among Noland's students were artists Thomas Downing, Howard Mehring, and Anne Truitt. The artists formed a little Bohemian subculture, and Mary Meyer could enter it whenever she felt inclined, always able to return to Georgetown. The artists went to parties at each other's houses, visited each other's studios, and drank beer together at the Bayou in Georgetown or the Showboat Lounge or the Bohemian Caverns, legendary Washington jazz clubs on the black side of town that attracted such jazz greats as Thelonious Monk and Miles Davis. Black musicians had only recently become able to sell their records in "white" record stores, and jazz musicians' spontaneity and experimentation with atonality appealed to the abstract artists.

Elsewhere in the country, the Beat movement was under way. Allen Ginsberg's poem "Howl," expressing his disgust with materialistic, conformist America, was called obscene in 1956. By the end of the decade the beatniks' language was becoming part of the American lexicon: "a gas," "groove," "chick," and "make the scene." The Washington artists were not Beats. On the surface they were as conservative as their town: all crew cuts, rep ties, button-down collars, loafers, and tweed blazers. But, like the spies in their midst, they were not what they seemed.

When Mary threw herself wholly into the art scene after her separation from Cord, Ken Noland was already the leader of a group of Washington artists working in the color field style, one in which the importance of color superseded form. Noland's self-described artistic philosophy was: "No graphs; no systems; no modules. No shaped canvases. Above all, no thingness, no objectness. The thing is to get the color down on the thinnest conceivable surface, a surface sliced into the air as if by a razor. It's all color and surface. That's all."[29] But during his romance with Mary, while he was achieving Greenberg's cool, nonreferential ideal, Noland's work looks much more passionate than it was to become. Robert Hughes called his paintings from that period "hedonism for the eye."[30]

Noland and the artists who became known as the Washington Color School stained color on canvas in repetitive forms—bull's-eyes, circles, chevrons, stripes. Eventually Noland became a success, followed later by lesser-known artists who had studied with him, including Mary's friend Anne Truitt. In the early sixties Anne Truitt also began working in a mode that elevated color over form, not on canvas but on simple wooden structures of sometimes monumental size that she designed and had built by carpenters. By the end of the 1960s, the work of Noland and other Color School artists favored by Greenberg was being shown in New York and sold to collectors.

The Color School style was not for everyone. Art critic Harold Rosenberg, the other preeminent 1950s critic and Clement Greenberg's nemesis, found some of Greenberg's favorite artists shallow and rejected Greenberg's celebrification of artists. For Rosenberg, the purpose of abstract art was uninhibited self-expression, not the mannered, formalistic work Greenberg was promoting. The Color School had an empty and purely decorative aspect, Rosenberg argued. He described Noland's art as "bound by rules and principles rather than by an effort toward the realization of individuality."[31]

The Color School artists worked in the capital of the cold war in a style that elevated cool and rejected sentimentality. Like the spies among them, they communicated in a secret language comprehensible to others in their group but cryptic to outsiders. These canvases that Clement Greenberg admired could be seen as metaphors for American society, cool and serene on the surface, in turmoil below. The United States was booming economically, and efficient gadgets kept the burgeoning suburbs running smoothly. General Eisenhower was in charge, cleaving to the middle road. Yet there were the bomb shelters and the duck-and-cover exercises and experimental aircraft being mistaken for UFOs, all referring to a mortal danger that never really showed itself. The secret signs of menace were visible only to men such as Cord Meyer, the cold warriors who believed they were all that stood between the United States and the dread disasters of Communist takeover and nuclear war. For them, the surface was never all it seemed.

At the height of their romance in the late 1950s Noland often spent the night with Mary at her house in Georgetown, where she had a canopy over her bed and Spode china tucked away in the closet. The house was oddly designed: the kitchen and bathroom were in front, and a long living room in back ended at French doors to the garden. The floors were covered with yellow rugs and the windows had lace curtains. Mary had a small hole put in one wall so the family cats could come and go freely. The music room held a piano used by her sons. Quentin lived with her when he was home from the Salisbury School in Connecticut. Mary tended her garden religiously and before long it was a profusion of flowers, which she proudly showed to visitors. She also grew her own salad greens. In those years Mary became close to Noland's young daughter Lynn, a blue-eyed child with silky long blond hair. She let the little girl play with a marvelous East Indian toy carriage and fed her carrot sticks served on ice. Even after the relationship with Noland ended, Mary sometimes went to the fence near little Lynn's school and watched her from afar during recess. Lynn Noland regarded Mary as a woman "in command of herself and always in charge," in contrast to some of the other adults in her life.[32] For two years Noland and his three children summered in Milford with Mary and her boys. This raised bemused eyebrows in Georgetown and enraged Cord Meyer, who referred to Noland not by name but as "the younger painter" (Noland was four years younger than Mary) and worried about the artist's effect on his sons.

Mary's two sons adapted differently to the new arrangement. Her youngest son, Mark, was more easygoing and accepting and remained close to Noland for years. Quentin was more hostile toward Noland's presence and troubled by the fact of his parents' divorce.

Mary was an involved but not overbearing mother. She went to the boys' basketball games, drove them to after-school lessons, and invited their friends to play at her house. Still athletic herself, she played her powerful game of tennis with Quentin, passing on to him what Amos had taught her. But the boys were also expected to make it on their own. With Cord in charge of their schooling, they were sent to camp in the summer and went away to boarding school in New England as soon as they reached their teens.

Noland thought Mary tended to be a distracted, "perfunctory" mother, but women saw a devoted, almost overly protective woman. "Children were a big part of her life," said Barbara Higgins, a poet and longtime friend. "She was very, very motherly, but she didn't come on as 'Mom.' " After Michael's death, Mary grew closer to her youngest son, Mark, and was extremely watchful about him. Friends recall her going out to the little playground just a block away from the Georgetown house to watch both boys at play and to personally remind them to come home when it was time. Noland remembered that Mary was frustrated with Quentin's unhappiness, for she didn't like brooding people. She disciplined him in her own way. Once when he stole some money from a friend, she drove him back to the friend's house and made him personally hand back the money and apologize for it. She and Cord sent Quentin to a psychiatrist, who reported that many of their son's complaints had to do with ill feeling toward his mother, perhaps traceable to some "lack of affection" she had shown her firstborn as an infant. That blame-the-mother analysis, so popular in psychiatry in the 1950s, kicked off another round of animosity between Cord and Mary. Their eldest son's troubles became part of the postdivorce battle. In the margin of Cord's journal Mary wrote, "Push him into what he fears—for Christ sake don't let those fears harden out the [illegible] of the game."[33]

She took pride in the fact that she had sent her sons to the integrated, progressive Georgetown Day School before Cord moved them to St. Albans. She had a flowering peach tree planted at Georgetown Day School in Michael's memory. "She was very concerned that they have black friends," recalled Helen Husted, who lived at Mary's Georgetown house briefly in the early 1960s, after Helen's hospitalization for depression.[34] One of Mark's best friends was in fact a black schoolmate from Georgetown Day, Brent Oldham, who recalled many afternoons at play inside Mary's Georgetown house. Yet such was her fear for the boys' physical safety that when Quentin wanted to go down to the Mall in August 1963 to witness Martin Luther King Jr.'s march on Washington, Mary forbade him.

During her Georgetown years, Mary probably supported herself on a combination of Cord's alimony, income from her relatively small trust fund—worth no more than $60,000 in 1964—and her mother's Pinchot money. "Her mother really held the purse strings," Noland recalled.[35] But if Mary had cash flow troubles, no one saw the signs. She did not have to work for a living, although she was never lavish in her lifestyle, either. She had a housekeeper two days a week, and on those days she'd say she liked to "live rich." She liked a breakfast of eggs and bacon brought to her in bed, and a salad waiting for her when she came home in the afternoon.

With her sons less dependent on her, Mary put more time into her painting. She experimented with colors and imitated Noland's color field style. She started pouring and scrubbing paint into canvases laid on the floor and began a notebook of colors, keeping track of what she had mixed to achieve a particular hue. She began to favor round canvases with simple pie wedges of color. She took in the daughters of Georgetown friends and neighbors as art students. One of her pupils was Scottie Lanahan's daughter Eleanor. To Eleanor, Mary seemed extremely disciplined, focusing her teaching efforts on details such as brushstrokes. "My father remembers coming to pick me up and her praising to the skies the way I dried my brushes on the paper."[36]

Personally, Mary was a little better off. She was no longer married to Cord Meyer and immersed in a daily battle of wills with him. But her new boyfriend was as self-absorbed and dismissive in his way as her ex-husband had been. Although they were together for at least three years and she was deeply influenced by Noland's art, Noland could not ever recall seeing one of Mary Meyer's paintings. "The relationship was really in the context of my work," Noland said in an interview. "She was very private about her work. . . . She wasn't a professional artist and she didn't have any pretensions about being a professional. It didn't seem like we really talked about it that much. I never gave her criticism. It wasn't in our relationship. I vaguely remember seeing one of Mary's paintings at Cicely Angleton's."[37] This was after Mary's death.

Indeed, the work of women in Noland's contemporary-art milieu was just about invisible. The women who got noticed owed such attention to their links to men: Helen Frankenthaler, for example, was married to abstract expressionist Robert Motherwell. Mary might not have wanted to show her work to Noland. She shared studio space with women artists, first Anne Truitt and later V. V. Rankine. The Washington artists trying to become noticed in New York were all working in an extremely defined style and there was not room for them all to succeed. Noland recognized the competition, and some of his contemporaries have suggested he might have felt threatened by Mary, who had appropriated his method and was showing ability. If so, she still had a long way to go to actually pose a threat. Mary "had an instinct" for her art but had begun following it too late in her life, said curator Alice Denney.[38] But Mary was a dedicated novice with a strong will and she knew the right people and moved in the right circles. Mary's friends believed she was on the right track. She was disciplined about her work and seemed to idolize the lifestyle of artists she admired. "There was nothing phony about Mary. She didn't pose as an artist," said one Georgetown friend who grew close to Mary in the early 1960s. "She was earnestly engaged in art. I thought she went overboard sometimes because I don't think artists are necessarily all that fascinating. But for her they were romantic figures."[39]

To Kary Fischer, Mary's art was part of her effort to overcome emotional turbulence. Self-discipline was her balm. She tried to work on her painting a certain number of hours a day, and she took long daily walks on the towpath to force herself into a routine. "She was not at peace," Fischer recalled. "There was a lot of turmoil beneath the calm surface. She tried hard to keep possession of herself, and although she didn't acknowledge it, art was a sort of therapy for her. She saw art as a way into herself."[40]

The discipline paid off, and Mary's art eventually was noticed. Shortly before she died, several of her paintings were selected to be part of a Pan American Union show set to tour Central and South America. The show included the works of a number of younger Color School artists. Artist Sam Gilliam, whose work was also in the exhibit, met Mary at that opening. "Her language was the same as every other strong abstract artist. There was this sense of concentration on the idea of painting and what was new. She pointed out to me that she was unable to recognize whether my painting was oil or acrylic. I said I had a way of flattening oil so it looked acrylic and she said, 'You should be given credit for that.' "[41] Among the Washington artists, there was great attention paid to who got credit for what, and Mary was very aware of that, particularly since Noland was concerned that his innovations be credited to him.

Throughout the 1950s Noland periodically visited Clement Greenberg in New York and brought him paintings. In 1954 Greenberg chose a Noland painting and a Morris Louis painting for an exhibit, and by 1959 he was showing Noland's work regularly. The two men had a close personal and working relationship. Noland occasionally brought Mary with him when he visited Greenberg in New York. The Greenbergs visited Ken at Mary's Georgetown house and spent a weekend with them at Milford. In both places the Greenbergs were impressed by Mary's style, her country ease, and the "tattiness" of her house, which Greenberg's wife, Jenny, thought seemed "just perfect." The Greenbergs also became acquainted with some of the other Washington women, including Anne Truitt. Jenny Greenberg found them all to be "classy girls." "They were cultivated, except that 'cultivated' implies a tone and they didn't have a tone. They were straight-arrow kind of people. I'm very keen on the difference between the real thing and perhaps an assuming of it, a sense that you have acquired something. These people had strong personalities as women on their own."[42]

But not so strong that Mary ever talked about her own painting in front of Ken Noland and Clement Greenberg. Jenny Greenberg said she never thought of Mary as a painter. She was just the attractive woman on Ken's arm, tweedy and casual. Jenny Greenberg was so impressed with a beige wide-wale corduroy trench coat Mary wore that she went out and bought one herself and wore it for years. She remembered Mary as vibrant but, in the manner of the times, very deferential toward men. "She was all there, but like many of the women of her day, she would pay more attention to men. I think she wanted to learn from Clem. If a man and a woman were talking, she'd listen to the man. That was what one did. I ran into that a lot, unfortunately. It was true of all those wives."[43]

Noland was impressed by Mary's spirit and body, not her art. To him she was lissome, graceful, feminine. "She was kind of fey, very soft-appearing and soft-voiced and delicate and mannered in the way privileged women sometimes are," Noland said. "That was kind of the style in Washington at that time, Ivy League, a certain kind of humor, lots of catch phrases and things." She also had, Noland discovered, a strong will. "She did whatever she wanted to do," he recalled.[44] She was dedicated to adventure. She was searching for something or someone to set her right again after the death and the divorce, and she was more than willing to try something new. When he suggested they both go to see a Reichian therapist in Philadelphia, she agreed.

Wilhelm Reich began his career as a Marxist psychoanalyst in Germany. In the 1920s he began developing his theory that orgasm was the source of fundamental human energy and sexual dysfunction the source of all neuroses. The therapy involved body work to loosen the resistance to pleasure and emotion that had been built up by years of traumatic events and social conditioning. In his book *The Function of the Orgasm*, Reich defined the core of all neuroses as "dammed-up sexual energy," and through graphs and detailed descriptions of male and female sexual functions he attempted to outline a course of treatment for what he called "orgasm anxiety." He was particularly concerned that children be allowed to fully experience their sexuality rather than have their capacity for pleasure socialized out of them before adulthood, through fear and training.

Eventually Reich began to define a kind of metaphysical theory of orgasmic energy. He tried to capture this basic life energy in orgone boxes—specially constructed, metal-lined closetlike boxes inside which patients were supposed to spend time absorbing energy. Reich emigrated to the United States in the 1940s, but he quickly got in trouble with the U.S. government in the 1950s when he began to advertise that his orgone boxes could cure cancer and other diseases. After a long legal battle at the end of which the Food and Drug Administration forced him to destroy his orgone boxes, he died in prison in 1957. He left behind a group of disciples in the United States, psychoanalysts who had studied with him and who carried on his work.

One of these followers was Dr. Charles I. Oller of Philadelphia. Ken Noland first learned of Oller and Reichian therapy around 1950 and underwent therapy for nine years. He introduced others, including Mary, to Oller. In the ongoing search for pure creative impulse, trips to Dr. Oller became very popular among the Washington abstract artists and their admirers, a "kind of a cultish thing" for the Color School artists for a time, said one woman close to the artists. Mary in turn may have introduced other people to the doctor.

The therapy relied on a series of sessions aimed at removing people's emotional blocks with physical as well as intellectual effort. Those emotional blockages, it was believed, took root in various parts of the body, "armoring" the person against pleasure. Therapy involved strenuous exercises beginning with the facial muscles and moving downward. It could be quite physically demanding. The breathing exercises gradually evolved into crying, screaming, gagging, and raging, pounding on couches and rug-covered walls, and freewheeling dancelike movements to banish the demon of resistance to pleasure. Eventually, if the therapy worked, the client would see results in all areas of his or her life, but the primary source of that improvement would come from healthier, more vigorous sexuality.[45]

Mary saw Oller for a few months during her relationship with Noland. The Reichian therapy approach became obvious to her family. Her son Quentin observed that "my mother is trying to learn how to be uninhibited." When Mary saw that note in one of Cord's journal entries, she wrote next to it: "Let old Q. take a little pleasure in himself and he won't act like such a scared bunny. Let him now—so he won't be awed by pleasure when he is 42."[46]

Noland believed Reichian therapy profoundly affected his art during the late 1950s, especially during the making of the series of circle paintings that coincided with the first years of his relationship with Mary. The paintings are of concentric circles, often with deep, pulsating orange in the middle, surrounded by circles of blues and greens and white, with names like *Heat, Plunge, Split, Luster,* and *Stretch.* They have the almost physical effect of sucking the viewer into a small, intensely warm, even ecstatic space. The splattered edges and the choice and arrangement of colors with their throbbing centers are much more overtly sensual than the crisp lines and official colors Noland began to prefer in the early 1960s, after he had moved to New York and away from Mary.

The romance was very passionate, at least in the beginning. "Ken was absolutely crazy about Mary," Jenny Greenberg remembered.[47] "They really were attached," recalled Elizabeth Eisenstein. "That was quite an intense affair."[48] Noland was physically and emotionally captivated. Mary occasionally talked about her son's death, and her sadness had a magnetic effect on him. "There was attraction and empathy and sympathy," he said. "It's natural to feel that in people, whether you know the nature of the wound or not. You could sense it in her, the deep sadness."[49]

But she was not an easy woman for Noland—or many of the men of her generation—to be with. He thought she did what she wanted to do, at a time when men were accustomed to women doing what men wanted to do. Noland's daughter remembered Mary as always "being in charge," not a very popular feminine trait then. For her part, Mary found Noland attractive. She also enjoyed the access he had to the New York art world.

Taking her lead from Noland's distillation of sexual experience into intense circles of color, Mary tried to experience as much as she could and reduce experience into its essence in color. She determined to live by her senses, to taste, smell, feel, see, and hear, and to cast off the bourgeois conventions of her social group—without alienating friends and losing her social place entirely. Her art was less intense and explosive than Noland's, her choice and arrangement of colors more subdued, her overall work less mature and accomplished. She painted one large circle with four hues of deep red, each one almost imperceptibly different from the other. In many of her canvases, she favored blues. Still within the formal color field style, she experimented with nongeometric, curving yin and yang shapes.

Writing about her own work, Mary employed language that Noland used repeatedly, and which Anne Truitt still used decades later. "Someone wanting to paint poppies in a wheat field is probably wanting to put *that* color red against *that* color brown, so why not head straight for the real thing?" Mary wrote of her later work. "These paintings are not linear; the edges simply exist as a byproduct of the color fields. Where one color stops and another starts there is an edge, but it is the result and not the cause of the color shapes or forms. In my paintings the color *is* the form."[50]

Although Anne Truitt and Mary were profoundly different, it is possible to gauge Mary's artistic direction by looking at the life and art of her friend. Anne Truitt's art was intricately connected to her relationship with Mary and Ken Noland. Her husband, James Truitt, was one of the first journalists to write about the Color School; some of the artists believed he had coined the name. Anne's personality differed greatly from Mary's. Where Mary was expansive, Anne was obsessively introspective, and where Mary could be reckless, Truitt was fastidious and took herself very seriously. But the two women's artistic lives were entwined. In one of the three books she has published about her work as an artist, Truitt dates her art epiphany, as it were, to a weekend in New York with Mary Meyer in November 1961, during which they visited an exhibit of work by Barnett Newman and Ad Reinhardt at the Guggenheim Museum; the exhibit changed her view of art. "For once in my life enough space, enough color," she wrote. That night the two women slept at Mary's mother's Park Avenue apartment, where Anne was too stimulated to sleep and spent the night "sitting wakeful in my bed like a frog on a lily pad. Even three baths spaced through the night failed to still my mind, and at some time during these long hours I decided, hugging myself with determined delight, to make exactly what *I* wanted to make. The tip of balance from the physical to the conceptual in art had set me to thinking about my life in a whole new way. What did I know? What did I love?"[51]

This epiphany soon led to her working in colors derived from what art critic Brooks Adams called "white picket fences and dark green, Waspy club rooms"[52]—two essential settings in Anne Truitt's life experience, and perhaps incidentally also the colors of the white marble and green foliage of official Washington, D.C. Her first creation was a white fencelike structure she called *One*. By the next year she had moved away from work that was referential in any way and discovered the technique that occupied her for decades: painting plywood columns of varying height. Her early work attracted Clement Greenberg, who told her she was daringly close to "non-art," exactly what minimalists were striving for.[53]

Through the 1970s and 1980s Anne Truitt carved out a place for herself as a minor artist whose work is exhibited occasionally and purchased by a few small regional museums. She produced monolithic blocks and columns of fragile plywood that had to be weighted at the bottom in order to stand up. She did not build the sculptures herself, but had cabinetmakers in Maryland construct them. She experimented with color. Her published journals are the reflections of a woman who has read widely in philosophy and thought deeply about herself. In them she charts her progress as an artist and echoes her friends Mary Meyer and Ken Noland in their concern with color over form.

Anne and James Truitt were divorced in 1971. In one journal Anne lamented the effect of World War II on the men of her generation and, by extension, on women such as herself. She wrote of the "subtle sorrow" experienced by these women and especially of the loneliness felt in their relationships with the men who had fought in the war. "Confronted by the probability of their own deaths, it seems to me that many of the most percipient men of my generation killed off those parts of themselves that were most vulnerable to pain, and thus lost forever a delicacy of feeling on which intimacy depends. To a less tragic extent we women also had to harden ourselves with them."[54]

Unlike Anne Truitt, after her own divorce Mary did not abandon hope of finding happiness with a man of her generation. On the contrary, she was sometimes irresponsible in her relationships with them. "Mary was bad," said one close friend, simply, of her behavior with men.[55] She hurt people. Some of her wildness may have been a reaction against Cord's infidelities. And perhaps, having been hurt deeply herself by her own failed marriage and the death of her son, she rebelled by inflicting emotional pain. The full extent of her affairs with men, married or single, is something unofficial Washington gossiped about after her death and most likely exaggerated. In the absence of her diary the real facts are unavailable. She told Noland that after her divorce and before her long affair with him she had dated a teacher at her son's school and a television journalist. Several friends said she had an affair with Jim Truitt, her best friend's husband, and that Anne learned of the relationship only after Mary's death. Jim

Truitt was openly entranced by Mary and came to think of her as his spiritual twin, someone he believed he could communicate with even after death.

Men adored Mary but did not know what to make of her. One ex-lover rather ungratefully called her "a starfucker." To some, she was that classic female type, the "collector" of men, a woman who attached herself to men who were rising in politics or the arts in order to gain power herself. But her friends regarded her affairs as something she did for her own fulfillment, not to gain any political or social cachet. "We thought of her as an independent, free spirit in a way, having left Cord and then shacking up with Ken," said one Georgetown friend. "She was not a feminist. She was much too seductive and fond of men. She was very fond of the men. I don't think gender entered into her consciousness at all. She didn't have the cause in mind at all."[56]

No feminist, she was no golddigger, either. Mary Meyer was an American aristocrat with funds from her mother and alimony from her ex-husband. Firmly ensconced in Georgetown society, she didn't need men for social ascension or financial support. But men were her teachers and they brought her into places women didn't enter on their own, from the jazz clubs of black Washington to the Oval Office of the White House. She also genuinely enjoyed their company and attention. She studied them the way a scientist or a connoisseur would, and became known to her friends as an astute and humorous observer of the meaning behind peculiar male behavior. Anne Truitt described Mary as "an acute judge of masculine character."[57]

One man who assumed the role of teacher and admirer was LSD guru Timothy Leary. On a spring afternoon in 1962 Leary was working in his office at Harvard's psychology department, where he had been conducting tests of hallucinogenic mushrooms on himself and his graduate students for several years. He had just taken his first dose of LSD. He was about to be relieved of his duties by skeptical department heads who thought Leary's experiments were out of control. "I looked up to see a woman leaning against the door post, hip tilted provocatively, studying me with a bold stare," Leary wrote in his autobiography. "Flamboyant eyebrows, piercing green-blue eyes, fine-boned face. Amused, arrogant, aristocratic. 'Dr. Leary,' she said coolly, 'I've got to talk to you.' " She introduced herself as Mary Pinchot.[58]

Leary was a collector of beautiful women. Adventurous models, dancers, and heiresses were flocking to the good doctor to offer themselves as subjects for his fabled tests. Often the intimacy of the drug experience led them into emotional and sexual experiments as well. Leary took Mary home with him that first afternoon, where his girlfriend at the time, a Moroccan model who went by the name of Malaca, and British LSD guru Michael Hollingshead were waiting. The foursome took a low dose of hallucinogenic mushrooms. In the middle of the experience, Leary said, Mary gave a lecture on the CIA's interest in using such drugs for brainwashing and interrogation. Leary wrote that even though the four had a "pleasant, conspiratorial feeling of those who are sharing a psychedelic session," he was uneasy with Mary Pinchot: "There was something calculated about Mary, that tough hit you get from people who live in the hard political world." Leary wrote that she said she wanted to learn how to "run an LSD session." She told him she had already tried LSD herself, but wanted to learn how to administer it properly to "this friend who's a very important man." Leary said she told him she and a group of women were planning to get their men high. According to Leary, she said: "Washington is run by men. These men conspiring for power can only be changed by women."[59]

Mary's relationship with Leary continued for the next two years. He said she periodically dropped in without warning, sometimes called him from a hotel in Boston, and had him up to her room where they shared champagne and discussed the fantastic possibilities offered by what he called "utopiates." She seemed to him the ultimate female insider, a kind of Mata Hari of drugs. At one meeting in a hotel room at the Ritz in Boston, Leary said she told him the CIA had actually started the American Veterans Committee, of which he, like Cord, had been a member. She also told him the CIA had created radical student organizations and was running them "with deep-cover agents." The latter was eventually revealed to be true. He claimed she then asked him for drugs to take back to Washington, and at that point Leary decided Mary was wilder than he. "I want to learn to brainwash," he claimed she said, to which he responded, "That doesn't sound very ladylike."[60]

Leary sent her information on how to run an LSD "session" (and presumably drugs, although he never admitted to it). According to him, Mary seemed to know things about the government's tacit approval of his drug testing. "I told you they'd let you do anything if you kept it quiet," she said at one meeting after he was fired from Harvard. Seeing her again in 1963, Leary wrote that he was "struck again by the brittleness this aristocratic woman had picked up from those stern-eyed, business-suited WASPs working for Wild Bill Donovan in Zurich, for Allen Dulles in Washington, for Henry Luce as bureau chiefs." He also said she told him not to worry about failing to create an LSD factory in Mexico (one of Leary's many schemes), because more drugs were sure to arrive soon. Mary told him, Leary wrote, "I can give you a contact in England. They'll sell you everything you need. And if things go the way I hope, we'll be seeing lots of good drugs produced here at home."[61] If she gave him such a contact, Leary never wrote of it later and did not recall it in several interviews shortly before his death in 1996.[62]

It is not known how Mary came to experiment with drugs. She might have discovered drugs through the art world. Like their counterparts in New York, the Washington abstract artists believed they were working on the very edge of the new. Their idea of originality was more than a revolt against tradition; it was an intimate search for the roots of creativity that involved a wholesale rebirth, a self-creation. In order to achieve it, all sorts of new therapies and drugs were tried. Many artists experimented with marijuana and sometimes LSD. "There was this idea of wanting to see and experience color," said Washington artist Sam Gilliam, a student of Noland's.[63]

Another, perhaps more likely avenue for Mary's initiation into drug experimentation was her friend Jim Truitt. Truitt was an eclectic intellectual, a man whose interest in Eastern art might have led him to experiment with the more holistic Eastern religions. In the minds of drug pioneers such as Leary, the tenets and occasional practice of Oriental religions were quite enmeshed with LSD use. In later years, Truitt became interested in the practice of Huichol Indian religion, which involved the use of hallucinogens, and built an altar decorated with psychedelic colors and symbols in his house in Mexico. He also grew peyote on the rooftop of the same house.[64]

As to the other part of Leary's story, as Cord Meyer's wife, Mary could have learned about CIA infiltration of various academic and other organizations. No public documents link Cord Meyer to the CIA's extensive drug experiments, but at his level in the hierarchy he would have had access to such information. The CIA's search for mind-control drugs started in the very early part of the cold war with the zombielike confessions of Soviet dissidents at the purge trials in Eastern Europe. The confessions provoked fears at the CIA and the Pentagon that the Russians had developed some kind of mind-control drug or procedure. A search was begun for drugs that could probe minds for secrets, change personalities, or make agents invulnerable. The cold warriors were influenced by Aldous Huxley's *The Doors of Perception*, about LSD. "He made something totally impossible seem possible," CIA psychologist John Gittinger recalled. The experiments involved academics and researchers in universities across the country.[65]

Over the years, under a project code-named MK-ULTRA, the agency funded thousands of experiments involving drugs (including LSD) that promoted sleep, illogical thinking, and hallucinations. The agency also experimented with induced unconsciousness, hypnosis, paralysis, amnesia, and shock treatments. As early as 1950 a CIA memorandum from the Interrogation Research Section addressed the "problems involved in finding a psychiatrist" who might work on a mind-control project. One potential worry was that "his ethics might be such that he might not care to cooperate in certain more revolutionary phases of our project."[66]

The CIA was fascinated by the possibilities inherent in LSD, especially because such a small amount was so powerful. One CIA man told writer John Marks the agency was obsessed with the fact that "a two-suiter suitcase could hold enough LSD to turn on every man, woman and child in the United States." Public water supplies were vulnerable, they believed.[67] CIA psychologist John Gittinger recalled that the army was at one point very worried about the drug being administered through air-conditioning systems, and so the CIA researched the possibility of delivering LSD to large groups unwittingly. "You got entirely different reactions when it was administered unwittingly than you did when you knew you were taking it," Gittinger said. "I was engaged in a very foolish project trying to make it an aerosol spray, but we were never able to do it."[68] At one point in the early 1950s a rumor passed to the CIA that the Swiss company Sandoz, which then had a monopoly on production of the drug, was about to put twenty-two pounds of it on the open market. Allen Dulles personally authorized the purchase of the entire stock with $240,000 delivered by agents in a black bag. It turned out the rumor was not true, but Sandoz agreed to take the money and send the CIA weekly shipments of the drug. The CIA funded research into LSD, disguising the source of funds through false foundations. One of them was based at Georgetown University Hospital. The hundreds of experiments conducted for the CIA used witting and unwitting subjects, and some were conducted under clearly unethical conditions. In one CIA-funded experiment, seven men in a Kentucky prison were kept on LSD for seventy-seven days straight. After another, an army officer who had been unwittingly administered LSD committed suicide.[69]

Not all the subjects had bad trips, however. The CIA's LSD research occurred at hospitals and prisons but also at some of the nation's top universities, including Harvard and Stanford. Graduate students were some of the first Americans exposed to the drug. One of them was Ken Kesey, a student in a Stanford writing program. The experience led him to become the original Merry Prankster and preceded his writing of *One Flew over the Cuckoo's Nest*. Kesey and many other test subjects later promoted LSD use when the drug became widely available through the black market. Thus the CIA's tests were a catalyst for the acid scene of the 1960s. "No one could enter the world of psychedelics without first passing, unawares, through doors opened by the Agency," John Marks concluded. "It would become a supreme irony that the CIA's enormous search for weapons among drugs—fueled by the hope that spies could, like Dr. Frankenstein, control life with genius and machines—would wind up helping to create the wandering, uncontrollable minds of the counterculture."[70]

In the early sixties, when Mary Meyer used it, the people trying LSD still wore suits and ties and got regular haircuts. The drug itself was legal and was something of a fad among the intellectual elite. Henry and Clare Booth Luce, publisher and ambassador, were among the establishment types who tried the drug. LSD was also being used as a tool by some psychoanalysts. One patient who reportedly underwent LSD treatment was Ethel Kennedy.[71]

Some CIA officers who officially tested the drug later spoke reverentially of it. John Marks interviewed a CIA officer who recalled LSD as a transcendental experience; he saw all the colors of the rainbow coming out of cracks in the sidewalk.[72] But if some CIA officers and friends had formed a "cell" in Washington to use the drug privately, none has admitted it. And there is no one who has come forward to say that Mary was involved in any organized effort to "turn on" powerful men. That notion had been around since Aldous Huxley started experimenting with the drug, and there was at least one organization in California nominally devoted to that goal.

Mary might have spontaneously arrived at the idea herself, however. She was already a bit contemptuous of Washington, and once she had had the LSD experience, she might have decided it could change the world. While other avid LSD users could only daydream about getting it into the water supply of a large city, Mary was connected enough—by 1960, she was an intimate of the president-elect of the United States—to promote or disseminate the drug at high levels.

By 1960 Mary was no longer a suburban housewife. She had a circle of Georgetown friends with whom she could sit up late into the night and discuss art, politics, books. She shared studio space with Anne Truitt and was trying to be a disciplined artist. She was attracted to the new and unconventional; she seemed "hungry" for experience and fame, Noland thought. She had traded in her Plymouth station wagon and bought herself a sporty cream-colored Studebaker. She wore peasant blouses and blue tights and sometimes carried around a velvet drawstring bag filled with semiprecious gems—peridots, aquamarines, amethysts, lapis, and citrines. She had a casual style, but she was a meticulous dresser with a distinctive look. "She could walk into a secondhand dress shop and immediately pick the one perfect dress on the racks," one friend recalled.[73] She liked bright colors and would wear a huge hot-pink flower in the buttonhole of a mango-colored knit suit. She was offbeat.

She was attracted to glamour and to dramatic types. She made a point of meeting movie and theater people who came to town. When Otto Preminger came to Washington to film *Advise and Consent* inside an abandoned mansion north of Georgetown, she met Preminger and managed to get a walk-on part, and persuaded Kary Fischer to come along as an extra.[74]

She paid attention to her own emotional health. Throughout those years, except for her episode with the Reichian therapist, she saw a conventional psychoanalyst and started to "really work on herself," said one friend. But the Reichian therapy left a lasting impression. She had learned to pay attention to what she *felt*. She was drawn to the kind of physical and emotional experience not commonly available or even desired among the Georgetown wives. Pleasure became, if not a mantra, an important objective in her daily life.

One Sunday afternoon in 1962 a hardware store in Georgetown caught fire. Mary called a friend and begged her to accompany her to watch the fire. The friend reluctantly agreed. When they arrived the three-story building was at a full blaze, and sparks and smoke were flying onto the sidewalk. Mary wanted to get as close as possible to the blaze, but her friend was afraid the building was going to collapse. Mary seemed literally turned on by the sight, the woman recalled. "She kept saying, 'Oooh, I wish it would just explode, don't you?' " Fearing that would in fact happen, the other woman left, leaving an ecstatic Mary laughing with glee as the flames devoured all the little tools that went into making a home. "Mary tended to be courageous and foolhardy. If she wanted to do something crazy, she would just do it," said the friend.[75]

She was intensely interested in danger, perhaps because the writer-reporter in her was still curious. When a couple she knew were robbed at gunpoint inside their Georgetown house, Mary demanded a minute-by-minute account of what had happened. She was fascinated by the idea of experiencing such a thing without fainting.

In winter Mary and her friends skated on the frozen canal, and they tried to extend the skating season as long as possible. She happily took risks on the ice. One afternoon in the early 1960s Mary and Kary Fischer took their skates out even though there were patches where the ice was melting. Most of the crowd stayed to the edges. Fischer skated out until he broke through. She helped pull him out, the icy water sloshing around her legs and filling her skates. He finally emerged, coated with mud from the chest down.

Mary's quest for intense experience and her new interest in pleasure might have been related to her son's death and her divorce. She did not wear her pain on her sleeve, but her sadness was a palpable part of her. Noland attributed her extremes of behavior—her reeling between artistic self-discipline and emotional heedlessness—to the tragedy. He felt the death had "unbalanced" her.[76] The boy's death "was the point where she broke loose," said her longtime friend David Middleton. "I think she wanted to build another world for herself, which she had been trying to do back in New York in the forties, mixing the social world with the theater, the glamour. She really wanted to be something of her own, rather than being an ornament or spectator."[77]

Women were inspired by her independent spirit. Eleanor McPeck lived in a house across the street from Mary on Thirty-fourth Street, and they had drinks in Eleanor's garden occasionally. Mary laughed a great deal, McPeck recalled. Although Mary was near her forties then and McPeck in her twenties, McPeck felt they were about the same age.

"Feminism was rarely discussed then, but I always thought of her as an independent spirit," McPeck said. "She was quite ahead of her time." McPeck also liked her because, unlike most of the Washington crowd, Mary didn't seem so embroiled in the politics of the era.[78]

She took pride in standing outside the in crowd, knowing that she could always slip inside at will. Jackie Kennedy visited her in the afternoons, sometimes bringing her daughter Caroline along. She was a favorite at Washington political and social doyenne Alice Roosevelt Longworth's house, and also a friend and visitor of Joseph Alsop. When she visited them she often brought Ken Noland. She attended parties at the Bobby Kennedys' when that family moved into Hickory Hill after JFK and Jackie moved out. Noland recalled leaving one of the Hickory Hill parties in a rage one night while Mary was urging everyone to strip and jump into the pool.

"She had this sense of *la vie en bohème* and the *outré* and the way-out," said her friend Elizabeth Eisenstein. "She wanted to be on the cutting edge of what was happening. A lot of people were like that in the sixties." Mary persuaded Eisenstein, a rather conservative university professor, to see the cult film *Mondo Cane*. The film intersperses footage from anthropological documentaries of head-hunting tribes with scenes from Chinese restaurants that serve very fresh dog and scientific film of radiation-sickened animals on Bikini Atoll, all to make a point about human beastliness. Eisenstein recalls being disgusted within the first five minutes and wanting very much to walk out of the theater. "We came out and I said, 'God, that was repulsive,' and she said, 'That's what it was meant to be,' " Eisenstein recalled. "She was astounded at my reaction. I had given her what she felt was a philistine response."[79]

Kary Fischer, who married the writer Jane O'Reilly in Mary's garden in 1962, nursed a secret love for Mary. Although she spent many hours talking to him at Martin's, a favorite bar in Georgetown, and inside her home, a romance never developed. Fischer was one of the friends who knew Mary in Georgetown as a woman who would stay up into the wee hours after black-tie dinners, sipping bourbon and water and talking about art and philosophy. She liked doing the same thing at home. She gave casual dinner parties, serving fried chicken and mashed potatoes cooked by her maid. She herself always prepared an onion tart appetizer for the gatherings, although the maid had to roll out the crust. She was an avid reader of fiction and poetry, and books covered walls of her living room. Kary Fischer became for her an older Bob Schwartz, an educated man who adored her and with whom she could talk about the higher questions. Unlike Noland, Fischer took her seriously. He saw the same side of her personality that Schwartz had. "Politics rather bored her. She was not political, she was aesthetic," Fischer recalled, echoing a man he had never met.[80]

"I think Mary was a serious person," said Marian Schlesinger. "She had a philosophical turn of mind, and she was really quite different from many of the other women in the scene. I found her most sympathetic and at the same time, elusive and very private, on the periphery and observing the passing show. She was an experimentalist, as shown in her painting. Nothing she did would surprise me."[81] Kary Fischer called her a "doubting" person, one who questioned everything and would not settle for conventional wisdom. "She was ready to try almost anything," he thought.

After the divorce, Mary and Cord occasionally ran into each other at cultural events—Cord rarely missed a poet's reading if he could help it. But otherwise, their lives only intersected over their sons. Cord wanted to date women, but he was having a difficult time. He squired many young Georgetown women around town but didn't seem to connect with any of them. His dates thought he was too quick to pounce. He drank heavily and began to show the argumentative, confrontational side for which he became known during the Vietnam War. Said Marian Schlesinger: "Cord you met at cocktail parties and he was always drunk." One woman who dated him then remembers that he seemed very well read but "he loved to hear himself talk."[82]

Mary and Cord and the boys continued to spend Christmases together as a family. The two parents communicated about tuition, about sporting events, and about sending the boys to summer camp, to Milford, to Cord's family farm in New Hampshire, and to their prep schools for the winter. In his teens Quentin began having more problems at school, and Cord and Mary squabbled over which parent had caused the divorce. Cord's mother had never much liked Mary, who was too independent for her taste. When Cord told her they were getting divorced, she replied, "I divorced Mary a long time ago."[83] During one of Quentin's visits to the Meyer family farm in New Hampshire, the elder Mrs. Meyer told her grandson about his mother's affair with the Italian, which greatly upset the boy.[84] Quentin remained troubled, although he completed prep school, went to Yale, and even served in Vietnam.

Mary was worried about her eldest son and apparently concerned that he would grow up conflicted and self-doubting, like Cord. As Quentin became an adolescent, he and Mary had more frequent arguments, and Mary often called Cord to come and settle them. In one journal entry, Cord wrote that Quentin felt betrayed by the divorce and wanted to get back at "God and the universe" for Michael's death. Mary responded: "Everyone of us, every yellow last one of us has those feelings—Jesus, the daily bread has to be baked—Goose the wonder boy!"[85] During these years, Jim Angleton came to play a greater role in the Meyer family affairs. He took it upon himself to be a second father to the boys, taking them fishing and checking in on them periodically. Eventually he was overseeing their trusts and intervening for them at their colleges.[86]

Mary's love affair with Ken Noland was fading by 1959. He was moving to New York, and she had her life in Washington, where she was committed to her children and her friends. Mary and Ken eventually agreed to see other people, and Mary may have already begun having flings with other men, some of them married. It was an amicable ending.

Mary remained a member in good standing of a social world to which Noland had never belonged. Her sister, Tony, was married to one of Georgetown's most powerful men. Although the two sisters' lives were very different—Mary's madcap, single lifestyle was the polar opposite of Tony's married life with Ben Bradlee and six children—Mary was close enough to the Bradlees to drop in on them occasionally. With her fresh views and attractive face and figure, she was a welcome addition at the Bradlees' and at other Georgetown social venues. The men of Mary's generation in the world of power politics were happy to have a newly single woman in their midst, especially one who might be called a "swinger," a woman who could do the Twist, drink and smoke, keep up with the action, and, above all, get the joke.

One evening in the spring of 1959, before their breakup, Mary and Ken dropped in at the Bradlees' for drinks. Ben's friend and Georgetown neighbor John Kennedy was also there. The very suave senator from Massachusetts was about to announce he was going to run for president in 1960. Mary and Kennedy greeted each other with some familiarity. To Kennedy, Mary was a trusted member of his crowd, someone who got the wink and the nod. A few years before, Mary had housed one of his young girlfriends, Pam Turnure, at her house on Thirty-fourth Street, at Kennedy's request, after the girl had been kicked out of a rooming house for associating with a married man.[87] And as the four of them sat there, drinks in hand, Noland noticed what he called "a stirring" between Mary and Kennedy. She was coming alive in a way Noland remembered from the early days of their own affair.

Later that same year, Noland rented a house on Long Island for a few weeks in the summer with his children. Mary drove up north to Provincetown alone and rented a one-room shack out on the end of a pier and stayed there by herself for two weeks before coming down and joining Noland at his rented place. In later years Noland attached some significance to the fact that Mary's little cottage in Provincetown was within a few nautical miles of Hyannisport.

# 7

# Jack and Mary

*The females imported from New York for the occasion had been spectacular again.*

BEN BRADLEE
ON A KENNEDY WHITE HOUSE DANCE

One of pop artist Tom Wesselmann's three "nudes" hanging at the Washington Gallery of Modern Art's "Popular Image" show in 1963 offended the gallery's board of trustees. Wesselmann had started out painting only nudes and feeling indifferent about color. One night he had a dream about the colors red, white, and blue that provoked his "Great American Nude" series. The resulting collages contained silhouettes of nude women with pictures of televisions, American flags, toasters, house cats, plastic fruit, and official portraits of presidents. They had already been displayed in New York, but in Washington the work was provocative. Lincoln with a generic nude was one thing, the women on the gallery board thought, but President John F. Kennedy with a nude Marilyn Monroe next to him? The implication went a little too far. Abstract art was often incomprehensible, but at least it wasn't politically offensive. This, on the other hand, simply wouldn't do.[1]

The "Popular Image" show was a groundbreaking cultural event in Washington. It signified exactly how current the new gallery would be. Until then the contemporary art that had made its way down the Atlantic seaboard from New York to Washington was the art of the 1950s, abstract expressionism, sometimes minus the expression. The nonreferential and apolitical art of Ken Noland and his followers was becoming acceptable, and Georgetown was beginning to purchase and hang such works in the living room near the eighteenth-century oils and silver-framed wedding photos. But the "Popular Image" show brought something unsettling to the city. Just when people had accepted abstract art, pop art arrived and proclaimed itself the reaction against and the opposite of abstract art. Pop art was more than referential; it was often the real thing. Sinks and shower heads, car dashboards, soup cans, and Marilyn Monroes—all the detritus of American popular culture and commerce was presented as art. To some, this represented a rather unhappy cultural shift. One might hang an abstract black canvas above the inherited terra-cotta urns, but an unframed Chevrolet dashboard still looked better in the garage.

In 1963, long before Robert Mapplethorpe's bullwhips and Andres Serrano's *Piss Christ*, people took offense at a painting that paired a framed portrait of the president of the United States with the silhouetted nude body of a movie star. Previewing the "Popular Image" show, members of the new museum's board questioned the propriety of the collage. Katharine Graham, Marie Harriman, and some of the other trustees called for a personal meeting with Alice Denney. They demanded that she remove Tom Wesselmann's *Great American Nude No. 44* from the show.[2] "It was ironic, because we all knew what was going on at the White House," said Denney's assistant at the time, Eleanor McPeck. "Kay Graham and Marie Harriman and some others insisted this picture be taken down and taken out of the show. The board was very conservative. They were simply not prepared for it."[3]

Alice Denney objected, but the board members were the mu-

Ruth Pinchot

*Before her marriage, Mary's mother was a feisty Greenwich Village journalist who supported the labor and women's suffrage movements.*

Schlesinger Library, Radcliffe College.

Amos Pinchot

*Mary Meyer's elegant father was famous for tilting at windmills. He opposed U.S. entry into World War II and became a bitter critic of FDR.*

Courtesy of Grey Towers National Historic Landmark, USDA Forest Service, Milford, Pennsylvania.

Grey Towers *Life at the Pinchot estate was both formal and Bohemian. The women sunbathed nude, and the family entertained prominent American writers, artists and political figures around the water table at night.*

Courtesy of Grey Towers National Historic Landmark, USDA Forest Service, Milford, Pennsylvania.

MARY WITH HER PONY
*Her childhood was filled with tennis, riding lessons, and a French nanny whom the girls called "Mademoiselle."*

William A. Gaston.

MARY AND HER SISTER, TONY
*Four years older than Tony, Mary was also more outgoing and athletic. The sisters grew up to look similar but have very different styles.*

William A. Gaston.

MARY AND TONY IN *MADEMOISELLE*
*Women's magazines in the 1930s sought out the daughters of socially prominent New Yorkers to model fashions, and the Pinchot sisters of Park Avenue were happy to oblige.*

Photograph by Tony Frissell. Courtesy of *Vogue*. Copyright © 1935 (renewed 1963, 1991) by Condé Nast Publications, Inc.

MARY'S HALF-SISTER,
ROSAMUND

*Sometimes at night, Mary was awakened by the pounding of hooves—Rosamund liked to ride bareback in the moonlight.*

Graduation from Vassar, 1942

*Mary's classmates selected her to be part of the Daisy Chain, a group of the school's prettiest girls who wore white and carried flowers on commencement day.*

Courtesy of Special Collections, Vassar College Libraries, Poughkeepsie, New York.

As a glamorous New York debutante in 1938

*Mary was much in demand, but not always satisfied by the party life. At home, her father was growing dangerously depressed.*

Courtesy of *Vogue*. Copyright © 1938 (renewed 1966, 1994) by Condé Nast Publications, Inc.

Mary as a reporter for *Mademoiselle*

*With the men away at war, the women worked. As a journalist, Mary wrote about such daring subjects as venereal disease and the very modern "marriage classes" popular with young college women.*

Photograph by Genevieve Naylor. Courtesy of *Mademoiselle*. Copyright © 1944 (renewed 1972) by Condé Nast Publications, Inc.

MARY'S WEDDING TO CORD MEYER JR. IN 1945

*They were twenty-four and seemed perfect for each other.*

New York Times Pictures, New York Times Company.

MARY AT A WORLD FEDERALIST MEETING IN LUXEMBOURG

*As a young wife and mother, she supported Cord's crusade for world peace. One participant at the convention recalled how "swish" she seemed in that company.*

Photograph courtesy of Tom Hughes.

MARY AND CORD

*Cord's soaring reputation brought Mary publicity, too, but took him away from home too often.*

Photograph by Peter Martin. Courtesy of *Mademoiselle.* Copyright © 1948 (renewed 1976) by Condé Nast Publications, Inc.

MARY IN THE EARLY 1960S
*Her experimental mood led her to LSD, to guru Timothy Leary at Harvard, and to abstract painting that elevated color over form.*

Corbis-Bettmann LLC.

JFK WITH MARY *(far right)*, TONY, AND RUTH IN 1963
*After this picture was taken, the president retreated into the Pinchots' "little house" to look at baby pictures of Mary and Tony with their mother, who was already contributing to Barry Goldwater's campaign.*

Photo by Cecil Stoughton, a U.S. Army Signal Corps photographer on active duty assigned to the Office of the Military Aide to the President.

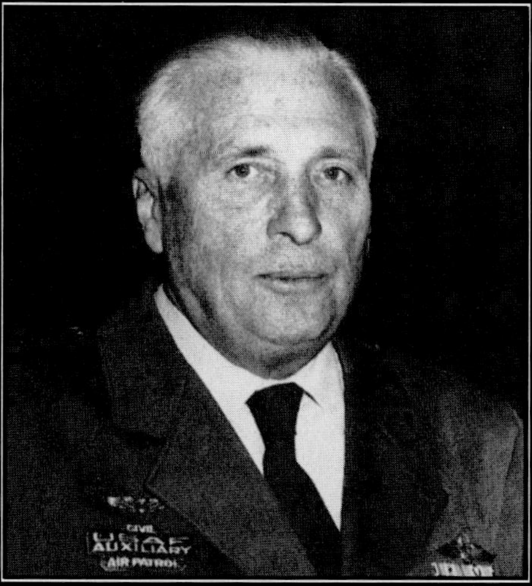


ONE OF THE TOP CRAFTERS OF CIA POLICY DURING THE COLD WAR

*Cord Meyer's work was so clandestine, he never got the public acclaim he had once craved.*

New York Times Pictures, New York Times Company.

JAMES JESUS ANGLETON

*The CIA's counterintelligence chief took charge of Mary's diary and personal papers after her death, destroying some of them. He later boasted that he had wiretapped her phone and bugged her bedroom.*

George Tames / New York Times Pictures, New York Times Company.

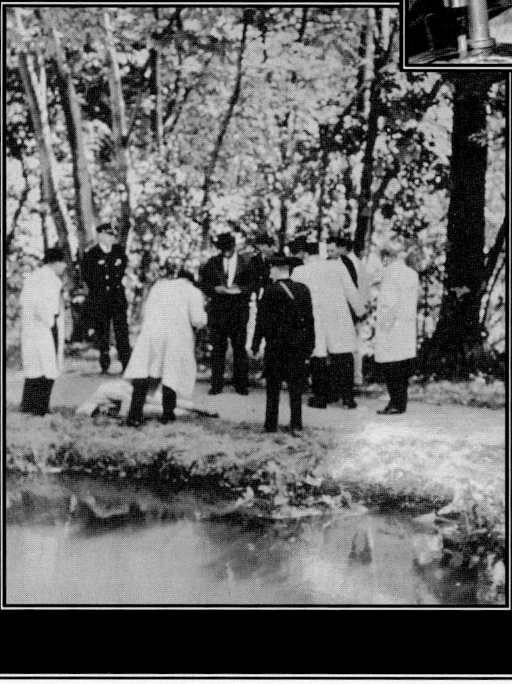

THE GEORGETOWN TOWPATH WHERE MARY WAS KILLED IN OCTOBER 1964

*The news photographer at the canal found it odd that there were so many men in suits at the crime scene and that journalists were kept at such a distance.*

Copyright © Washington Post by permission of the D.C. Public Library.

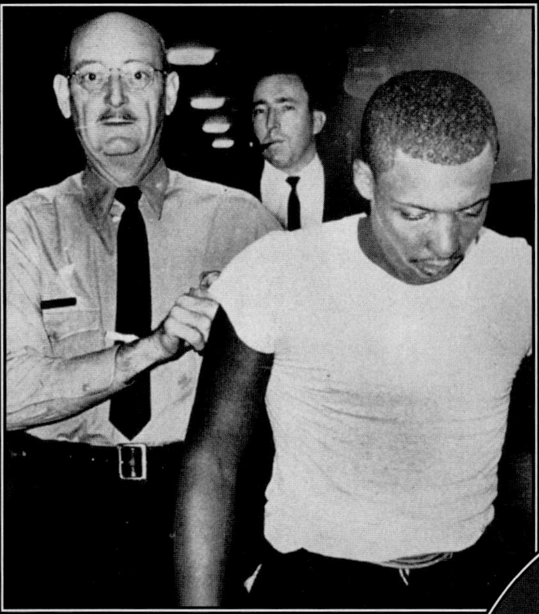

THE ARREST

*Washington resident Ray Crump had recently been released from jail when he was arrested on the towpath. He told police he had been fishing near the crime scene.*

Copyright © Washington Post by permission of the D.C. Public Library.

DOVEY ROUNDTREE

*Crump's attorney was a soft-spoken but fierce advocate. She portrayed Crump as a "little man" in danger of being railroaded by the white establishment.*

Courtesy of Dovey Roundtree.

AL HANTMAN

*The prosecutor was confident his circumstantial case would persuade a jury.*

Photo supplied by Alfred Hantman.

seum's financial lifeline. Reluctantly the curator prepared to take the Wesselmann down. But behind the scenes the matter had come to presidential attention. Mary Meyer, by then one of the president's occasional lovers and a confidante, told him about the little art imbroglio. She described the Wesselmann collage with the Monroe nude beneath his official portrait. She told him about the ladies of the gallery board, all in a dither. The image of grande dames such as Marie Harriman scrambling to protect his reputation was too funny. The president laughed at the story and told Mary to tell the little Gallery of Modern Art that he wanted the Wesselmann to hang. The collage stayed in the show.[4]

President John F. Kennedy represented a changing of the guard from the old generals of World War II to the young company officers. He could laugh at the image of the prudish gallery board aghast at the pairing of his image with that of a nude actress. If they only knew. A decorated World War II veteran, Kennedy approached government as he had approached war: as a macho, high-stakes game relieved as often as possible by the sinful delights of shore leave. His image floated along on good looks and a sharp wit. His election elevated a new generation of federal government employee: expensively educated, well bred, and schooled in the subtle art of cold-war relations. These men kept him and his image on course. They coined the notion of a "New Frontier," which was more than just a political slogan. Kennedy and his administration were going to conquer space, Communists, the jet age, nuclear power. All of modern culture lay before them, a vast twinkling newness to be explored, staked out, and named for America.

As the first television-age president, Kennedy deftly manipulated the new medium. He institutionalized the televised presidential press conference. Americans were dazzled by this telegenic, witty man, a president who looked like a movie star and who had real guts. The Kennedy style was everything middle America longed for: moneyed but casual, nautical, all salt air, wind, and ease, clad in Ray-Bans and khakis, apparently bounding with good health and wholesomeness. He could express all that on camera. Norman Mailer was awed at the way Kennedy, who looked his full age in person, seemed to drop ten years in front of the cameras and microphones and metamorphose into "a movie star, his coloring vivid, his manner rich, his gestures strong and quick." Mailer thought Kennedy "had a dozen faces."[5] Behind the wit and grin, his war record and his vitality had been embellished by some of the best political strategists in the nation, and his intellect was bolstered by the work of his speechwriter, Ted Sorensen.

His proverbial ship of state looked on TV and seemed even to those on board to be navigated with a steady hand on calm waters. But by the time Kennedy took the oath of office on a snowy morning in January 1961, Fidel Castro had signed an economic agreement with the Russians, and U.S. assets in Cuba had been appropriated by the Communists. Gary Powers, a U2 pilot shot down over the Soviet Union and captured, to the great embarrassment of the U.S. government, was serving a seventy-year prison sentence in a dank Moscow prison.

Kennedy was the nation's hottest cold war president. Earlier he had staked his political career on the declaration of a missile gap with the Russians and the notion that America needed to beef up its nuclear capability, and that position had helped propel him into the White House. "We are facing a gap on which we are gambling with our survival," he had said at campaign stops for months.[6] With that oft-repeated line, he had introduced into American consciousness the notion that the Russians had more, and more effective, nuclear weapons than the United States. He had implied that the Russians might actually win an all-out nuclear war or, short of that, threaten America into submission. During the 1960 campaign Eisenhower and Nixon had looked weak compared with him, while Kennedy appeared to be the grim soothsayer. It did not matter that Kennedy was aware, thanks to classified information shared with him, that the missile gap might not in fact exist.[7] He was further assured of American might when he met Eisenhower on the eve of his inauguration, January 19, 1961. There the outgoing president told his successor that whatever had been said during the campaign about Soviet missiles and nuclear strength, the United States had a strategic edge because of nuclear-equipped submarines patrolling the coasts of the Soviet Union. "You have an invaluable asset in Polaris. It is invulnerable," Eisenhower told him.[8]

The next morning poet Robert Frost set the tone for the coming thousand days of international tension in his inaugural poem, "For John F. Kennedy," which he wrote but was unable to finish reading because the wind blew it off the podium. In the poem, the white-haired New Englander had written, "Of a power leading from its strength and pride / Of young ambition eager to be tried / Firm in our beliefs without dismay / In any games the nations want to play."

In 1961 any nations that didn't want to play East versus West were in the game anyway. The American intelligence agency believed it was on top of the game. By the time of Kennedy's inauguration, the CIA was at its peak; but Kennedy's more hands-on style and the disastrous Bay of Pigs episode signaled the beginning of the agency's decline. The agency was initially pleased to find in the White House New Frontiersmen who understood the international cowboy style. Attorney General Robert Kennedy saw Cuba as the gateway to Communism in Latin America and became involved early on in discussions with the CIA about what to do. In March of 1961 the CIA continued its attempts to assassinate Castro, a process begun under Eisenhower. Poison intended for Castro was handed off to a mobster named Johnny Roselli.[9] In April the Bay of Pigs invasion was launched, with Cuban exiles landing on Cuba believing they were going to be backed up by American jets. The jets never came, and the invaders who did not escape were captured by Castro's forces. It was not the first time the CIA had encouraged a deadly rebellion against Communism only to fail to back up the rebels. In Hungary, thirty-two thousand people had died in 1956 in an anti-Communist uprising encouraged by the CIA in radio broadcasts.[10]

The CIA was not discouraged. On May 30, 1961, Dominican

Republic president Rafael Trujillo was assassinated with CIA assistance. As the Kennedys were flying to Paris on Air Force One for a summit with Russian leader Khrushchev in Vienna—the trip on which Jackie Kennedy, with her elegance and fluent French, would score a public relations triumph in France—the dictator Americans had installed in the Dominican Republic thirty-one years before was shot to death on Avenida George Washington.[11] He was killed by so-called Dominican dissidents supplied with American weapons, delivered via a series of coded messages also begun under Eisenhower. Earlier that month, the U.S. deputy chief of mission in Ciudad Trujillo, Henry Dearborn, had cabled the State Department: "The members of our club are now prepared in their minds to have a picnic but do not have the ingredients for a salad. . . . Last week we were asked to furnish three or four pineapples for a party in the near future, but I could remember nothing in my instructions that would have allowed me to contribute this ingredient."[12] Shortly after that the American guns arrived and Dearborn gave them to the dissidents. As Trujillo lay dead, Kennedy and Charles de Gaulle rode in a convertible limousine up the Champs Élysées to the Tomb of the Unknown Soldier under the Arc de Triomphe. It was raining and the streets were lined with black umbrellas.[13]

Kennedy went on to the Vienna summit with Khrushchev after announcing, "I am the man who accompanied Jacqueline Kennedy to Paris." But the Kennedy style failed to charm the Russian who nine months before had pounded his shoe on a desktop at the U.N. General Assembly in New York. Kennedy's talks with Khrushchev resolved nothing. Worse than the impasse was the fact that Kennedy was proclaimed the loser. Upon his return from Vienna (with his back so painful he had to be lifted off the plane),[14] one of the first questions Kennedy wanted answered was how many Americans would die in an all-out nuclear exchange with the Russians. The Pentagon's answer was about seventy million people.[15] The president spent the rest of the summer of 1961 dealing with the Berlin crisis and watching the Berlin Wall go up in August.

In October 1961, just six weeks after the Berlin Wall was erected, Mary Meyer's name appeared for the first time on a White House Secret Service gate log, signed in to see the president in the evening. Jackie was away with the children in Newport. The handwritten logs kept by the Secret Service recorded the names of all visitors entering the White House and the person they meant to see.

President Kennedy had spent the first few days of October vacationing in Newport, Rhode Island, with Jackie and some Washington friends, including journalist Charles Bartlett, Bartlett's wife, Martha, and William Walton. Kennedy described it as "the best vacation I've had in a long time."[16] Upon his return, Kennedy spoke at a *Washington Post* book luncheon observing the publication of the John Adams papers. That night, October 3, at 7:40 P.M., according to the gate log, "Mary Meyers" had an appointment with Evelyn Lincoln, the president's personal secretary, and was authorized by Lincoln to enter the White House.[17]

The world Mary Meyer entered that evening was the slippery but stardusted deck of the cruise ship Kennedy had been piloting since his election. With the end of Eisenhower's eight years, the midwesterners had been pitched overboard along with their isolationist tendencies and provincial morality. In their place, the new social arbiters in the capital elevated "swingers," men and women who were sophisticated about world travel, art, politics, and sex. Washington then barely resembled the workaholic city of policy wonks it would become in a few decades. Smoking and heavy drinking were the norm, and a certain kind of sophisticated sin was synonymous with life in the capital. Jean Friendly, one of the socially prominent women of the time, recalls the sheer "naughtiness" of their crowd, crowned by the outrageous infidelities engaged in by the president himself. In those days, few cared. "There was no horror to it," recalled Friendly in 1995, a white-haired grandmother who was still receiving visitors in the sitting room of the same Georgetown house that had seen so many wild parties then. "It was a little like a game. There wasn't the kind of desperation to the city there is now."[18]

Women who wanted to be "in" with the Kennedy set understood the ground rules. A quick act of love shared between a willing man and a willing woman, whether married or not, was one of the small pleasures of a life well lived. It was accepted that one code of behavior applied to the peasants and middle class, another to the sophisticates, who were better equipped to handle certain emotional ambiguities.

Kennedy had spent the better part of thirteen years in Georgetown before his election, and he tried to retain his connections to the casual, intimate lifestyle of the community.[19] Georgetown was thrilled that one of their own was in the White House. Joseph Alsop later described his first evening in the presidential residence after the Kennedy ascension. The old mansion had yet to be redecorated, and Mamie Eisenhower's "vomit green and rose pink" color scheme, as Alsop put it, was still in evidence. But signs of better times ahead were available, too, as Jackie Kennedy scoured the White House for something in which to serve ten pounds of caviar from Palm Beach friends and finally dumped it into a gold bucket.[20] "Suddenly this inbred old-style society that was utterly foreign to the rest of the country was on the stage," said former White House correspondent Hugh Sidey, who covered Kennedy for *Time*. "Washington society was visible all over the world. They were young people who liked a good time. They were very self-satisfied but also idealistic. That formed a new Washington."[21]

On the night of his inauguration, Kennedy went to a party at Joseph Alsop's house, where the columnist had been surprised after midnight by uninvited guests in inaugural finery. Alsop fortunately had in his pantry plenty of champagne plus frozen Maryland terrapin and the pounds of butter and gallons of sherry required to cook it. The surprise showing by Kennedy around midnight was unusual, but Pam Turnure (formerly one of Kennedy's girlfriends, later ensconced as Jackie Kennedy's press secretary) recalled that after the election both Kennedys "tried to go out and tried to continue the pattern of Georgetown life, and the natural thing to do was to come back to a small dinner, but it was a difficult thing to do and it got to be a strain."[22] Instead of going out, the Kennedys started having Georgetown in. Ben and Tony Bradlee and Mary Meyer became frequent White House guests. But there was a difference between the parties to which the Bradlees were invited and those Mary attended.

Kennedy's sexual escapades were legendary in Georgetown. To the rest of America he was a family man with a beautiful wife, a man of caution, wit, and strategy. In private he was dazzlingly reckless. There was an aura of Hollywood around Kennedy even though he was not of it himself, and the women around him were fashioned a little after nameless starlets, even if they were actually secretaries on Capitol Hill. Some of his most infamous sexual liaisons were with real actresses on the West Coast, women procured with the help of his brother-in-law, the actor Peter Lawford. Lawford ran with Frank Sinatra and Dean Martin, who converged with Kennedy and various actresses and prostitutes for wild parties at the Lawford beach house in Santa Monica. Dean Martin's first wife, Jeanne, would later say, "The things that went on in that beach house were just mind-boggling."[23] Among the actresses Kennedy was linked with before and during his marriage were Marilyn Monroe (introduced by Peter Lawford), Angie Dickinson, and Gene Tierney.

Kennedy brought some of that swinging style to the national capital. He was genuinely jet-set before he even entered politics and began traveling the country as a campaigner. His cares had never been those of an ordinary man. His father had endowed each of his children with ten million dollars in trust, ensuring they would never have to work.[24] Kennedy's concern for the downtrodden was born not of personal shared hardship but of imagination and compassion. Some journalists who met him felt he had a hard time comprehending poverty, although he was deeply moved by it when he saw it firsthand in places such as West Virginia.

In his rarefied world he had developed certain habits few common men could match. One was an obstinate, often foolish risk-taking, a need—like Mary Meyer's—to establish himself as an individual outside the expectations and confines of the sheltered, upper-class world into which he was born. His behavior with women was compulsive, perhaps even addictive. "I can't go to sleep without a lay," he told Clare Booth Luce.[25] A more recent version of that notion came from legendary Washington lobbyist Bobby Baker, who told Seymour Hersh that Kennedy had said, "You know, I get a migraine headache if I don't get a strange piece of ass every day."[26] Inside the White House he supposedly established a gambling pool with his friends—the kitty went to the first man to have sex with a woman other than his wife in the Lincoln bedroom.[27]

Kennedy's way with women was no secret to the press. Journalists during the Kennedy years were agog at White House affairs to which lovely young things were invited down from New York. It was well-known that when Kennedy had a free night he liked to have lots of pretty girls around. Ben Bradlee, writing about the White House scene in *Conversations with Kennedy*, gives the impression that the Kennedy dances involved a portable seraglio of nameless beauties. "The females imported from New York for the occasion had been spectacular again," he wrote of a March 1963 dance. At the same dance, Kennedy surveyed the beauties, turned to Bradlee, and said wistfully, "If you and I could only run wild, Benjy."[28]

Journalists, muckrakers, and now academic historians have confirmed that Kennedy was in fact, by conventional standards, "running wild." Various writers have since speculated that his sexual appetite was fueled by frequent injections of cortisone, meant to prevent death from Addison's disease, a disorder of the adrenal gland. However, it is testosterone, not cortisone, that increases the sex drive, and the theory does not hold up. Some biographers have attributed Kennedy's behavior to psychological idiosyncrasies as well. Throughout Kennedy's youth his father, Joseph Kennedy, had been a flagrant philanderer, even going so far as to install actress Gloria Swanson on a cruise ship along with his wife, Rose. The Kennedy boys expected wives no less long-suffering than their mother. Compounded by the intense competitiveness of the family, the Kennedy upbringing made for men who were not much interested in "that delicacy of feeling on which intimacy depends," as Anne Truitt put it in another context.

The president's private "naughtiness" was an open joke among the women of Georgetown. "Everybody was having an affair with JFK and everybody was in analysis" was how one of the president's Georgetown paramours recalled the times.[29] The male journalists close to Kennedy officially overlooked the rampant stories of his sexual voracity and his infidelity to Jackie. The small number of female journalists on the beat wouldn't have thought of writing about it, either. Not for publication, maybe, but among themselves the Georgetown wives did talk. One prominent Georgetown woman who did not find it hard to resist Kennedy recalled being in a car with "a bunch of women" once during the Kennedy years. "John Kennedy's behavior was unbelievable to me," she recalled. "I never understood the attraction, and I said, 'I don't believe all those stories about him.' And there was a great giggle—every woman in the car had either had an affair or been propositioned by him."[30]

Kennedy's was a phallocentric world. He and the men around him discussed events in terms of the relative safety of their testicles. There were "nut-cutter" situations or "castrating" events to be avoided or survived intact. "He feels like he's been kicked in the balls," Kennedy said of his little brother Teddy after the revelation that he cheated on a Harvard exam.[31] Kennedy's civil rights coordinator, Harris Wofford, recalled that Kennedy ridiculed anyone who advised against the Bay of Pigs invasion by saying they were "grabbing their nuts" in fear.[32] Kennedy habitually used words like *prick* and *fuck* and *nuts* and *bastard* with "an ease that belied his upbringing," Ben Bradlee wrote.[33]

The "females" who were officially part of their lives, their wives and staff, were on the sidelines. They came around sometimes with children or party plans, but they were by and large decorative elements. Cecil Stoughton's White House photographs of the Bradlees sporting with the Kennedys are even more telling than Bradlee's frat-boy prose. On the skeet shooting range, Kennedy took aim while

Jackie Kennedy and Tony Bradlee sat demurely on a bench watching, legs crossed at the knees, sweaters on shoulders. On the golf course, the women sat primly on a golf cart while Ben and Jack walked the greens, swinging clubs. The men rolled with the children on the grass while the women sat nearby, always watching, never acting. Although Jackie was a great rider and an athlete in her own right, when Kennedy was with his male friends Jackie was not involved in their games. Politics was a man's game, too, and she grew to dislike it for a time. At an early campaign event, Bradlee recalled, his own wife, Tony, and Jackie Kennedy "stayed in a stairwell, totally ignored," throughout the speeches.[34]

When Kennedy first encountered Mary Pinchot as the date of his friend Bill Attwood during Kennedy's senior year at Choate, in 1935, as Attwood later recalled, Mary was "the best"—the prettiest girl at the dance. Kennedy kept cutting in on him.[35] Their paths crossed again while Mary was at Vassar and Kennedy dated some of her classmates, and again at the U.N. organizing convention in San Francisco in 1945. Their backgrounds were somewhat similar in terms of wealth and politics. Kennedy's father, Joe, like Amos Pinchot, had been notoriously opposed to U.S. involvement in World War II.

Mary and Kennedy met yet again in Washington while he was still a senator. Her insouciance, an unusual quality in protocol-conscious Washington, was one they had in common. Light irony was her style, and she got his sense of humor. She was his kind of woman. Besides agreeing to house Pam Turnure for a brief period in 1958, Mary saw Kennedy socially in Georgetown with Ben Bradlee when Kennedy was still a senator.[36] After Joe Alsop's impromptu inaugural party, Kennedy's first attendance at a Georgetown supper as president was on January 31, 1961, at Ben and Tony Bradlee's. According to Kennedy secretary Evelyn Lincoln's personal records, Mary Meyer was at that supper party, along with Bradlee's parents and Helen and

Walter Lippmann, although Bradlee did not mention Mary in his account of the dinner in his 1976 book about Kennedy.[37]

The White House relationship between Mary Meyer and President Kennedy was first revealed by journalist James Truitt in 1976, and later corroborated by Ben Bradlee's eyewitness description of Mary's diary and by Tony Bradlee's comments to journalists. Mary apparently told the Truitts about her meetings with the president while they were happening, and Truitt kept notes with dates, times, and details.[38] It is unclear whether Mary knew of or approved of Truitt's note-taking, although she did tell a female friend during this period that she regarded her trysts with Kennedy as interesting history.[39]

Secret Service gate logs and White House social lists document many of Mary Meyer's evening visits to the private residence of the White House, and they corroborate Truitt's account, although Truitt was unaware of the first evening visit in October 1961. White House gate logs show Mary Meyer signed in to see the president at or around 7:30 P.M. on fifteen occasions between October 1961 and August 1963, always when Jackie is known to have been away from Washington, with one exception when Jackie's whereabouts are not verifiable by White House records or news reports. Truitt claimed there were at least thirty White House meetings. The gate logs do not tell the entire story of who was in the White House, because there were other entrances and many occasions when people have said they were inside the White House without being signed in. Frequently a Kennedy retainer such as David F. Powers would sign in at seven-thirty with only the notation "Powers plus one." The fact that Mary Meyer's name is so often entered means she was not hidden and was probably there more often than the logs indicate.

Jim Truitt said the pair also met outside the White House, at houses in Georgetown. He told all to the *National Enquirer*, which published the revelations in 1976. Tony Bradlee then confirmed the liaison to the *Enquirer* but insisted it be called a "fling."[40] In Truitt's account, Mary Meyer's sexual relationship with Kennedy began in early 1962. Gate records and White House social logs indicate Mary was at a White House dance in the late fall of 1961. There, according to Truitt, Kennedy first propositioned her, and she refused.

Kennedy aides, while still clinging to the fiction that Kennedy was always true to his wife, admit Mary Meyer was one of his favorite women and that it was never a surprise for them to find her in the private residence with the president after a workday. White House counsel Myer Feldman recalled that Mary was almost part of the furniture around Kennedy. Unlike with some of the other women—and men—in the White House, the president did not ask her to leave the room when he discussed business. So frequent was her proximity to the president, and so obvious Kennedy's admiration for her, that Feldman felt Mary might make a good conduit to the president's ear if and when Kennedy was unavailable to discuss matters of state with him. Feldman played tennis with her occasionally and remembers that she expressed an interest in his special area, Israel, and in other foreign issues. Kennedy "had a great attachment to her," Feldman said, though he said he never saw any indication that they were lovers. "I'd walk in and out of the office all the time and I would see her in the Oval Office or over in the residence," Feldman recalled. "Around eight-thirty, when the day was over, often I'd walk over to the residence and she'd be sitting there. There wasn't any attempt to hide her the way there was with some of the other women."[41]

Other Kennedy aides were also aware of Mary Meyer's relative status in the president's life. The mere mention of her name was considered helpful for job seekers. Arthur Schlesinger Jr. wrote a two-page memo to Kennedy in December 1962 urging the president to hire historian Trumbull Higgins to write the official White House version of the Bay of Pigs fiasco. Higgins was seeking access to information and had written a letter to Schlesinger. Schlesinger wrote that he thought it might be useful to get the White House account of the crisis recorded before too much time had passed and other versions took precedence. "I know Higgins slightly," Schlesinger wrote. "He is an old friend of Mary Meyer's, who knows him better."[42] Higgins eventually wrote a history of the Bay of Pigs. Longtime Kennedy aide Dave Powers recalled about Mary Meyer that "Jack loved to talk to her and he talked to her about just about anything." Powers said their relationship was "extremely warm," but he too would not describe it as a romantic relationship. "He trusted her and he didn't feel he had to restrict himself around her," Powers said. Powers also corroborated the fact of her presence at private evening parties.[43]

Kennedy aides have publicly insisted that Kennedy was always true to his wife but they were sometimes complicit in delivering women to him. Mary Meyer and other female favorites were usually escorted to evening parties with the president by Kennedy friends and retainers who served as beards. Mary was usually escorted by Bill Walton, a former tough-guy war correspondent who headed the Fine Arts Commission. Walton loved power, art, and society. He was a favorite of Jackie Kennedy and frequently advised her on White House decor. After the president was assassinated, he combed history books to find out how the White House had been draped in mourning after Lincoln was shot and proceeded to array the mansion accordingly.[44]

With Mary at these parties were friends of the president, including Charles Spalding, Bill Thompson, Lem Billings, and Timothy "Ted" Reardon.[45] These men were known around the White House as part of Kennedy's social crowd and they had no official duties within the White House, although Reardon did hold an official post as a presidential aide. Their function was to party with the president, help him relax, and feed him social gossip and jokes.[46] On the nights when she joined them, Mary stayed for the evening and then Kennedy would have a car sent around to pick her up and take her back to Georgetown around or after midnight.

The president's flings and liaisons, including his romance with Mary Meyer, while carefully hidden from the public eye, were no secret to various institutions within and without the government, and as the years of his administration passed, his escapades put him in an increasingly vulnerable position. J. Edgar Hoover collected information on Kennedy and his girlfriends and even had tapes made of his trysts.

Kennedy was in awe of Hoover's information. "Boy, the dirt he has on those senators," Kennedy told Ben Bradlee after one meeting in which Hoover probably discussed FBI information on Kennedy's romps with an East German woman, Ellen Rometsch.[47] This information might have helped Hoover keep his job during the years when Kennedy's friends were urging him to fire the FBI director. It also might have served as leverage when Hoover asked Attorney General Bobby Kennedy for permission to wiretap Martin Luther King Jr.[48] Hoover's arsenal of information on the president included the fact that Kennedy had had an affair with Scandinavian beauty Inga Arvad, a friend of Hitler's during World War II; the fact that Kennedy's father had paid half a million dollars to hush up a threatened breach-of-promise suit by a woman Kennedy had allegedly impregnated; Kennedy's affair with Marilyn Monroe; and his relationship with Rometsch. His affair with Frank Sinatra's friend Judith Campbell ended only after Hoover formally notified Kennedy that the FBI knew of the affair and branded Campbell an associate of hoodlums. Records the FBI has released have not confirmed that Mary Pinchot Meyer was one of the women the FBI investigated, but it is conceivable that her relationship with the president was known to federal agents.

The CIA was also interested in Kennedy's indiscretions, since the potential for blackmail was always a threat to national security. Allen Dulles admitted in 1963 that the CIA used sex as bait in intelligence work. Naturally, the intelligence community believed the KGB employed the same techniques. Information such as Hoover had on Kennedy's sex life was probably collected by James Angleton, as head of the counterintelligence office. No evidence exists that he taped Kennedy or Mary Meyer, but Angleton boasted of it and had already shown his capacity for making surreptitious tapes of unwitting Georgetowners at play when he recorded a dinner party and played it for Dulles's amusement.[49] More dangerously, the Mafia and the Teamsters were also collecting tapes and information about Kennedy's extramarital sex life as a defensive weapon against the administration's crackdown on crime.[50]

In this climate a less reckless man might have curtailed his urges. But Kennedy was not going to be hemmed in. Early in his administration he began devising ways to elude his Secret Service guards. His appetite for women and fun reached a peak in the summer of 1962, the period when Mary Meyer was logged into the White House most frequently for private visits with him, which also coincided with resumed atmospheric testing of nuclear weapons, heightened tensions with the Soviet Union, and dalliances with different women every week.

While Hoover, Angleton, and a variety of other Kennedy-watchers had been aware of Mary Meyer and other women, after Truitt's story about Mary was published in the *National Enquirer* in 1976 the Kennedy entourage was quick to deny it. The vehemence of the denials suggests they felt there was something to hide. Kenneth O'Donnell, for example, told reporters that Mary Meyer was never brought in "through the back door" and that she was not in the White House *only* when Jackie was away.[51] In fact, gate records and phone logs indicate that all but one of Mary's 7:30 P.M. visits occurred when Jackie Kennedy was verifiably away.[52] Kennedy press secretary Pierre Salinger denied that he remembered Mary Meyer at all, even though Ben Bradlee recalled getting a sympathy phone call the day she died from the man the president had nicknamed "Plucky."

Some of these men began late in their lives to respond with a wink and a nod about Kennedy and his women, but they always agreed on one thing: Kennedy's aides did not believe Kennedy was ever intellectually influenced by any woman, including his mother, his wife, or Mary Meyer. Dave Powers said that while Kennedy adored Mary's company, he probably didn't have much use for her opinions—or any other woman's, for that matter. Myer Feldman agreed. "Kennedy could not be swayed by any woman," Feldman said. "He might be called a chauvinist today. He did not think most women were his equal, and that was true of Mary Meyer."[53]

Mary Meyer's friendship with Kennedy was no secret to Jackie Kennedy. The two women were friends themselves. They shared some life experiences, not the least being the death of a child. They had been neighbors in McLean in 1956, when Jackie experienced the stillbirth of her first child while Kennedy was away on a yacht in the Mediterranean. Both had attended Vassar—Jackie five years after Mary—and both women had complicated relationships with their fathers; Jackie's father, "Black Jack" Bouvier, had been an alcoholic roustabout who doted on his daughter but was rarely available to her. They both were molded into women of impeccable speech and manners by cotillions and girls' prep schools. And both had married World War II veterans who were ambitious, powerful players on the national scene.

There, however, the resemblance ended. Mary was private and casual in her personal relationships and relaxed and unassuming in public. Jackie had been thrust onto the public stage by her husband's political career, a situation she both accepted and rejected. She belonged to the world of fashion designers and hunt club members. She enjoyed lavish parties and antique furniture, which she collected to restore the White House. In a famous incident she completely ignored the presence of Martin Luther King Jr. next to her in a White House elevator, so excited was she at the discovery of an antique chair in the basement. Both women were aesthetes, but from vastly different schools. Jackie's taste ran to prerevolutionary France. Mary was thoroughly modern. Rather than become an artist herself, Jackie was the grandest arts patron of them all, bringing the nation's musicians, poets, and artists to Washington and fêting them at White House balls. Many of her friends were people who took pride in their knowledge of art without actually practicing it. Jackie too painted, but unlike Mary Meyer, who was actually trying to paint with the painters and understand the reasons behind the new style, Jackie Kennedy's paintings were old-fashioned albeit witty illustrations. She had a Special Committee for White House Paintings help her select paintings to purchase for the White House; they bought Americana and some of the French impressionists. Her interest in the arts and in White House events such as the dinner for Nobel Prize winners gave the Kennedy administration an aura of high culture, but the president himself was uncomfortable around intellectuals and knew little about art. It is possible Mary Meyer talked to him of her work in the Color School, though. When Jackie showed the president a red, yellow, and blue finger painting by Caroline and pretended it was an abstract painting by William Walton, Kennedy responded with, "Pretty good color."[54]

Jackie Kennedy's greatest triumphs were in the presentation of herself and the pageantry of the White House. The Kennedys hosted sixty-six state receptions during the thousand days of his administration and scores of smaller parties for close friends. One of the most fabulous dinners was the July 1961 state dinner held in honor of Pakistan's President Mohammed Ayub Khan. Jackie hired 150 workers to arrange the event at Mount Vernon, George Washington's estate, a few miles down the Potomac from Washington. The presidential yacht, *Honey Fitz*, and three navy ships ferried 132 guests to the event. Mrs. Kennedy, wearing a white organza dress with a chartreuse sash, greeted them on the lawn, where they drank mint juleps from silver cups and listened to four musical groups including Lester Lanin and the National Symphony. The tables were decorated by Tiffany's and the guests ate French food by candlelight.[55]

Kennedy had married a woman who was above him in class and taste by the standards of the day, and he liked that about her. "There was an awful lot of the Irish mick in him about his attitude toward women," journalist Laura Bergquist said. "In marrying Jackie he in a sense knew that he was outclassed, that he was married above his station. He said to Red [Fay], a longtime Kennedy aide, 'She's everything that a woman ought to be. She's beautiful, she paints.' What she does in short is very graceful and charming and talented. But nothing very major certainly."[56] Robert Kennedy told *Look* magazine: "Jackie has always kept her own identity and been *different*. That's important in a woman. Who wants to come home at night and talk to another version of himself? Jack knows she'll never greet him with 'What's new in Laos?' "[57] Kennedy was awed by his wife's style, her ability to speak French and move among the effete. He told Laura Bergquist she was "romantic by temperament in the old-fashioned sense of the word, fey even."[58] Across the country, college girls took to imitating her breathless little voice. Women copied her sleeveless sheaths and her pillbox hat and her famously bouffant hair. Jackie Kennedy was a natural queen.

Mary Meyer had no equivalent sense of personal grandeur. She had a curiosity about life and the world, and she had never been exposed to the kind of public pressure Jackie had. "Mary was not in the boiler room, and she didn't have to react against politics the way Jackie did," said Marie Ridder, a friend of both women.[59] Mary might have asked Kennedy what was new in Laos. She also had personal simplicity. "She had the style of an artist," recalled Helen Husted. "Everything was beautiful but simple and clean and airy."[60] Her short, windblown hair was never covered with a pillbox hat. Mary Meyer was not immune to the thrill of her nearness to power, but she had not lived her life with a consuming need for it, either. She did not have the financial means to live Jackie's jet-set lifestyle. She borrowed dresses from friends to wear to the White House.

Mary and the other women in Kennedy's stable of girlfriends were never sure exactly how much his wife knew. It was part of Jackie's mystique to seem unconcerned about such matters. "There was some question about why we did this, knowing Jackie," said one woman who was an occasional lover of the president's. "But there was kind of a sense of Jackie felt it was okay. She knew he had this problem."[61] The same woman recalled a particular White House ball in 1962 at which guests were seated at round tables for ten. Jackie had seated this woman on one side of Kennedy and Mary on the other, at a time when both were having occasional romps with him. "I always wondered what that meant, and I'm sure Mary did, too," the woman said.

On another occasion, the March 1961 dinner for eighty, Mary was seated on one side of the president and her sister, Tony Bradlee, on the other, at the same table with Helen Husted, recently divorced from a Russian prince, and the journalists Rowland Evans and his wife, Kay, a close friend of Mary's from Vassar days. The women filled the role once held by dancing girls in the courts of sultans.

They were there to amuse the president visually, conversationally, and in some cases in bed. Usually both the women and the men on the guest list were selected by no one other than his wife. Mary Meyer, much older than the retinue of regular party girls who danced attendance at the Kennedy White House, clearly matched his tastes.

Mary's involvement in the arts might have given Kennedy a more realistic appreciation of American art than his wife's position as a patron did. By 1961 Mary Meyer was a working artist. She had to scrape paint off her skin and from under her fingernails before going to the White House. With the grand opening of the Washington Gallery of Modern Art in 1962, she and other artists finally had a venue for the kind of work they most admired. The gallery was dedicated to the new and it had attracted the financial backing of some of Georgetown's biggest names, including a payload of well-heeled cold warriors and their wives: Attorney General and Mrs. Robert Kennedy, Treasury Secretary and Mrs. Douglas Dillon, Defense Secretary and Mrs. Robert McNamara, Arms Control Director and Mrs. William Foster, Assistant to the President and Mrs. McGeorge Bundy, Assistant Defense Secretary and Mrs. Paul Nitze, Ambassador and Mrs. Chester Bowles, and their journalistic friends Walter Lippmann, Joseph Alsop, Arthur Krock, and others. On the board was Katharine Graham, wife of *Washington Post* publisher Philip Graham.

Tom Wesselmann was just one of twelve artists in the gallery's "Popular Image" show in 1963. Andy Warhol contributed a Campbell's Soup can and four Marilyn Monroe oils in hues he called mint, grape, cherry, and peach. Roy Lichtenstein had submitted a giant cartoon. Claes Oldenburg had a large stuffed canvas called *Big Hamburger* and another called *Bacon, Lettuce and Tomato Sandwich*. Robert Watts hung the decorated dashboard of a Chevrolet, and Vern Blosum had provided a series of paintings of a parking meter with different amounts of time left on it. Robert Rauschenberg and Jasper Johns, the fathers of the pop art movement, were also represented.

The show included Washington's first-ever "happening," called

*Stars: A Farce for Objects.* Designed by Claes Oldenburg and involving twenty-one players, the happening lampooned official Washington and satirized the capital's iconography. One piece was a huge sewn miniature of the Washington Monument moving around by means of seven people huddled inside. One scene involved a very well-endowed naked woman coming down some steps, and included such absurdities as a roller skater, a waiter carrying a tray and spilling colored foam rubber bits, a girl brushing her teeth, two men spraying room deodorant, a woman undulating inside two mattresses, a girl ironing, and a child dishing out blue frosting. It was accompanied by drumbeats and a rendition of "Sweet Leilani." Each action was repeated twenty-four times. It was received with annoyance by the art critic for the *Washington Evening Star*, who found the whole event tedious. The show, he wrote, "will be repeated and repeated and repeated tonight."

That sort of criticism only fueled the sense among the artists of being apart from and above the philistines who shared the city with them. The artists appreciated the fact that the Kennedy White House was art-friendly, but the avant-garde scene was hardly democratic. One either belonged to the aristocracy of consciousness or one did not. Mary belonged. She could also cross the line and be one of the few female White House insiders.

Mary had avoided Washington society throughout her years in McLean. Now, through her relationship with Kennedy, she was at the top of Washington's A-list. Besides seeing the president privately, Mary Meyer was invited to many of the big White House dances and smaller dinners organized by Jackie Kennedy. The dance of the moment was the twist, danced to the tune by Chubby Checker. Phil Graham split the seat of his pants at the White House doing a particularly energetic twist at one party. The twist represented youth and the end of the dreary 1950s. Mary Meyer "knew exactly how to do it, and Jack just adored it," said Helen Husted. "Mary had this sense of perfect taste, and she dared to do things other people wouldn't."[62]

As one of the president's favorites, Mary Meyer was both discreet and nonchalant. She had drinks in the Oval Office, danced in the

Green Room as a guest of both President and Mrs. Kennedy, dined in the private residence, and even—Truitt claimed—left her slip behind only to have it sealed in a White House envelope and returned to her. But very few people understood how close she was to Kennedy. She told Kary Fischer about her frequent dinners with the president and observed to him that she didn't believe all the women who said they'd had flings with Kennedy. "She seemed to think that more often than not he had these women over to talk, to test out his ideas on them," Fischer said. "She felt his relations with women were exaggerated."

But Mary also believed Kennedy and not the First Lady was responsible for her many invitations to White House events. "She rather liked it, being put on display by the president of the United States," Fischer said. Mary told him her relationship with Jackie was not warm and that Jackie did not particularly enjoy the fact that her husband was so fond of both Mary and her sister, Tony. "She never felt Jackie had any feeling for her," Fischer said. "Mary liked to have some kind of conversation with people, in the metaphorical sense, and she did not have that with Jackie. Jackie was impenetrable."[63]

All of Washington was dying to be part of the new in crowd, and she was there. She was more inside than most men, including her ex-husband, who would never find his name on a White House guest list even though he was at the very pinnacle of the intelligence community. When Kennedy was elected, Cord Meyer had hoped that his long wait in bureaucratic obscurity during the Eisenhower years would end with the advent of a Democratic administration. But that was not to be. The bad blood between him and Kennedy precluded that, as did the president's apparent fascination with his ex-wife.

First Cord tried for a diplomatic post. Jim Angleton asked Ben Bradlee to recommend Cord to Kennedy as ambassador to Guatemala. But Bradlee, who disliked Cord Meyer and for whom the feeling was returned (probably as a result of Bradlee's role in the European husband-dumping trip), never passed on the recommendation to Kennedy. Bradlee later wrote that he knew Kennedy did not like Cord and neither did he, owing to Cord Meyer's "derisive scorn for the people's right to know."[64] In the book where he mentions his and Kennedy's dislike for Cord, he fails to mention the anecdote, widely discussed in Georgetown, about the night a drunken Cord Meyer lunged for Bradlee's neck across a dinner table.[65]

As chief of the CIA's International Organizations Division, Cord Meyer sometimes met personally with Kennedy and his staff. Cord might have been involved in the anti-Castro plots, although his direct involvement was not revealed in public documents available as of 1997. He was certainly aware of them. In his private journal he described a 1960 meeting with a man named Pepe Figueres (probably José Figueres, president of Costa Rica, whose nickname was "Don Pepe") at which they "talked about what to do about Castro/Trujillo."[66] He met often with Robert Kennedy after the Bay of Pigs. In October 1961 President Kennedy called Cord into the Oval Office to privately ask how to gain agency support for replacing CIA director Dulles with John McCone. Cord came away from that meeting feeling Kennedy was "much more serious and less arrogant than I'd known him before."[67]

Cord was aware as early as October 1961 of Kennedy's interest in his ex-wife. Jim Angleton was paying keen attention to the young president's personal life and he had obliquely warned his old friend, although it doesn't appear he told Cord all he knew at the time. He later told Joan Bross, whose husband, John, was a high-ranking CIA official, that his bugging revealed that when Kennedy first called Mary, she went to the White House and found herself alone, and she asked to be taken home again. In his journal, Cord wrote that Angleton had told him Mary "baffles" Kennedy and that even with money and power, Kennedy "still yearns for a respect that eludes him from such as myself."[68]

Cord eventually became troubled by the situation, although he never grasped the real nature of the relationship between his ex-wife and the President. In a long and melancholy journal entry in 1963 in which he listed his problems one by one, he wrote of "the peculiar relationship that exists between me and the President." Charles Bartlett, a mutual friend of Cord and the president, had spoken to

Kennedy about a political appointment for Cord but "was told by JFK that due to some incident that occurred at the U.N. conference in San Francisco in 1945 there was no possibility."[69]

Cord was always confused when Kennedy inexplicably seemed to know details of his personal life and plans. Cord noted in his journal that Kennedy had "learned, how I don't know, that I was thinking of leaving the government to take up freelance journalism. Kennedy said if the roles were reversed he would do the same thing. . . . To this strange competitiveness, he adds a curiosity about and interest in my private life that I find unexplainable, even to the point of asking about a bathing suit that was sent anonymously to someone and that I returned to Mary, thinking it was hers."[70]

Still, Cord savored his rare closeness to the center of world power. In a letter to Quentin dated August 1, 1962, he wrote, "I did get a chance to go up to Camp David and see the bed where Khrushchev slept and play on Eisenhower's little golf course."[71]

Mary let Cord know she communicated with Kennedy on a more intimate level than did he. On one occasion Mary told him that Kennedy believed Cord had difficulty addressing him as "Mr. President" upon first meeting him after the inauguration. "So by these signs and portents I conclude that a public career is closed to me so long as he remains in office," Cord wrote in his journal.[72] Even without hope of getting a position, Cord did not give up. He jockeyed for a position in the social world around Kennedy. During most of the Kennedy years he dated a young woman named Jill Cowen, one of the two women in the Kennedy White House nicknamed "Fiddle and Faddle." The other was Patricia Weir. The two Baltimore-born socialites assisted Pierre Salinger and Evelyn Lincoln, respectively. In their pumps, Jackie-styled hair, and tight skirts and jackets, the two young women were the objects of endless salacious speculation about their real positions vis-à-vis the president.

Mary and Kennedy were friends before, during, and after the period during which they were romantically involved. Truitt thought the sexual interval in their relationship began in 1962. In early 1962 Kennedy was coming off what his brother Bobby called "a very mean year." The new year began on a much more upbeat note, with the animated Mary Meyer as his occasional bedmate and frequent dinner companion. The beginning of what would be his fling with Mary Meyer also coincided with a heating up of the cold war. Kennedy's threatening rhetoric in 1961 had caused the Russians to become alarmed. On Veterans Day 1961 Kennedy had asserted the United States was ready to face war. "There is no way to maintain the frontiers of freedom without cost and commitment and risk," he said. "There is no swift and easy path to peace in our generation."[73]

The threat of nuclear war became more real than ever in 1962. In February Kennedy's defense secretary, Robert McNamara, secretly told senators the American nuclear force could survive a surprise attack. By late March, Kennedy had told Stewart Alsop the United States was prepared to initiate nuclear war if necessary.[74] This severely damaged U.S.-Soviet relations. Kennedy continued to boast of American nuclear superiority. In this atmosphere, there was no chance the Russians were going to allow on-site inspections for a test ban treaty. With the Russians testing atomic weapons, Kennedy's aides advised him to prepare to start testing the weapons again.

On the night of April 25, 1962, American nuclear bombs were exploded over Christmas Island, the first such tests since 1958 and the first of forty tests over the following six months. *Life* magazine described the scene as tourists in Hawaii lined up on the beaches to watch the atomic spectacle over the Pacific. "The blue-black tropical night suddenly turned into a hot lime green. It was brighter than noon. The green changed into a lemon pink . . . and finally, terribly, blood red. It was as if someone had poured a bucket of blood on the sky."[75]

Diverting attention from the terrifying displays of fire and warlike rhetoric was the parade of intimate dinners and glamorous fêtes at the White House. The charred images of atomic warfare hovered over the festivities like the plague in "The Masque of the Red

Death," Edgar Allan Poe's short story. At one of these dances, if Truitt is correct, Kennedy first propositioned Mary.

On the raw fall night of November 11, 1961, the Kennedys hosted a dinner-dance for more than eighty in honor of Mrs. Kennedy's sister, Princess Lee Radziwill. (The Kennedys often tried to find people to "honor" as excuses for their parties, and sometimes it backfired. In one case the honorees actually thought they were supposed to invite their own friends. The Kennedys had to disinvite some of their own favorite people, including Mary Meyer.)[76] All of Georgetown was invited, including a number of the women the president enjoyed seeing privately. The candlelight did wonders for female guests such as Anne Chamberlin and Mary Meyer, nearly twenty years out of Vassar and suddenly glowing regulars at the hottest parties in the nation. Fashion designers, journalists, politicians, and diplomats tippled and danced until the wee hours, serenaded by strolling musicians and escorted through the corridors of the White House by solicitous men in uniform. The guests dined on duck and did the twist to the Marine Corps Band and Lester Lanin's orchestra. A pre-party *Post* item about the event was reverential: "The last time there was a White House dinner dance for Lee Radziwill, the richest, brainiest, wittiest, prettiest couples of the Kennedys' acquaintances were gathered—with international set names rubbing elbows with working newspapermen—for merry-making against the background of historic White House grandeur. The chandeliers gleamed long into the night."

Mary refused that night's advance, according to Truitt. Ten weeks later, on January 22, 1962, with Jackie away at Glen Ora, the refurbished Virginia estate where she escaped from Washington, Kennedy's offer to send a White House limousine to Mary's townhouse proved irresistible. Kennedy had attended Sunday morning mass in Washington, helicoptered to Glen Ora, and then choppered back from Virginia the next day, leaving his wife and children at the estate. Monday night, "Mrs. Meyers" was signed into the White House by Evelyn Lincoln to see the president at 7:30 P.M.[77]

Apparently based on what Mary herself had told him, Truitt believed that this winter night was the night Mary became one of the president's lovers. Earlier that morning, with Jackie still away in the country, her mother, Mrs. Hugh Auchincloss, had substituted as White House hostess to sixty wives of governors of the Stock Exchange Association who had come to see the new White House decor.[78]

In February 1962, the Kennedys hosted another White House dinner-dance to which Mary was invited. Jackie Kennedy invited everybody who was anybody and the president personally scrutinized the guest list, dropping people he thought shouldn't be invited and suggesting other names.[79] Tony and Ben and possibly Mary Meyer dined first at Bill Walton's; then the sisters and Ben went to the White House, where the dance was under way in honor of Stephen and Jean Kennedy Smith. Bradlee, like the rest of Washington, was awed by the scene, which he described as "a dazzling mixture of 'beautiful people' from New York, jet-setters from Europe, politicians, reporters (always reporters) who are friends and Kennedy relatives. The crowd is always young. The women are always gorgeous, and you have to pinch yourself."[80] During that dance, Kennedy fed Bradlee the story of the return to America of U2 pilot Gary Powers, and Bradlee called it in from the White House to the *Washington Post* for the morning's paper, a major scoop.

That dance lasted until 4:30 A.M., and the next day Kennedy and Bradlee rehashed the evening with copious appraisals of the women. Bradlee recalled: "The conversation ended, as these conversations often ended, with his views on some of the women present—the overall appeal of the daughter of Prince Paul of Yugoslavia and Mary Meyer. 'Mary would be rough to live with,' Kennedy noted, not for the first time. And I agreed, not for the first time."[81]

In a brief interview in 1997 Bradlee tried to explain that remark. "Mary was a very independent woman, not like the other women then, who would usually do whatever the men wanted to do. She did what she wanted to do and that was unusual. So she would have been rough to live with by the standards of the day. Not a pain in the ass, just difficult."[82] Bradlee has always insisted he had no idea at the time that Kennedy and Mary were intimately involved with each other.

Another dance that spring for thirty-five people in honor of economist and ambassador to India John Kenneth Galbraith took place on the same day the *New York Herald Tribune* reported Harvard doctors' prediction that the nation's physicians could not cope with a nuclear attack. Publishing their findings in the *New England Journal of Medicine*, the doctors predicted that 2.2 million people, including most of the medical professionals, would die in a firestorm in the Boston area alone in the event of a nuclear attack.

That evening Jackie choppered in from Glen Ora to host the private dinner. Mary Meyer was one of the guests.

During the summer and fall of 1962 Mary was logged into the White House frequently—in one case, several times in a week—while Jackie was away on a three-month vacation that included stays in Virginia, Newport, Cape Cod, and Rome. The routine at the White House was always the same. Mary arrived at around 7:30 P.M., often delivered by a White House driver, after having been phoned by the president or one of his aides earlier in the day. She was ushered into a private dinner with the president. The dinners sometimes included other guests, usually Kennedy's close male buddies Kenneth O'Donnell and Dave Powers, sometimes Representative Torbert MacDonald, a Kennedy buddy from his congressional days. Pam Turnure has said that when he got together with his Boston Irish pals, Kennedy cut loose and sang Irish songs with them.[83]

When Mary and Kennedy ate dinner with a group in the private residence, conversation revolved around politics and Washington gossip; state secrets of the Castro-assassination variety were not discussed. Kennedy might have met with Cord Meyer and his CIA colleagues earlier in the day, but the subjects and the meetings stayed off the record. The rest of the White House staff derisively called Kennedy's dinner pals his "social retainers," men who did not involve themselves in the real business of the White House.[84] After dinner the men would retire, leaving Mary alone with the president.[85] Frequently she would call his private phone line the day after the dinner, and they would talk.[86]

The Kennedy aides were correct that Mary Meyer was not a surreptitious guest at the White House. She was never as hidden as some of Kennedy's other girlfriends, whose names were not even entered in the official logs.[87] But discretion was always observed when Mary visited the White House. The true nature of her relationship with the president was not obvious to the other dinner guests. Those who were not in on the secret could be confused by the refined woman so incongruously present among the ribald Kennedy retainers. Banker James Reed, a Kennedy friend, recalled that at one of the intimate dinners with Kennedy he concluded Mary was there as an extra single woman and that Kennedy was trying to "fix me up with this beautiful woman."[88]

The private evening visits were random. Sometimes they coincided with historic events or statements; other times Mary was merely a pleasant diversion after a long day of mundane ceremonial events. Sometimes the visits were preceded by private telephone calls, also logged by Kennedy's secretary. On March 13, 1962, Mary called the White House and was transferred to the president. On March 15, 1962, with Jackie away on her famous visit to India, Mary signed in for an evening with the president. That afternoon Kennedy gave a press conference and answered one of the first questions about shipping arms to Laos. That night he called the Secret Service at 11:50 P.M. for a car to pick up "Mrs. Meyer" at the South Gate.[89]

By the time their relationship began, Kennedy was physically a study in contrasts. He exuded vigor on TV but suffered from a life-threatening disease and excruciating back pain. He sometimes used a cane and crutches. Seeking cures for the pain, Kennedy was open to a variety of experimental drugs and treatments. His doctors tried unapproved treatments on him, and when they worked he continued them whether they were sanctioned or not. One of his doctors, Max Jacobson, went by the nickname "Dr. Feelgood" because of his talent for devising injected cocktails of vitamins and speed that rejuvenated the weary jet setters. His patients included Truman Capote and Eddie Fisher. He frequently taught them how to inject themselves, using oranges for practice.[90] He later experimented with LSD on his patients.[91]

Some writers have wondered about the effects of these drugs on Kennedy during crucial episodes during his administration. When Kennedy met Khrushchev in Vienna, the president had been severely hampered by his back pain. Throughout the course of the summit he not only received regular procaine injections, but may have also been injecting himself with Dr. Feelgood's amphetamine cocktails. Historian Michael Beschloss has written a sympathetic analysis of the Vienna episode. Kennedy "found himself locked into a summit with Khrushchev, doubled over with pain, and surrounded by advisors admonishing him to extinguish any suspicion Khrushchev had that he might be soft or indecisive on Berlin or other matters." Under such circumstances, with the fate of Western civilization believed to be at stake, injections of speed would have seemed no more morally repugnant than a couple of aspirins.[92]

On the evening of July 16, 1962, "Mrs. Myers" was signed in for an appointment with the president at 7:30 P.M.[93] Kennedy had returned that day after spending the weekend on Cape Cod, where Jackie and the children were to remain throughout July.[94] That morning the head of the Business and Professional Women's Federation had again blasted the president in the press for failing to appoint women to his cabinet. Color television pictures were beamed across the Atlantic via satellite for the first time that night.[95] That evening, according to Truitt, Kennedy and Mary smoked marijuana together.

The White House was due to hold a conference on narcotics in a few weeks, and the irony was not lost on Kennedy, who mentioned it to Mary. Jim Truitt claimed he himself provided Mary with the pot. The president smoked three of the six joints Mary brought to him. At first he felt no effects. Then he closed his eyes and refused a fourth joint. "Suppose the Russians did something now," he said.[96] Kennedy then told Mary the pot "isn't like cocaine," and told her he would get her some of that.[97] White House phone logs for the next day indicate Mary Meyer was the first caller on the morning log to the president, at 6:43 A.M., followed by two calls from Mrs. Kennedy.[98]

The pot-smoking story received much ink after the *Enquirer* published Truitt's account in 1976. But pot, as every antidrug message would warn Americans for years to come, was only the top of a very slippery slope; Mary's visits to Timothy Leary during the time she was also Kennedy's lover suggest that Kennedy knew more about hallucinogenic drugs than the CIA might have been telling him. No one has ever confirmed that Kennedy tried LSD with Mary. But the timing of her visits to Timothy Leary do coincide with the dates of her known private meetings with the president. Angleton later said Mary took one low dose of LSD with Kennedy after which, Angleton said, "they made love." Angleton said he got this information out of Mary Meyer's diary.[99]

No one has ever corroborated Truitt's account of the drug use, or even speculated on how people who were not regular drug users might keep their eyes open after inhaling three joints in a single evening. If Kennedy did experiment with drugs, his aides had no idea about it. Former Kennedy aide Myer Feldman finds the very notion of Kennedy using recreational drugs completely out of character. "He never drank more than a glass of wine," Feldman said. "And he was a control freak."[100] Journalist Hugh Sidey also recalled that Kennedy avoided strong drink and occasionally told journalists that he had enough trouble maintaining his energy and control without using alcohol.[101] On the other hand, Kennedy was not averse to using drugs that hadn't been approved by the FDA as long as they made him feel better. He was so enamored of Dr. Feelgood's shots that, according to Secret Service agent Larry Newman, "After lunch, he was done for the day if he didn't have a boost."[102]

The private evenings continued through the summer of 1962 while Jackie remained away from Washington. On July 30 "Mary Meyers" arrived at the southwest gate of the White House with Kennedy friend Bill Thompson for a seven-thirty dinner with the president. A week later she was with Kennedy on August 6, the night after Marilyn Monroe killed herself in Los Angeles.[103] The suicide by pills intimately involved the Kennedys. Marilyn had been close to their brother-in-law Peter Lawford, and Lawford had introduced her to the Kennedy brothers and arranged their meetings. Published reports have linked both the president and his brother Bobby with the blond actress.

The star's suicide was one of those private crises that made all the other craziness of Kennedy's life stand out in bold relief. At the White House on August 6, with Marilyn Monroe's death the banner headline in all the papers, telephone records indicate mob moll Judith Campbell called for the president from Los Angeles in midafternoon and was told no by Evelyn Lincoln, indicating Kennedy was not taking her calls. "Mrs. Mary Myer" called a little later and left her number. Judith Campbell called again that evening shortly before Mary Meyer was logged in, and phone records indicate Mrs. Lincoln again put her off, telling her the president was in a conference. That evening, while Mary was with Kennedy at the White House, Mrs. Kennedy called from New York at 7:50 and was told the president was out. At quarter to nine, Peter Lawford, in the thick of the suicide story by virtue of having spoken with Marilyn just before she died (reports claim he was talking to her when she passed out), called Kennedy from Beverly Hills and got through. At 11:28 Kennedy called for a car to be sent to the South Gate, presumably to take Mary home.[104]

As the summer passed, the situation with the Soviets reached a critical level. Threats and counterthreats had made Cuba the crisis point. Meanwhile, the evening meetings with Mary and other women increased. On nights when Mary was not at the small White House dinners with the president, other women with whom Kennedy has been linked arrived on the arm of one of the retainers or alone. Their presence, and Mary's, were recorded on White House gate logs in notations of "Dave Powers plus one" or "William Walton plus one" at the usual social hour of seven-thirty. There are several dozen such entries throughout the summer of 1962 and into early 1963.[105]

Another of Mary's White House visits that summer coincided with a memorable crisis. Domestically, race tension and violence were rampant in the American South as civil rights workers clashed with white racists all summer long. On September 30, 1962, the situation exploded. That day an attempt to integrate the University of Mississippi by bringing James Meredith to register resulted in a six-hour riot that killed a London newspaper correspondent and a resident of Oxford, Mississippi, and wounded scores of others. In his last dispatch, the British correspondent, Paul Guihard, reported by phone that the crowd sang "Dixie," and a banner was unfurled from one of the college windows proclaiming "A black America will lose its greatness." The correspondent described the growing frenzy: "The mob sings and laughs under the hot October sun and from the first minute one realizes that this mob is completely unconscious of the enormity of its gesture."[106] Kennedy went on television and spoke about the race violence for nine minutes that night, asking for order. Kennedy addressed white Mississippians directly, appealing to their sense of honor. "You have a great tradition to uphold," he said. "The eyes of the nation and all the world are upon you."[107]

Kennedy stayed up until dawn the next day with his brother and staff trying to address the crisis. That night, October 1, Mary Meyer was logged in for a dinner with Kennedy.[108] While she was at the White House, Mississippi's segregationist governor, Ross Barnett, who had been urging Mississippians via TV and radio broadcasts not to "surrender," spoke on national television to accuse the federal government of inciting the violence. "The responsibility for this unwarranted breach of the peace and violence in Mississippi rests directly with the President," Barnett said.[109]

The fall of 1962 closed an era of reckless fun for the president. The final sobering event came in October, when Kennedy learned that the Russians had delivered missiles to Cuba. Kennedy's response brought the world closer to nuclear war than it had ever been. By then Jackie had returned to the White House.

Mary Meyer remained on the First Lady's A-list. On October 10, 1962, one day after Jackie returned from her three-month holiday, the First Lady threw a small dinner party for eight at the White House, where guests ate rockfish soufflé ambassade as a main course and drank a 1959 Pouilly-Fumé, a 1955 Château Mouton Rothschild, and a 1952 Dom Pérignon. Anne and James Truitt were two of the invited guests, along with Bill Walton and Mary.[110]

On the night of October 22, 1962, Mrs. Kennedy hosted a small dinner party that included Mary Meyer, Bill Walton, and Mrs. Kennedy's favorite designer, Oleg Cassini, among others. The assembled dined on sole Hortensia, *canard à l'orange*, wild rice, *épinards aux croutons*, and *soufflé au chocolat*, accompanied by a 1959 Pouilly-Fumé, a 1955 Château Hautbrion, and a 1955 Piper Heidsieck.[111] An hour before joining the guests, Kennedy went on national television to announce that the United States planned to blockade Russian ships heading toward Cuba unless the missiles were removed. The statement was taken as a declaration of war, and for several days the world was on the brink of annihilation. Millions watched on October 24 as American television cameras showed Russian ships steaming toward a line of demarcation in the ocean, beyond which Kennedy had promised to stop them. A television announcer's voice choked with emotion as he counted down the miles and waited for U.S. ships to open fire. They did not. Other Russian ships did not approach the line.

Behind the scenes, a series of tense meetings between the Soviet ambassador and Robert Kennedy had been under way during the middle of the night, invisible to newsmen and other diplomats.[112] Through that back channel Kennedy was able to secretly agree to remove U.S. missiles from Turkish bases in exchange for the public

Russian removal of missiles from Cuba. The missiles were removed with much relief on all sides, ending an episode that made Kennedy look tough and uncompromising with the Soviets.

The crisis had changed his thinking. He knew, though the American public was unaware of it, that his repeated talk of American nuclear superiority had helped push the Soviets into the Cuban missile response. His machismo and Khrushchev's bullying had almost obliterated the planet. During the second week of the crisis he told the British ambassador that something had to be done about the nuclear situation "because this is just too much."[113] During that week in October he had asked Jackie to clear the evening schedule and make sure she was home so he could spend time with his children. The awesome responsibility of his position and the effects of his nuclear brinkmanship had hit home.

That fall and winter the glowing White House balls and dinners continued, and Mary Meyer remained on the guest list. One week in November she was at the White House two nights in a row, once for an informal dinner whose guests included Isaiah Berlin and Joe Alsop and then at a dinner-dance for fifty.[114]

At some point the affair between Mary and Kennedy cooled into friendship. The end of 1962 was a transitional period for Kennedy. The cares of office, particularly the Cuban missile crisis, had sobered and deepened him. He talked more about the world's children and his responsibility to see that they did not perish in a thermonuclear war.

In January 1963 an event occurred that surely alarmed Mary and worried the president. *Washington Post* publisher Phil Graham, suffering from alcoholism and manic-depression, had broken the unwritten code of Washington journalists and mentioned Mary Meyer's affair with John F. Kennedy at a convention of American newspaper editors in Phoenix. Graham had attended the convention without being invited to speak. In the middle of the proceedings he stumbled to the podium, grabbed the microphone, and began a rambling tirade that included a story about the president's "new favorite," Mary Meyer. It is a testament to the discretion of the newspaper editors in those days and their unquestioning reverence for the highest office in the land that not one newspaper carried a whisper of Graham's revelation. Perhaps the fact that Graham was also taking off his clothes onstage affected his credibility with the editors. In any case, the outburst by the consummate Washington insider was deemed so astonishing and such a threat to the status quo that the White House itself provided a government jet to get Graham's doctors to him quickly. Back in Washington, Graham was committed to the care of a private mental institution.[115] Later that year he shot himself to death. It is possible that the Graham outburst prompted Mary and Kennedy to break off their relationship.

Blair Clark, then vice president of CBS News, was Mary's escort to a White House dance on a snowy night in the last winter of Kennedy's presidency. Clark had met Mary in Paris on her husband-dumping tour and was pleased to be asked to escort her. He had no clue that the woman he was squiring to the ball was actually one of the president's mistresses. Clark noticed nothing out of the ordinary at the dance except that Mary wore a pastel chiffon dress very much out of season when there was still snow on the ground, and that she disappeared in the middle of the evening for an hour or two. "I finally caught up with her and found the bottom of her ball gown was sort of wet and she looked a little odd. I said, 'Mary, where have you been?' I can still see the bedraggled bottom of her dress. She said, 'I've been out walking around the White House.' I said, 'In the snow?' I remember thinking she must have been upset, although I have no memory of her not being in control of herself." The party lasted until past three in the morning, and Clark and Mary and the Bradlees were among the last to leave. Kennedy and Jackie saw them off at the front portico of the White House, everyone teetering a bit from the effects of the endless bottles of champagne. "That night he told her they were through," Clark said he was later told by purveyors of Kennedy gossip.[116]

Without Mary's diary, it is impossible to know for certain whether that night or another event marked the end of the sexual part of the relationship. In 1963 Kennedy and Mary stayed in touch, sometimes talking on the telephone and occasionally seeing each other in the White House residence when Jackie was out of town. Mary was one of a small number of guests invited to a birthday party Jackie threw for the president in May aboard a yacht floating in the Potomac. At least once Mary was the first person Kennedy wanted to see after being away. She dined with him the night of July 3, 1963, on the day he had returned at two in the morning from a ten-day European trip. She spent two private evenings with Kennedy in June 1963: on June 12, the day civil rights leader Medgar Evers was shot, and again two days later. That weekend she and Marian Schlesinger played tennis on the White House courts. She dined privately with Kennedy in August 1963, two days after *Post* president and mutual friend Phil Graham shot himself.[117]

As his presidency wore on, Kennedy retired from some of his congressional romping ways. The furtive ducking into closets and lunches with nymphets in the White House swimming pool became less frequent. But unlike the actresses and secretaries, Mary made the transition from plaything to family friend. She kept up a cordial relationship with Jackie Kennedy. When Mrs. Kennedy's last pregnancy ended with her son Patrick dying several days after a premature birth, Mary Meyer sent off a handwritten letter of sympathy on stationery with her mother's New York address. "Dear Jackie," she wrote in her rounded, left-leaning handwriting, "Anything that I write seems too little—but nothing that I feel seems too much. I am so so so very sorry."[118]

In the fall of 1963, just two months before he was assassinated, Kennedy undertook a precampaign trip through the western states to talk about conservation. His first stop was Milford, Pennsylvania, and Grey Towers, where he accepted the old stone château and hundreds of acres of the grounds as a gift from the Pinchot family to the U.S. Forest Service. The official donor was Mary's cousin, Gifford Bryce

Pinchot. Kennedy insisted that the Pinchot sisters fly from Washington to Milford with him. They landed at a military base near Newburgh, New York, and helicoptered into Milford. Film of the event captured the two Pinchot sisters standing on a bunting-draped dais among other dignitaries. As the president walked past them and the crowd began to roar at the sight of him, Mary appeared to be laughing and cast a sidelong look at her sister Tony, who primly stared straight ahead, unwilling to share the private joke.[119]

In his remarks, Kennedy referred to Amos Pinchot several times, even though the late Governor Gifford Pinchot, renowned as a conservationist, was the main subject of his speech. He dedicated the grounds to "the greater knowledge of the land and its uses" and christened Grey Towers and the donated grounds the Pinchot Institute for Conservation Studies. The old stone house soon became a financial burden on the Forest Service as the cost of its upkeep far exceeded its value as a tourist attraction, but it remained in government hands and still served as a center for the study of conservation and forestry in 1997.[120] After his speech, Kennedy insisted on visiting the little house where the Pinchot sisters had spent so many summers. Ruth Pickering Pinchot was by then a rabid conservative and Goldwater supporter, but she welcomed him cordially. A photographer snapped Kennedy standing with the elderly Mrs. Pinchot, Tony, and Mary at the steps of the little house. Ben Bradlee described the photo as "one of history's stiffest set of smiles." Yet Mary, in her dark glasses and yellow coat with a scarf knotted at her neck, was still grinning broadly. Afterward, the president looked at baby pictures of Tony and Mary with their mother.[121]

In the following week Kennedy traveled with the press corps to the western states, where the scheduled topic was conservation. But at a stop in Montana, Kennedy was surprised at the fervent crowd reaction he received when he mentioned the passage of the nuclear test ban treaty. Realizing he had struck a popular note with the bomb-fearing American populace, he spent the rest of the trip extolling the virtues of disarmament.[122] The western trip concluded with a wild party in Las Vegas organized by Frank Sinatra and Peter Lawford.[123]

On November 22 news of the president's death reached Washington minutes after the shooting. Shocked Georgetowners congregated at each other's homes in front of the television. Many of Mary's friends huddled at the Bradlees' house on N Street as the awful news unfolded.[124] But the only record of Mary's behavior and feelings that day is a single telephone call to the White House, logged by Kennedy's personal secretary at 5:14 P.M.—long after the president had died—and including her return phone number.[125] That night Ben and Tony Bradlee went to the White House to be taken to Bethesda Naval Hospital, to greet Jackie Kennedy in her bloodstained pink suit.

The following Monday, Mary and Tony attended the president's funeral in St. Matthew's Cathedral, a light-colored stone church in downtown Washington. Afterward the sisters joined the long funeral procession to Arlington National Cemetery.[126]

After Kennedy's assassination, Mary Meyer went back to her routine with a vengeance. She continued her therapeutic daily walks and put in hours at her studio. She felt, she told Kary Fischer, a great concern about what Kennedy's assassination said about the human condition. "I remember sitting with her a little after his death and she asking me with great urgency what I thought of it. She wasn't crying, but she was not far from tears. She wanted to know how to deal with it, what it meant. She wasn't looking for a political explanation; she was looking for some bigger, wider explanation having to do with fate. I remember her inability to fathom the violence. It was more than a personal loss for her. I remember saying I thought here was a punk, rejected by all, looking for a golden boy, the one upon whom all riches and power and beauty had been bestowed, as his victim. And she seemed to agree with that." Fischer said Mary, like most Americans at the time, accepted the idea that Oswald was the lone assassin.[127]

Around this time folk singer Pete Seeger was popular, and Mary was particularly enamored of one of his songs, "Where Have All the Flowers Gone?" which would become the antiwar anthem of Vietnam protesters in the next few years. She asked Fischer to try to find the album for her, which he did. She began turning out many canvases during this time. She told Fischer she wanted to give him a painting, but so great was her sense of inadequacy and the constant need for improvement that she was never able to decide which one he ought to take home. Fischer acquired one only after she died.[128]

Some writers have speculated that Mary Meyer was the one mistress for whom President Kennedy really had deep and lasting affection and an intellectual connection. Followers of Timothy Leary who regard Mary Meyer as a capital-city pioneer of the drug culture have gone further and suggested that it was to her credit that Kennedy became more interested in nuclear disarmament and rapprochement with Cuba toward the end of his life.[129] While his sexual relationship with Mary was under way, Kennedy was still carrying on relationships with many other women, but there is certainly truth to the notion that she meant more to him than most of the women with whom he was on intimate terms. James Angleton, when asked by journalists in the 1980s how Kennedy could have felt strongly about Mary and still carried on affairs with other women, replied, "There's a difference between sex and love."[130]

Friends of Mary who knew her during the Kennedy years do not believe she was seriously in love with the president. "She was over forty years old and the president wanted her in his bed," said one friend.[131] "She was having fun." Another woman who was simultaneously involved with Kennedy for occasional trysts recalled that she and Mary both had "real lives" apart from the glamorous playpen of the White House and were pursuing serious relationships with other men. But if Mary had another lover during this time, her friends were not aware of him. The Kennedy affair "was kind of an adventure."[132] Although some of Mary's close friends at the time were not in on the secret, one felt that in hindsight there were clues. "I was not surprised about the affair, though she never spoke of it," said one Georgetown friend who spent a great deal of time with Mary during the summers of 1962 and 1963. "There were many interesting moments of 'Well, I don't think I can go to the movies this evening, I might have something going on.' I sort of wondered what she was doing hanging around Washington in the summer."[133]

President and Mrs. Kennedy exemplified a certain ideal of postwar America. Mary Meyer was closer to the female reality. She had endured some unfulfilling years as a suburban CIA wife and embarked on an odyssey of escape. An extramarital fling with the president of the United States was part of her awakening. With her short blond hair, dark glasses, and pedal pushers, she was a bit like Jean Seberg in *Breathless*, a well-bred ingenue out looking for fun and getting into trouble along the way. Mary Meyer was a risk taker. The nonchalant artist and pleasure seeker inside her were amused by her access to Kennedy. But the other Mary Meyer—the half-sister of Rosamund, the teenager who craved glamour, and the Vassar graduate who sought to distinguish herself in a dramatic way—must have been more than amused. She was probably thrilled to the marrow. For all her modern independence, she was still Amos's daughter and in awe of powerful men.

Women as a group made some political gains during Kennedy's presidency. His administration presided over one of the milestones in working women's battle against sex discrimination with the Equal Pay Act, signed into law in 1963. The Equal Pay Act had limited effect—it mandated equal pay only for women doing work equal to what men were doing, ignoring the majority of women in sex-segregated jobs. But it marked the entrance of the federal government into the business of safeguarding women's employment rights.[134] Kennedy also established a Commission on the Status of Women, which in its final report emphasized equal opportunity for working women.

Kennedy genuinely enjoyed the company of women who amused him, but that didn't translate into rewarding women with jobs in his administration. His ten Senate-confirmed appointments of women were five fewer than those made by Eisenhower or Truman.[135] His record of placing women in political posts was no better than that of previous administrations, a great disappointment to his many female political supporters. Democratic women's organizer Katie Louchheim and other women who had worked for Kennedy in the campaign gave lists of names of women to Ralph Dungan, who was in charge of finding appointees for the administration, but Dungan claimed never to have seen them.[136] From that, Louchheim concluded: "I think they had a healthy disregard for what women could accomplish or contribute." Louchheim was rewarded for her campaign efforts with the post of special consultant to the assistant secretary of state for educational and cultural affairs.

A case can be made that the most significant role women had in the Kennedy administration—other than the obvious social and less obvious sexual ones—was in unofficial service as couriers or undeclared lobbyists. Judith Campbell was only the most notorious example of a woman in the role of courier and presidential girlfriend. The voluptuous California brunette was apparently an unwitting messenger between the administration and the anti-Castro mobsters. White House phone logs indicate Kennedy was still getting calls from Judith Campbell long after J. Edgar Hoover had informed Kennedy the FBI considered her to be an "associate of hoodlums." Campbell has publicly acknowledged ferrying yellow manila envelopes to the president from mobsters.[137]

Journalist Anne Chamberlin was another prominent female whose relationship with the president was probably chaste but who served in unofficial friendly ways. Ken Noland believed she might have arranged some meetings between Kennedy and her friend Mary outside the White House.[138] According to Myer Feldman, Kennedy asked Chamberlin to discover the sources of negative articles written by her fellow reporters, particularly from the unfriendly southern newspapers.[139]

Another female who played a messenger role of some interest was ABC reporter Lisa Howard. After interviewing Castro, Howard realized he wanted to restore communications with the United States. She introduced Kennedy's U.N. delegate William Attwood (whose date with Mary years earlier had occasioned the first meeting between

Mary and Kennedy) and Cuban U.N. ambassador Carlos Lechuga in September 1963. The meeting between Attwood and Lechuga led to consideration by Kennedy of a back-channel communication with Castro. Howard later informed Attwood in late October 1963 that Castro wanted an American to fly from Key West to a secret airport near Havana. Kennedy was considering how to respond to Castro about a secret meeting when he took his fatal trip to Texas.[140] After Kennedy's assassination, the Cuban exercise was "put on ice," Attwood later wrote, "where it has been ever since."[141]

Sleeping with the president conferred upon a woman in those years a certain power. Many women during the Kennedy years in Washington would have relinquished their sense of propriety for a chance to be one of the president's favorites; in fact, more have claimed they did than was probably humanly possible. Whatever shame there was in it was more than rewarded by the social ascendancy to be gained from such a position, if one was willing to risk a little social disapproval. Georgetown was perhaps more forgiving of the president's infidelities than the rest of America would have been, both then and now. But the requisite secrecy that went along with an affair with the president was tremendously repressive. Mary was very likely awed by the fact of his power, of his human hand on the nuclear button. Close to him, she was on the adventure of her life. She had to tell somebody about it, and Jim Truitt, with his journalistic inquisitiveness and quirky disregard for convention, apparently seemed to her a good choice.

Although only the Truitts, Mary's psychiatrist, and a very small number of women knew at the time that Mary Meyer had slept with the president, she was generally known in the Kennedy circle to have access to the president's ear, and in that she had potential power. Such access to presidents is highly valued. People have always paid large sums of money for it. At those many dinners with the president, she could have delivered messages to him from White House staff or people who wanted Kennedy's attention. If White House counsel Myer Feldman considered Mary a possible conduit, undoubtedly others in the White House and perhaps outside did as well.

As a mistress and friend of the president, Mary Meyer certainly heard talk at high levels and knew about private presidential matters that spies, diplomats, and political office seekers would have "given their nuts for," in the parlance of the crowd. Kennedy's aides admit that "Kennedy loved to talk to her."[142] But the subject matter was probably not dirty state secrets such as Castro assassination plots and government links with the American Mafia. That Kennedy wouldn't have talked to her about certain official matters was consistent with his personality and with what scholarly research has revealed about his governing style. Kennedy compartmentalized his life.[143] "He liked to talk with his women, he liked to ask you questions and get a view of your opinion," said one of Kennedy's occasional Georgetown girlfriends. "He'd pick your brains at dinner about what was happening in your world, but it is unthinkable that he would have anything to say beyond that."[144]

On the other hand, Mary Meyer was not a lightweight. She was grounded and had depth, and as her old friend Bob Schwartz had noticed so many years before, she was "serious about being serious." She certainly would have discussed such matters as civil rights with Kennedy the night after the bloody Mississippi riot. Without her diaries, it is difficult to know what the president shared with her. Kennedy aide Feldman believed the president, his chauvinism aside, might have discussed substantial issues with her. "I think he might have thought more of her than some of the other women and discussed things that were on his mind, not just social gossip."[145]

Even if Mary was simply in it for fun, just having access to the president could have made her seem like a secret agent to her Georgetown contemporaries and to the spies and agents who made it their business to watch Kennedy's women. "People told her things," insisted one Georgetown friend who remained convinced her murder was somehow connected to her relationship with the president, although she had no evidence or idea what those "things" might have been.[146]

Having a fling with President Kennedy could be destructive to a woman, although it is not clear that any were actually in mortal danger. The president's women made certain types of men very nervous. Females with access to the president's body had access to his ear, and women with such access could be baffling. Who knew, the men of the FBI and the CIA thought, what other men those women answered to and who was controlling *them*? Some of the women were believed to be as dumb as the proverbial box of rocks. That might make them harmless, but stupidity could spell danger, too.[147] Women could be especially dangerous if they became emotional about being treated in the casual, unfeeling style that was the Kennedy hallmark. Marilyn Monroe was one who objected to being used and tossed away. Her instability and her very public persona created a serious threat to the Kennedy image in the month before she committed suicide.

Judith Campbell's life was made miserable by the constant spying of FBI agents, and eventually she did fear for her life. Her house was broken into, and it is possible the home invaders used something they took to blackmail the president.[148] East German call girl Ellen Rometsch was abruptly deported when her affair with the president threatened to become a scandal.[149] It is possible some pressure or secret attention was brought to bear on Mary. The summer before she died, Mary Meyer sometimes thought someone had been inside her house while she was away. On one occasion, the maid found the doors to the garden open on a January morning, while Mary and her sons were asleep upstairs. Mary filed a report with the police. On another occasion, she found a heavy wooden door ajar in her basement—a door neither she nor her sons could open without help. She more than once wondered aloud, "What *are* they looking for in my house?"[150] "She did say to me she was scared about seeing somebody in her house," Elizabeth Eisenstein recalled. "She thought she had seen somebody leaving as she walked in. She was frightened."[151]

Women who slept with the president became suspect in the eyes of the national-security apparatus. At that time, spies in the American security system, led by Jim Angleton and J. Edgar Hoover, were spying on each other and on the president of the United States, in addition to spying on the Russians. "There were things happening, serious matters the public wasn't aware of, dangers that we considered to the peace of the world," said Feldman. "In that context you have the CIA. There were serious problems of secrecy in the environment in which Mary Meyer lived. I think there was more covert action in the Kennedy days than there was in any succeeding administration. We were so security-conscious then. It exceeded anything that exists even today." With her combination of access and disregard for convention, Mary Meyer became a female type, the classic dangerous woman. "If she were an agent, she'd have been a terrific one," said Feldman. The fact that people viewed her that way would have provoked both her throaty laugh and a little secret pride.

# 8

# Crump

*It looks like you got a stacked deck.*

RAY CRUMP
TO POLICE WHEN CONFRONTED
WITH HIS ABANDONED JACKET

The Chesapeake and Ohio Canal was begun in 1828, intended to cut through the Appalachians and transform Georgetown into a major trade center. But the canal builders stopped a few hundred miles away at Cumberland, Maryland, and Georgetown was destined to remain a regional transshipment center. Georgetowners made use of the old canal anyway. The canal towpath was perfect for a pastoral stroll in good weather. Journalist Walter Lippmann and his wife, Helen, walked their beloved poodles on it every day. Jackie Kennedy sometimes walked there in the days before she became First Lady. But it was also a sanctuary for derelicts. The path where mule teams had once pulled tons of cargo through the locks formed a gravelly divide between the canal itself and the bottomlands along the Potomac River to the south. Drunks stumbled and slumbered in the area between the path and the Potomac, obscured by a tangled growth.

The canal itself was a combination of beauty, filth, serenity, and danger. No longer used for transport, its sluggish water collected algae, lily pads, and garbage. "I had occasion to watch it drained once," said a Georgetown police officer. "I'll never forget what I saw at the bottom."[1] But it had beauty, too. Ducks floated in pairs on the surface, and farther out of the city, the observant eye might spy a great blue heron, still as a branch, or a family of raccoons gamboling at the water's edge. Elm, mulberry, and other river bottom trees shaded the path at intervals.

The wilderness between the towpath and the river to the south was littered with broken glass and laced with poison ivy. It had once been a forest of old-growth trees, whose strong roots withstood regular flooding. But years of careless smoking by mule-drivers and boatmen and the campfires of fishermen and bums had destroyed many of the older trees in the forest, allowing honeysuckle vines and weedlike "trash trees" to thrive in their place. Between fallen trees and weeds and vines, the area was nearly impenetrable. To walk in it, one had to cleave to an old trolley track that ran through it, below an embankment alongside the canal and parallel to the towpath. It was not unusual to find men sleeping in those woods or under the Key Bridge or one of the smaller footbridges that crossed the canal. Women especially stayed away from the area or went in pairs. But there had been only one violent crime on the path in the twenty years before 1964. A few years earlier a robber had badly beaten a man walking along the path several miles away from Georgetown.[2]

Mary Meyer's affinity for the forests of her childhood drew her to the towpath nearly every afternoon when she was painting. The walks provided both daily discipline and leisure. The derelicts didn't bother her. She had never met one she couldn't deflect. There was nothing to fear in her private world and never had been. On her walks, there were only the colors and the crunch of her feet on the gravel. Every afternoon was an exercise in a finer discernment of nature's intricate arrangements of leaves, birds, and sky. The tree colors seemed to change slightly all the time, not just in the fall, and the shifting blues and grays of the mid-Atlantic sky inspired her.

It was Mary's habit to approach the canal walking downhill on Thirty-fourth Street, which hit the towpath just as the major thoroughfare of M Street split away from the canal and became the broad and curving Canal Road. That point marked one end of the Francis Scott Key Bridge, which connected Washington with Virginia, across the Potomac. The bridge was named after the Washington lawyer who once owned a house on the site, where he first read "The Star-Spangled Banner" to his glee club.

On her last day, October 12, 1964, Mary might have waited briefly above the path on Thirty-fourth Street. Helen Stern had mentioned she might be interested in going along for a walk this afternoon. But after a few minutes Mary decided Helen was not going to make it. Helen did show up later, but, noticing the police cars, she turned back, unaware that her friend was the reason for the commotion.

Mary then crossed one of the footbridges that connected Georgetown with the towpath, which was across the canal from the city. At this point, about twenty minutes after noon, a jogger passed her. She was walking west and the jogger was heading east. About two hundred yards later, the jogger passed a black male walking behind Mary in the same direction as she was. The jogger would remember that the man wore a light-colored jacket, a dark golf-type hat, and dark slacks. The jogger remembered that the man had his hands in the pockets of his jacket. He recalled Mary as "a middle-aged woman in a light blue parka."

Mary walked away from the city, passing the ruins of an old lime kiln along the towpath. A rendering plant and a foundry belching smoke were the last vestiges of the port industry that had been Georgetown's economic mainstay. Clanging and fumes marked the city's edge. Beyond them was the great wild expanse of vines and scrubby trees. She passed the city's oldest surviving boat club, the Potomac Boat Club, with its docks and green outbuildings. Past that point the towpath became country, even though some of the greatest homes of Washington proper were located in the tree-shrouded hills to the north. The secluded path sometimes offered panoramic views of the Potomac River to the south, a wide silvery blue ribbon cleft by massive rocks. Across the river was McLean and all its sad memories. Large houses were visible on the cliffs overlooking the river. During the years of her marriage, Mary had spent evenings there at one party or another, looking back across the Potomac at the twinkling lights of Georgetown and Capitol Hill. The only sign that the towpath was still in a city was the distant whoosh of traffic on Canal Road, across the canal itself from the path and situated about thirty feet above the water level. A stone wall and vine-tangled hill separated the canal from the street above. Occasionally the tops of passing cars were visible from the path. There was no sidewalk along Canal Road, however, and people did not normally travel it on foot.

Mary walked at a healthy clip. It was a gloriously sunny day. She carried no purse and her arms swung free at her sides. Near the point where Kary Fischer had fallen through the canal ice a few winters before, Mary Meyer met her death. The encounter lasted less than a minute and ended at twenty-five minutes after noon. The sun was high, and at first she would have had no reason to fear the person who approached. Then something, a gesture or words, revealed danger. Mary did not submit easily to the assailant. Her self-confidence remained intact, probably until the moment the gun was drawn, and she was physically strong. She fought and screamed, attracting attention to her struggle.

On Canal Road above the scene, two men had just arrived to service a stalled Rambler. William Branch and Henry Wiggins were mechanics employed by an Esso station near Key Bridge in Georgetown. Wiggins was a black Korean War veteran in his mid-twenties who had served as a military policeman. The two men had just stepped out of their truck when they heard a "howling, like someone was being hurt," Wiggins said later.[3] They thought at first that drunks were fighting and ignored the noise. Then they heard a gunshot and a weak voice calling, "Somebody help me!" The words floated across the water and up the hill and over the gray stone wall onto Canal Road. Not until after he heard the first shot did Wiggins begin to walk over to the wall that separated the road from a view of the path below. His partner, Branch, was frightened and stayed near the truck. As Wiggins was walking toward the canal wall, Mary was already bleeding from a head wound that would have killed her. Down on her knees and mortally wounded but still pulsing with the remains of life, she clung to a small tree. One gloved hand pushed weakly at the attacker, touched her bleeding head, then went back to the tree. The attacker tried to pull her off the tree and down the wooded embankment out of sight of the road. Using her last ounce of vitality, bleeding profusely from the head, she stood up and ran across the path toward the canal water and toward the wall and the street above, only to fall to the ground near the water's edge. While she was down and probably in severe shock from the head wound, the gun was reapplied, this time to her back. That bullet shattered her shoulder blade, severed the aorta, which carries blood to the heart, and came out of her chest on the other side.

The struggle between gunshots lasted ten seconds. In that time, Wiggins had crossed Canal Road and reached the stone wall above the canal. He heard the second shot just before he looked over the wall and down at the path. There, about 120 feet from him, Wiggins saw a black man with a light tan jacket and dark cap leaning over the prone body of a woman. Wiggins watched for half a minute, then, fearing he would be shot if the man turned to look at him, bobbed back down below the wall. When he peered back over the wall, the man stood up and put something Wiggins could only identify as a dark object into the pocket of his zippered jacket, turned and looked up toward Wiggins, then walked away from the body, down the embankment into the dense growth that separated the canal from the river.

Looking at Mary's body coiled in a fetal position on the path, it was clear to Wiggins that something terrible had just happened. The other mechanic stayed near the wall above the body while Wiggins drove back to the Esso station near the Key Bridge, approximately a minute's drive away, and called the police. Before he hung up a squad car was pulling into the gas station.

The report of a body quickly mobilized the Seventh Precinct police officers, whose headquarters were in a pillared building overlooking the Georgetown University campus, a few blocks from the towpath. Within four minutes, according to police estimates, the conventional exits from the towpath were sealed. Those were the Water Street exit near the edge of Georgetown, the Foundry Underpass exit, about two tenths of a mile east of the body, and another exit a mile to the west of the body, called Fletcher's Boathouse. Officers then began a foot search of the area between the exits, walking through the woods toward each other and the murder scene. With the conventional exits closed, the killer had the option of crossing the muddy canal and trying to scale the very visible twelve- to fifteen-foot high stone wall up to Canal Road to the north, or wending his way through the dense woods south of the Potomac and swimming across that broad river. The police believed swimming the river was the only way out because officers and onlookers, including the mechanic who had stayed behind on Canal Road, would have sighted a man climbing the wall and running across Canal Road in the moments after the crime.

More than a dozen officers participated in the foot search. Officers east of the body at the Foundry Underpass walked west toward it, and officers at Fletcher's Boathouse walked east, toward the body. Officer Rick Sylvis was walking east from Fletcher's Boathouse along the trolley tracks in the river bottom when he saw a black male poke his head out of the woods in front of him and look down the tracks, then disappear back into the woods. Sylvis estimated the head appeared a bit less than a mile west of the body at about 12:45 P.M.[4]

About thirty minutes later Officer John Warner was walking west toward the body, having started at an entry to the towpath closer to the city. He stopped at one of the cement culverts along the canal that had once been used to water the towpath mules. The culvert was about five hundred feet east of the murder scene and dropped about fifty feet into the Potomac. Warner checked under the culvert and saw nothing, then stepped out onto the tracks and looked along the clearing they made in the undergrowth. About thirty feet in front of him stood a small black man clad in white T-shirt and black pants, soaking wet, covered with bits of weed, with a bleeding hand, torn pants, and an open fly. As Warner approached, the man made no effort to flee. When asked, the man produced a driver's license identifying himself as Raymond Crump Jr., age twenty-five, resident of Washington, D.C. Warner asked him what he was doing in the area and he said he had been fishing but that he had fallen asleep, dropped his pole into the water, and then fallen in the river himself. Warner asked to see the fishing spot and Crump walked Warner back toward the murder scene and stopped about ten feet below it, telling Warner the fishing spot was "just around the bend." As Warner walked with Crump, he asked Crump about his bloody right hand and a cut over his eye. Crump said he had cut himself climbing out of the river.[5]

Warner walked Crump toward the murder scene, and as the officer and his charge came into view, Wiggins, who was standing near the body with several police officers, including the chief homicide detective, excitedly pointed at Crump and said he was the man who had been standing over the body just after the second gunshot. Crump was patted down but no weapon was found. He was handcuffed and placed under arrest. Forty-five minutes had elapsed since Wiggins heard the shots. Chief homicide detective Bernard Crooke later told journalists he asked Crump why his fly was open and Crump answered, "You did it."[6]

Later that afternoon, police recovered a light tan zippered jacket floating in the river within a thousand feet of the murder scene. In a pocket was a half-pack of Pall Mall cigarettes, Crump's brand. The jacket was torn. Crump's wife, Helena, identified the clothing as his.[7] When confronted with the jacket at the jail, Crump burst into tears and said, "It looks like you got a stacked deck." He then began to sob inconsolably.[8] His fishing pole was found in his closet at home the evening of the murder. The next day police fished a dark plaid cap out of the Potomac near the crime scene, which was also identified as Crump's.

At his arraignment Crump told the fishing story again and added that he had heard shots. "I don't know what happened myself. I almost got shot myself."[9] He was held in jail without bond as officers tried to identify the dead woman. She was beautiful and there was something about her even in death that suggested money and importance. "She even looked beautiful with a bullet in her head," Crooke said later.[10] She carried no identification except for the faint cleaner's mark "Meyer" on the inside of her soft leather glove. The only personal effect on her body was a tube of Cherries in the Snow lipstick in her pocket. She was not wearing underwear. It took police eight hours of phone calls to all the Meyers in the Washington, D.C., phone book to finally identify her relationship to *Newsweek*'s Washington bureau chief Ben Bradlee. That night the journalist undertook the grim task of identifying his sister-in-law's body in the morgue.

Mary Pinchot Meyer was a debutante in the middle of her first year at Vassar when Ray Crump Jr. was born February 25, 1939, in a hamlet called Norwood in the south-central Piedmont region of North Carolina. He was the first of three boys born to Martha and Ray Crump. His birth was duly recorded in the separate "colored" birth register by the Stanly County recorder of deeds. His first home was just outside Norwood proper, among a close-knit concentration of rural black families whose houses were located on the rich bottomlands near the confluence of the Uwharrie and Yadkin Rivers. As far as the eye could see from around his house lay the cotton fields his forebears had tended as slaves for two centuries. The mixed fragrances of pine tar and freshly plowed fields filled the air. There were rivers to fish and swamps with great fallen trees to explore. As a boy he lived as his parents and grandparents and great-grandparents had, in the security of families who had weathered hard times and good times together since the days before anyone could remember.

Ray and all the black Crumps in Norwood were descended from slaves owned by the white Crump family that had owned the land and the cotton. Black and white Crumps lived side by side in the Norwood region for two centuries and still did when Ray was born.

White Crumps were the descendants of people who had migrated to Virginia from England in pre-Revolutionary times. James Crump, the first Crump to arrive in North Carolina, was a captain in the Revolutionary army and, according to family lore, served as a page to George Washington. James Crump was a slaveholder before he arrived in North Carolina. In the 1740s, his father, John Crump of Virginia, had bequeathed "negroes" named Sambo, Bange, Harry, Sam, Robin, Cook, Hannah, and Nan to his heirs in his will. James Crump and a brother acquired land shortly after the Revolution and started raising cotton with the help of a growing stock of slaves.[11] When plantations such as the Crumps' were just beginning, master and slaves worked the land side by side because there was so much clearing to be done. As the plantations grew and began to show a profit, the work was divided and slaves took over the coarsest jobs, cutting their hands raw on the sharp black stalks of the cotton plants. The master stayed inside and an overseer took control of the slaves' lives.[12] Throughout the nineteenth century, the Crump family's landholdings in North Carolina increased along with their use of slaves. In 1810 four Crumps in the area had a total of 57 slaves. By 1830 the family had 68 slaves.[13]

Slaves were watched by an overseer who would, if the mood struck him, beat the weary or recalcitrant with his hoe or worse. On some early farms before prosperity was achieved, slaves were not cared for in the most basic ways. Visitors to North Carolina right after the Revolutionary War found many slaves nearly naked and starving. Usually each slave was allotted one blanket and slept on the ground or on a bench. Once a year each slave received a suit of coarse woolen cloth, some shirts, and a new pair of shoes. They were barely sustained on a diet of maize and sometimes fish. To supplement the meager provisions, slaves learned to harvest wild vegetables and local wildlife. Opossum, bats, owls, and turtle became part of the fare. Slaves who married were in danger of being separated through sale. Rape was a constant threat. If the woman was not producing enough children, the master might force men upon her in the effort to get more slave children and increase his wealth. The property value of slaves was always foremost in the master's mind.[14] Crump family records indicate that their slaves were worth a great deal. In 1859 three Negro children owned by Crumps were valued at eight hundred dollars, and a sale of slaves on the Crump estate brought more than eight thousand dollars.[15]

From such a history the Ray Crump family of Norwood emerged in the first part of the twentieth century, poor people with a grim and terrible past. Their hope for the future lay away from the land of their slave forebears, and their faith was fueled by Martha Crump's intense religious belief. The Depression hit blacks hard. If anyone was going to lose a job in North Carolina, a black man would lose his before a white man. Ray Crump's father was a WPA worker when Ray was born, and his mother was a housewife.[16] But work was unstable and the rural lifestyle was harsh, with disease rampant and doctors for blacks few and far between.

When Ray was about ten he, his parents, and two younger brothers moved north. The family joined a quiet exodus that was changing the demographics of the old South and the inner cities of the North. Black people had been leaving North Carolina and the South in general since World War I. The mass migration quickened in the 1940s. North Carolina lost 5 percent of its black population in the decade after the First World War; it lost nearly 15 percent of its black population in the decade after World War II.[17] The cotton-growing region around Norwood needed fewer and fewer hands because farms were consolidating and machinery was replacing field help. Damage from floods and the boll weevil destroyed more agricultural jobs. Area textile mills closed up during the Depression or afterward. Farm laborers in the South made just one dollar a day. Blacks believed they would get better treatment as human beings in the North. They believed the North might offer their children better educations and themselves voting rights.[18]

Seeking a better life, the Crumps and tens of thousands of black families like them bought tickets on northbound trains, dubbed the "Chicken-bone Express" after the country-style meals rural travelers brought aboard, heading for points along the eastern seaboard.[19]

Railroads had to add extra cars to their passenger trains to accommodate the demand. Some passengers got off in Washington, D.C. Others rode until they reached Philadelphia, Newark, or New York.

The Crumps arrived in Washington and settled in the quadrant of the city known as Southwest. The neighborhood was the smallest and poorest of the capital city's four sections, but it was held together by southern roots, shared hardship, and deep religious feeling kept alive by the neighborhood churches. In the early 1950s twenty-three thousand people lived there, three fourths of whom were black. But the majority lived in wooden shacks more than fifty years old. Half of the houses had no indoor plumbing; a quarter were without water at all and without electricity. Most had no central heating.[20] Some people literally lived in small shacks constructed in alleys. Health conditions were hardly better than they had been in rural North Carolina.

When they arrived, Martha Crump took a job as a laundress in a white section of the city. Ray senior took on construction jobs when he could find them. Martha Crump joined the Second Baptist Church and became a mainstay, never missing a service, and traveling back to North Carolina for tent revivals when she could get away. Young Ray and his brothers attended one of the all-black schools. The family stayed in the neighborhood as the city housing authority systematically demolished the old shacks and moved families into other neighborhoods under the social experiment known as urban renewal. The Crumps' rented house was on Carrollburg Place and one of the few that remained standing. The redevelopment was likened by one resident to "living in a war zone." The remains of demolished buildings often erupted into fires, which the city fire department rarely bothered to extinguish. Fires smoldered for days. Family dogs abandoned by those who had been forced to move roved in feral packs among the charred ruins.[21]

Crime in the black ghettos of Washington was rampant but largely ignored by white Washington. A 1950 report described the rising crime in the black communities. The report did not become table talk in official Washington. It was an embarrassment to the whites, who preferred to believe that conditions for black people had improved since emancipation. The only whites who confronted the problem were the police officers, who tended to attribute it to innate black depravity. "Frustrated, idle blacks hung around street corners, shot craps, got into the rapidly spreading numbers racket, beat up wives, begot illegitimate children, assaulted and stole from passers-by, burglarized and sometimes finished off brawls with manslaughter. . . . As long as the lawbreakers old or young confined themselves to colored neighborhoods the press paid little attention to them."[22]

The small capital city was utterly divided. Separate social traditions and communication systems operated on different sides. Whites controlled the institutions of government and the media; blacks found support, community, and information inside their churches. Martha Crump found her network at the Second Baptist Church. Such churches gave strength to the civil rights movement and connected the struggles of black Birmingham to black Washington.

Segregation in Washington's public and quasi-public places remained the norm into the late 1950s. If the Crumps wanted seafood in their Southwest neighborhood, they could get carryout food from the fish restaurants along the Potomac, but they could not dine inside them. Their children went to movie theaters where white children were allowed, but whites-only theaters barred blacks. Black children were excluded from white playgrounds and city swimming pools. Blacks who worked downtown had to walk to a government cafeteria to eat lunch or bring their own food from home. The National Theater closed down for a season in the mid-fifties rather than allow blacks; it was not desegregated until new owners came in. Schools were strictly segregated. It took a Supreme Court decision in 1954 to force restaurants, schools, and parks in the national capital to begin to admit blacks.

The fight for desegregation in Washington was relatively nonviolent, compared to what was under way in the South by the early

1960s. The federal government was desegregated and had been employing blacks for decades, making Washington home to many solidly middle-class blacks. In 1951 Harris Wofford, who became President Kennedy's point man on civil rights, organized some Howard University law students to picket the segregated lunch counter of a downtown department store. Other pickets and protests followed, largely peaceful. A violent exception was a riot over swimming pool access in June 1949, which the *Washington Post* deliberately ignored. The peaceful tenor of the civil rights movement in Washington began to change in the early sixties, when Marion Barry rose to power as an organizer of the growing legion of unemployed black men in the capital.

Kennedy's years in office were some of the bloodiest in the civil rights movement, especially in the South, and fears and rumors of imminent black violence unnerved Washingtonians. The city had been majority-black since the early fifties. Incidents of black-on-white street crime were increasing. In June 1963 the *New York Times* ran a series of stories about the racial problems in Washington, D.C. The first one opened with anecdotes about street violence instigated by black perpetrators: an Ohio tourist beaten and robbed by "a band of fast-moving Negro girls"; an elderly clergyman beaten to death by four black youths for $1.29; two college girls from Pennsylvania raped by a gun-wielding black male. Violence was a symptom of the urban decay behind the postcard facade of the capital city.[23]

Minor race riots occurred in the District twice during Kennedy's term, both centered on sporting events. The mere fact that they had occurred led white residents to fear more violence. Agnes Meyer, wife of the owner of the *Washington Post* and Katharine Graham's mother—no relation to Cord—warned of racial violence in editorials and speeches unless certain social conditions were immediately addressed, specifically the joblessness of black youth.[24] Black leaders picked up on the fear and used the threat of black violence as a political tool. In May 1963 Malcolm X came to town and New York democratic congressman Adam Clayton Powell Jr. warned that Washington "will be the scene of one of the worst race riots in the history of America" unless social conditions for the city's poorest blacks were improved.[25]

Members of Kennedy's subcabinet group on civil rights and the State Department pressed city realtors and businesses and banks to let up on racial discrimination. Robert Kennedy, Charles Bartlett, and other Georgetown men resigned from the Metropolitan Club when it continued to exclude blacks. But while nominally for civil rights, Georgetowners did not get actively involved with the black community until after 1968, when a black mob looted and burned a portion of the city. Polly Wisner Fritchey said in hindsight, "We should have seen it coming. We—the city of Washington and we—were not treating them the way they should have been treated. I think that it was a time that none of us should be very proud of."[26]

Georgetown was aware of the potential for racial disaster in the United States but remained focused on international issues. While most of its liberal white residents supported black equality, among the cold-war hawks there was always the suspicion—shared by Hoover—that domestic chaos caused by King's nonviolent protests might benefit or even involve Communists. The Communist Party was an early supporter of civil rights. The potential for Communist infiltration of the civil rights movement eventually became an obsession for the FBI and the CIA, both of which launched domestic spying efforts to make sure the black activists weren't really Reds.

The segregationist politicians who controlled the House of Representatives' District of Columbia Committee were less concerned with the Communist threat than with maintaining order the good old southern way. They promoted the use of police dogs and stiffer jail sentences as a cure for the growing crime problem in the capital. They and the city's white police were of the same mind. In their opinion, black crime was due more to an innate deficiency in the people than to any societal cause. After all, the federal government had just invested in the nation's first and largest public housing program to clear away Washington's slums. D.C. police chief Robert V. Murray expressed his view on the incorrigibility of the black criminal at a District Committee hearing on Capitol Hill in 1961: "The ones that commit the crimes would not work under any circumstances. They do not want to work. They want to get their money the easy way and even with employment at an all-time high, you are not going to get any of those people to take a job. They do not want a job."[27]

Two months before Mary was murdered, the capital was thick with race resentment and fear. "District Heads Warned to Act Lest Wrongs Spark Outburst," read one headline in the *Washington Post.* A thirteen-man black delegation warned that violence was a real and imminent possibility unless various black grievances involving police misconduct and housing problems were addressed. "The present possibility of violent protest and long-standing, still-unrequited grievances require accelerated action by our city and its leadership which will help insure order," the delegation announced.[28] Mary's own attitude toward civil rights was progressive. Her black maid felt she genuinely "liked black people," and she made sure her sons had black friends. Still, the threat of violence frightened her and she refused to let her eldest son go to King's march on the Mall.

By 1960, when Ray Crump Jr. was twenty-one, he had attained his full adult height of five feet six inches. He was a small man, physically unassuming, with strong shoulders and a head that seemed a little large in proportion to his body. His eyes didn't quite match and he sometimes wore glasses. His mother regarded her firstborn son as "the runt of the litter" because of his small size and learning difficulties. His drinking problem became apparent as a young adult, and he did jail time for public intoxication. In 1962 he was beaten in a robbery attempt on him that might have injured his head. On August 24, 1963, he was ordered to spend sixty days in jail for petit larceny.

Unlike his two younger brothers, who graduated from high school and got jobs (one as a D.C. police officer, the other at the Government Printing Office), Ray dropped out of one of the city's four all-black high schools a year before graduating. In 1958 he married his neighbor Helena Blair at his mother Martha's place of worship, the Second Baptist Church. Helena was seventeen on their wedding day and already five months pregnant with the first of their four children. The couple moved into one of the housing projects in Southeast Washington on a wide, treeless street called Stanton Terrace. The Stanton Terrace housing project was a community started on farmland obtained by the federal government along the banks of the Potomac River and devoted to housing black people. It was originally established by freedmen and refugees from the Civil War who built homes on one-acre plots of land set aside by the Bureau of Refugees in 1865. The original residents constructed their own homes at night by lantern and candlelight using lumber donated by the government. They policed the community themselves.[29] But in the 1940s the old houses were torn down and replaced with new standard-issue housing projects, a move that uprooted families and destroyed the small-town feel of the community. The Crumps' house was half of a yellow brick townhouse, set at a crooked angle to the street in a grassy but otherwise barren lot. With four square windows and a small concrete stoop before the screen door, it was identical to fifty more townhouses on the street. After Crump's arrest the *Washington Post* sent a reporter out to interview his neighbors and deemed the housing project "prosperous and pleasant."

Crump worked as a day laborer. He suffered excruciating headaches and blackouts, and while physically present could seem to be "not there" at times. When drunk, he became extremely violent, especially toward the women in his life.[30] His wife, Helena, "abhorred his drinking." She believed his trouble with the law had something to do with his drinking and never visited him in jail.[31] If he was drunk on the day of his arrest, there is no record of it; blood alcohol tests were not performed.

On the day he was arrested for Mary Meyer's murder, Crump was supposed to be doing construction work. He and other unemployed men got temporary work by lining up at dawn at a parking lot in northwest Washington. Companies needing an extra hand that day sent trucks that loaded up the men and delivered them to the jobsite. On the morning of the murder, although he left his house on Stanton Terrace early and seemed to be headed to work, Crump failed to show up at the job line.[32]

Crump never gave a coherent account of what he was doing on the towpath the day of the murder or why his fishing gear was home while he was supposedly fishing in the Potomac. He never explained why he'd dropped his hat and jacket into the river. He did eventually tell his defense attorney that he had actually gone out to the towpath with a prostitute, not to fish. In other accounts he gave, he simply woke up and heard gunfire.[33] After his arrest, word went around Crump's Stanton Terrace neighborhood that he had been hauled up on a rape charge.[34]

News of the murdered woman on the towpath traveled fast in white Washington, and some of Mary's friends suspected immediately the victim might be their friend. That night police took Ben Bradlee to the morgue in a squad car to identify the body of his sister-in-law. One of the officers who accompanied the newsman was Detective Sam Wallace, a junior officer on the homicide team. Wallace remembers thinking the tragedy taught this liberal newsman one very good lesson about the real nature of crime in Washington. "I said, now you get to see what you've been writing about. All that let 'em out of jail stuff comes home to roost."[35] In fact, Bradlee had little experience with black urban crime. As he noted in his memoir, in his early days as a reporter at the *Washington Post* he would hear about a crime on the police radio and ask whether he shouldn't go and cover it. "Naw, that's black," the night city editor would reply.[36]

Unaware that their friend was dead, the Angletons went to a poetry reading. At the Library of Congress, Reed Whittemore spoke on "Ways of Misunderstanding Poetry and Being Dismal." One of the misunderstandings about poetry was the notion that poetry must be "pure," he told his listeners. He compared the sterile concept of pure poetry with the lifeless center of Washington, "all those monuments, all that turf, all those inscriptions, all those marble pillars and steps and busts—and not a delicatessen or sidewalk café for miles."[37]

The first news reports of the murder were being written that night. At the *Washington Evening Star*, a reporter called one of Mary's Vassar classmates, Scottie Lanahan, who described her friend as a woman who was "never afraid." William Walton, her escort at White House dinners, described her as "one of the most beautiful women I have ever known." He called her art "feminine, glowing and lyrical." Neighbors told reporters about an "elegant" woman who usually dressed in blues and greens "which seemed to alter the color of her light eyes to match them." One report in the *Washington Post* described her as "a close friend of the John F. Kennedys from the days when Mr. Kennedy, then a Senator, lived near her N Street studio." None of the news reports identified her ex-husband as a CIA official. He was described as an author and former U.N. delegate. The first reports quoted police as saying they suspected the motive was "a criminal assault." In later accounts the word *rape* was mentioned. There was, however, no evidence that a rape had occurred. And since Mary was not carrying a purse, robbery was discounted as a motive.

Back on N Street the night of the murder, the grieving Bradlees fielded two phone calls that Ben Bradlee remembered years later. One was from President Kennedy's press secretary, Pierre Salinger, in Paris, expressing his condolences. The second call was from Anne Truitt in Tokyo, claiming a matter of some urgency. She said Mary had asked her to take care of her personal diary if anything ever happened to her. Truitt asked whether they had found such a diary. The Bradlees said they had not looked.[38]

The complicated chain of events that followed became a matter of dispute among all involved. Their early denials and later competing accounts have contributed much to the aura of mystery surrounding Mary Meyer's life and death. Anne Truitt and Cicely Angleton contend that when word of Mary Meyer's death reached the Truitts in Tokyo, Anne Truitt called and reached Jim Angleton at the Bradlees' house on N Street. Anne Truitt claimed Mary had explicitly requested that if anything happened to her while Anne was in Japan, she should instruct James Angleton to take charge of her private diary.[39]

One of Angleton's nicknames was "the Locksmith," reflecting his professional skill at black-bag jobs. His overall reputation as a master of intrigue had the curious effect of inspiring trust in him among his friends. "His aura of clandestine genius drew people into his web of intrigue, prompting them to entrust him with their most intimate confidences, as if the secret would be somehow safer in his keeping than in theirs."[40] Perhaps that explains why Mary or her friends believed the diary was safest in his hands. It is also conceivable that Anne Truitt deemed Mary's relationship with Kennedy a matter of national interest and took it upon herself to involve the CIA man.

It is impossible to confirm whether Mary really wanted Angleton involved. Ben Bradlee thought not. Anne Truitt and Cicely Angleton contended she did. The two women wrote a letter to the editor of the *New York Times Book Review* in 1996 after a review of Bradlee's memoir, refuting Bradlee and claiming it was Mary's explicit wish that Angleton take her private papers. Cicely Angleton said she wrote the letter to defend her husband's "honor."[41]

Bradlee offered a completely different recollection of events. In Bradlee's book Angleton was described as an uninvited visitor to Mary's house and studio. Bradlee remembered that he and Tony were twice surprised to bump into an embarrassed Jim Angleton wearing gloves and carrying tools, breaking into Mary's house and studio, searching for the diary that Anne Truitt had sent them all to find. The first incident occurred the morning after the murder, according to Bradlee; he and Tony went to Mary's townhouse on Thirty-fourth Street, where they found Angleton already inside. "We found his presence odd, to say the least, but took him at his word," Bradlee wrote. The search party did not find the diary on that round. Later that day, as Bradlee remembered it, he and Tony decided to search Mary's studio in the alley behind their house. There again they stumbled upon Angleton in the process of picking a padlock. "He would have been red-faced if his face could have gotten red, and he left almost without a word," Bradlee wrote.[42] Bradlee and Tony then went inside the studio and eventually found the diary. The Bradlees read it later that night. According to the newsman, the diary was six by eight inches, with fifty or so pages, mostly filled with paint swatches and descriptions of how the colors were mixed. About ten of the pages contained "phrases" which described a love affair, and "after reading only a few phrases it was clear that her lover had been the President of the United States, although his name was never mentioned."[43] But Tony Bradlee told a reporter for the *National Enquirer* it was more explicit and that "there were some JFK's in it." She also told the tabloid's Jay Gourley "it was nothing to be ashamed of."[44]

In Cicely Angleton and Anne Truitt's account of the diary search, a group of Mary's friends, including Tony, the Angletons, "and one other friend of Mary Meyer's," together searched for Mary's diary. At some point, according to the two women, Tony Bradlee discovered the diary and "several papers bundled together" in Mary's studio. After she and Ben looked at the diary, Tony gave the bundle and the diary to Angleton and asked him to burn it all.[45]

The Bradlees' reaction to their new knowledge of Mary's relationship with Kennedy was confusion and betrayal, Bradlee recalled. Yet Ben Bradlee was also admiring. "There was a boldness in pulling something like that off that I found fascinating," he wrote. Tony was more disturbed. "She felt she was Jack Kennedy's friend, at least as much as Mary was, and all of a sudden she had come to realize that there was this difference. She had been kept in the dark by her sister and her friend." They also recognized they held a political hot potato in their hands. "We both concluded this was in no sense a public document, despite the braying of the knee jerks about some public right to know," he wrote.[46]

So they gave the diary and private papers to Jim Angleton. Angleton later told journalists Philip Nobile and Ron Rosenbaum that he went through the papers, catalogued them, and offered some letter writers the option of repossessing their letters. Angleton said he had read the diary, that two other people, whom he cryptically identified to the two journalists as "M" and "F," had read the diary, and that Mary's eldest son, Quentin, was also allowed to read it.[47] Angleton then burned the loose papers that were not repossessed, mostly personal letters; Angleton later personally assured Ken Noland he had burned the artist's letters to Mary.[48] But the counterintelligence chief did not destroy the diary, and on this matter the women and Bradlee agree. Several years later he gave it back to Tony Bradlee. At that point, according to Anne Truitt and Cicely Angleton, the final erasure of Mary's private life was accomplished in almost ritual fashion by Tony Bradlee and Anne Truitt. According to the women, Tony burned the diary herself, "in the presence of Anne Truitt."[49]

Some parts of the diary may have been preserved and passed around for a short period. Helen Stern used Mary's own writing about her art, taken from the papers left after her death, to create the brochure for a posthumous art show in 1967. Angleton believed some of her papers were still stored at Milford. Over the years, other people close to the family have suspected that Mary's diary was never really burned but is stored at the summer house. If that is so, the Pinchot-Pittman family has not admitted it.[50]

In death, thanks to Anne Truitt's machinations and James Angleton's professional curiosity, Mary's private life came to seem a matter of national security. In later years, as his reputation grew, Angleton cast a long and sinister shadow over the story. It is very possible Angleton did keep a copy or notes on the diary somewhere. Like J. Edgar Hoover, Angleton had preserved his position at the pinnacle of national security by collecting secrets, not discarding them. Richard Helms claimed he never saw the diary. Other CIA men, including those instructed to go through Angleton's safes after he was forced to resign in 1976, also said the diary was not in his papers. Helms said that if Angleton had taken the diary to the CIA—and Helms would not confirm that he did—Angleton was justified because it might have embarrassed the president. "That's something you can blackmail the president of the United States with, you know," Helms said. "Just because he's dead doesn't mean people wouldn't try to protect his memory."[51] And just because he was dead did not mean the diary was valueless to Angleton.

Angleton's involvement in this diary caper was similar to other errands he undertook involving papers that mentioned John F. Kennedy or his assassination and the CIA. In 1971 he traveled to Mexico and pried a manuscript out of a CIA widow's hands. The manuscript was a memoir by Mexico City CIA station chief Winston Scott. Before Scott was buried, and before Scott's son could stop Angleton, he had acquired the manuscript and flown back with it to the United States, where he secreted the papers in a safe at Langley. Scott's son sued the CIA for access to his father's papers but in 1997 still had not seen them. The papers possibly included a CIA photograph of Lee Harvey Oswald at the Cuban embassy in Mexico City.[52]

As deliberately as Washington's best fixers or the CIA's master conspirators, Mary's sister and friends set out after her death to achieve what they felt would be the best possible image of her and of their own private world. In so doing, they all but obliterated the written record of her life.

The inner circle delicately edged around the fact of her relationship with Kennedy. Most of the first news reports of her death on the towpath included the anecdote, supplied by unnamed "friends," that she had been a dear and close friend of Jackie Kennedy's and that the two women had often walked together hand in hand on the towpath. In later interviews other unnamed friends confided that it was "doubtful" such an event ever occurred. Angleton even went so far as to state to journalists once that "they weren't friends."[53] But in death, the woman who had avoided dinner party small talk got the label she would have spurned, "a Georgetown socialite."

Two weeks after her death, a friend of Mary's, Washington architect James Hilleary, wrote "an appreciation" of Mary Meyer, in which he said her death had "stilled one of the truly creative talents in the Washington metropolitan area." He tried to explain what kind of artist she had been. "Her contribution to this [Color] school has been described as lyrical and emotional rather than coolly calculated, though carefully thought out. Recently she favored circular paintings which seem to revolve as a pinwheel in motion. Though not a pioneer of the 'Colorists' movement, her work of the past few years has brought her into the mainstream of their approach and her development as well as her reputation have been advancing steadily. She was an artist moving toward, rather than having arrived at, her fullest potential."[54]

The private details of family grief fell to Mary's sister and mother. Tony went through Mary's house the day after the murder and found a whole turkey and other groceries out on the kitchen counter. Mary had planned to have a birthday dinner party for herself. Later, Ruth Pickering Pinchot, seventy-eight years old and sitting at the desk upon which she had penned so many wry articles as a young woman, read and signed the papers that settled her murdered daughter's estate. There were bills to pay, for Mary Meyer had credit at all the small shops in Georgetown. She owed seventeen dollars to Powder and Smoke; a few dollars for books recently purchased at the Savile Bookshops, a popular bookstore occupying three quaint townhouses on Wisconsin Avenue; money to the grocers for boxes of goodies sent to Mark and Quentin at their boarding schools the week before her murder. She owed the Becker Paint and Glass Company for two gallons of turpentine and some Stanley blades. Ruth received the catalogue of Mary's house and belongings in which china, unframed watercolors, silver beaker, four-poster canopy bed, and everything from the telephone stand to the metal andirons to a Magnavox record player–radio were assessed. None of it would ever be of any interest to a Sotheby's auctioneer. The Queen Anne–style settee, enamel bookcases, boys' beds, faience pillbox, the writing desk—everything that had been Mary's was now reduced to its monetary value so that it could be divided evenly into two halves of equal value for her surviving sons. Her jewelry was listed and assessed. There was not much of that. The most valuable item she owned was a turquoise necklace worth twenty dollars. There was a large lot of costume jewelry, earrings, pins, and bracelets, a gold-framed opal, a gold necklace with agates and bloodstones, and a little Mexican silver. Ruth had her paintings transferred to storage. Many of them, untitled and unframed, spent years in rolled-up piles at the little house at Milford. The total value of her personal estate, $63,550.70, was divided between Mark and Quentin.[55]

A month after Mary's death, Cord Meyer, who was apparently kept out of the diary caper but who would have been apprised of the diary's contents by Angleton if he did not actually read it himself, embarked on a previously planned trip abroad. He had sobbed at the funeral but he did not spend time grieving with his motherless sons. Cord put on a stiff upper lip and insisted his sons do the same. "He told them not to cry," Peter Janney recalled. "It was awful." Cord's attitude can be seen in a letter he wrote two weeks after Mary's death to foreign service officer Edward Barnes in Germany asking him to introduce journalist Charles Bartlett to "the organization" in Munich: "The boys have taken it with a great deal of courage and there is nothing much more to be said."[56] Mark and Quentin went back to their respective boarding schools in New Hampshire and Connecticut. Before Cord went overseas, he shifted his belongings into the Thirty-fourth Street townhouse, a quick move that unnerved some of Mary's friends. In 1966 he purchased Mary's share of the house back from Ruth Pinchot. The next year Quentin bought his mother's car from Ruth.

Cord did not mention his ex-wife's murder or his feelings about it in his journal for five months. He finally made a single mention of her death in a brief entry dated March 7, 1965: "The wind was raw today but the sun is beginning to be warm again. I went into the garden of the 34th Street house where I've been living now and found the green shoots of the daffodils already 3 or 4 inches high. Also found Mary's trowel and rake where she must have left them that morning. She was murdered in October on the towpath along the canal by a total stranger at noon. The boys live with me now when they are not away at school."[57]

# 9

# Justice

*The Bible says, "Father, forgive them, for they know not what they do."*

— DOVEY ROUNDTREE

Dovey Mae Johnson was eleven years old in 1925 when she and her grandmother boarded a trolley car into Charlotte from their home on the outskirts of town. The little girl in pigtails had never been on a trolley before, and she sat down in one of the yellow cane-backed chair seats near the front to watch the driver steer the big vehicle down the tracks ahead. Before the car moved, the driver, a white man, turned and spat angrily, "You know that tar baby don't belong up here." Her grandmother reluctantly hurried the child back to the "colored" section of the car, and then the two got off at the next stop and walked the rest of the way into town. After a day's business in the city, they walked back home as well. At dinner that night, the grandmother, her fine-boned face reflecting mixed Native American, African, and French blood, told the day's story and admonished the children at the table to remember that no matter who told them what, they were as good as white people and deserved no less.

Dovey took that lesson to heart. Born in 1914 outside Charlotte, Dovey and her mother and sisters went to live with her grandparents in 1919, after her father died in the 1918 influenza epidemic. Her grandfather was a preacher who lost his pulpit because of drinking. Dovey was infused with strong religious faith from infancy. The trolley incident wasn't the only reason Dovey developed an early distrust of white men. Her female forebears had learned to fear and hate the white boss and his son, who had raped and occasionally impregnated them, and that sentiment was passed from generation to generation of black women. She was taught to fear the white salesmen who came out to her grandmother's house every so often selling cheap trinkets. In the lore Dovey grew up with, those same men insinuated themselves into the beds of black girls, who then gave birth to half-white babies who were shunned by the white community and left to the blacks to raise. As James Baldwin wrote, integration worked fine after the sun went down.

Little Dovey Johnson eventually became Dovey Roundtree, Esq., a respected criminal attorney in Washington, D.C. Her life story was as full of parables as the New Testament. "Racism is the black man's cross," her grandfather told her, but the grinding unfairness of white racism was obvious to a child in 1920s North Carolina. Dovey was precocious: "Even as a child I was able to talk the fat off a hog," she recalled. She did well in school but had no money for college. She and her mother took work as a domestic "team" for a wealthy white family. Eventually the two of them saved enough money for Dovey to enter Spelman College in Atlanta, a school for black women.

While she was in college, the white family for whom she continued to work, mistrustful of black education, eventually had her arrested for stealing from them, a charge Dovey denied. A white attorney got her released from jail. The incident taught her the power of the law. She graduated in 1938 and resolved to become an attorney.

After serving as a captain in the Women's Army Corps during World War II, she married William Roundtree and entered Howard University Law School. She was one of five women in her class and passed the D.C. bar in 1951. The D.C. bar was strictly segregated then, and even the courthouse law library was not open to blacks. She and other black attorneys congregated near the courthouse and took what cases they could, for the small sums their clients could pay. Dovey liked to say she worked for eggs and collard greens. But her church connections eventually brought business, first church and property tax work; then a funeral home came on as a client. Eventually she was able to right one of the wrongs she had witnessed as a girl. She successfully pressed the case of a black woman military officer who had been denied a seat on a Trailways bus in Florida because all the "colored" seats were taken. The Interstate Commerce Commission ruled for her. Dovey framed the judgment and sent it to her college as a gift.

Dovey got her start in Washington criminal defense under the mentorship of a slightly older man, Julius Robinson, who became her law partner and close friend. When Robinson died suddenly of a heart attack in the late 1950s, Dovey was devastated. She herself suffered heart problems, and during one hospital stay she felt herself "called" to the church. She went back to Howard and studied theology, becoming an ordained minister in the African Methodist Episcopal Church in 1961 (one of the first women so designated). She considered abandoning the law for the pulpit, but as she finished up her late partner's business she was drawn back into the practice. She began taking on criminal cases. She eventually opened an office on Eleventh Street, in an old townhouse painted bright light blue. Next door was a sign for the Beautorium, a beauty salon.

In October 1964 the pastor of the Second Baptist Church, attended by Martha Crump, visited Dovey Roundtree. Martha's son was in jail, accused of murdering a white woman. Would she please take the case, he asked. The church community had raised a little money for Martha Crump to hire a private attorney, although Dovey recalled only getting taken to lunch a few times and being paid one dollar. But for her, taking the high-profile case was not about money. "I think in the black community there was a feeling that even if Crump was innocent, he was a dead duck," Roundtree recalled. "Even if he didn't do it, he's guilty. I took that as a personal challenge. I was caught up in civil rights, heart, body, and soul, but I felt law was one vehicle that would bring remedy. The churches were there for me, too, in prayers and in hopes and faith. And that was just putting me in the briar patch because anybody who knows anything about me knows I am highly religious."[1]

In the days after his arrest, Crump's case quickly became a minor cause inside the black church community. Here was this black man, small of stature and possibly not of sound mind, picked up without a weapon in the vicinity of a well-to-do white woman's body. It sounded like every other trumped-up case that had led to lynchings in the South. In the atmosphere of the growing civil rights movement, the matter had the makings of another scenario in which a black man would be martyred to white racism.

On the day of Mary Meyer's funeral, Martin Luther King Jr. was awarded the Nobel Peace Prize. King donated his $54,000 prize to the civil rights movement. Dovey Roundtree was herself deeply involved in the movement, emotionally and professionally. Weekdays she advocated with lawyerly sobriety inside the courtroom before a judge, usually a white man. But on Sundays she spoke from the pulpit in the burning language of righteousness. She was regarded as one of the best black defense attorneys in the city.

Dovey Roundtree joined the Crump defense on October 15, three days after Mary Meyer was murdered and one day after her funeral, the same morning the U.S. attorney took the case to a grand jury and received an indictment for first-degree murder. At that hearing Crump testified that police had beaten him, which detectives denied. The case was moving fast. Prosecutors had already dispensed with a preliminary hearing, a fact that Dovey would object to and appeal. A trial date was set for November 11, 1964, less than a month away. Dovey immediately got a continuance.

Crump had been locked in the D.C. jail, an old stone building some compared to a dungeon, for three days when Dovey met him. She was struck by his small stature and his utter dejection. He was being kept in solitary confinement and was withdrawn and depressed. "He just kept crying and crying and crying," she recalled. She also found him apathetic and uncommunicative, more so than any client she had ever had, which made it hard for her to plan his defense. She attributed his strange behavior to jailhouse fear. "He was this little man, completely terrified. He didn't know why he was there. He couldn't even remember."[2] Martha Crump was sure her son was going to be killed by white guards or inmates inside the jail, and she called Dovey night and day with pleas to get Ray out of the building. Crump himself began to believe he might be poisoned by the prison food, a fear Dovey tried to allay with logical advice. "I told him to run his fingers through his food before he ate it," she said. At night the guards, all white, urged him to confess. Dovey told her client to demand his attorney, in a voice loud enough so other inmates could hear him, whenever guards approached.

The first thing Dovey Roundtree did for Crump was try to get him ruled insane and unfit for trial. The combination of Crump's fears in the jail and his oddly apathetic behavior and depression convinced Dovey to ask for a mental competency hearing. "I just couldn't get through his crying," she recalled. The reasons she gave in requesting a mental examination of Crump were that he suffered blackouts, had "excruciating headaches," and was "somewhat addicted to alcohol and was drinking, or had been drinking on the day of his arrest."[3] In mid-November he was removed from the jail and taken to St. Elizabeths, the public mental hospital, where psychiatrists examined him. Sixty days later, after observation and interviews with the accused, doctors pronounced him fit to stand trial.

But the trial was still months away. Dovey Roundtree was not about to let the prosecution railroad her client to a death sentence or life in prison, the two options if he were convicted. She put up a pretrial fight that called upon every courthouse maneuver in the book, beginning with pretrial motions to suppress evidence, which she argued and lost. She formally objected to the fact that he had been indicted without a preliminary hearing. That objection went up to a higher court on an appeal, and the government won on the grounds that a grand jury had already found cause to indict him. In January the prosecution notified her that police in the jail were going to cut a piece of Crump's hair for evidence. She argued that taking hair from his body violated his right against self-incrimination. Two months later, after an appeal, that motion was rejected and hair was taken from his head. Crump struggled and claimed to have been injured during the haircut. Dovey demanded a private doctor, but the court sent him to the jailhouse physician, who pronounced him uninjured and in good health. After the haircut, Dovey moved to suppress the evidence against Crump, not only his hair but also the clothes that had been taken from him at the jail. After lengthy written arguments from both sides, that too was denied.

On July 20, 1965, the trial began. Much had changed since the day of the murder. The old rules were under attack, as were the men among Mary's set who played by those rules and who, in many cases, made them as well. American soldiers were fighting another war. Vietnam was home to 190,000 Americans, and the names Da Nang and Mekong Delta were becoming familiar to Americans. More than a thousand Americans had already died there. A group of antiwar protesters planning to destroy the Washington Monument, Statue of Liberty, and Liberty Bell had been arrested. Timothy Leary issued his famous dictum, "Drop out, turn on, tune in," in a journal called the *Psychedelic Review*. Poet Allen Ginsberg coined the term "flower power." LSD was available on the streets. The Berkeley Free Speech Movement was spreading across the nation's campuses as baby boom youth rejected their parents' conformity. Across the city of Washington, as in other American cities, street crime and racial tension were acknowledged problems. A new era in race relations was beginning.[4]

Crump's trial literally pitted the old white establishment against the black underclass at a moment in history when few whites wanted such a fight. The Washington elite and by extension the national establishment was represented not only in the victim herself, but in the white police force and in the prosecutor's office, which was still under the control of Attorney General Robert Kennedy. The U.S. attorney for the District of Columbia, appointed by Bobby Kennedy, was David Acheson, son of cold warrior and former secretary of state Dean Acheson. Acheson belonged to the Georgetown crowd. His sister was married to Kennedy advisor McGeorge Bundy. He had been a personal friend of Mary Meyer's, attended Yale with Cord, and knew Cord was more than the generic government clerk he was labeled in the newspapers.

The judge assigned to preside over the case was a younger man, new to the bench and, some felt, possibly not ready for such a high-profile, tense murder trial. But the trial date had caught the more seasoned trial judges summering in the country with other Washingtonians of means. Judge Howard Corcoran had been appointed to the federal bench by Lyndon Johnson shortly after Johnson became president. Corcoran was connected to Washington power not via Georgetown but from the other end of town, Capitol Hill. His brother and sometime law partner, Thomas "Tommy the Cork" Corcoran, was a legendary congressional lobbyist and operator, a man whose name was for decades attached to clichés of smoky back rooms, ice clinking in whiskey glasses, and envelopes stuffed with cash. Howard Corcoran's nomination to the bench was regarded by several as Johnson's way of repaying Tommy the Cork for some legislative favor. But he played by the book. He was determined in his rulings to follow the law and not be overturned on appeal. Corcoran's law clerk for the trial was a young lawyer fresh out of law school named Robert Bennett, who decades later would represent President Bill Clinton against a sexual harassment lawsuit.

With this firepower arrayed before him, Crump's trial could easily have become a cartoon of white power massed against a tiny black man. But weighing against a "railroad" case was the fact that the Supreme Court, led by Justice Earl Warren, was in its heyday, and zealous prosecutors and police were being forced to become more cautious by rulings that increased the rights of those arrested. Defendants had to be handled more gently and evidence collected scrupulously or the case would be thrown out of court. Judge Corcoran allowed Dovey Roundtree to make all her motions and objections.

Crump also had the good fortune to face a prosecutor who, although accomplished, was not known for creativity. Alfred Hantman was a twenty-five-year veteran of the District of Columbia criminal courts and had handled scores of murder cases and high-profile felonies. A retired air force officer, he was dark-haired and pleasant-looking but uninspired in his courtroom style. What he lacked, and what Dovey Roundtree had to her fingernails, was charm. Hantman was, alone among the white men in the courtroom, not privy to the social connections that linked the victim, the U.S. attorney, and the CIA.

Dovey Roundtree was not privy to those connections, either. Every attempt she made to understand Mary Meyer had met with failure. "It was as if she existed only on that towpath on the day she was murdered," Roundtree felt.[5] She knew that Mary Meyer was divorced, and somewhere in her investigation the lawyer had come to believe that the divorce decree had granted custody of her children to her husband—an incorrect notion based on the fact that he had been granted control over their educations, but one that intrigued her for what it implied about the dead woman's character. Other than that, she felt stymied in her efforts to find out anything about Mary. As a black female, Roundtree could not even walk around Mary's Georgetown neighborhood without arousing suspicion; even the black postman inquired about her business in the area. She knocked on the doors of a few of Mary's neighbors, and some talked to her from their steps. Elderly neighbors described the victim as "Bohemian" and as someone who might have had more than the usual number of gentlemen callers. Roundtree thought that if the dead woman had been promiscuous, she might raise the possibility of a jilted lover or even an angry ex-husband as the killer.[6] But Judge Corcoran, in pretrial admonishments, refused to allow either side to mention the private lives or children of the defendant or the victim.

July 20, 1965, was a hot day, but the District of Columbia

courthouse was new and had air-conditioning. The sixty men and women assembled in the pool of jurors were comfortable. Selected from voter registration rolls, the prospective jurors were a cross-section of the city, mostly black, mostly over forty, and the vast majority government employees. What they saw on the first day was the contrast in the attorneys. Dovey Roundtree, a soft-featured woman with a neat graying coiffure, wore a pastel dress; she always wore light-colored dresses to court to offset the darkness of the business at hand. She had a North Carolina accent and spoke in a comfortable vernacular with the cadence of a preacher. At the opposite table was the prosecutor, still bristling with the precision of the air force officer he had once been. Hantman had tried hundreds of felonies and thought of Crump as "that scoundrel."[7] He expected to send him to jail for life—at the very least. His physical stature and grimness were in stark contrast to the woman at the defense table, who could have been taken for the young defendant's mother. Crump himself sat quietly at the defense table, head bowed, wearing a new suit his mother had bought him for the occasion.

The courtroom was packed with journalists, including a young man named Sam Donaldson who would achieve television fame in the coming decades. Cicely Angleton attended the entire trial. She noticed that the audience was filled with black people, presumably friends of the defendant's churchgoing mother. Cicely was unnerved by the racial tension in the room.[8] Dovey Roundtree glanced around and noticed what she thought of as all the "high-class" white people in the crowd, especially a lot of "men in gray suits."[9]

When the judge asked the prospective jurors how many had read or heard about the case, two dozen hands shot up—more than any court observers could recall from previous cases. Still, Dovey Roundtree was not interested in a change of venue. The usual options were Philadelphia and Baltimore, and she didn't think her client would do any better away from his home turf. She hoped to find sympathetic members of the community right here, near his own home and hers too. By the end of the first day the jury had been selected. Eight women and four men were picked—two of whom were white, according to Hantman—with an average age older than forty.[10] Most were government employees or housewives. The man selected as foreman, Edward Savwoir, was a black federal employee who worked for the Job Corps of Economic Opportunity. "I thought I had a fair jury when all was said and done," Roundtree recalled.[11] Hantman too was satisfied.

Hantman delivered his opening statement on the second day of the trial. Striding back and forth before the jury, he ticked off a minute-by-minute account of Mary Meyer's final walk on the towpath, her death struggle "at the high noon of her life," the two bullets, and Wiggins's account of the screams and the man standing over the body. He then recounted with stopwatch precision the arrival of the police on the towpath, the closing of the two nearest pedestrian exits "at 12:24" and "at 12:28," the foot search, and the discovery of Ray Crump soaking wet about five hundred feet east of the body just forty-five minutes after the shooting, with his bloody head and hand, his fishing story and no fishing pole. Hantman described the evidence he had: an eyewitness who would identify Crump as the man standing over the body; Crump's jacket found at the water's edge 684 feet west of the body; his cap found another 426 feet beyond that; the shoes and slacks he'd worn that day, matching the identification made by the witness. Hantman promised to bring in a map of the towpath that would prove there was no way out of the area for Crump except running west or swimming the Potomac; photographs of the crime scene showing drag marks where the struggle occurred; the police officers who found the defendant "soaking wet." He promised to bring in the very tree that Mary Meyer had clung to in her last desperate seconds of life.[12]

Hantman was confident. It was an open-and-shut circumstantial case. He'd tried dozens of them. His opening statement was a powerful indictment of the defendant. He was so confident that he opened his remarks by admitting that there would be no weapon and no blood linking the defendant to the victim. The .38 caliber Smith and Wesson murder weapon was never found despite extensive and expensive efforts that involved several branches of government. The morning after the murder forty police officers combed fifteen hundred feet of the dirt and dense brush around the murder scene on foot, and the search went on for two days. The U.S. Park Police, who technically had jurisdiction over the towpath, closed a lock upstream and drained the canal, but there was no gun in the mud near the murder scene. Park police scuba divers searched the murky water farther away and found nothing. Harbor police searched the Potomac River from shore to fifty feet out using grappling hooks and magnets. Six navy divers searched the bottom of the rocky river. No weapon was ever found.

Ben Bradlee, Washington bureau chief for *Newsweek*, was the first witness Hantman called to the stand. Bradlee established that the dead woman had indeed been Mary Pinchot Meyer, his wife's sister, and that he had identified the body himself the night of the murder. Then Hantman asked Bradlee a series of questions that, had Hantman been better informed, could have led to the revelation that the victim kept a diary that certain people very much wanted to keep away from public notice. Hantman asked the newsman under oath, "Did you make any effort to gain entry to this studio that was occupied by Mrs. Meyer?" Bradlee replied affirmatively. "Now besides the usual articles of Mrs. Meyer's avocation, did you find there any other articles of her personal property?" Bradlee replied, "There was a pocketbook there." In the pocketbook, he testified, were keys, wallet, cosmetics, and pencils. On cross-examination, the defense asked Bradlee, "You have no other information regarding the occurrences leading up to her death?" Bradlee replied in the negative and was excused.[13]

After Bradlee, the city medical examiner testified to the nature of the wounds that Mary Meyer suffered. The first shot had come from someone holding a gun to the back and side of her head, and the bullet traversed the base of the skull, lodging at the other side. It was the medical examiner's opinion that someone with such a wound might move twenty to twenty-five feet before losing consciousness. He testified that during those seconds she had instinctively brought her hands up to her temples, hence the blood on her gloves. The second shot went through her shoulder blade and severed the artery carrying blood to the heart. The medical examiner observed what he called "dark haloes" on the skin around both entry wounds. FBI experts testified that those haloes meant the shots had been fired at close range, possibly point-blank.[14]

The prosecution then brought in the government's first piece of evidence, a fifty-five-foot-wide map of the towpath, designed by a Park Service employee. Hantman wanted to tack the map to the courtroom walls for the next several days as witnesses and police came in and testified. Hantman planned to mark their locations on the wall map with a pointer and in ink as they testified. The size of the map was unusual, and Corcoran ruled it might be prejudicial to leave it on the wall when it was not being used in testimony. Hantman was left with the laborious task of putting up the giant map and then pulling it down between witnesses.

The mapmaker, Joseph Ronsisvalle, a career government employee and engineer, testified that there were only five ways out of the towpath within miles of the area where Mary's body had been found. But Ronsisvalle turned out to be a disastrous witness for the prosecution. Roundtree, in the first of a series of objections that eventually made Hantman lose his temper, demolished the map's credibility. On cross-examination she elicited the fact that Ronsisvalle had never walked the towpath area himself and therefore was unaware of what she described as numerous small and unofficial paths in the towpath and river area. The mapmaker conceded, "I can only indicate from the records of my office that the records indicate that these are the exits of the towpath between Chain Bridge and Key Bridge." Hantman rose with an objection, but he was overruled. "If he doesn't know, he doesn't know," Judge Corcoran said. The jury, familiar with Washington topography, probably knew well enough that the area around the Potomac River was a weed-choked jungle and that official records in some government office might not tell the whole story.[15]

Years later Hantman still stubbornly defended the map. "Best thing we had was that fifty-five-foot topographical map the Department of

Interior made," Hantman said, shaking his head. "We showed them exit by exit how quickly it was shut down while the police were scouring the area and coming across the scoundrel."[16]

Tuesday afternoon, the government's star witness took the stand. He was Henry Wiggins, the twenty-four-year-old mechanic. The government had subpoenaed Wiggins's boss at the Esso station to tell the court about the stalled Rambler, but he was out of the city on business when the trial commenced. Neither Wiggins nor anyone else in court knew whose Rambler it was or why it was parked at that particular spot. Wiggins testified that he heard Mary's screams for about twenty seconds, then heard the shots, then saw a man standing over the body. The man, Wiggins testified, did not seem to be in much of a hurry. Wiggins had all the makings of a credible witness. Years later Dovey Roundtree said she had "qualified" him in her mind as a good witness. As an MP in Korea, he had once worked on a murder case. His identification skills were unassailable. When Wiggins called police from the Esso station to report the shooting, he described the suspect as a black man clad in a light tan jacket and dark cap, about five feet eight inches tall, and weighing about 185 pounds.

Fortunately for Crump, those measurements overestimated his real height by about three inches and his weight by forty or fifty pounds. Crump's small size became the deciding factor in his defense. Wiggins and the jogger both guessed the presumed killer's height at five foot eight. When Crump arrived at the D.C. jail after he was arrested, he was measured at five foot five and a half, 145 pounds. Dovey Roundtree proclaimed in court that his driver's permit had him at five feet three inches tall and weighing 130 pounds. Her client was, in words she would use repeatedly and to great effect in her closing statement, just "a little man."

Cross-examining Wiggins, Dovey Roundtree pounded home the discrepancy between the initial report and the short man sitting at the defense table. After establishing that Wiggins did tell the police on the telephone that the man above the body was five foot eight and 185 pounds, she asked Wiggins whether "that would be an accurate estimate of the man you saw." Wiggins replied, "That wouldn't be an accurate estimate, no, ma'am." Roundtree: "Well now, are you telling us now you gave them information which was not accurate?" Wiggins explained that he had been looking down from the height of Canal Road upon the scene of the crime. "I tried to do my best," he said. Wiggins was on the stand for a day and a half answering questions about every aspect of his report and behavior once the police arrived.[17] After the trial, he complained that the police had failed to back up his identification of Crump with a full police investigation that might have bolstered the charges. Wiggins was upset that the entire case had been made to hang on his identification of Crump. "It was me against Crump," he said after the trial.[18]

But the city police officers had very little to add to Wiggins's testimony. A half-dozen white officers testified that they had responded as promptly as possible to the report of a murder. They closed the known towpath exits and began patrolling the area near the scene immediately. It was the government's belief that police had arrived before the murderer could have escaped. Roundtree gently ridiculed their testimony. Did they have stopwatches on the towpath that day? she asked. How, then, could they be so sure they had arrived at precisely four minutes after the crime?

The police also testified about the conflicting reasons Crump gave for his presence in the area and his condition, soaking wet, bleeding from his right hand, pants torn and unzipped. He told the first officer he had cut his hand on some rocks trying to retrieve his fishing pole from the water. He told another he had cut his hand on a fishhook. He told one he'd fallen into the river while walking away from his fishing spot and another that he'd fallen into the river while asleep.[19] Neither pole nor hooks nor bait was ever found at the scene, although his pole and fishing box were found later that afternoon in a closet at his house. But Hantman did not give the conflicting stories much significance. He allowed them to be stated randomly by different officers and never came back to them in his opening and closing statements. Crump's incessant jailhouse crying and dubious mental stability were not part of the trial.

The prosecution of the case depended on a precise depiction of the murder scene itself and on putting Ray Crump in it. The government had a theory about Crump's movements after the crime. They said he had run west through the woods about a mile, dropping first his cap and then his jacket into the river, poked his head out of the woods and spotted an officer, run back east toward and then past the body by about five hundred feet, and got wet trying to swim around the open culvert before running into Officer Warner on the trolley tracks. But the moment of the murder itself was invisible, and Hantman was not able to re-create it. Nobody really knew what had happened on the towpath just before or during the time when the shots were fired. There were only a bloody tree, drag marks in the gravel, a body with two bullet holes and a scraped knee, and a witness who heard shots and screams, then saw a man standing over the body just seconds after the shots were fired. From these, the government had constructed a detailed theory of the struggle that preceded the murder itself.

Officers testified about drag marks on the towpath, two grooves across the path leading from the body to the edge of the forest on the Potomac side. Those marks, according to the government's case, appeared there because Ray Crump had dragged Mary Meyer on her knees toward the dense woods, to get her out of view of Canal Road. That dragging had torn her slacks at the knee and bruised her knee. Dovey Roundtree suggested the grooves might have been horseshoe tracks or marks left by running shoes.

The trial recessed on Thursday and didn't resume until Monday of the following week. By the weekend recess, Hantman was beginning to feel a little queasy. Somehow Dovey Roundtree had managed to subvert his case—and she hadn't even made an opening statement yet. His witnesses were not holding up under her cross-examination and neither was his evidence. Her constant objections had begun to fray his temper. At one point she interrupted his questioning of one of his witnesses to exclaim, "Don't testify, counsel." He blew up in open court. "If your honor please, I am either going to put on my case or I'll sit down and let counsel put on the Government's case." Judge Corcoran admonished him and ordered Hantman's angry outburst stricken from the record.

The second week of trial began with more police officers and the FBI agents who had conducted lab tests on the bullets, Mary Meyer's clothing, Crump's clothing, and Crump's hair. Roundtree injected doubt into the testimony of almost every witness. A firearms expert testified that because Crump was in the water before he was tested for gunpowder, he could have washed any trace of nitrates—proof of having fired a weapon—from his clothes and hands. Nitrates, he testified, are water-soluble. But Roundtree elicited from the man that when hands were tested for gunpowder in the lab, they were often washed after the first test on unwashed hands, and then tested a second time. The implication was that water might not in fact wash away all traces of a recently fired weapon, and she argued that since no traces were found on Crump, he hadn't fired the weapon.

Another FBI agent testified that Crump's hair—the hair obtained by force and which Roundtree had tried to suppress—matched hairs found inside the plaid cap in twenty-one of twenty-two characteristics. Such matching indicated to the FBI agent that the hair in the cap was almost certainly Crump's hair. Dovey Roundtree had been studying the literature on hair testing and she brought a dozen books into the courtroom with her, conspicuously piled on the defense table. She quizzed the agent in the witness chair about the literature, much of which he admitted he had not read. The sheer number of books and scientific disagreements she cited reduced to absurdity the notion that hair matching was an exact science. She asked the witness whether all hair analysts agreed on method and outcome. "Well," he responded, "in the area of neutron activation of hairs there is a great controversy raging right now. Some say we can make positive identification, some say we cannot."[20] The defense attorney forced him to admit that he had never studied hair analysis at any accredited university. He was unfamiliar with the names of the experts she cited.

Hantman's biggest psychological defeat came toward the end of the trial. He had promised the jury they would see the bloodstained tree trunk to which Mary Meyer clung in her last moments. The defense felt it was inflammatory. Hantman fought hard even as Judge Corcoran expressed incredulity. "What has the tree got to do with it?" the judge asked Hantman in an exasperated sidebar. "How big is this tree?" Hantman backtracked: "It is just a limb, your honor. . . . about thirty inches long. You can hold it in one hand." The tree, he said, went directly to the heart of the struggle between Mary Meyer and the assailant, which was central to the government's account of events on the towpath. Corcoran thought Hantman could simply describe the tree by having the analyst who identified Mary's blood on it explain where the blood came from. Hantman would not relent. "You're making a mountain out of a molehill," Corcoran told him. The tree was ruled "inflammatory" and not allowed. After this colloquy and Hantman's reluctant acceptance of the judge's ruling, the two lawyers continued to argue at the bench. Hantman said he thought the defendant was getting a fair trial. Roundtree said she was "worried." Corcoran stepped in: "I think he is getting a fair trial," he told Roundtree. "I don't want this jury to go out with passion and decide this case, I want them to go out cool."[21]

In another sidebar Judge Corcoran told Hantman he was overtrying the case. The prosecutor wanted to project a slide photograph of Mary Meyer's injured knee onto a screen. The jurors had already heard about the injured knee and seen photographs of the crime scene and body. Corcoran took Hantman aside and tried to pull him back. "It is just hurting your case," Corcoran said. "Just because you have a lot of material, counsel, it doesn't necessarily mean you should put it all in evidence." Hantman accepted the ruling but did not change his tactics.[22]

Roundtree had allowed Hantman his rope and done nothing but cross-examine his witnesses and raise objections as often as possible. She had not even made an opening statement, and the prosecution was about to rest. Hantman had no idea what she was up to. The courthouse was rife with speculation that her entire case was going to hinge on Crump's testimony. Hantman could barely wait to get his hands on Crump in the witness chair. He would nail the man to the wall with his own conflicting accounts of events on the towpath that day. But Hantman was in for a surprise.

The weekend before the second week of the trial, Dovey Roundtree sat on her back porch in the shade and sipped lemonade. On her lap was the yellow legal pad where she was writing her opening and closing arguments. She wanted to put Crump on the stand. He was so shy and innocuous, she felt he could only help himself with the jury. But her colleagues were strongly opposed. They argued that from where they had been sitting, away from the defense table, Hantman's twenty-seven witnesses and nearly fifty pieces of evidence had not proved the case. With Wiggins's wrong measurements, the government had not even placed Crump on the scene, let alone put him there with a missing murder weapon. Why, they asked Dovey Roundtree, give Hantman a chance to shred Crump in front of the jury? On Monday morning Roundtree rode the elevator up to the courtroom. The elevator operator, a black woman, took her by the arm and told her that the white prosecution team had been joking in the elevator about how they couldn't wait for her to put Crump on the stand. "Sometimes people will say things in front of a certain type of person that they wouldn't say in front of other people," Dovey Roundtree, daughter of domestics, observed later. The image of a group of white men chortling about her strategy and oblivious to the listening ears of the black elevator operator was the final kick that ultimately persuaded her not to give Crump to Hantman.[23]

Tuesday morning Roundtree went to court in a dress she had bought especially for the occasion at a Washington department store, a pink and white pinstriped seersucker with a thin white belt. She put on white pumps, white earrings, and a necklace of round white buttons.[24] She made her opening statement short and simple. The first part of her argument had been made for her, she said, because the government had been unable to prove Crump guilty in the week of trial. "There are a number of things which, at the proper time, we shall pull out from that great quantity of evidence and show to you in substantiation of our contention that you may not find from this evidence that Raymond Crump, Jr. was the person who fired the gun on that fatal afternoon causing the death of Mrs. Meyer," Roundtree said, preparing the jury for her closing argument.[25] The second part of her defense was the evidence before them in the person of Ray Crump Jr. "Exhibit A," she said. "Look at Raymond Crump, Jr., and then you weigh him beside the evidence that you have before you these long and tedious days of trial."

She told the jury that "evidence of good character may be sufficient alone . . . to raise a reasonable doubt, and having raised a reasonable doubt in your minds, then you may not convict Raymond Crump, Jr. as charged of murder in the first degree." She presented three character witnesses, friends of Martha Crump's from the Second Baptist Church. They said that they knew Ray from church and that he was peaceful, orderly, and calm, not violent. Their testimony lasted twenty minutes. Hantman asked a few questions, trying to prove the witnesses barely knew Crump. They were steadfast. After just twenty minutes Roundtree rested her case. A dumbfounded Hantman approached the bench. "If your honor please, I am caught completely flat-footed at this moment because I never anticipated in my wildest dream that counsel would rest her case."[26] The court went into recess to allow the government to prepare for jury instructions.

The tortoise had just overtaken the hare.

The two court reporters for the *Washington Evening Star* and *Washington Post* had watched the entire trial and they were stunned at what had just occurred. Roberta Hornig of the *Star* was convinced the defendant was guilty. She knew more than the jury had been allowed to hear about the evasive way Crump had behaved when apprehended, including his comment that the evidence was stacked against him, and she was focused on his conflicting stories about fishing or sleeping. She was convinced Hantman had blown the trial. He had failed to point out that Wiggins overestimated Crump's height because Crump was wearing two-inch heels the day he was arrested. The "little man" had been physically elevated on the day of the crime. Hornig and another reporter did a lot of "journalistic soul-searching" about what to do. As reporters, they were committed to impartiality. Yet they were convinced a guilty man was about to go free, and they finally resolved to go and talk to Hantman. "A lot of the defense case hung on how short he was—yet in evidence were these two-inch heels," Hornig said. "Finally we went to the prosecutor and said, 'Why haven't you argued this?' "[27]

In her closing argument, Dovey Roundtree made the estimated size of the presumed killer the centerpiece of her defense. She also took apart other aspects of the government's case. If there really was a body-to-body struggle, surely blue angora fibers would have rubbed off Mary's sweater onto Crump. If the police had been able to find a small button from Mary's sweater and tiny angora fibers on the tree, why hadn't they—working with the best military divers—found the murder weapon? She answered her own question: Obviously the gun was nowhere near the towpath if those experts could not locate it. The real killer had walked out of the park with it, on one of the many uncharted paths overlooked by the government mapmaker. She had proven the only case she needed to prove. Her client was known to be of "peace and good order." The government had done the rest for her. "I leave this little man in your hands," she concluded. "And I say to you fairly and truly, if you can find he is five feet and eight inches tall, that he weighs 185 pounds, irrespective of what he wore that day—if you can find—I cannot from this evidence—and I say you must have a substantial and reasonable doubt in your minds, and until the government proves its case beyond such doubt, then you must bring back a verdict of not guilty."[28]

Hantman tried to recoup on Wednesday. When he had submitted the shoes as evidence early in the trial, he had described them as black wingtips to precisely match the description Wiggins would give. He had failed to point out their heels. In his closing arguments, he carried the shoes to the front of the room and placed them on the lectern. "Look at the heels on these shoes," he said. "They are practically Adler-heel shoes. There are at least, as I look at it, and you will have to make up your own mind, two inches of heel on that pair of shoes." The shoes gave Crump the extra inches of height to make him the size described by Wiggins and the jogger. "Do we quibble with two and a half inches when the defendant was wearing the shoes with heels as you see here?"[29]

Hantman still thought he had a chance of conviction, despite the growing sense that he had been outfoxed by the defense attorney. He thought Roundtree's closing argument had been sermonlike, and he himself was no preacher. His closing argument was flat in comparison, but he trusted that logical minds would prevail. "If he didn't shoot and kill with malice and premeditation why did he throw clothing away?" Hantman said in his final arguments, pointing at Crump. "Why did he abandon it as much as 1,100 feet away from the scene?" And where were the bait box, the knife, the fish hooks? "I ask you to think with your heads, not your hearts," he begged the jury in his last minutes. "Thank you very much."[30]

Thursday morning Judge Corcoran gave the jury its instructions. He explained that Crump was not required to take the stand and that the fact that he hadn't was not to be taken as admission of guilt. He defined "reasonable doubt." The government, he said, was not required to prove guilt to mathematical or scientific certainty. Reasonable doubt would cause "a reasonable person to hesitate or pause in the graver or more important transactions of life." He instructed them about the elements of first-degree murder, with which Raymond Crump was charged, which included malice and premeditation. First-degree murder was punishable by death by electric chair or life in prison, Corcoran said, and the jury would have to choose between the two. If the government did not prove Crump guilty of the elements of first-degree murder, the jury might still convict him of second-degree murder, which required only malice, not premeditation.

At three that afternoon the jury went into deliberations. At ten-thirty that night, foreman Edward Savwoir sent a note to Judge Corcoran. It was read in open court with Crump present. "Your Honor, after eight and a half hours, we have eight jurors who have reached a decision and four who have not. Do you consider this jury deadlocked?" The judge sent back a note: "We do not consider the jury to be hopelessly deadlocked." Because of the lateness of the hour, the jurors were told to retire for the night.[31]

Late Friday morning, after deliberating a total of eleven hours, the jurors announced they'd reached a verdict and filed back into court just before noon. Hantman noticed two elderly white women jurors were weeping—a bad sign for him, he felt. Roundtree noticed that the jurors looked at her, always a good sign. The conventional wisdom was that if they were going to convict, jurors never made eye contact with the defense lawyer.[32] She thought these jurors smiled her way.

Ray seemed unsteady on his feet. Martha Crump was behind him. Cicely Angleton was in the back of the room. The verdict was handed to Judge Corcoran. He opened it and admonished the jury to rise. "Members of the jury, we have your verdict which states that you find the defendant Ray Crump, Jr. not guilty, and this is your verdict, so say you each and all?" The jurors indicated their affirmation.

At the defense table where he was standing, Raymond Crump swayed forward and appeared about to faint. Dovey Roundtree gave him a hug and turned to take congratulations from her law partners. Martha Crump rose and began singing praises to the Lord. Hallelujahs rang through the courtroom as her church friends rose in jubilation. Hantman cast one furtive glance at Roundtree. He would not congratulate her, and Dovey Roundtree would later say he never spoke to her again. His opinion of the outcome had been molded by the sight of those two white women crying. A racial verdict, he thought, or a matter of lawyerly personality. Judge Corcoran remained impassive. "Raymond Crump," he said, "you are a free man."[33]

Crump didn't move. Roundtree took him by the arm and walked

him out through the throng of well-wishers from his mother's church and past the reporters. In the hallway Martha Crump wiped away tears and told reporters, "I'm so proud. I'm thanking the good Lord for giving me my son back free."

Reporters staked out the jury foreman, Edward Savwoir, on his way out of the jurors' lounge. What had swayed the jury? they clamored. "There were many missing links," Savwoir said. "We just didn't get the man on the scene."[34] He wouldn't say how the jury had been divided the night before. In days to come anonymous racist threats were sent to his home. Savwoir turned the hate mail over to the FBI, but the source was never discovered.[35]

Al Hantman had just lost his most important case. Before the trial he had been oblivious to Mary's social connections. He hadn't known about the diary or her connections to JFK, but if he had, it wouldn't have made a bit of difference to him. Immaterial to his case. Not evidentiary. They had their man, Crump, and Hantman was sure he was guilty. "It all hung on the presentation of the case and the summation given at the end," Hantman said years later. "I'm not a preacher and my argument didn't go over too well. But if you base it on logic and to what conclusion reasonable minds might come, there was a fair argument that he was the one." After the trial ended, Hantman received a call from Ben Bradlee, who wanted to get his assessment of what went wrong. "I told him it's a flip of the coin. You could describe it as jury nullification. If the jury were true to its oath it would follow the law and the only way it could come out would be with a verdict of guilty. But if they don't like personality or race, they go off and do whatever they want. And here was a guy that just walked."[36]

Roundtree would later say that Crump was such a timid little man, if he had been guilty, he would have confessed everything on the spot as soon as the police had him. It was not her practice to keep tabs on her clients after they were acquitted, but Crump was so high-profile, she worried for his safety. She put her client on a bus back to his relatives in North Carolina. He stayed there for a month, then returned to Washington. Dovey Roundtree's case notes from the Crump trial went to the Columbia University Law School, where they were used to teach law students the ideal way to defend a circumstantial-evidence case. She later lectured on the subject.

Dovey Roundtree the advocate would always contend in public that Crump was innocent and that if he "got into a little trouble," as she put it, in the years after his acquittal, it was due to the trauma of months spent in jail charged with a heinous crime he didn't commit. A defendant's guilt or innocence was not really her business, anyway; it was the Lord's. Decades after Crump's acquittal, as an eighty-two-year-old woman with a long and illustrious career behind her, Roundtree explained her philosophy with an anecdote that had all the force and logic of a parable. Once she had been asked to defend a woman who had butchered her husband's girlfriend with a kitchen knife. There was no doubt about her guilt. "She got a butcher knife and cut this woman as long as she could swing it," Roundtree recalled. "The next day, a reverend called and asked me to go down to the jail. And I saw under her fingernails blood. And I covered her hands with my hands and we just sat there. She said what many people say who have taken the life of another: 'If she hadn't, I wouldn't have.' And we both cried and both prayed. And the case was dropped. That's prayer. Nothing any courts can do about that. It is stronger than the courts. She is back in church and I'm sure she's still singing in the choir. I felt she had forgiven herself. That's the first step to forgiveness. The Bible says, 'Father forgive them, for they know not what they do.' But you've got to also forgive *yourself*. I have represented brothers who killed brothers, sons who killed fathers. Everything. And I found the key for me is, Can you forgive?"[37]

# 10

## "Half Light"

*Axel wondered if this was what his father meant by the dream world of women. Unsuited by temperament to the hard realities of government and politics, they lived in a half-light of illusion; they turned the facts to mean what they wanted them to mean, and perhaps in that way achieved their heart's desire.*

WARD JUST
ECHO HOUSE

When Ray Crump was acquitted, Mary's Georgetown friends reacted with silent and stoic resignation. It was a small chink in the psychic dike protecting them from what really threatened them, much closer to home than Khrushchev or the Communists in Southeast Asia. Cicely Angleton reported to Cord Meyer, who reported to Ruth Pinchot, that the trial had been well conducted but the jury had not found the evidence conclusive.

Georgetown soon looked away from Crump and got on with the business of the cold war and national politics. Crump became the invisible man he had been before his arrest and trial. Decades after the acquittal, Ben Bradlee still believed that Crump "was escorted to the city limits . . . and told never to set foot in the District of Columbia again."[1] Of course, by 1965 the justice system would never have allowed police officers in the South, let alone the nation's capital, to exile a man found innocent by a jury of his peers. For all Bradlee knew, Crump spent the rest of his life outside the city limits. His violence in the next three decades never reached the white part of town and certainly never made the pages of the *Washington Post*.

If Mary's closest friends felt her murderer had walked away, there was nothing they could do or say. Their privilege had become an albatross of white guilt and their neighborhood a place to be defended. The sense of civic peace that had prevailed in Georgetown was gone. Homes and women had to be protected with locks and security guards. Black unemployment was three times higher than white unemployment.[2] The civil rights movement had raised awareness of white transgressions. Small incidents on the street—a pushing match between a black woman and a white woman at a trolley stop, for instance—became citywide racial events requiring delicate negotiations, compromise, committees, and reconciliation.[3] Predictions of coming racial violence haunted the pages of the local papers. "It was not a time when you wanted to press a case against a black man too hard," said one of Mary's friends.[4]

Two weeks after Crump was acquitted, a riot across the continent in the Los Angeles ghetto of Watts inaugurated an era of urban racial violence. Fires raged and bullets ricocheted for six days beginning on August 11. Thirty-four people died, a thousand were wounded, and acres of property reduced to ash. Four thousand people were arrested, and fourteen thousand National Guardsmen were called out to quell the violence. In Washington, a black leader who spoke anonymously to the *Washington Post* warned that the capital was in danger of even worse violence. "Washington has been restless for two years," the leader said. "It was right on the verge of trouble last year. . . . On a 95-degree day come down to 7th Street and anything can still happen. If the center blows here, it will spread quickly and could make Los Angeles look like a small affair."[5] The next summer Chicago and Cleveland saw riots, then Detroit; finally in April 1968, Washington got its turn when a riot erupted and mobs looted and burned parts of the city. Images of soldiers standing guard over the smoking rubble of America's capital finally exposed the fallacy behind the cold warriors' notion that the real threat to the nation lay abroad. The destruction occurred across Rock Creek Park from Georgetown, but it was close enough for smoke and ash to drift past the leaded glass panes and settle in the gardens.

After his return to Washington a month after his acquittal Ray Crump got work at construction jobs putting up the glass and steel block buildings that were replacing the old townhouses in downtown Washington. One of his many jobs over the years put him on a site right across the street from the *Washington Post* building.[6] He helped construct a number of the buildings that eventually housed the offices of lawyers and lobbyists and national journalists who worked in Washington in the decades to come.

Dovey Roundtree would later say her former client "got into a little trouble" after his acquittal. In fact, arson and assault with a deadly weapon became the distinguishing habits of a repeat offender. The available record shows twenty-two subsequent arrests in the Washington area and a pattern of violence.[7] In 1969, within four years of his acquittal, he was charged in Washington, D.C., with assault with a deadly weapon. The circumstances surrounding that case and the disposition of it have been discarded. Two years later, in 1971, he was charged in Washington with carrying a gun. Again, details of the underlying incident were lost in the records system.

His first wife, Helena, who never visited him while he was in jail on murder charges, officially separated from him after his arrest. She left their four children with his mother to raise. Martha Crump and her husband and son had bought a new house shortly before Ray's murder trial to house the children, probably purchased with help from Martha's church. Helena filed for and was granted a divorce in

1969. She then left the area and went into hiding. Her whereabouts in 1998 were not known.[8]

In April 1971, Ray Crump married Lois Taylor and was living with her and her children in Palmer Park, Maryland, a tract-house suburb near the Beltway. According to court records, Ray committed an arson there. He bought a gallon of gasoline and, with the family inside, he doused the building with gas and set it aflame. Lois and the children escaped unhurt. Crump was arrested and taken to jail in Upper Marlboro, Maryland, the county seat. Crump pled guilty to the crime of "malicious burning" and was sentenced to eighteen months in jail, beginning in April 1972. The jail sentence was "a great hardship" for the family, his attorney told the judge, and had forced them to apply for public assistance. In June 1972, after Crump had been in jail two months, he was released early and ordered to attend an alcohol rehabilitation program.[9]

Six months later, a Maryland probation officer asked another judge to put Crump back in jail. Crump had committed several violent crimes, in violation of his probation. He was arrested for drunk driving without a permit and for assaulting a police officer. He was arrested again in September on a charge of assault with a deadly weapon. He had pointed a gun at his wife, Lois, in their second-floor apartment. To escape, she jumped out of the window, fracturing her collarbone and breaking an ankle.[10]

Between 1972 and 1977 he was charged with assault with a knife, grand larceny, another arson, and several individual charges of destroying property. During that period, he spent seven months in jail.[11]

In January 1978, according to court records, Crump set a fire in the entryway of the building where his new girlfriend, Ann L. Johnson, lived. He had repeatedly threatened to kill her over the course of several days in January. On the night of January 24 he carried a gasoline can to the Hunter Gardens apartment complex in southeast Washington. A witness watched as Crump poured gasoline on the first-floor landing and stairs and struck a match. The police arrested Crump on the basis of the witness's identification but he was released pending trial.[12]

Several months later, Crump was charged with a rape in Arlington, Virginia, across the river from Washington. He allegedly took the seventeen-year-old daughter of a friend on a shopping trip in Arlington and then took her to an apartment. There, police told news reporters, he allegedly raped the teenager when she went into a bedroom to comb her hair, and he later dropped the girl off at her mother's house.[13] That case was never prosecuted and the Virginia authorities have lost all records of it.

A few months after the Virginia rape charge, Crump went on trial for the January arson at his girlfriend's apartment. He was convicted and spent the next four years in the D.C. prison until he was paroled in June 1982.[14]

In Washington in 1983, Crump committed another fire-related crime, this time torching a neighbor's car.[15] Before he was sentenced for this crime in 1985, the judge ordered a mental competency hearing. The court psychiatrist concluded after examining him that Ray Crump demonstrated no signs of mental illness. His age, forty-six, was cited as a possible factor for "reduced aggressivity." He showed certain memory defects, "probably the result of organic brain damage related to his chronic alcohol abuse," the psychiatrist reported. He could not subtract serially by sevens and could not remember the names of the presidents prior to Richard Nixon. He was sentenced to two and a half to ten years in prison.[16]

After his parole in 1989, Crump and his third wife moved to Albemarle, North Carolina, near Ray's birthplace, Norwood. There he committed another arson, tossing a homemade gasoline bomb into the home of an auto mechanic with whom he was in a dispute over money.[17] That arson won him a sentence of twelve years in North Carolina's prison system. But because it was also a D.C. parole violation, Crump was extradited back to the District of Columbia to spend two more years in prison. In June 1996, he was released from parole and returned to his mother's neighborhood.

In 1997, Ray Crump was fifty-eight years old. He suffered a mild heart attack. He found work as a day laborer wherever light construction jobs were under way in his neighborhood. He blended in.

His mother, Martha, was old and ailing. She had little to say about her eldest son. She did the best she could for her children. "I worked every day and nobody ever gave me anything," she said. She went to church every Sunday all her life. "None of us know what happens on the street," was all Martha Crump said about Ray's arrest for murder in 1964.[18]

Ray Crump's episodes of drinking and violence made him a kind of Dr. Jekyll and Mr. Hyde to people close to him. Some days he was a good provider for his wife and family, but one person close to him for a period of time said: "He pretends he can't remember what he does when he is drinking but he uses it as an excuse. He uses drinking like a medicine to help him carry out what he plans, like Dr. Jekyll. He knows what he's doing."[19]

Criminologists working for the Bureau of Alcohol, Tobacco and Firearms have found a strong link between repeat arsons and other types of violent crimes, especially rape. Seventy-four percent of serial killers are also arsonists. The link between the crimes, the researchers believe, is a need for power and control. Fire begins as an obsession and becomes a tool for revenge and violence. Studies are showing that "arsonists are much more violent people than we had thought," said one expert in the field.[20]

Only Ray Crump can ever tell the world exactly what he was doing on the towpath on that sunny day in October 1964, near the scene of a brutal murder. His conflicting explanations have left many questions. Why did he toss his hat and coat in the water? Why did he tell police he was fishing when his pole and tackle were at home in a closet? If he wasn't fishing, what was he doing there? How did he get the cuts on his hand and head and the rip in his pants if he was not fishing? Why did his wife at the time so fear him that she fled, leaving her children behind, after his arrest? In a letter to the author in September 1997 Crump wrote that he did not want to discuss the case and remembered nothing of that day on the towpath.[21]

Because he was acquitted, Ray Crump is innocent of murder in the eyes of the law. The police considered the case closed and threw away the evidence after twenty-five years, as is their practice. Thus it is impossible to apply new scientific techniques to try to solve the murder now. Whatever happened on the towpath, it is certain that Mary Meyer did not go easily. "She was fearless," said her friend Kary Fischer. "She would have fought back."

In the week after Mary Meyer was murdered, a white cross appeared on the towpath at the spot where the crime had occurred. Someone also scrawled on the Key Bridge the words "*Mauvais Coup*, Mary" in white paint. The phrase is a French idiom that translates roughly as "Bad luck, Mary."

For twelve years after her murder Mary's secrets remained buried. Tony Bradlee released one bit of writing from Mary's diary as part of a brochure for a posthumous art show in 1967. The show was roiled by art and power politics. First, Ken Noland opposed having Mary's work shown at the Washington Gallery of Modern Art in a small room alongside a retrospective of the work of his friend and fellow "jam session" painter, Color School pioneer Morris Louis.[22] But Tony Bradlee and Mary's friend Bill Walton pushed it, over his objections, using paintings from her last months of life. Among them were six "tondos," or round canvases painted with pie wedges of color. One was red, charcoal, black, dark blue; another was blue, yellow, light blue; another orange, pink, violet, and light olive green. There was also a small landscape painting with an orange horizon line "evoking Noland," the curator wrote. In the brochure for the show, Charles Millard, director of the Washington Gallery of Modern Art, wrote: "It has become increasingly apparent to those who knew her well, that at the end of her life Mary Meyer began, in her painting, to come to grips with problems of more than ordinary importance."[23]

*Washington Post* art critic Andrew Hudson reviewed the Morris show at length and gave Mary two paragraphs at the end. He described Mary as "one of the lesser members" of the Washington School. "Her paintings have a certain probity in the way they are concerned with testing out color, but express little in the way of feeling," Hudson wrote. "Whether, after all her color experiments, Miss Meyer might have plucked up the courage to break out into something more personal is impossible to say."[24]

Hudson was fired by Ben Bradlee within weeks of writing that review. The art critic believed his bad review of the editor's sister-in-law had something to do with his firing, although he admitted they had never gotten along. "Bradlee never talked to me, then one morning about a week before the show he came to me. He was literally physically trembling. He said, 'I don't know what to do about this show of Mary Meyer's coming up, whether we should review it.' It made him nervous that these women who had little talent in the art world were showing their work. All he cared about was power and politics."[25] Hudson was offended when, the day after the opening night of the Louis/Meyer show, the paper ran an article in the social pages about the prominent men and women who had convened for a dinner honoring the show. The article equated the two artists by inference and began: "Over 350 friends, admirers and colleagues of the late Mary Pinchot Meyer and the late Morris Louis" attended the opening followed by a preshow dinner hosted by "Mrs. Meyer's close friend," Mrs. Philip M. Stern.[26]

As the 1960s wore on and America got crazier and crazier, Mary's old friends fell out and feuded with each other. Some of the men fell victim to alcohol or the soul-deadening pursuit of power. Their wives retreated deeper into their rarefied world. Alcoholics drank more, spies became more suspicious, and the ambitious grew sharper elbows. Betrayals provoked lifetime vendettas. Marriages cracked. Friendships dissolved into private wars. Jim Angleton and Ben Bradlee stopped speaking in the late sixties after Bradlee wrote a review of English spy and traitor Kim Philby's book about duping the American intelligence agency, a book in which Angleton figured prominently as a gull. By reviewing the book and naming him in the *Post*, Angleton argued, Bradlee had blown his cover. Bradlee would later tell journalist Tom Kelly "Cord [Meyer] can't stand my guts.

Angleton . . . thinks I'm a traitor."[27] Bradlee presided over Watergate and Deep Throat and was photographed by Richard Avedon for *Rolling Stone*. Tony and Ben separated, and Ben remarried an attractive younger reporter at the *Post*, Sally Quinn. People close to the couple attributed the breakup partly to Tony Bradlee's increased reclusivity and consuming interest in mystical spiritualism after her sister's murder.

James Truitt drank more and began showing signs of manic-depression. In 1969 Anne Truitt sought a conservatorship for her husband's financial affairs based on a physician's certification to the court that he was suffering from a mental illness "such as to impair his judgment and cause him to be irresponsible,"[28] and the couple was divorced two years later. In 1969 he had been fired from his position as a top *Post* editor, and the double breakup left Truitt in a shambles. He even wrote Cord Meyer, apparently seeking a job at the CIA, in 1969. After his firing Truitt moved to Mexico with a new wife and settled in San Miguel de Allende among a community of American expatriates, many of whom were retired CIA agents. He grew increasingly erratic. He had five small dogs, was desultorily writing an archeological book on the Huichol Indians, and cultivated peyote on the roof of his house in the dry Mexican sun.[29]

Anne Truitt focused much of her energy on her art, creating monolithic pillars of fragile cabinet wood, painted over and over with layers of color. She published three artist's journals describing her childhood in Easton, Maryland, and her feelings about her children and her failed marriage. She contemplated how her personal history interacted with the painting of large wooden boxes. In the three journals she mentioned her old friend Mary Meyer exactly twice—once to explain her own art epiphany and once in passing, to recall Mary's keen understanding of masculine character. She took a job teaching art at the Madeira School for girls and at the University of Maryland for a time and spent summers at the artist colony Yaddo in upstate New York, where she eventually served in an administrative post.

Jim Angleton continued to drink multiple martinis at lunchtime and pursue his mole hunt based on his "monster plot" theory of endemic Communist infiltration. His daughters came home from college politically converted and marched against the United States presence in Vietnam. They eventually converted to the Sikh religion. Cicely Angleton, after leaving her husband several times, stayed on but buried herself in the study of medieval history. In 1976, with the press on a post-Watergate hunt for excesses in the national security system, Angleton was forced to resign from the CIA after revelations that he had spent several decades overseeing an illegal domestic mail-opening project.

Cord Meyer remarried in 1966. After he was exposed in newspapers as the brains behind the CIA's infiltration of American student organizations, his career seemed to stall. Instead of getting promoted to the top of the covert-action department, in 1973 he was shifted to London, where he served as the CIA's station chief. He resigned from the CIA after that posting and began writing newspaper columns with a hard right edge as a partner with his old friend Charles Bartlett. He wrote a book about his career, but it was more of a treatise in defense of the CIA's involvement in various international events, from Iran to Chile, than a personal memoir. He gave away little about his own real work for the agency. His reputation for argumentativeness never abated. In his seventies he was diagnosed with cancer, and in 1997 he was still living in Mary's Thirty-fourth Street townhouse.

His sons Quentin and Mark went to Yale, and gradually both turned toward religion. Mark became a missionary for the Seventh-Day Adventist Church in China before returning to the Washington area, where he reportedly translates Chinese for the government. Quentin also lives in Washington. Neither has ever married.

In the years following the murder, Georgetown whispered about Mary Meyer and the rumored diary. Mary's affair with JFK remained known for certain only to the privileged few: her closest women friends, the Bradlees, the Truitts, the Angletons, and her psychiatrist. But in time the security fence of propriety was breached by tabloid attention. Cocktail gossip was as far as talk about Mary went until

February 23, 1976, when the *National Enquirer* published a front-page story headlined "Former Vice President of *Washington Post* Reveals . . . JFK 2-Year White House Romance." The article included prominent pictures of James Truitt in a black turtleneck, vaguely resembling James Coburn, and appearing to be rolling a cigarette; Mary Meyer looking young and plump and also with a cigarette in her hand; Angleton sporting a sly smile beneath the rim of a felt hat; and half of a photo of the Bradlees and the Kennedys on a White House couch, showing only JFK and Tony Bradlee. The story's biggest bombshell was Truitt's allegation that the president and Mary had smoked marijuana joints that Truitt had provided. The story also revealed that Kennedy had hidden "one of Mary's undergarments in the Presidential safe." Truitt claimed Mary loved Kennedy but realized their romance would never be more than an illicit affair. To report the story, the tabloid sent reporters down to San Miguel de Allende to interview Truitt. The tabloid also contacted Tony Bradlee and Angleton and tried to talk to Ben Bradlee.

Bradlee was furious. When the *Enquirer* sent a reporter to talk to him in his *Post* office, the editor erupted in a shouting rage and had the reporter thrown out of the building.[30] Bradlee and Truitt went way back together, socially and professionally, and Truitt's betrayal hit Bradlee especially hard. Both had worked in the Washington bureau of *Newsweek* and both had been right-hand men to Phil Graham. When the newspaper fired Truitt, as part of his settlement he took $35,000 on the written condition that he not write anything for publication about his experiences at the *Post* that was "in any way derogatory" of the *Post* company, Phil Graham, or the Graham family.[31] Because he had been an assistant to Graham as well as a party buddy, it was presumed he had knowledge of a great deal of the publishing family's dirty laundry.

No one knows exactly what motivated Truitt to sell Mary's story. Some journalists who talked to him believed he wanted to embarrass Bradlee in the wake of his 1976 best-seller, *Conversations with Kennedy*. Truitt was disgusted that Bradlee was getting credit as a great champion of the First Amendment for exposing Nixon's seamy side in

Watergate coverage after having indulgently overlooked Kennedy's hypocrisies. He wrote Bradlee a letter when he heard about Bradlee's plans to publish his Kennedy book and demanded to know whether Bradlee would expose Kennedy's affair with his sister-in-law. At the time the *Post* was running editorials demanding the White House "let it all hang out" in the Watergate matter. Bradlee mentioned Mary five times in his book, never divulging a hint of the true nature of her relationship with the president, with the coy exception of the comment that Kennedy had once noted that "Mary would be hard to live with." Truitt also might have wanted to hurt his ex-wife, Anne. He probably did not betray Mary for the money: The *Enquirer* paid him just one thousand dollars for his story in 1975 and didn't run it until after the revelations about Judith Campbell Exner's affair with Kennedy were made public during House hearings into the Kennedy assassination the following year.

Advance word of the upcoming tabloid scoop provoked the *Washington Post* to cover it. Ben Bradlee was vacationing in the Virgin Islands with his new wife, Sally Quinn. Reached there, Bradlee objected to running the story until he could get a "clear focus" on it, but the editors vetoed waiting. "We're not going to treat ourselves more kindly than we treat others," one of the editors, Harry Rosenfeld, said.[32]

A *Post* reporter was dispatched to see Truitt in Mexico, where Truitt again recounted the details of Mary's private life. The *Post* ran an article on page one filled with the denials of Kennedy aides. One of them, Timothy Reardon, told the *Post* "nothing like that ever happened at the White House with her or anyone else." Kenneth O'Donnell called Mary "a legitimate, lovely lady" and denied that there had been a romance. Angleton told the *Post* he had assisted the Meyer family in a purely private capacity and said Mary had been a "cherished friend" of his wife. He refused to say whether there had been a diary.[33]

Mary's women friends were angered by the *National Enquirer* story and horrified that the husband of one of their own had been the source of the disclosures. Their efforts to counter the revelations came in the form of unsourced quotes later found in small items in venues such as *Time*. While not denying the sex outright, they tried to put it in a more ladylike context, away from the insinuating tabloid sordidness. "She was not the kind of person to get into a dalliance," insisted "one old friend of the Meyer family" to *Time*. "This wasn't some tawdry affair."[34]

The least horrified person involved seemed to be Mary's sister, Tony Bradlee, who matter-of-factly confirmed the fact of the romance but insisted that it be described as a "fling," not an affair. "Neither the relationship of Mary with JFK nor the existence of the diary has ever been made public before," Tony told *Enquirer* reporter Jay Gourley. "It was nothing to be ashamed of. I think Jackie might have suspected it, but she didn't know for sure." Later she told the *Post* that the tabloid had taken her words out of context "to make it appear that I corroborated their story." But she denied none of it.[35]

In 1981 James Truitt committed suicide with a gunshot to the head in Mexico while his college-age son was visiting from Washington. Truitt's widow, Evelyn Patterson Truitt, stayed in Mexico and knitted her own set of conspiracy theories. She claimed that Truitt's papers, including copies of Mary's diary, had been stolen from her after his suicide by an ex-CIA agent named Herbert Burrows. Burrows was in fact a retired CIA agent living in San Miguel de Allende before his death in the 1980s. Evelyn Truitt claimed her husband's papers covered thirty years "of close work with government" and that his "personal friend" Jim Angleton wanted them.[36] Angleton *was* a personal friend of Truitt's, but by the time of Truitt's death he had been out of the CIA for five years. The CIA, of course, denies anyone was assigned to steal Truitt's papers.

After Truitt's revelations about Mary's affair with Kennedy, her officially unsolved murder took on new depths of meaning in a variety of circles. The revelations came during the election year of 1976 and coincided with the post-Watergate atmosphere of deep distrust of the U.S. government and especially of the CIA. The CIA was being investigated on Capitol Hill, and national newspapers were still revealing assassination plots, poison pills, testing of psychoactive drugs, and domestic mail opening, all conducted during the years when Mary Meyer was alive and closest to the center of power. The Kennedy assassination itself was under review in Congress, and ugly secrets about the administration's Mafia links were being revealed.

One legacy of the 1960s was paranoia. The deep paranoia of the security services about domestic unrest and Communist infiltration—epitomized in the minds of James Angleton and J. Edgar Hoover—provoked an equal and opposite reaction of paranoia on the left. The condition seeped into the culture at large. Literary critic Morris Dickstein, analyzing the work of writer Thomas Pynchon, defined the paranoia of the 1960s as involving "a sense at once joyful and threatening that things are not what they seem, that reality is mysteriously over-organized and can be decoded if only we attend to the hundred little hints and byways that beckon to us, that life is tasteless and insipid without this hidden order of meaning, but perhaps appalling with it."[37]

Similar sensations accompanied LSD experiences. The drug often provoked the simultaneously beautiful and terrifying sense of wholeness and interconnectedness of all matter in the universe. The first public person to try to decode the mysterious reality of Mary's life and death was her old friend Timothy Leary, by 1976 a fading cultural icon but still the caricature of the dangerous criminal he had been branded by federal agent G. Gordon Liddy and the U.S. government. Serving time in San Diego's Metropolitan Correctional Center on drug charges, Leary read the tabloid news of Mary's affair with the president and especially the shared marijuana joints with happy amazement. Was it possible the president himself had turned on? The acid movement's fondest hope might have actually come true without Leary's even knowing it. The implications drove him to even wilder speculation. Could there be a hallucinogenic link in the Kennedy assassination? He had been convinced from the first news of Mary's murder that there had been "a cover-up," that things were not what they seemed. When he read of her death in 1964, Leary learned for the first time that the beautiful woman he knew as Mary Pinchot had been married to Cord Meyer. In one of fate's strange coincidences, Leary knew Cord from the days when both were members of the American Veterans Committee. Leary recalled loathing young Cord's efficient campaign to wipe out the left-wing element in that organization. He knew from mutual acquaintances that Cord was now at the CIA, conducting even vaster secret campaigns. And anything the CIA touched became a hall of mirrors. Mary's death was in that labyrinth, and he decided to investigate and expose it.

Leary did not pursue the matter until he got out of jail. An investigator he hired to look into the murder was inexperienced; the investigator was unable even to locate the Crump trial transcripts (a fact Leary attributed to a possible government cover-up), and did not bother to pull Crump's criminal record. The investigation led nowhere, but that didn't stop Leary from penning an article in an alternative magazine called *Rebel* in 1983 that detailed the comings and goings of the mysterious blonde from Washington and ended with speculation about her death. Leary hinted but never stated outright that Mary dropped acid with the president. Even in later interviews he always hedged. When asked whether he thought Kennedy took LSD with Mary, he went no further than coy suggestions. He had no proof. What proof might exist could be found only in Mary's diary, and the CIA, he thought, had taken care of that.[38]

Given the subversive image LSD had in the American public's imagination by 1964 and the CIA's apprehensions about the drug, a woman's knowledge that the recently assassinated president had actually tried LSD might have made her diary and her personal papers items of great interest. Former CIA director Richard Helms believed that if Angleton took the diary it was because Angleton wanted to ensure that the president was not "embarrassed" posthumously.[39] Since Washington was rife with women who had been intimate with Kennedy and whose papers were of no interest to the CIA, Angleton probably was interested to see whether Mary Meyer's diaries and papers contained references to something more embarrassing than a romp in the Lincoln bedroom.

Leary's acolytes in California and elsewhere seized the Mary Meyer story and made it their own. They embellished it and turned her into a feminist drug icon who had been trying to sow world peace through "the intelligent use of psychedelics" before she was shot down in a noon-hour hit authorized by the enemies of peace and drug use. An alternative magazine called *Mondo 2000* published in 1992 an article by a woman named Nancy Druid headlined "America's First Psychedelic President?" In it, the writer imagined the scene between Kennedy and Mary as they did drugs together and then described the theory popular among Leary's followers that Mary had been part of a "cell" of Washington women who actively plotted to turn on the president and other powerful men. According to this theory, Mary was in cahoots with journalists Lisa Howard and Dorothy Kilgallen—two women who died of mysterious overdoses after Kennedy's assassination. Mary "became that person most dreaded by the intelligence agencies—the 'runaway wife,' " Druid wrote. Howard's death appeared to be a suicide or accidental overdose. Dorothy Kilgallen's death in 1965—shortly after she had a private interview with Jack Ruby, the man who shot Lee Harvey Oswald—is mysterious. Just days before she died of what a medical examiner described as a lethal combination of alcohol and barbiturates, she had boasted of the assassination, "In five more days, I'm going to bust this case wide open."[40] Although Washington was a small town, there is no evidence Mary associated with either Howard or Kilgallen. Nonetheless, Leary and his followers regarded Mary Meyer as a martyr in the battle to bring hallucinogenic peace and wholeness to the world.

From there the legend grew. Another man to publicly associate Mary Meyer's death with a conspiracy to assassinate Kennedy is writer and self-proclaimed former CIA contractor Robert Morrow. Morrow has claimed in two books to have been involved in acquiring Mannlicher rifles to kill Kennedy. He claimed he provided sophisticated communications devices to three hit teams that killed the president and made counterfeit money used to undermine Castro's regime. According to Morrow, the assassination was the work of a conspiracy between the mob, the intelligence agencies, and "the leaders of our nation." In a second book, published in 1992, Morrow brought Mary Meyer into his conspiracy theory for the first time. He claimed that shortly before the Warren Commission's report came out, Marshall Diggs, deputy comptroller of the treasury under Roosevelt and one of those people in the federal government Morrow claims was witting of the conspiracy, "requested an urgent meeting" with Morrow about two weeks before Mary's murder. Morrow wrote that Diggs told him that "a prominent lady here in Washington knows too much about the Company, its Cuban operations and more specifically about the President's assassination." In Morrow's account, Diggs said that Mary Meyer had told a close friend of his "she positively knew that Agency-affiliated Cuban exiles and the Mafia were responsible for killing John Kennedy." Morrow claims Diggs also told him that CIA official Tracy Barnes was "concerned" about Mary and that the Cuban exile leaders ought to be informed. Morrow passed it on and the exile leader, Robert Kohly, supposedly replied, "Tell Diggs I'll take care of the matter." A week later Mary Meyer was dead.[41]

Morrow's story is rife with holes. First, conveniently for him and inconveniently for investigators, everyone involved in the discussions he described is dead—except him. There is no written or taped record of such discussions if they ever took place. Second, if Mary had inside knowledge about Kennedy's assassination—and it is not clear who might have passed such knowledge on to her—she shared it with no one, not friends and not even, if Bradlee's account is to be believed, her diary. Finally, Morrow is regarded by investigators who interviewed him for the House Select Committee on Assassinations as an unreliable source whose other stories have not checked out.[42] Although he seems to have been involved in some Cuban exile activity, his allegations about the Kennedy assassination have never been validated by investigators for the congressional committee that looked into the assassination, nor by scholars and researchers.

Another dedicated purveyor of conspiracy in Mary Meyer's death was the late author Leo Damore. Damore was a New England journalist who wrote a best-selling book about Ted Kennedy's Chappaquiddick accident. In the late 1980s he turned to the Mary Meyer murder. A meticulous researcher, he compiled lists of the names of all the police officers who were involved in the foot search and investigation and interviewed Dovey Roundtree at length and Al Hantman for a lesser period. He never located Crump (who was in prison at the time) or expended much effort to find out what Crump did after the murder acquittal. He explained Crump's fishing lie and ripped clothing as the behavior of a confused but innocent black man in a racist world. After several years of research, Damore began telling his copious interviewees that he was quite certain Crump was innocent.[43] He also boasted that a figure close to the CIA had told him that Mary Meyer's death had been a professional "hit." Damore's never-ending vortex of conspiracy led to nothing solid. He died of a self-inflicted gunshot in the presence of a nurse and a police officer after calling 911. No book was ever published.[44]

The legend continued to grow. In recent years, the Internet became the ideal venue for disseminating Mary Meyer conspiracy theories. On a random day in 1997 there were 141 Internet "hits" on Mary Pinchot Meyer, most involving speculation about drugs and the CIA. In one Internet theory, Mary was a pawn in the CIA's mind-control experiments and JFK the ultimate MK-ULTRA project guinea pig. The writer posits the question, "Was Mary Meyer playing some sort of clandestine game? Was she some sort of Mata Hari? Or was she perhaps unwittingly being used by someone in that capacity?" The message is from a four-part series published in the conspiracy magazine *Steamshovel Press* and titled "The High and the Mighty: JFK, Mary Pinchot Meyer, LSD and the CIA." For the price of a subscription, one could buy the story in detail. Another Internet writer proposed that Timothy Leary himself was in the CIA and that Mary Pinchot Meyer served as some kind of courier or connection between Leary and the agency. Another message from Conspiracy Nation linked her murder to every suspicious or tragic national event between 1963 and 1974, beginning with Phil Graham's suicide and ending with Watergate.

That said, it is clear the CIA had an interest in Mary Meyer—or at least the counterintelligence chief did. A photographer for the Associated Press who took pictures on the canal when Mary's body was discovered later recollected that he had found the crime scene rather odd. "The police kept us on the other side of the canal for a long time," Arthur Ellis said. "I took the picture with a long-angle lens, and when I look at it now I wonder who all those men in the picture were. There were Park Police there, which is normal for the C&O Canal, and homicide police as well. There just seemed to be so many plainclothesmen there. I'm curious, in light of what we know about the CIA now, who those men were."[45] On the other hand, experienced investigative journalists Philip Nobile and Ron Rosenbaum, who interviewed two of the story's main participants when they were alive—Angleton and homicide investigator Crooke—still came to the conclusion that "no one has ever pointed to a better suspect than Ray Crump."[46]

The conspiracy theories about Mary Meyer have been nourished by the mere presence of Jim Angleton in her life and death. Angleton's involvement in Kennedy's assassination and the investigation remains mysterious and the subject of legitimate inquiry. As the millions of pages of classified documents about the Kennedy assassination begin to be released, his role is still not clear. Angleton had kept close tabs on the writing of the Warren Commission report, and the final document was greeted with relief by the CIA, which had escaped without the commission's revealing the existence of, much less opening, a Pandora's box of curious and embarrassing facts about assassination plots and Mafia ties. The incompleteness of the report later served to raise suspicions about the assassination. Among the pieces of information the commission omitted was the fact that the CIA had been keeping track of Lee Harvey Oswald for some time, even to the point of taking his picture in Mexico City the year before the assassination. The commission also failed to mention the numerous ties connecting the CIA, the Kennedy administration, and the Mafia in assassination attempts on Castro. The report focused on

Oswald so intensively that Kennedy biographer William Manchester suggested it ought to be subtitled "The Life of Lee Harvey Oswald."

The CIA conducted its own investigation into the assassination. Although he was not its official head, the man who took ultimate control over the CIA's internal investigation and the CIA's relationship with the Warren Commission was Mary Meyer's friend and her ex-husband's closest confidant, James Jesus Angleton. Angleton apparently manipulated the Warren Commission through former CIA director Allen Dulles. In January 1964 he debriefed a Russian defector named Yuri Nosenko, whom he personally believed to have been sent by the Russians to trick the Americans. Nosenko defected just after Kennedy's assassination and told the CIA that although the KGB knew of Oswald before the murder, the KGB had not been behind his actions on November 22, 1963. Through Dulles, who was a member of the Warren Commission, Angleton made sure the commission's report was sufficiently hedged that if in fact Nosenko was proven to be a liar, the CIA would not look duped.

In a memo sent to a CIA official in July 1964, reference was made to discussions with Dulles regarding Nosenko and how best to handle Nosenko's information without having "a negative effect on the standing of the Commission's report." The memo concluded that Angleton would be "the most suitable person to work with [Dulles] directly" on the matter. [47] Dulles and Angleton kept the commission away from the curious ties between the CIA and the Mafia, the Kennedy brothers' involvement in those ties, and the CIA plots to assassinate Castro using American hoodlums. The final report contained no mention of those activities, and it took another decade before they were officially admitted by the agency.

The CIA man officially in charge of the agency's internal investigation of Kennedy's death eventually testified to the House Select Committee on Assassinations. He said that Angleton's involvement was improper but that Helms refused to end it. The CIA official, identified by the false name "John Scelso," was chief of the CIA's Central America and Mexico operations when Kennedy was killed.

He was placed in charge of the investigation by Helms, but Angleton "immediately went into action to do all the investigating," Scelso testified. When Scelso complained, he said Helms refused to act but said "you go tell him" to back off. Helms never denied the incident took place but said that "everyone" was involved in the investigation.[48]

Scelso also told investigators Angleton was aware of the CIA's plots with the Mafia, and he claimed that others in the agency believed Angleton had personal ties to the Mafia. Scelso based this allegation on the fact that Angleton had vetoed a CIA plan to trace mob money to numbered accounts in Panama. Angleton said it was the FBI's business, but Scelso said he discussed the matter with another CIA man, who "smiled a foxy smile and said, 'Well, that's Angleton's excuse. The real reason is that Angleton himself has ties to the Mafia and he would not want to double-cross them.' "[49] Angleton was stationed in Sicily during his early years with the OSS during World War II, where he recruited agents for the Allies.

From his position as a great collector of secrets, Angleton was well placed to manipulate the flow of information from the CIA about Kennedy and the assassination in the post assassination years. He seemed to speculate that a conspiracy was behind the assassination when he said, "A mansion has many rooms and there were many things going on. . . . I am not privy to who struck John."[50] Typically, Angleton never explained that remark. History is left to ponder whether he was simply indulging his taste for metaphoric language or implying knowledge of a conspiracy.

In the legend of Mary Meyer's death, the fact that the Warren Commission report was released just before she was killed is deemed very significant. Conspiracy theorists tend to believe she might have known *something*—what she might have known is of course unknowable and therefore open to wild speculation—but something that was perhaps at odds with the commission's report. Fate often flings strange coincidences around public assassinations and baffling crimes such as

Mary's murder. Those seeking a framework of order and purpose in the chaos and intrigue of the early 1960s see endless links and coincidences between her killing and Kennedy's. Both occurred in broad daylight, almost at high noon. Both victims were killed by two bullets, "hit" style, to the head and upper body. Both of the men arrested were physically short misfits from mean circumstances, and both were ciphers about whom little was understood and therefore much could be suggested. So just as the conspiracy theorists believe that Oswald was set up, they believe that Crump was lured to the towpath and that the mechanics who witnessed a black man in a tan jacket and a dark cap standing over the freshly killed woman were lured to the spot to make an identification that might protect the real killer.

The theories vary in scope and in devotion to known facts, but they all have one common element: The purveyors desire to identify some order behind the randomness represented by Mary Meyer's death, to find some controlling hand. Lacking God and faith, and full of suspicion about the secret activities of the U.S. government, they turn to the all-powerful CIA and are willing to believe its agents designed a murder in broad daylight to snuff out a woman they regard as the leading female figure in the movement for psychedelics and world peace, or at least the leading lady in John F. Kennedy's secret life.

The people who might have put such stories to rest have not. In Georgetown, a protective silence around Mary Meyer remains. Ben Bradlee initially felt her diary did not belong in the hands of the police or the public. Bradlee had excoriated Cord Meyer for *his* "derisive scorn" for the people's right to know in the 1960s, but the rules changed when the subject of a story was his sister-in-law. In that case, the written record of a private life (whether or not it might bear on her murder) was too personal, and it was justifiably burned, Bradlee thought, not in the family fireplace but in a CIA furnace. Those were the good old days before what Bradlee calls "celebrification"—when the private lives of public officials were nobody's business and the CIA might be called upon to keep them private.

The First Amendment champion of the Watergate investigation admitted in his memoir that he gave Mary Meyer's diary to the CIA because it was "a family document." He and Tony gave the diary to Angleton "because he promised to destroy it in whatever facilities the Central Intelligence Agency had for the destruction of documents. It was naive of us, but we figured they were state of the art."[51]

Other Georgetown journalists who might have investigated the story also felt too close to the people involved to ever talk about it, let alone write about it for publication. "Oh, I just can't. Too many of my friends are part of that one," said a nervous Charles Bartlett. Kay Evans, wife of journalist Rowland Evans and a close friend of Mary Meyer's, was a journalist in her own right and another Vassar girl. She told friends she could not imagine a book written about Mary "without all the sex."

James Angleton might have answered some questions, but he cultivated his aura of mystery just as assiduously as he cultivated his orchids. Journalists and writers fascinated by the Angleton legend continued to approach him for years, seeking tidbits from the master's files. Angleton greatly amused himself in retirement playing cat and mouse with journalists. Scott Armstrong, a reporter hired by Ben Bradlee at the *Washington Post* in the year just after Watergate, received a dangerous dose of Angleton's mischief. Armstrong was assigned to help investigate the Mary Meyer story in 1976 after the *Enquirer* article. He started with an interview with Tony Bradlee, and after talking with her about the Kennedy relationship (which she again confirmed), he went to James Angleton's suburban house in Arlington, Virginia. It was dark and no one answered the doorbell. Armstrong intrepidly wandered back to the dark greenhouse where the orchids were grown. As Armstrong was entering the greenhouse Angleton shouted at him from behind an unlit window in the house to stay out. He had been watching all along. Angleton then invited Armstrong in and offered him drinks. The young reporter was impressed by the bizarre deliberation evident in the ex-spook's every move: Angleton placed the drink glasses at one end of the counter and walked the entire length of the room with a pair of tongs, bringing one ice cube at a time back to the glasses. When he had the drinks made, he retired to another room to put on a formal tweed jacket. Then he squatted in front of a foot-long glass block ashtray and talked off the record, a cigarette perpetually hanging from his lips and dripping ash into the tray.

Like Scheherazade, Angleton filled the young reporter's ears with marvelous and tantalizing tales of seamy Washington. He told Armstrong that Jim Truitt and Phil Graham had done LSD together and that Mary Meyer had had an affair with Phil Graham, among other men. He claimed her diary had been destroyed. He also told Armstrong that Truitt had been paid "hush money" by the *Post* not to tell stories such as the one he had just sold to the *National Enquirer.* He talked of many other Washington affairs and dirty laundry, piling on so much that Armstrong could barely keep it straight. Whenever Angleton stepped out of the room to fetch another drink, Armstrong scrambled to write a key word in ink on his ankle, trying to record the fastball revelations coming at him from the former spymaster. When he finally stumbled back to the *Post,* drunk, dazed, and dazzled, his editor called him into a private meeting and demanded to know what he had been up to. The editor, Leonard Downie Jr., had just received a call from the publisher, Katharine Graham, who had just received a call from James Angleton. Angleton told Graham that Armstrong had come to his door asking questions about the very embarrassing and private things Angleton had just divulged to the reporter. Armstrong's job was barely saved by the editors.[52]

When Bradlee returned from the Virgin Islands, Armstrong told the editor he thought the *Post*'s "hush money" to Truitt—the $35,000 agreement—was news. Bradlee refused to see it that way. Flipping open a file on Truitt and half-showing it to Armstrong, Bradlee told him the fact of the financial agreement was not newsworthy because it had already been revealed ten years earlier in a right-wing journal called *Human Events.* Bradlee flashed the article in Armstrong's face. Armstrong backed down, and none of Angleton's revelations ever saw print.[53]

Angleton delighted in rope-a-doping reporters like that. He also took a mischievous pleasure in parceling out mysterious little facts and opinions that could not be confirmed, feeding grist to the conspiracy mill. He told one writer that Mary Meyer wrote in her diary that she and JFK had used a small amount of LSD together, after which they "made love." But he never mentioned that again, and Cicely Angleton—who claims never to have seen the diary herself—denies that her husband ever said such a thing. During a two-hour interview with another journalist that included seven martinis he implied that Mary was a woman who influenced policy with her pacifist beliefs.[54] He also said that a number of men and women had read the diary, not just him and the Bradlees.

After the publication of David Martin's *Wilderness of Mirrors*, Angleton was offended by the media portrayal of him as being deeply paranoid and possibly mentally unbalanced. With few supporters left, he turned for help to the right-wing media-watchdog group Accuracy in Media. His collection of secrets made him an imposing figure, and the folks at AIM were delighted to have so revered a cold warrior join their camp, but the sight of this once-powerful man forced to turn for help to a group of conservative agitators was rather sad. He boasted around the AIM offices that he still had Mary's diary and that it would show everyone "the real JFK." He never produced it, however.

Angleton alternately lied about destroying the diary and told the truth about the affair. He became an unofficial godfather to the Meyer children and a sort of surrogate older brother to Cord. Throughout the last part of his life, Angleton watched over the Meyer boys, even minding their money and meeting with headmasters or college deans when they were in trouble. One of Mary's sons lived in a Washington apartment Angleton owned. In his will he left Cord Meyer five hundred dollars, one bequest among ten of the same amount to his closest male friends. He died of lung cancer in 1986, and on his deathbed, according to Cicely Angleton, his last words were, "I've made so many mistakes."[55]

The image of the CIA as the all-powerful and all-knowing Oz capable of sinister acts that were yet to be exposed survived in the minds of the children and wives of the cold warriors, who carry with them forever the sense of having been kept in the dark from great secrets by these men. The revelations of the 1970s and the Church Committee only deepened their sense of unease. Jane Barnes learned about her father Tracy Barnes's real deeds at the CIA only after his death in 1972. She began to see her father as a man with evil and good sides, with operative E. Howard Hunt as his dark side's agent. She learned her father had probably overseen the operation in which terror leaflets were dropped on Guatemala during the CIA-backed coup there and that he probably knew that men and women who disagreed with United Fruit and the new regime were taken to concentration camps and shot. Suddenly her image of the aristocratic daddy who wore dancing pumps to dinner every night darkened. In the 1980s she ventured down to a Florida hotel room and a meeting with Hunt to talk about her father's CIA work. That meeting, when she was in her forties, served as a kind of strange healing, enabling her to ask and say things she had not been able to communicate about her father.[56]

Peter Janney's parents, Wistar and Mary, were close friends of the Meyers. Wistar was a career CIA officer, a decorated World War II veteran who had won the Navy Cross. Like Cord, he emerged from the war adamant that there should never be another, and he was attracted to the early idealistic vision of the CIA. Like many of his CIA contemporaries, Wistar loved Ian Fleming and would take his entire family to James Bond movies. Young Peter would quiz his father about spy gadgets and wonder if he was also able to bed as many women as Bond. But Peter never really reconciled with his father before the elder Janney's death. "It is human nature that a boy wants to know what his father does in the world. . . . But as I now sit in the midyears of my life I am painfully aware that something is missing."[57]

The Vietnam War and the youth upheavals of the 1960s tore the Georgetown CIA families apart. The fathers were hawks, the children against the war. "My father's explosive temper was my personal Tet offensive," said Janney. "I was shocked by the behavior of my government; not only was it too close to home, it was home." Peter and Wistar fought constantly about Vietnam and in the fall of 1969 were thrown out of a restaurant during a heated confrontation after Peter told his father he planned to avoid military service. The same revolt was played out in the Meyer family, although Quentin did serve in Vietnam for a brief stint. Cord visited his sons at their prep schools, and later at New Haven, and the political arguments would spill over so that days later he was sending them letters, still arguing his point. Even with his sons, Cord was a man who could not give an inch when national policy principles were at stake. "My parents and their CIA friends were outraged that their secrets had been betrayed, but never got beyond that," Jane Barnes said. "They could never admit that they were mistaken or had embraced an ideal of secrecy and toughness that might have been damaging to family relationships."

Mary Meyer's vibrant life cut short was a simmering subject in this atmosphere of intergenerational distrust. Peter Janney grew convinced the CIA had had something to do with the murder. To him Mary Meyer was an icon, a rebel who posed a threat to national security. In the 1970s Mary's teenage nephew, Andy Pittman, and a close friend decided to "investigate" the murder themselves. They collected information but were left with more questions than answers. More poignantly, Mary's eldest son, Quentin, remained haunted by her death. By the 1990s he was closing in on fifty years old and still wondering about his mother's unsolved murder. In the middle of the night during that period, Timothy Leary received a call from a man who identified himself as Quentin Meyer. "What happened to my mother?" he asked. Leary had no answer.[58]

The Georgetown of today is worlds away from the Georgetown of Joseph Alsop's dinner parties and dances at the Sulgrave Club, of ice clinking in glasses of hard liquor around swimming pools on steamy nights, of touch football games with Bobby and Jack and Ethel and Jackie. No one does the twist anymore. In the new Washington, there is little humor and zest left, and to the older generation it sometimes seems that the art of conversation has been lost. The wives of the policy makers in contemporary Washington are less likely to be artists than to be lawyers or to work in the government like their husbands. The Georgetown ladies who painted and wrote live among relics of the 1960s avant-garde with a Tworkov on this wall, a Noland or a Barnett Newman over there. Upon meeting them, there is always something slightly jarring about such old people surrounded by art that strove for and captured the essence of "new."

In 1964, right before she died, Mary Meyer finished a painting she named *Half Light*. It belongs to the National Museum of American Art in Washington, D.C., a gift from her sons, but it is not on display. Because Mary is considered a minor artist, the museum keeps the work, a round canvas with four pie wedges in aqua, lavender, olive, and mossy brown, in a storage space. It can be viewed only by appointment.

Like *Half Light* and Mary Meyer's other paintings, much of the art produced by the women in Mary's set is obscure, hanging in family living or dining rooms, printed in self-published books, passed around among family members, reviewed by friends. In the decades after she died, her friends continued to paint, sculpt, and write. They worked quietly in an eclipsed world once removed from the public plane on which their men exercised national power. They turned inward and toward the philosophical and the mystical. Tony Bradlee became a devoted follower of Gurdjieff, whose mystical spiritualism attracted many of Europe's wealthiest men and women in the 1920s. In the 1990s Tony Bradlee still attended Gurdjieff classes nearly every weeknight. Anne Truitt also became a sometime student of Gurdjieff. "His analysis of process into octaves is fascinating to me," she wrote in one published journal. "The point at which decision is brought to bear on process is that at which two opposing forces meet and rebound, leaving an interval in which a third force can act. The trick of acting is to catch this moment."[59] Truitt and another woman artist continued to hold séances together into the 1980s.

The occult had always beckoned. In 1968 Ben and Tony Bradlee and Jim Truitt visited a Methodist minister and part-time spiritual "reader" named Ted Swager, seeking a link with Mary in death. Swager had been publicized in articles in the *New York Times* for his ability to communicate on a spiritual plane, sometimes with the recently dead. Truitt was working on a *Newsweek* cover story on the occult when they met. In the 1970s Swager left the Methodist Church to devote his full efforts to traveling around the country doing readings.

Among the practitioners of his art, Swager considered himself a professional. No crystal balls or candles and contrived darkness for him; his readings were done in natural light. He sat in a recliner in his own living room in Waldorf, Maryland, and went into a trance and talked; his wife, Lois, took notes and taped him on a reel-to-reel Wollensak. Truitt later wrote Swager thanking him for his contact with Mary Meyer. "The most amazing part came at the end with you suddenly saying 'Mary Mary Mary, etc.,' " Truitt wrote Swager in September 1968. He found what emerged about Mary "remarkable."[60]

Truitt later told journalists that Swager contacted Mary at one of the sessions, and she described her grave in Milford and spoke of the Kennedy brothers. "Jack is here. Bobby is here now," she supposedly said through the medium.

The occult has always attracted Washington wives, so often kept in the dark on the worldly plane. Tony and Mary's aunt Cornelia Pinchot regularly consulted psychic Jeane Dixon in Cornelia's home on Rhode Island Avenue. By the 1990s Anne Truitt was holding weekly spiritual meetings called *satsang* sessions at her home. The women who attended, including Cicely Angleton, Helen Stern, and Tony Bradlee, subscribed to a kind of ersatz Buddhism involving reincarnation and based on the idea that they were all on the way to becoming "perfect masters." Anne Truitt herself came to believe she had a special spiritual connection to Alexander the Great. She often spoke of Mary Meyer as though she were still around, "a shade" who might still be contacted, according to one person close to her.[61] For Mary's friends and contemporaries, the occult led back to the mysteries of the cold war. Over and over again they tried to recover the knowable and grasp the secrets they missed when they were young and behind the screens their husbands erected in their own homes.

For these women, there remained a continuing possibility that their men were engaged in or aware of conspiracies and awful acts still to be revealed. Fully one half of their history—the world inhabited by their men—was dark to them. Cicely Angleton's self-published poetry in a book called *A Cave of Overwhelming* refers to this darkness obliquely and directly. The cave of the title refers to a place of "overwhelming dark" where a clever little fox tries to lure the writer. Angleton's poetry is mostly about old age and longing, the ruminations of a woman recalling Italy, the 1940s, and a man who falls asleep after asking, "Did you come?"

Anne Truitt's paint-coated boxes are open to interpretation. One is that they neatly contain emotions such as fear—an emotion that was understandable during the cold war, yet denied. For Anne Truitt and the women of Mary Meyer's old group, fear was never really conquered. They remained permanently haunted by the real and imagined deeds of the cold warriors they knew so intimately. In the late 1980s Truitt and some friends stored their artwork in a suburban Virginia warehouse. The warehouse itself became another repository for the sinister, in her mind: She came to believe that the building had been purchased by a shadowy corporation and was being outfitted with soundproof metal. Then the janitor was mysteriously shot.[62] Once again the women confronted new mysteries, not of heaven or the everlasting fire, but of the human beast living in and among us all, engaging yet again in some secret plot.

Like their men, these women gave the best parts of their lives to the cold war. Cord Meyer's desire to banish war by consolidating world power in a single benign and rational authority was shared by the women. But kept in the dark about their husbands' work and raised to believe that the public sphere was reserved for men, they did not address the greater problems themselves. Like Katharine Graham, the women of that generation assumed "women were intellectually inferior to men, that we were not capable of governing, leading, managing anything but our homes and our children."[63]

The secrets of the cold war years are personal matters to these women. They guard their pasts carefully because they never know what some outsider will excavate, what new coup or illegal domestic plot will be linked to their husbands or male friends through deed or knowledge. And so it is with Mary Meyer. Their friend's life and death remains a blot of sorrow and doubt on their minds, a part of the past that baffles and embarrasses them. They remain wary of the possibilities of awful revelation—about her sex life and about her murder. Anne Truitt has turned down all requests to discuss her friend or explain why she was so certain Mary would have wanted her diary to be safeguarded by CIA counterintelligence chief James Angleton. Cicely Angleton and Anne Truitt remain bound with other elderly Georgetown women by their knowledge, not of conspiracy, but of their friend's freedom, her sexual expression, and her reckless pursuit of experience through her senses.

Just as their fear slipped out from time to time, so did their ambivalence about Mary. In one of her published journals Truitt described the way her son Sam moved. "He rises on his toes when he walks, a habit that Mary Meyer, an acute judge of masculine character, always claimed marked interesting men." Whether that remark is meant to be a cut or a compliment will probably never be known. Similarly, Cicely Angleton called Mary a "beautiful, mysterious woman," but "not at all representative of her generation."

Most of the other women of Mary Meyer's generation did not as eagerly make the shift from their postdebutante world to the colored-tights milieu of the 1960s. When she was murdered, Mary Meyer was already immersed in psychedelia and the holistic worldview that would become the basis for New Age philosophy. She died before assassinations, war, racial strife, and sexual and youthful rebellion spun the old Georgetown right off its axis and into the chaotic future. For the men, the solution was to appropriate more and more power to stave off change. The women retreated into Gurdjieff and *satsang*, poetry, and thin wooden boxes painted over and over and over again. As these women grow old and come to the end of their lives, hindsight conferred by two decades of social evolution allows us to recognize that Mary Meyer's attempts to venture into the new were not really so shameful. And the very fearlessness and assurance she possessed—not some sinister and ultimately unknowable conspiracy—ultimately led to the circumstances of her death.

# Notes

The majority of the 152 interviews for this book were conducted on the record with people who did not object to their names being used. Six people were uncomfortable speaking freely and on the record if they were going to be named in the book. I have identified them as "unnamed sources."

In four other instances, interviews were conducted or information offered under strict agreement of confidentiality because the sources did not want their names revealed under any circumstances. These people are identified as "confidential sources."

*Chapter 1* ~ Murder in Georgetown

1. Otakar "Kary" Fischer, author interview, 1997.
2. Polly Wisner Fritchey, author interview, 1996.
3. Washington journalist Charlie Peters and retired CIA officer Samuel Halpern, author interviews, 1996. The CIA refused to confirm or deny any use of the garage.
4. United States District Court for the District of Columbia, *United States of America v. Ray Crump, Jr.*, transcript, volume I, page 290.
5. Evan Thomas, *The Very Best Men: Four Who Dared: The Early Years of the CIA*, Simon & Schuster, 1995, page 103.
6. "Bishop at Meyer Rites Asks Prayer for Killer," *Washington Evening Star*, Oct. 15, 1964, page B2.
7. Eleanor M. McPeck, author interview, 1996.
8. Cord Meyer Papers, Library of Congress, Manuscript Division, Container 1.
9. The document was obtained through the Freedom of Information Act. William C. Sullivan was operationally in charge of

all FBI criminal, intelligence, and espionage investigations. He put in thirty years of service to the FBI between 1941 and 1971. He died in a hunting accident just before his book critical of the FBI was published. The Soviet press agency, TASS, claimed the death was suspicious, but the U.S. government ruled it accidental.

10. Tom Mangold, *Cold Warrior: James Jesus Angleton: The CIA's Master Spy Hunter,* Simon & Schuster, 1991, pages 53–5.

11. Joan Bross, author interview, 1997.

12. Kary Fischer.

13. Howard Bray, *The Pillars of the Post,* W. W. Norton, 1980, page 67.

14. Mary Truesdale, author interview, 1996.

15. Cicely Angleton, author interview, 1996.

16. Myer Feldman, author interview, 1996.

17. Myer Feldman.

18. C. Wyatt Dickerson, author interview, 1996.

19. June Dutton, author interview, 1996.

20. Unnamed source.

21. Susan Mary Alsop, author interview, 1996.

22. Barbara Howar, *Laughing All the Way,* Stein and Day, 1973, page 84.

23. Philip Nobile and Ron Rosenbaum, "The Mysterious Murder of JFK's Mistress," *New Times,* Oct., 1976, page 25.

## *Chapter 2* — Grey Towers

1. Naomi Nover, "Memories of a Weekend at Grey Towers," provided by Grey Towers National Historic Landmark.

2. Carol Severance, curator, Grey Towers National Historic Landmark.

3. William Gaston, author interview, 1996.

4. Carol Severance.

5. Amos R. E. Pinchot Papers, Library of Congress, Manuscript Division, Family Correspondence, 1863–1941, Container 3.

6. Confidential source.

7. Carol Severance.

8. Amos R. E. Pinchot, *History of the Progressive Party 1912–1916,* edited and with a biographical foreword by Helene Maxwell Hooker, New York University Press, 1958, page 17. (Referred to hereafter as Hooker.)
9. Hooker, page 13.
10. Hooker, page 12.
11. Max Eastman, *Love and Revolution: My Journey Through an Epoch,* Random House, 1964, page 29.
12. Hooker, page 17.
13. Carol Severance.
14. Gifford Pinchot Papers, Library of Congress, Manuscript Division, Container 369. Feb. 1, 1939, letter from Gifford to Amos.
15. Hooker, page 10.
16. Ronald Steel, *Walter Lippmann and the American Century,* Vintage Books, 1980, page 226.
17. Hooker, page 64.
18. Gifford Pinchot Papers, Library of Congress, Manuscript Division, Container 314.
19. Max Eastman, *Enjoyment of Living,* Harper & Brothers, 1948, page 336.
20. Ruth Pinchot, "A Deflated Rebel," from *These Modern Women: Autobiographical Essays from the Twenties,* edited and with an introduction by Elaine Showalter, Feminist Press, 1978, page 60.
21. *These Modern Women,* pages 64–5.
22. *The New Republic,* May 11, 1921, page 323.
23. *The Nation,* volume 128, number 3319, pages 202–3.
24. Amos R. E. Pinchot Papers, Family Correspondence, 1863–1941, Container 3, July 22, 1922, Ruth to Amos.
25. Amos R. E. Pinchot Papers, Family Correspondence, 1863–1941, Container 3, July 2, 1923, Ruth to Amos.
26. *These Modern Women,* page 62.
27. Amos R. E. Pinchot Papers, Family Correspondence, 1863–1941, Container 3, July 2, 1922, Ruth to Amos.
28. Amos R. E. Pinchot Papers, Family Correspondence, 1863–1941, Container 3, July 2, 1923, Ruth to Amos.

29. Amos R. E. Pinchot Papers, Family Correspondence, 1863–1941, Container 5, May 29, 1935, Amos to William Eno.
30. Amos R. E. Pinchot Papers, Family Correspondence, 1863–1941, Container 4, Apr. 8, 1927, Amos to his older children.
31. *These Modern Women,* pages 125–26.
32. *The WPA Guide to New York City: The Federal Writers' Project Guide to 1930s New York, prepared by the Federal Writers' Project of the Works Progress Administration,* with an introduction by William Whyte, New Press, 1992.
33. Amos R. E. Pinchot Papers, Family Correspondence, 1863–1941, Container 4, Oct. 14, 1929, Amos to Nettie.
34. Gifford Pinchot Papers, Container 314, Nov. 9, 1931, Amos to Gifford.
35. Gifford Pinchot Papers, Container 369, Apr. 10, 1933, Amos to Gifford.
36. Robert S. McElvaine, *The Great Depression,* Times Books, 1984, pages 204–5.
37. Ibid., page 79.
38. Amos R. E. Pinchot Papers, General Correspondence, Container 59.
39. Amos R. E. Pinchot Papers, Family Correspondence, 1863–1941, Container 5, Dec. 12, 1938, Amos to William Eno.
40. Amos R. E. Pinchot Papers, Family Correspondence, 1863–1941, Container 5, Dec. 12, 1938, William Eno to Amos.
41. *New York Times,* Apr. 26, 1937.
42. Amos R. E. Pinchot Papers, Family Correspondence, 1863–1941, Container 5, July 1, 1941, Amos to William Eno.
43. David Middleton, author interview, 1996.

## *Chapter 3* ⁓ "PINCHOT"

1. *New York Times,* Nov. 11, 1934.
2. Frances Kilpatrick Field, author interview, 1996.
3. Brearley Yearbook, 1938.

4. William Attwood, *The Reds and the Blacks: a Personal Adventure,* Harper & Row, 1967, page 133.
5. Carol Severance.
6. *Park Avenue Social Review,* Nov. 1938.
7. Barbara Blagden Sisson, author interview, 1996.
8. *Life,* Nov. 14, 1938, cover story on Brenda Duff Frazier.
9. David Middleton.
10. *Life,* Nov. 14, 1938.
11. *Park Avenue Social Review,* Nov. 1938.
12. *Life,* Dec. 6, 1963, page 133.
13. David Middleton.
14. Mary McCarthy, "The Vassar Girl," from *On the Contrary: Articles of Belief, 1946–1961*, Curtis Publishing Co., 1961, pages 195–97.
15. Mary Truesdale, author interview, 1996.
16. Frances Prindle Taft, author interview, 1996.
17. Unnamed source.
18. Mary McCarthy, pages 202–3.
19. Mary Truesdale.
20. Frances Field.
21. "Futility," *Vassar Review and Little Magazine,* Apr. 1941, pages 5–6, 22.
22. Wayne Koestenbaum, *Jackie Under My Skin: Interpreting an Icon,* Plume, 1996, page 193.
23. Amos R. E. Pinchot Papers, Family Correspondence, Container 5, Sept. 30, 1941, Amos to Giff.
24. Gifford Pinchot Papers, Container 369, Nov. 17, 1939, Amos to Gifford.
25. Deborah Davis, *Katharine the Great: Katharine Graham and the Washington Post,* National Press, 1987, page 52.
26. Amos R. E. Pinchot Papers, Family Correspondence, Container 5, May 1, 1940, Amos to Giff.
27. Amos R. E. Pinchot Papers, Family Correspondence, Container 5, July 9, 1940, Amos to Giff.

28. Amos R. E. Pinchot Papers, Family Correspondence, Container 5, Sept. 30, 1941, Amos to Giff.
29. *New York Times,* Aug. 8, 1942.
30. Mary Brier Goodhue, author interview, 1996.
31. Barbara Gair Scheiber, author interview, 1996.
32. Perez Zagorin, author interview, 1996.
33. Bob Schwartz, author interviews, 1996 and 1997.
34. Gifford Pinchot Papers, Container 397, Feb. 7, 1944, Ruth to Gifford.
35. Gifford Pinchot Papers, Container 397, Mar. 1, 1944, Ruth to Gifford.
36. Gifford Pinchot Papers, Container 397.
37. For an insightful description of the role marriage courses played in the lives of women in Mary Meyer's generation see Betty Friedan, *The Feminine Mystique,* Dell, 1974, pages 115–16 and 354–55.
38. "Credits for Love," *Mademoiselle,* Aug. 1944, pages 251–52.
39. Lois Gordon and Alan Gordon, *The Columbia Chronicles of American Life, 1910–1992,* Columbia University Press, 1995, page 334.
40. Barbara Sisson.
41. Marie Ridder, author interview, 1996.
42. Barbara Scheiber.

## *Chapter 4* — The Idealists

1. Cornelia Bryce Pinchot Papers, Library of Congress, Manuscript Division, Box 410, May 2, 1945, Ruth to Cornelia.
2. *New York Daily News,* Apr. 20, 1945.
3. Cord Meyer Papers, Container 5, journal entries, Dec. 20–27, 1961.
4. Cord Meyer Papers, Container 5, journal entries, July 6, 1958.
5. Croswell Bowen, "Young Man in Quest of Peace," *PM Magazine,* June 1947, page M6.
6. Ibid.
7. Ibid., page M7.
8. David Challinor, author interview, 1996.

9. John Costello, *The Pacific War,* Atlantic Communications, Inc., 1981, page 484.
10. Cord Meyer, "On the Beaches," *Atlantic Monthly,* Oct. 1944, pages 42–45.
11. Costello, page 485.
12. Cord Meyer, *Facing Reality: From World Federalism to the CIA,* Harper & Row, 1980, page 29.
13. Mary Goodhue, author interview, 1996.
14. Bishop Paul Moore, author interview, 1996.
15. Richard L. Neuberger, "Marginal Notes at San Francisco," *Saturday Review,* May 26, 1945, page 6.
16. E. B. White, "A Reporter at Large," *The New Yorker,* May 12, 1945, page 44.
17. "San Francisco Album," *Fortune,* Sept. 1945, page 157.
18. E. B. White, "A Reporter at Large," *The New Yorker,* May 5, 1945, page 45.
19. Harris Wofford, *Of Kennedys and Kings: Making Sense of the Sixties,* Farrar, Straus, Giroux, 1980, page 29.
20. Descriptions of the genesis of Kennedy's dislike for Cord Meyer can be found in Ben Bradlee's book *Conversations with Kennedy* (Pocket Books, 1976), page 35, in which he says Kennedy never forgot Cord's refusal to be interviewed and decided to "get even." There is also some discussion about the uneasy relations between the two men in Cord Meyer's own journal entries, in which he chalks it up to Kennedy's class inferiority. The animosity and the anecdote about the interview were confirmed to the author by Kennedy aide Dave Powers through Myer Feldman.
21. Meyer, page 39.
22. *PM Magazine,* June 1947, page M9.
23. *New York Times,* Sept. 4, 1945.
24. Cord Meyer Papers, Container 5, journal entry, Nov. 23, 1945.
25. "Modern Man Is Obsolete: An Editorial," *Saturday Review,* Aug. 18, 1945, page 5.
26. Confidential source.

27. "Steps to Peace: The Cord Meyers, Jr.," *Mademoiselle,* Sept. 1948, page 198.
28. Annalee Jacoby, "Too Early, Too Late—Or Soon?" *World Government News,* Sept. 1948, page 21.
29. Meredith Burch, author interview, 1996.
30. *Glamour,* July 1947, page 27.
31. Lee Charell, "*Mademoiselle*'s Third College Forum: World Government," *Mademoiselle,* Aug. 1946, page 327.
32. Cord Meyer Papers, Container 5, journal entry, July 2, 1947.
33. Cord Meyer Papers, Container 5, journal entry, undated, between Dec. 1945 and June 1946.
34. Cord Meyer Papers, Container 5, journal entry, Nov. 13, 1946.
35. Cord Meyer Papers, Container 5, journal entry, Mar. 23, 1946.
36. Cord Meyer Papers, Container 5, journal entry, Nov. 12, 1945.
37. Meyer, page 52.
38. Ibid.
39. Ibid.
40. *PM Magazine,* June 1947, page M9.
41. Tom Hughes, author interview, 1996. Hughes, a world federalist who also later joined the CIA, recalled Mary Meyer as particularly "swish."
42. Cord Meyer Papers, Container 5, journal entry, Jan. 3, 1950.
43. Confidential source.
44. Cord Meyer Papers, Container 1, correspondence in 1950 and 1951 between Cord and Dean Acheson, Averell Harriman, McGeorge Bundy, and Arthur Schlesinger. These letters give a good indication of Cord's early connections to the men who would eventually figure prominently in Kennedy's administration.
45. Robin Winks, *Cloak and Gown,* William Morrow, 1987, page 440.
46. Alfred McCoy, *The Politics of Heroin,* Harper & Row, 1972, page xvii. Also discussed in Victor Marchetti and John Marks, *The CIA and the Cult of Intelligence,* Knopf, 1974, page 312.
47. Meyer, pages 64–5.

48. Freeman Dyson, "The Race Is Over," *New York Review of Books,* Mar. 6, 1997, page 4.
49. Martin Walker, *The Cold War: A History,* Henry Holt, 1994, page 27.
50. Walker, page 58.
51. Lois Gordon and Alan Gordon, *The Columbia Chronicles of American Life, 1910–1992,* Columbia University Press, 1995, page 408.
52. Cord Meyer Papers, Container 5, journal entry, Mar. 18, 1950.
53. Confidential source.
54. Cord Meyer Papers, Container 5, journal entry, May 24, 1951.
55. Cord Meyer Papers, Container 5, journal entry, undated, 1951.

## *Chapter 5* — CIA Wife

1. Jane Barnes, author interview, 1996.
2. The Freedom of Information Act process is slow and there is no reason to believe the CIA doesn't have more documents mentioning Mary Meyer. FOIA requests made in 1996 and 1997 are pending and further documents, if they exist, should be released within five years of the date the inquiries were made. A third document was released toward the end of the writing of this book, but it shed light only on the CIA's continuing obsession with security regarding anything from its files, even those forty years old. The document was ten pages long and in the form of a letter with every single line except the date at the top redacted—blacked out with a marker, allegedly for national security reasons. The date, Oct. 20, 1953, suggests the letter has something to do with Cord Meyer's battle for his job after a McCarthyite attack on his political associations.

Although President Clinton issued an executive order in 1995 declaring that records over twenty-five years old will be presumed declassified beginning in 2000, little has been accomplished in beginning the process at the CIA. Theodore Draper reported in the Aug. 14, 1997, *New York Review of Books* that by January 1997 the

CIA had declassified only 19,600 pages of the 165.9 million pages subject to Clinton's order. For more information on the subject, see *Secrecy: Report of the Commission on Protecting and Reducing Government Secrecy,* chairmen Daniel Patrick Moynihan and Larry Combest, Government Printing Office.

3. Tom Braden, author interview, 1996, is the source for the entire anecdote about being lost in the French countryside with the Meyers.

4. *Counterspy,* Apr. 1981, page 17. The article describes the effects of CIA labor infiltration in Japan and the Philippines.

5. Cord Meyer, *Facing Reality: From World Federalism to the CIA,* Harper & Row, 1980, page 66.

6. Sallie Pisani, *The CIA and the Marshall Plan,* University of Kansas Press, 1991, page 143.

7. Peter Coleman, *The Liberal Conspiracy: The Congress for Cultural Freedom and the Struggle for the Mind of Post-war Europe,* Free Press, 1989, pages 46–8.

8. Kai Bird, *The Chairman: John J. McCloy, the Making of the American Establishment,* Simon & Schuster, 1992, page 484.

9. Tom Braden, "I'm Glad the CIA Is Immoral," *Saturday Evening Post,* May 20, 1967, pages 10–4.

10. G. W. Domhoff, *The Higher Circles,* Random House, 1970, pages 262–63.

11. Victor Marchetti, author interview, 1996.

12. Tom Mangold, *Cold Warrior: James Jesus Angleton: The CIA's Master Spy Hunter,* Simon & Schuster, 1991, page 55.

13. Meyer, pages 70–1.

14. Ibid., pages 69–80.

15. "Famous African Insulted by D.C. Cafés, Sails Home," *Washington Pittsburgh Courier,* Sept. 23, 1950, page 1.

16. This was true until the Kennedy administration, when embarrassment over the discrimination faced by black diplomats from recently decolonized nations after arriving at the airport in New York finally led to action. According to Marie Ridder, Robert Kennedy sent a deputy to drive up Interstate 95 between

Washington and New York, stopping at each café and gas station and personally instructing managers to serve blacks.

17. Constance Green, *The Secret City: A History of Race Relations in the Nation's Capital,* Princeton University Press, 1967, page 314.

18. The book was so cozy, one reviewer noted, "Nothing is written here which would prevent the author from being invited back," according to Robert Merry, in *Taking on the World: Joseph and Stewart Alsop—Guardians of the American Century*, Penguin, 1996, page 466.

19. Evan Thomas, *The Very Best Men: Four Who Dared: The Early Years of the CIA,* Simon & Schuster, 1995, page 105.

20. Merry, pages 156 and 377. Merry writes that Stewart Alsop actually had been a spy.

21. Carl Bernstein, "The CIA and the Media," *Rolling Stone,* Oct. 20, 1977. Bernstein wrote that congressional investigators looking into the CIA's domestic associations found the CIA to be most intensely protective of the identities of the journalists who had helped the agency, either on the payroll or as unpaid sources.

22. Deborah Davis, page 286. By the 1970s, the CIA was seen as an unsavory ally and Bradlee and other journalists were extremely upset about assertions that they had ever been associated with it even unofficially. Davis published a Justice Department memo from an assistant U.S. attorney involved in the Rosenberg case which specifically indicated that Ben Bradlee was helping the CIA manage European propaganda regarding the Rosenbergs' spying conviction and death sentences. Bradlee denied working for the CIA. Pressure from Bradlee and Katharine Graham, who wrote that an assertion that Phil Graham helped the CIA was Davis's "CIA fantasy," apparently played some role in persuading Davis's first publisher to shred printed copies of the book. But according to Carl Bernstein, a former deputy director of the CIA said, "It was widely known Phil Graham was somebody you could get help from. Frank Wisner dealt with him." Davis included the Bradlee memo in a second edition, published almost ten years after the shredding of the first copies.

23. Thomas, page 106.

24. Bernstein, page 60.

25. Cord Meyer Papers, Letters 1943–1970, Container 1, and journal entries, Container 5.
26. Confidential source.
27. Confidential source.
28. Marie Ridder.
29. Confidential source.
30. Constance Casey, "Mixed Blessings," *Washington Post Magazine,* Apr. 19, 1992.
31. Peter Janney, author interviews, 1996.
32. "No Time for the Girls," *Washington Post,* May 8, 1959, page D4.
33. Polly Wisner Fritchey.
34. Polly Wisner Fritchey.
35. Eleanor Lanahan, author interview, 1996.
36. Joan Bross, author interview, 1997.
37. Eleanor Lanahan, *Scottie, The Daughter of . . . ,* Harper Collins, 1995, page 214.
38. Peter Janney.
39. John Gittinger, author interview, 1996.
40. John Gittinger.
41. Mangold, page 51.
42. Tim Weiner, "The Spy Agency's Many Mean Ways to Loosen Cold-War Tongues," *New York Times,* Feb. 9, 1997, page E7.
43. Victor Marchetti.
44. Elizabeth Eisenstein, author interview, 1996.
45. Eleanor Lanahan.
46. Cord Meyer Papers, Container 5, journal entry, Oct. 9, 1961.
47. Letitia Baldrige, author interview, 1996.
48. David Middleton.
49. Anne Truitt, *Turn: The Journal of an Artist,* Penguin Books, 1986, page 35.
50. Ben Summerford, author interview, 1996.
51. Mangold, page 238.
52. Ibid., pages 238–39.

53. Jane Barnes.
54. Thomas, page 207.
55. Peter Janney.
56. Jane Barnes.
57. Letitia Baldrige.
58. Unnamed sources.
59. Cord Meyer Papers, Container 5, journal entry, summer 1965.
60. Unnamed source.
61. Confidential source.
62. Godfrey Hodgson, "Cord Meyer: Superspook," *London Sunday Times Magazine,* June 15, 1975.
63. Cord Meyer Papers, Container 5, journal entry, Feb. 1, 1954.
64. Cord Meyer Papers, Container 5, journal entry, Nov. 8, 1954.
65. Confidential source.
66. Confidential source.
67. Cord Meyer Papers, Container 5, journal entry, Oct. 18, 1956.
68. Ben Bradlee, *A Good Life: Newspapering and Other Adventures,* Simon & Schuster, 1995, page 159.
69. Blair Clark, author interview, 1996.
70. Cornelia Bryce Pinchot Papers, Container 61. Which of the three Giffords she is referring to is unclear.
71. Cornelia Bryce Pinchot Papers, Container 61.
72. Cord Meyer Papers, Container 5, journal entry, Oct. 18, 1956.
73. Cord Meyer Papers, Container 5, journal entry, Feb. 27, 1955.
74. C. David Heymann, *A Woman Named Jackie,* Lyle Stuart, 1989, page 85. The Bouvier sisters' scrapbook, called *One Special Summer*, was eventually published in 1974.
75. Thomas C. Reeves, *A Question of Character: A Life of John F. Kennedy,* Prima Publishing, 1992, page 115.
76. Cord Meyer Papers, Container 5, journal entry, Oct. 18, 1956.
77. Cord Meyer Papers, Container 5, journal entry, Oct. 18, 1956.
78. Thomas Reeves, pages 137–38.
79. Cord Meyer Papers, Container 5, journal entry, Oct. 18, 1956.
80. Thomas Reeves, page 139.

81. Peter Janney.
82. Confidential source.

*Chapter 6* ⁓ EXPERIMENTS

1. "D.C. Gets a New Kind of Gallery," *Washington Post,* Oct. 13, 1957.
2. Ibid.
3. James Truitt told reporters for *Time* magazine the psychoanalyst was named Dr. Eden.
4. Kenneth Noland, author interviews, 1996 and 1997.
5. Alice Denney, author interview, 1996.
6. Cord Meyer Papers, Container 5, journal entry, Jan. 14, 1957.
7. Cord Meyer Papers, Container 5, journal entry, Sept. 3, 1957.
8. Kenneth Noland.
9. Washoe County Court document No. 175609, *Mary P. Meyer v. Cord Meyer, Jr.*
10. Cord Meyer Papers, Container 1, letter from Pittman to Meyer, Apr. 11, 1957.
11. Washoe County Court document No. 175609.
12. Marie Ridder.
13. Confidential source.
14. Brent Oldham, author interview, 1997.
15. Confidential source.
16. Cord Meyer Papers, Container 5, journal entry, Nov. 1, 1958.
17. Cord Meyer Papers, Container 5, journal entry, May 25, 1963.
18. Calvin Tomkins, *Off the Wall: Robert Rauschenberg and the Art World of Our Times,* Doubleday, 1980, page 30.
19. Richard Layman, ed., *American Decades 1950–1959,* Gale Research Inc., 1994, page 33.
20. Barbara Rose, *Frankenthaler,* Henry Abrams, 1981, page 32.
21. Ben Summerford.
22. Marian Cannon Schlesinger, author interview, 1996.
23. Ben Summerford.
24. Alice Denney.

25. Mary Orwen, author interview, 1996.
26. Tomkins, page 46.
27. *Washington Evening Star,* March 14, 1961, page A1.
28. Ed Kelley, author interview, 1997.
29. Kenneth Noland.
30. Robert Hughes, *The Shock of the New,* Knopf, 1981, page 156.
31. William C. Agee, ed., *Kenneth Noland: The Circle Paintings 1959 to 1963,* Museum of Fine Arts, Houston, 1993, page 16.
32. Lynn Noland, author interview, 1997.
33. Cord Meyer Papers, Container 5, journal entry, May 25, 1963.
34. Helen Husted, author interview, 1996. At the time she was using her married name, Helen Chavchavadze.
35. Kenneth Noland.
36. Eleanor Lanahan.
37. Kenneth Noland.
38. Alice Denney.
39. Elizabeth Eisenstein.
40. Kary Fischer.
41. Sam Gilliam, author interview, 1996.
42. Jenny Greenberg, author interview, 1996.
43. Jenny Greenberg.
44. Kenneth Noland.
45. Morton Herskowitz, *Emotional Armoring: An Introduction to Psychiatric Orgone Therapy,* handbook for practitioners, printed by Herskowitz.
46. Cord Meyer Papers, Container 5, journal entry, May 25, 1963.
47. Jenny Greenberg.
48. Elizabeth Eisenstein.
49. Kenneth Noland.
50. The brochure for Mary's posthumous art show was composed by Helen Stern, who put it together with some portion of Mary's diary shared with her by Tony Bradlee.
51. Anne Truitt, *Turn: The Journal of an Artist,* Penguin, 1986, page 150.
52. Brooks Adams, "Solid Color," *Art in America,* October 1991, page 113.

53. Truitt, *Turn,* page 164.
54. Anne Truitt, *Daybook: The Journal of an Artist,* Pantheon, 1982, page 200.
55. Unnamed source.
56. Unnamed source.
57. Truitt, *Daybook,* page 165.
58. Timothy Leary, *Flashbacks: A Personal and Cultural History of an Era,* G. P. Putnam's Sons, 1983, page 130.
59. Ibid., pages 128–29.
60. Ibid., page 155.
61. Ibid., page 178.
62. Timothy Leary, author interview, 1996.
63. Sam Gilliam.
64. Cornelia Reis, author interviews, 1996 and 1997.
65. For a full description of the CIA's search for mind-control drugs with experiments on unwitting civilians, military men, students, prisoners, and hospital patients based on Freedom of Information Act documents, see John Marks, *The Search for the Manchurian Candidate: The CIA and Mind Control,* W. W. Norton, 1991.
66. John Marks Documents, National Security Archive, Washington, D.C., Box 1.
67. Marks, page 62.
68. John Gittinger.
69. Marks provides a well-documented description of the CIA's LSD tests, pages 57–133.
70. Marks, page 130.
71. Martin A. Lee and Bruce Shlain, *Acid Dreams: The CIA, LSD and the Sixties Rebellion,* Grove Weidenfeld, 1985, page 93. The therapy supposedly occurred at Hollywood Hospital in Vancouver, and the anecdote is attributed to a now-dead therapist.
72. Marks, page 74.
73. Unnamed source.
74. Kary Fischer.
75. Unnamed source.

76. Kenneth Noland.
77. David Middleton.
78. Eleanor McPeck.
79. Elizabeth Eisenstein.
80. Kary Fischer.
81. Marian Cannon Schlesinger.
82. Barbara Gamarikian, author interview, 1996.
83. Confidential source.
84. Cord Meyer Papers, Container 5, journal entry, Mar. 26, no year.
85. Cord Meyer Papers, Container 5, journal entry, May 25, 1963.
86. Angleton's presence in the Meyer sons' lives is evidenced in various letters between Cord Meyer and his sons over the years. In one 1969 letter about money Cord told Quentin that "Jim and I are going to turn it over to you to squander as you please."
87. Thomas Reeves, page 242, on Pam Turnure.

## *Chapter 7* — Jack and Mary

1. Alice Denney, Eleanor McPeck.
2. Alice Denney, Eleanor McPeck.
3. Eleanor McPeck.
4. Alice Denney, Eleanor McPeck.
5. Norman Mailer, "Superman Comes to the Supermarket," *Esquire,* November 1960.
6. Richard Reeves, *President Kennedy: Profile of Power,* Simon & Schuster, 1993, page 58.
7. Michael Beschloss, *The Crisis Years: Kennedy and Khrushchev, 1960–1963,* HarperCollins, 1991, pages 26–27.
8. Richard Reeves, page 33.
9. Thomas, pages 228–29.
10. Ibid., pages 142–48.
11. Richard Reeves, pages 140, 151.
12. Ibid., page 142.
13. Ibid., page 150.

14. Hugh Sidey, author interview, 1996.
15. Richard Reeves, page 175.
16. *Washington Post,* Oct. 4, 1961.
17. The Secret Service required everyone entering the White House gates to be signed in, with the time and the person they were intending to see also recorded. When a visitor was going to see the president, the gate logs indicate it by "Evelyn Lincoln," "Mansion," "Residence," or "President." The handwritten logs, organized chronologically by month and year, are available for public inspection at the John F. Kennedy Library at Columbia Point, Boston. The gate logs are probably only a partial record of Mary Meyer's visits. They indicate Mary Meyer's name, sometimes misspelled, fifteen times, usually entering around 7:30 P.M. Other nights, she may have been inside but was escorted by one of Kennedy's aides. On those occasions, she and others are indicated in the gate logs with notations that read "Dave Powers plus one," or "Bill Thompson plus one," or "Bill Walton plus one." For purposes of these notes, cites referring to these logs will read: Secret Service Gate Logs, date, JFKL.

Mary Meyer's name also appears on guest lists preserved at the JFK Library in the White House Social Files, which are indexed by guest name. Full guest lists and menus for each event are preserved in those files. For purposes of these notes, cites referring to those documents will read: White House Social Files, JFKL.

18. Jean Friendly, author interview, 1995.
19. Pamela Turnure, oral history, JFKL.
20. Joseph W. Alsop, *I've Seen the Best of It: Memoirs,* with Adam Platt, W. W. Norton, 1992, pages 437–38.
21. Hugh Sidey.
22. Pamela Turnure, oral history.
23. Tony Summers, *Goddess: The Secret Lives of Marilyn Monroe,* G. K. Hall, 1986, page 202.
24. Richard Reeves, page 313.
25. Ralph G. Martin, *A Hero for Our Time: An Intimate Story of the Kennedy Years,* Macmillan, 1983, page 49.

26. Seymour Hersh, *The Dark Side of Camelot,* Little, Brown, 1997, page 389.
27. Beschloss, page 615, attributed to Patricia Lawford.
28. Ben Bradlee, *Conversations with Kennedy,* Pocket Books, 1975, page 147.
29. Confidential source.
30. Confidential source.
31. Bradlee, *Conversations with Kennedy,* page 69.
32. Garry Wills, *The Kennedy Imprisonment: A Meditation on Power,* Little, Brown, 1981, page 35.
33. Bradlee, *Conversations with Kennedy,* page 131.
34. Ibid., page 27.
35. William Attwood, *The Reds and the Blacks: A Personal Adventure,* Harper & Row, 1967, page 133.
36. C. David Heymann, *A Woman Named Jackie,* Lyle Stuart, 1989, page 227. Confirmed to author by Kenneth Noland.
37. Evelyn Lincoln letter.
38. *San Francisco Chronicle,* Feb. 23, 1976, page 1.
39. Helen Husted.
40. Jay Gourley, author interview, 1997.
41. Myer Feldman.
42. National Security Archive collection of declassified documents, filed under "Mary Meyer."
43. David Powers, in response to written questions from the author, 1996.
44. Pamela Turnure, oral history.
45. JFKL, Secret Service Gate Logs, also from James Truitt and Kary Fischer.
46. Myer Feldman.
47. Hersh, pages 387–411 on Rometsch.
48. The official line of reasoning for spying on King was that he associated with members of the Communist Party, especially Stanley Levison, about whom the president himself had warned King. Surreptitious ties between King and Levison continued after the warning, arousing enough suspicion for Robert Kennedy to approve

the wiretap. Burke Marshall would later say the Kennedy brothers feared political damage to their own names and their belated support of civil rights if the Communist association became public.

Evidence exists that Hoover was also collecting dirt on Kennedy. Hoover's intense dislike of Bobby Kennedy and King is well known, and during the summer of 1963, while King was gaining power, Hoover continued a campaign to discredit him. It may or may not be a coincidence that the FBI was also collecting information on Kennedy's relationship with Ellen Rometsch while Hoover sought authority from Bobby Kennedy to tap King. On October 10 and October 15, RFK signed two wiretap authorizations, and at the end of that month Hoover and JFK had lunch.

Garry Wills believes there was a link. He wrote, "Robert had been appointed by his brother to contain the threat of Hoover—which made him acquiesce in Hoover's campaign to destroy King. That was a terrible burden to sustain; and it makes a mockery of any talk that John Kennedy's sexual affairs were irrelevant to his politics." (*Imprisonment of Power,* page 38.)

49. Tom Mangold, *Cold Warrior: James Jesus Angleton: The CIA's Master Spy Hunter,* Simon & Schuster, 1991, page 51.

50. Thomas Reeves, page 322.

51. "JFK Had Affair with D.C. Artist," *Washington Post,* Feb. 23, 1976, page A1.

52. The reconstruction of Jackie Kennedy's travel and Mary Meyer's recorded visits to the White House to see the president is shown below. Secret Service gate logs from the JFK Library, books, and newspaper clips were used to assemble the data. No official documentation of Jackie Kennedy's precise itinerary exists in the JFK Library, the National Archives, or the Library of Congress.

The following is not every instance Mary Meyer was in the White House; rather it is a record of the known appointments with the president recorded by the Secret Service, all but one (June 15, 1962) of which occurred when Jackie Kennedy was out of town.

—Tuesday, October 3, 1961. At 7:40 P.M., "Mary Meyers" is signed

into the White House, while Jackie and the children are at Newport. The president had returned from Newport that day.
—Monday, January 22, 1962. "Mrs. Myers" signed into the White House at 7:30 P.M., while Jackie is at Glen Ora.
—Tuesday, March 13, 1962. Mary Meyer calls the White House at 9:52 A.M. and is transferred to the president.
—Thursday, March 15, 1962. As Jackie Kennedy pulls out of the New Delhi train station in a special train outfitted with crystal, sandalwood soaps, and an embroidered cashmere bedspread, "Mrs. Myers" is signed into the White House to see the president at 7:35 P.M. At 11:50, the President calls for a car to be sent to the South Entrance for "Mrs. Myer."
—Friday, June 15, 1962. "Mrs. Myers" signed into the White House at 7:44 P.M.
—Monday, July 16, 1962. "Mrs. Myers" signed into the White House at 7:30 P.M. Jackie and the children are vacationing at Squaw Island, Cape Cod, for the month of July.
—Tuesday, July 17, 1962. "Mrs. Mary Meyer" calls the president at 6:43 A.M.
—Monday, July 30, 1962. "Mary Meyers" is signed into the White House at 7:30 P.M. JFK has just returned from a weekend at Hyannisport, where Jackie and the children remain.
—Monday, August 6, 1962. "Mary Meyers" is signed into the White House at 7:32 P.M. The morning papers carried news of Marilyn Monroe's overdose. Jackie flew to New York with eleven suitcases, tennis racquets, and a golf bag in preparation for an Italian vacation.
—Wednesday, September 5, 1962. "Mrs. Myers" signed into the White House at 7:29 P.M. Jackie is in Newport.
—Monday, October 1, 1962. "Mrs. Mary Myers" is signed in at 7:25 P.M. JFK and RFK began the day working until 5:30 A.M. on the civil rights situation. Jackie is still in Newport.
—Monday, January 28, 1963. "Mary Myers" signed in at 7:30 P.M. Jackie is at Glen Ora.
—Wednesday, June 12, 1963. "Mary Myers," Bill Walton, and Paul

Fay are signed into the White House at 7:35 P.M. Jackie is there, but Mary may be presumed to be Bill Walton's date.

—Friday, June 14, 1963. "Mary Myers" is signed into the White House at 7:50 P.M. Jackie and the children are at Camp David, where JFK will join them Saturday.

—Wednesday, July 3, 1963. JFK returns from a ten-day European trip at 2 A.M. "Mary Meyers" is signed in at 7:30 P.M. Jackie and the children are at Squaw Island.

—Monday, August 5, 1963. "Mary Meyers" is signed in at 7:40 P.M. Jackie, pregnant, is on Squaw Island.

—Wednesday, August 7, 1963. Baby Patrick is born on Cape Cod, five and a half weeks early, and dies on Friday.

53. Myer Feldman.

54. Bradlee, *Conversations with Kennedy,* page 159.

55. Thomas Reeves, page 317.

56. Laura Bergquist, oral history, JFKL.

57. Laura Bergquist, "Jacqueline: What You Don't Know About Our First Lady," *Look,* July 4, 1961.

58. Ibid.

59. Marie Ridder.

60. Helen Husted.

61. Confidential source.

62. Helen Husted.

63. Kary Fischer.

64. Bradlee, *Conversations with Kennedy,* pages 34–35.

65. James Truitt letter to Deborah Davis, Jan. 30, 1979. Truitt wrote that Bradlee described the incident to him and said it happened at a dinner party given "by a CIA type named Hunt, but not E. Howard."

66. Cord Meyer Papers, Container 5, journal entry, May 14, 1960.

67. Cord Meyer Papers, Container 5, journal entry, Oct. 18, 1961.

68. Cord Meyer Papers, Container 5, journal entry, Oct. 18, 1961.

69. Cord Meyer Papers, Container 5, journal entry, Mar. 21, 1963.

70. Cord Meyer Papers, Container 5, journal entry, Mar. 21, 1963.

71. Cord Meyer Papers, Container 1, letter to Quentin Meyer, Aug. 1, 1962.
72. Cord Meyer Papers, journal entry, Mar. 21, 1963.
73. *Washington Post,* Nov. 12, 1961.
74. Beschloss, pages 370–71.
75. Ibid., page 369.
76. Bradlee, *Conversations with Kennedy,* p. 143.
77. Secret Service Gate Log, Jan. 22, 1962, JFKL.
78. "First Lady's Mother Subs," *Washington Post,* Jan. 23, 1962.
79. Pamela Turnure, oral history.
80. Ben Bradlee, *Conversations with Kennedy,* page 49.
81. Ibid., page 54.
82. Ben Bradlee, interviewed by author's research assistant Mary Stapp, 1997.
83. Pamela Turnure, oral history.
84. Myer Feldman.
85. Kary Fischer, recalling Mary Meyer's description of events, confirmed to the author what James Truitt told the *Washington Post* and *National Enquirer* regarding the routine that was followed when Mary spent private time with the president.
86. Secret Service Gate Logs, JFKL, and White House telephone logs, JFKL. The phone logs are handwritten memos that were jotted down whenever the president received a call. The logs also indicate whether he took the call or not. They are also filed chronologically at the JFK Library.
87. Myer Feldman.
88. James Reed, author interview, 1996.
89. Secret Service Gate Logs, Mar. 15, 1962, JFKL.
90. Beschloss, pages 189–90.
91. Lee and Shlain, page 102.
92. Beschloss, page 190, and Hersh, pages 234–37.
93. Secret Service Gate Logs, July 16, 1962, JFKL.
94. Winzola McLendon, "President's Mother to Be His Hostess," *Washington Post,* July 16, 1962, page A12. The article detailed plans

for Rose Kennedy to host a state dinner for the visiting Ecuadoran president and gave Jackie's schedule for the summer. "The President's wife and two children are vacationing at Squaw Island on Cape Cod and plan to remain there throughout July. Then in August, the First Lady and four-year-old Caroline will go to Europe for a holiday on the Italian Riviera."

95. "BPW Head Blasts Kennedy for Bypassing Women in Cabinet," *Washington Post,* July 16, 1962.

96. *San Francisco Chronicle,* Feb. 23, 1976, page 1.

97. Ibid.

98. White House telephone logs, July 17, 1962, JFKL.

99. Heymann, page 375.

100. Myer Feldman.

101. Hugh Sidey.

102. Hersh, page 234.

103. Secret Service Gate Logs, July 30, 1962, JFKL.

104. Secret Service Gate Logs and White House phone logs, Aug. 6, 1962, JFKL.

105. Secret Service Gate Logs, June, July, and August 1962, JFKL.

106. *Washington Post,* Oct. 2, 1962, page A18.

107. *Washington Post,* Oct. 1, 1962, page A7.

108. Secret Service Gate Logs, Oct. 1, 1962, JFKL.

109. *Washington Post,* Oct. 1, 1962, page A7.

110. White House Social Files, JFKL.

111. White House Social Files, JFKL.

112. Anatoly Dobrynin, *In Confidence: Moscow's Ambassador to America's Six Cold War Presidents,* Times Books, 1995, page 85.

113. Beschloss, page 570.

114. White House Social Files, JFKL.

115. Katharine Graham, *Personal History,* Knopf, 1997, page 316.

116. Blair Clark.

117. Secret Service Gate Logs, June, July, and August 1963, JFKL.

118. White House Social Files. Mrs. Kennedy's correspondence is preserved in the social files.

119. Grey Towers National Historic Landmark, archived videotape.

120. Grey Towers National Historic Landmark, informational brochure.
121. Ben Bradlee, *A Good Life: Newspapering and Other Adventures,* Simon & Schuster, 1995, page 248.
122. Hugh Sidey.
123. Hugh Sidey.
124. Helen Husted.
125. Lyndon B. Johnson Library, White House telephone log.
126. Bradlee, *A Good Life,* page 262.
127. Kary Fischer.
128. Kary Fischer.
129. Timothy Leary made this point in a magazine article he wrote in the mid-eighties for an alternative journal called *Rebel,* and a writer named Nancy Druid posited the same notion in an article in the early nineties for *Mondo 2000.*
130. Philip Nobile and Ron Rosenbaum, "The Mysterious Murder of JFK's Mistress," *New Times,* Oct. 1976. page 33.
131. Alice Denney.
132. Confidential source.
133. Elizabeth Eisenstein.
134. Cynthia E. Harrison, "A 'New Frontier' for Women: The Public Policy of the Kennedy Administration," *Journal of American History,* Dec. 1980, page 642.
135. James Giglio, *The Presidency of John F. Kennedy,* University Press of Kansas, 1991, page 141.
136. Katie Louchheim, oral history, JFKL.
137. Hersh, pages 294–325. Hersh takes Campbell at her word.
138. Kenneth Noland.
139. Myer Feldman. Chamberlin did not respond to a letter asking for her version of this anecdote.
140. Beschloss, pages 638, 659.
141. Attwood, page 146.
142. Myer Feldman.
143. Richard Reeves posits this theory throughout his book.
144. Confidential source.

145. Myer Feldman.
146. Unnamed source.
147. Evan Thomas includes a derisive quote about Judith Campbell from her ex-husband in a footnote to help disprove the theory that she was a courier between the mob and Kennedy. "I couldn't imagine her being privy to any kind of secret information," William Campbell said. "She wouldn't understand it anyway. I mean . . . they weren't dealing with some kind of Phi Beta Kappa." Thomas, page 402.
148. Hersh, pages 317–20. Hersh takes Campbell at her word.
149. Hersh, Chapter 22, on Ellen Rometsch.
150. Confidential source.
151. Elizabeth Eisenstein.

## *Chapter 8* Crump

1. "Beauty and Filth in Old Georgetown," *Washington Daily News,* Mar. 22, 1952.
2. Lance Morrow, "Canal Walk Evokes Fear," *Washington Evening Star,* Oct. 14, 1964, page B1.
3. *United States of America v. Ray Crump, Jr.,* U.S. District Court for the District of Columbia, Criminal Case No. 930–64, transcript, testimony of Henry Wiggins.
4. Ibid., testimony of Roderick Sylvis.
5. Ibid., testimony of John Warner.
6. Philip Nobile and Ron Rosenbaum, "The Mysterious Murder of JFK's Mistress," *New Times,* Oct. 1976, page 24.
7. "Woman Painter Shot and Killed on Canal Towpath in Capital," *New York Times,* Oct. 14, 1964.
8. Nobile and Rosenbaum, page 24. Detective Sam Wallace, also in the police station with Crump when the coat was brought in, told this author that the police made a fatal mistake by trying the coat on Crump first. Crooke told Nobile and Rosenbaum, "It fit perfectly." But trying it on the suspect had also contaminated the evidence.

9. "Mary P. Meyer Believed Victim of Robbery Attempt," *Washington Post,* Oct. 13, 1964.
10. Nobile and Rosenbaum, page 24.
11. Stanly County Public Library, Albemarle, N.C., Local History Room, Crump Family Folder.
12. Jeffrey J. Crow, Paul D. Escot, Flora J. Hatley, *A History of African-Americans in North Carolina,* North Carolina Department of Natural Resources, Raleigh, 1992, page 12.
13. Stanly County Public Library, Local History Room, Crump Family Folder.
14. Crow et al., pages 15–16.
15. Probate Records, Settlement of Estates 1841–1859, Stanly County, N.C.
16. Stanly County Registrar of Deeds, Birth Records, 1939.
17. Crow et al., page 130.
18. Ibid., page 131.
19. Harry S. Jaffe and Tom Sherwood, *Dream City: Race, Power and the Decline of Washington, D.C.,* Simon & Schuster, 1994, page 26.
20. Elaine B. Todd, "Urban Renewal in the Nation's Capital: A History of the Redevelopment Land Agency in Washington, D.C., 1946–1973." Ph.D. dissertation, Howard University, Washington, D.C., 1986, page 135.
21. "Southwest Remembered: A Story of Urban Renewal," video, Dolores Smith, producer, Lamont Productions.
22. Constance McLaughlin Green, *The Secret City: A History of Race Relations in the Nation's Capital,* Princeton University Press, 1967, page 288. The crime report was prepared by the National Committee on Segregation in the Nation's Capital. Ninety people sat on the committee, including Eleanor Roosevelt; only thirteen were blacks from the city itself.
23. "Behind Washington's Postcard Facade: Change, Trouble and Danger Afflict Capital," *New York Times,* June 10, 1963, page A1.
24. "Mrs. Meyer Urges United Attack to Avert Race Disaster in Capital," *Washington Post,* Apr. 16, 1963.

25. "Powell Warns of Race Riot Peril in D.C.," *Washington Evening Star,* May 6, 1963.
26. Polly Wisner Fritchey.
27. "Fear of Racial Violence Haunts Capital," *New York Times,* June 11, 1963, page A1.
28. *Washington Post,* Aug. 1, 1964, page B11.
29. Sandra Fitzpatrick and Maria R. Goodwin, *The Guide to Black Washington: Places and Events of Historical Significance in the Nation's Capital,* Hippocrene Books, page 55.
30. Confidential source.
31. Dovey Roundtree, author interview.
32. *United States of America v. Ray Crump, Jr.,* U.S. District Court for the District of Columbia, Criminal Case No. 930–64, transcript, opening statement of the Government. Confirmed by Dovey Roundtree to the author.
33. Dovey Roundtree says that toward the end of his trial, Crump told her he had been on the towpath with a prostitute, drinking. Roundtree was never able to find the woman.
34. Author interview with Crump's Stanton Terrace neighbors.
35. Sam Wallace, author interview, 1996.
36. Ben Bradlee, *A Good Life: Newspapering and Other Adventures,* Simon & Schuster, 1995, page 125.
37. "Unserious Consultant in Poetry Tells You How to Misunderstand It," *Washington Post,* Oct. 13, 1964, page B1.
38. Bradlee, *A Good Life,* page 267.
39. "In Angleton's Custody," letter to the editor from Anne Truitt and Cicely Angleton, *New York Times Book Review,* Nov. 5, 1995, page 5.
40. David Martin, *Wilderness of Mirrors,* Harper & Row, 1980, page 206.
41. Cicely Angleton, author interview, 1996.
42. Ben Bradlee, *A Good Life,* page 267.
43. Ibid., page 268.
44. Jay Gourley, author interview, 1997.
45. *New York Times Book Review,* Nov. 5, 1995, page 5.

46. Ben Bradlee, *A Good Life,* page 269.
47. Philip Nobile, author interview, 1996.
48. Kenneth Noland.
49. *New York Times Book Review,* Nov. 5, 1995, page 5.
50. There are many who believe Angleton probably kept a copy of the diary for his files. He boasted of it once or twice. But he never produced it, and Cleveland Cram, who was charged with looking through Angleton's papers (those he left behind at the CIA, not all of them by any means) and writing a CIA history, never saw anything about Mary Meyer. But even Cram is not sure what Angleton took away with him when he left the agency.
51. Richard Helms, author interview, 1997.
52. "The Spy Who Loved Him," *Washington Post,* Mar. 17, 1996, page F1.
53. Nobile and Rosenbaum, page 33.
54. James Hilleary, "Mrs. Meyer Was a Lyrical Artist," *Washington Post,* Oct. 25, 1964.
55. United States District Court for the District of Columbia, Probate Court, Estate of Mary Pinchot Meyer, Deceased, Admn. No. 112755.
56. Cord Meyer Papers, Container 1, letter from Cord to Edward Barnes, Nov. 4, 1964.
57. Cord Meyer Papers, Container 5, journal entry, Mar. 7, 1965.

*Chapter 9* — JUSTICE

1. Dovey Roundtree, author interview, 1996.
2. Dovey Roundtree.
3. *U.S. v. Ray Crump, Jr.,* Criminal Case No. 930–64. Criminal Docket, "Motion for Mental Examination," signed by Dovey Roundtree. Roundtree said in an interview that the chief detective on the scene told her he smelled beer on Crump but that he did not think Crump was drunk.
4. Harry S. Jaffe and Tom Sherwood, *Dream City: Race, Power and the Decline of Washington, D.C.,* Simon & Schuster, 1994, page 41.

5. Dovey Roundtree.
6. Dovey Roundtree.
7. Al Hantman, author interview, 1996.
8. Cicely Angleton.
9. Dovey Roundtree.
10. This is Hantman's recollection of the jury. The court did not record the racial makeup of juries at the time. Bob Bennett also recalled the jury as predominantly black.
11. Dovey Roundtree.
12. *U.S. v. Ray Crump, Jr.,* pages 2–17.
13. Ibid., pages 45–7.
14. Ibid., pages 70–9.
15. Ibid., page 124.
16. Al Hantman.
17. *U.S. v. Ray Crump, Jr.,* pages 120–280.
18. Dovey Roundtree.
19. Police testimony at the trial revealed conflicting stories.
20. *U.S. v. Ray Crump, Jr.,* page 803.
21. Ibid., pages 540–49.
22. Ibid., page 693.
23. Dovey Roundtree.
24. Dovey Roundtree.
25. *U.S. v. Ray Crump, Jr.,* page 881.
26. Ibid., page 893.
27. Roberta Hornig, author interview, 1997.
28. *U.S. v. Ray Crump, Jr.,* page 944.
29. Ibid., page 948.
30. Ibid., pages 953–58.
31. Ibid., page 993.
32. Al Hantman and Dovey Roundtree.
33. *U.S. v. Ray Crump, Jr.,* page 995.
34. "Crump Acquitted in Towpath Slaying of D.C. Socialite," *Washington Evening Star,* July 30, 1965, page A1.
35. Savwoir family, interview with Mary Stapp, 1996.

36. Al Hantman.
37. Dovey Roundtree.

*Chapter 10* ~ "Half Light"

1. Ben Bradlee, *A Good Life: Newspapering and Other Adventures,* Simon & Schuster, 1995, page 270.
2. "Powell Warns of Race Riot Peril in D.C.," *Washington Evening Star,* May 6, 1963.
3. "Lessons of Los Angeles," *Washington Post,* Aug. 22, 1965.
4. Unnamed source.
5. "Lessons of Los Angeles," *Washington Post,* Aug. 22, 1965.
6. Confidential source.
7. The record comes from his official "rap sheet," prepared by the Superior Court of the District of Columbia, Social Services Division—Adult Branch, as part of a Presentence Report in 1986.
8. Helena Blair Crump filed for divorce from Ray Crump in 1969, stating that they had lived together until October 12, 1964, when Ray Crump was arrested and incarcerated. According to the divorce petition, when Ray Crump was released from jail in August 1965, he "never returned home" and the couple remained separated. In 1998, Helena Blair Crump could not be located. Her son Derrick Crump told his attorney in 1997 that his mother was afraid of his father and did not want her location revealed.
9. Prince Georges County, Maryland, Clerk of Court, microfilm records on Ray Crump, Jr.; author interview with Jack Salmon, 1996.
10. Prince Georges County, Maryland, Clerk of Court, microfilm records on Ray Crump, Jr.
11. Superior Court of the District of Columbia, Social Services Division Presentence Report and District of Columbia Department of Corrections record.
12. Superior Court of the District of Columbia, Criminal Division, Affidavit in Support of Arrest Warrant, Criminal Case No. FO0675-78.

13. "Rape Charged After Shopping Trip," *Northern Virginia Star,* Apr. 25, 1978.
14. Superior Court of the District of Columbia, Social Services Division Presentence Report and District of Columbia and United States Department of Corrections records.
15. Superior Court of the District of Columbia, Criminal Case No. FO6723-83.
16. Letter from Ben Zeichner, staff psychiatrist, Bureau of Forensic Psychiatry, Criminal Division Clerk, District of Columbia courthouse, May 22, 1985.
17. Confidential source.
18. Martha Crump, author interview, 1996.
19. Confidential source.
20. Carl Anglin, 1997.
21. Ray Crump, letter to author, Sept. 18, 1997.
22. A letter from gallery director Charles Millard to Ken Noland in 1967 acknowledges that "you'd been opposed to this," but that Mrs. Stern, Tony Bradlee, and Bill Walton "are all for it." Corcoran School of Art Archives, Washington, D.C.
23. Brochure, "Paintings by Mary Meyer," Washington Gallery of Modern Art, preserved at the Corcoran School of Art Archives, Washington, D.C.
24. Andrew Hudson, "Belated Tribute to a Washington Pioneer," *Washington Post,* Mar. 12, 1967.
25. Andrew Hudson, author interview, 1997.
26. "Gallery Show has 2 Artists," *Washington Post,* Mar. 4, 1967.
27. Tom Kelly, *The Imperial Post,* Morrow, 1983, page 141.
28. *Washington Post,* Feb. 23, 1976, page A1.
29. Cornelia Reis.
30. Jay Gourley.
31. Letter from Frederick S. Beebe, Chairman of the Board of the *Washington Post*, to Truitt, Dec. 23, 1970. Quoted in Victor Lasky, *It Didn't Start with Watergate,* page 27.
32. Howard Bray, *The Pillars of the Post,* W. W. Norton, 1980, page 138.

33. *Washington Post,* Feb. 23, 1976, page A1.
34. *Time* magazine, Mar. 8, 1976, page 42.
35. Jay Gourley.
36. Evelyn Patterson Truitt, letter to the author, Aug. 2, 1996.
37. Morris Dickstein, "Black Humor and History," *Gates of Eden: American Culture in the Sixties,* Basic Books, 1977. Reprinted in Gerald Howard, ed., *The Sixties,* Washington Square Press, 1982, page 289.
38. Timothy Leary, author interview, 1996. Shortly before his death, Leary continued to express the belief that Mary Meyer might have dropped acid with Kennedy but he admitted he had no proof. In his last days his continuing interest in Mary Meyer was evidenced by a well-thumbed copy of Cord Meyer's book near his bedroom, filled with marginal notes.
39. Richard Helms.
40. *Ramparts* cited Kilgallen's death as one reason to reopen the Kennedy assassination investigation in 1966.
41. Robert D. Morrow, *First Hand Knowledge: How I Participated in the CIA-Mafia Murder of President Kennedy,* Spi Books, 1994, pages 277–80.
42. Gaeton Fonzi, author interview, 1996. Fonzi, one of the House Select Committee investigators, interviewed Morrow and found he knew a lot about counterfeit-money schemes to fund the Cubans, but in the area of the JFK assassination "he was a bullshitter. He was concocting a lot."
43. Timothy Leary and Peter Janney were just two of Damore's interview/converts.
44. Lucianne Goldberg to the author, 1995. Goldberg was Damore's literary agent.
45. Arthur Ellis was interviewed for *People* in 1976.
46. Philip Nobile and Ron Rosenbaum, "The Mysterious Murder of JFK's Mistress," *New Times,* Oct. 1976, page 31.
47. National Archives, JFK Collection, RG 233, Memo from CIA Deputy Director for Plans, re discussions with Dulles.
48. Richard Helms.

49. "It Was Spy vs. Spy in JFK Probe / CIA Official Tells of Improper Contacts," *Newsday,* Oct. 6, 1996, page A19.
50. *New York Times,* Dec. 25, 1974, page A25.
51. Bradlee, *A Good Life,* pages 269–70.
52. Scott Armstrong, author interview, 1996.
53. Scott Armstrong.
54. Philip Nobile.
55. Tom Mangold, *Cold Warrior: James Jesus Angleton: The CIA's Master Spy Hunter,* Simon & Schuster, 1991, page 353.
56. Jane Barnes.
57. Peter Janney.
58. Timothy Leary.
59. Anne Truitt, *Daybook: The Journal of an Artist,* Pantheon, 1982, pages 118–19.
60. Ted Swager, author interview, 1997.
61. Unnamed source.
62. Unnamed source.
63. Katharine Graham, *Personal History,* Knopf, 1997, pages 416–17.

# Index

## A

# C

## D



## E



## F

# N

## Y

# About the Author

NINA BURLEIGH began her journalism career in the midwest at the Associated Press, and for five years covered national politics in Washington D.C., including the Clinton White House and Patrick Buchanan's 1996 run for the presidency. Her articles have appeared in *Time*, the *Washington Post*, the *Chicago Tribune*, *George* and other publications. Currently she is a contributing editor at *New York* magazine and lives in New York City.